ETERNAL
FLAME

Also by Jennifer Otter Bickerdike

Being Britney: Pieces of a Modern Icon

You Are Beautiful and You Are Alone: The Biography of Nico

Why Vinyl Matters: A Manifesto from Musicians and Fans

Joy Devotion: The Importance of Ian Curtis and Fan Culture

The Secular Religion of Fandom: Pop Culture Pilgrim

Fandom, Image and Authenticity: Joy Devotion and the Second Lives of Kurt Cobain and Ian Curtis (Pop Music, Culture and Identity)

THE AUTHORIZED BIOGRAPHY OF
THE BANGLES

ETERNAL FLAME

JENNIFER OTTER BICKERDIKE

GRAND CENTRAL

New York   Boston

Copyright © 2025 by Jennifer Otter Bickerdike

Jacket design by Amanda Kain. Jacket photograph by Sheila Rock.
Jacket copyright © 2025 by Hachette Book Group, Inc.

Hachette Book Group supports the right to free expression and the value of copyright. The purpose of copyright is to encourage writers and artists to produce the creative works that enrich our culture.

The scanning, uploading, and distribution of this book without permission is a theft of the author's intellectual property. If you would like permission to use material from the book (other than for review purposes), please contact permissions@hbgusa.com. Thank you for your support of the author's rights.

Grand Central Publishing
Hachette Book Group
1290 Avenue of the Americas, New York, NY 10104
grandcentralpublishing.com
@grandcentralpub

First Edition: February 2025

Grand Central Publishing is a division of Hachette Book Group, Inc. The Grand Central Publishing name and logo is a registered trademark of Hachette Book Group, Inc.

The publisher is not responsible for websites (or their content) that are not owned by the publisher.

The Hachette Speakers Bureau provides a wide range of authors for speaking events. To find out more, go to hachettespeakersbureau.com or email HachetteSpeakers@hbgusa.com.

Grand Central Publishing books may be purchased in bulk for business, educational, or promotional use. For information, please contact your local bookseller or the Hachette Book Group Special Markets Department at special.markets@hbgusa.com.

Print book interior design by Amy Quinn.

Library of Congress Cataloging-in-Publication Data has been applied for.

ISBNs: 9780306833342 (hardcover); 9780306833366 (ebook);
      9780306837906 (International)

CLA

10 9 8 7 6 5 4 3 2

*In gratitude for Terry Currier
You are a true, different light and real hero*

CONTENTS

Foreword — ix
Preface — xi
Introduction — xv

PART I: BEGINNINGS
1. 3
2. 13
3. 21
4. 31
5. 39
6. 45

PART II: COME TOGETHER
7. 63
8. 73
9. 80
10. 87
11. 93
12. 97
13. 110
14. 130
15. 140

16. 153
17. 164
18. 180

PART III: FAME
19. 205
20. 214
21. 223
22. 232
23. 247
24. 269
25. 286

PART IV: BREAKDOWN
26. 299
Epilogue 309
Legacy 311

Acknowledgments 315
Reference List 319
Notes 345
Index 379

vii

FOREWORD

They looked like they belonged together and they had...that rare chemistry of a band, that the whole is greater than the sum of the parts, but all the parts are exciting.

—PETER PHILBIN, A&R EXECUTIVE FOR COLUMBIA RECORDS, ON THE BANGLES[1]

From inception, the women who would become the Bangles were ambitious, focused, and intentional—their hard work and determination resulting in sales of millions of records across the globe before becoming the first entirely female band to have five top-ten hits. They toured the world, had number one records, and were collaborating with the biggest artists of the day. The foursome was the result of an entire generation of women musicians who weren't satisfied with being screaming fans; they envisioned themselves as being worthy of rock star adoration, though there was almost a complete absence of any real female role models. From angelic harmonizing to headlining huge concerts, the Bangles seemed unstoppable—until tensions within the group, artistic differences, and the pressures of sudden celebrity tore them apart less than a decade after first getting together.

With unprecedented access to Susanna Hoffs, Debbi Peterson, Vicki Peterson, and their inner circles,* this is, for the first time, in their own words, the story of a band breaking through invisible barriers and globally institutionalized misogyny, of a group of women who came together in a moment when being a female musician seemed almost unthinkable, burning a bright beacon for generations to follow.

This is the Bangles.

---

* Michael Steele declined to be involved in this project.

PREFACE

As a child growing up in the 1980s, seeing and hearing the Bangles was a revelation. The band was so much more than the pop stars I idolized as a kid; they were women who blazed a trail for what could be.

A key part of the Bangle origin story is the sheer focused chutzpah of the Peterson sisters, Debbi and Vicki, and Susanna Hoffs to form a band. Back in 2019, I decided to utilize the same tactic in a bid for the seemingly impossible: I wanted to write the story of the Bangles, focused specifically on their early years, the context they came from, and the reality of being an all-female group who achieved chart success in a male-dominated world.

For me as a young fan at that time, the band was all about power, talent, and prospect. Countless young women took direct inspiration from the Bangles, with everyone from L7 to Veruca Salt and the Donnas citing the foursome as lighting the way for their own artistry. The media was similarly fixated, but in a different manner: article after article focused on the band's gender and appearance, not their ability. A cursory dig into the press from the height of their popularity was shocking in its tone, with many pieces openly questioning if the women were playing their own instruments, a seeming impossibility for many a journalist to fathom. It was admittedly strange reviewing the same magazines, videos, and interviews that had informed my own values and world as an adolescent with adult eyes. Having now worked in and around the music business for over three decades, I was still gobsmacked at what I found on the internet, deep in the British Library archives, and in the memories of those who were around the band at the time.

The contrast is so striking between how I experienced the group—as a young girl hungrily looking for role models of strong women—and how the Bangles were written about and treated by the very industry that helped propel them to international celebrity. The male-centric music business was not easy to break into because of what Vicki once described as "things we can't help, like being female."[1]

Rock and roll has arguably been defined since its inception as "music played by men, especially white men, with guitars."[2] Runaways biographer Evelyn McDonnell calls this phenomenon "manhandling," a term she has coined to describe the "ideological" problem that systemically eradicates women from pop history, a distressing "way of seeing and presenting the world that is based on projections of power and control, not on reality."[3] The scariest part of manhandling may be its pervasiveness, so ingrained into our own belief systems and daily lives as to often go utterly unnoticed and be expected. For example, a piece in the UK music magazine *Mojo* labels the Bangles egregiously as "LA pop starlets,"[4] eradicating their years of sweat equity in various dubious Southern California venues and on the club circuit. From general belittling in articles printed in cultural tomes of the time to radio station playlists, being a female artist has historically been to be "other." McDonnell points to the "standard practice on classic rock radio, where women are relegated to token spots...and are never played back-to-back."[5] "We're already playing Sheryl Crow, so we can't play you," was a reply received by Lisa Loeb when she asked why her song was not added to FM rotations.[6] This reprieve is echoed by Liz Phair, who remarks, "We're [women] pitted against each other."[7] As Loeb points out, "If you got the slot [on the radio], then I didn't."[8] Artists' attempts to support each other were often denied, viewed as bad business decisions. "I remember talking to my agent about touring with another female, and the response was, 'You don't want to do that because it won't sell tickets,'" recalls Sheryl Crow.[9]

The Bangles are often referred to as "the girls," both by those around them and by themselves. Throughout this book, they will be mentioned by this, as it is what was and is used within their inner circles. It is utilized by them as both an empowering pronoun and one which displays the irreverence necessitated for survival. When I asked former tour manager Chris Lamson why this title is preferred, he explained how the band is "like a girls club. They're the girls because they were super fun, super flirty, and super friendly. They just didn't take themselves too seriously."[10] Such levity was arguably a mechanism for both creating an illusion of unity during times of inner band turmoil as well as playing to what was "expected" of the group while far exceeding most of their peers.

There is a prevailing sense that because they are female, the Bangles were incapable of being "real" artists. Within the world of mainstream music, women often found it hard to be promoted simply on their ability. "This is where the boy's club factor and some good old garden variety misogyny probably came into play," Henry Rollins tells me.[11] "I imagine it could be incredibly insulting. I don't think this is exclusive to Los Angeles, punk rock, or the 1980s. I think many women lineups were almost always infantilized or marketed as a 'girly' accessory to 'real' bands and again, not to be taken seriously. I don't know what women could have done in these instances besides fume and get on with things as best they could."[12]

The Bangles came to prominence as music videos dramatically changed how artists were experienced, promoted, and publicized, placing a higher value than ever before on appearance and personality. "I remember at one point, we had been on the road for eight or nine weeks," Vicki says.[13] "When we finally went home, I thought, 'I'm so sick of looking at myself in the mirror.' There was a real sense of pressure. Possibly for us, and other female musicians in the '80s, we were absolutely the minority. People didn't quite know what to do with us, especially men. Were we objects? We were complete aberrations of nature, being women on stage playing rock music."[14]

The frustration of this void is illustrated in a 1989 interview with Susanna, where she is asked what the Bangles are. "We're lumped into some kind of weird category....People can't really view us in the same breath as Guns N' Roses or U2....We're like in the strange all-girl-band category....People kind of lump us and then push us to the side: 'Oh yeah, they're an all-girl band, isn't that cute.'"[15]

Ultimately, against all odds, the Bangles proved that women *can* do and be anything. They provided a possibility model for young people encountering an uncertain world in a precarious cultural moment, changing not just the music business but the outlooks and prospects for legions of women to follow.

The real story of the Bangles is one of every band, and this band specifically. It is the often bald reality of changing objectives, miscommunications, naivete, disappointments, and the unpredictable consequences of fame. But more importantly, it is a study in hard work, aspiration, friendship, focus, and hope.

INTRODUCTION

Among the assembled crowd, the mood was jubilant as the globally chart-topping Bangles prepared to do a show at one of the most unprecedented venues to date: the opening of a freeway segment in Houston, Texas, known as Beltway 8. The stretch connected the I-10 and the US 290, providing new access to the area. Regardless of the unusual choice of performance space, the free gig was expected to draw just over twenty thousand attendees. The July sun was blazing and unrelenting, the freshly laid tarmac offering no relief from the sizzling ninety-four degree heat. "It was boiling hot," guitarist-vocalist Susanna Hoffs recounts of the day.

The band was exhausted, having been on the road virtually nonstop for the past seven years, promoting their albums with endless shows, appearances, interviews, and press junkets. The current tour, supporting their third LP, *Everything*, had been riddled with issues, from bad weather to band infighting.

The Houston show marked a strange choice made by the group's recently hired management, Arnold Stiefel and Randy Phillips; yet the band, as always, were keen to fulfill all of their obligations. "It was one of the more absurdist moments of my life," Susanna says, "but we went where we were told to go." A makeshift "stage" had been cobbled together "very high off the ground" on the thoroughfare itself.

As the attendees celebrated the chance to see their heroines in the flesh, the whole overpass started swaying under the weight of the carousing fans. The new freeway had been designed to hold the heavy, steady, moving weight of automobiles, not the up and down motion of tens of thousands of people simultaneously. Unbeknownst to the band, the cobbled together performance platform upon which they played began to break into pieces, making an already questionable choice of venues a possible death trap. "The lights above our heads were swinging and apparently the speaker cabinets were coming apart," drummer-vocalist Debbi Peterson says. "The structural engineer who built the toll way was worried. But you know, gotta get that extra buck no matter how much it endangers the band."

The new construction threatening to collapse under inexorable conditions was a fitting analogy for the precarious emotional and professional commitments keeping the band together. While playing "Crash and Burn," the audience, which had swelled to over seventy-five thousand, began to dance with abandon. "It felt like an earthquake," Debbi recalls, "the stage started bouncing up and down." Susanna concurs, saying, "All of a sudden, the whole toll bridge span started vibrating, almost in waves." The band did not know what was happening; though aware that something was desperately wrong, the shared inherent value of commitment to the group at any cost superseded personal safety. At first, Debbi thought older sister, guitarist-vocalist Vicki "was just stamping her feet really hard." Yet soon after the initial shift, Susanna left the stage. "I just thought, 'Oh my God, I've got to get off, it's going to collapse,'" she remembers. Bass player and vocalist Michael Steele soon followed, leaving the two Petersons on the improvised stage. "The Petersons went on playing, like the band on the *Titanic*," Susanna says. "I just thought, I need to get off of this thing before it sinks. It spoke to something about the dynamic in the band. Debbi and Vicki, they were going to go down fighting, no matter the circumstances."

PART I
BEGINNINGS

1.

Los Angeles is one of the largest counties in the United States, composed of 4,084 square miles. "It's so spread out and there are so many different communities within the community," says native Los Angeleno Debbi Peterson.[1] The third of four children, Debbi, and older sisters Pam and Vicki and younger brother Dave, grew up in Northridge, a neighborhood of San Fernando Valley, one of the many regions within the greater municipality of LA, an area referred to by locals simply as "the Valley."

"The Valley was a safe place back then," Debbi recalls of the town. "Endless shopping malls," adds musician Annette Zilinskas. "They were the cultural hubs of the Valley experience: movie theatres, miniature golf, a roller-skating rink." She goes on to elaborate, "There wasn't a lot to do. I liked it because it was just easy to get around, it's all a grid. It was suburbia."[2] The Petersons' residence was a spacious five-bedroom house with a pool smack dab in the middle of the bucolic setting. "It couldn't have been any more American middle class," says second oldest Peterson sibling, Vicki.[3]

Music was inherently important to their parents, Milt and Jeanne. "My parents were music lovers—they told us stories of their early dates sitting in my dad's house listening to jazz and comedy albums together," Vicki recalls.[4] Being the son of a carpenter, audiophile Milt built custom fifteen-inch woofers into the living room wall of the family home. When he could grab the rare moments of solitary relaxation, Milt would be found on the couch with a pair of headphones, reprive provided by classical music. "We had a big stereo in the living room," remembers youngest child, Dave. "My sisters would go out there and they'd blast tunes. I loved the records they would play, especially [oldest sister] Pam. She had a good LP collection. I was a pop music connoisseur when I was six."[5]

The interweaving of family, belonging, and music became an integral value to Vicki, with performance coming naturally. She pinpoints this love of being in front of an audience coming to fruition during family Sunday night parties. As Milt had to commute seventy miles every day to his aerospace engineering job at TRW in Redondo Beach, dinners as an entire family were rare. Even more infrequent were rainy Sundays in the placid Northridge atmosphere. Inclement weather would be the only reason the Peterson kids would be spared from Milt's regular chore rota, especially when it came to yard work. "We were always pulling weeds or hand digging trenches for my dad's irrigation system," Vicki tells me with a smile. "I don't even mind pulling weeds. What was annoying is that he would give us each a shopping bag to fill up. Once it was stuffed to the top, we would get a quarter. For a little kid, that's giant! I would hand him my full bag of weeds and he would take his huge Dad foot and go [makes a squashing down movement]! Big money dreams shattered."[6]

On these extremely rare, blustering weekends, the family would commune indoors, "stop everything and have a family party."[7] The accoutrements of the afternoons featured a fire in the underused hearth and the delicacy of "potato chips and onion dip," both notable as "very big important things which did not happen on other days."[8] More important to Vicki than the flicking flames or the titillating nosh was the opportunity to perform, her family the captive audience. "I would put on plays. Debbi was a willing participant. We would get our little brother Dave involved." Pam, being the oldest sibling, "kind of scorned it all," though occasionally could be coerced into partaking. "There would be commercial breaks," Vicki says, "and if it was during Christmastime, I would dance to *The Nutcracker*." "We were both just naturally drawn to performing," Vicki says of herself and Debbi.

1.

Milt and Jeanne sensed that a cultural shift would be marked with the February 1964 appearance of the Beatles on *The Ed Sullivan Show*. Not wanting their two oldest children to miss out on what could be a turning point in pop history, Pam and Vicki were both allowed to stay up late and watch the performance. "I think they actually got me out of bed," Vicki tells me, "which was absolutely okay because I was a nocturnal nightmare kid who would *never* go to sleep when I was supposed to."[9] More than half a century on, the evocation of the evening is tangible in Vicki's recollection. "I remember sitting on the vinyl floor with my sister, watching them on the black-and-white TV in our family room, this insane thing happening in front of me. I don't think I had yet heard of them at all." She smiles. "That was it for me, a life-long Beatles fan instantly born. The joy and energy of the music…[it was] strange but exciting. [I felt like] nothing was going to be the same. In a lot of ways, it wasn't."[10]

She concludes, "I was five."[11]

The annual Peterson pilgrimage from Southern California to Michigan also marked a key moment in musical awareness for the young girl. Every year, all six family members "plus suitcases, books, and toys" piled into a "very sleek" 1964 Buick LeSabre station wagon* and drove from California to Benton Harbor, Michigan, where Jeanne's parents and brother still lived.[12] Refreshment was provided by the "cooler full of orange juice and milk" and accompanying "bags of groceries." "Our breakfasts and lunches were eaten in a park or on the side of the road, never in diners," Vicki says. "I'm sure it was an absolute nightmare for our poor mom, four kids to keep occupied in an enclosed vehicle for five days, but I loved it."[13]

---

* The white Buick would be passed from kid to kid in the Peterson family, with each one in turn having ownership at some point. "We all drove it," says Vicki. "It was the car that stayed in the family until it finally died after my brother had a turn with it. I drove it and Debbi drove it. It was the vehicle that Debbi and I dragged our equipment around in when we were rehearsing and when we were driving all over Los Angeles County playing clubs in the late '70s and early '80s."

In retrospect, Vicki contemplates how much she enjoyed the road trips, the endless hours "of being in a packed vehicle with many other bodies" possibly training her for later life as a touring musician. The radio also was a constant companion, "always tuned to a pop station,"[14] underpinning a growing love with the Byrds, Buffalo Springfield, and the Mamas & the Papas.

One summer, upon arriving at her grandmother's house, Vicki found her uncle John in attendance, with a Beatles single in hand. "It was one of the early releases, with the A-side being 'Love Me Do' and the B-side 'P.S. I Love You,'" she remembers. It was the first time she had heard the group on wax. The girl was equally blown away with the recorded rendition of the performance as she had been with their appearance on *Ed Sullivan*. "I was fascinated with the sounds coming through the grill cloth of the speaker. I made him play it seven times in a row. He was the young, cool uncle, maybe eighteen, and he indulged me."[15]

Back at home, sister Pam was also a "guiding light" in the household, providing a template of connoisseurship for her three younger siblings to follow. "Pam was a full-on Beatlemaniac," Vicki confides.[16] "She got all the records."[17]

The first opportunity Vicki had to hold an instrument in her own hands required transgression into her father's sacred space. "When I was very little, I became aware that my father had a guitar in the closet of his den. It was a beautiful old Silvertone Jazz archtop guitar, a sort of tobacco color, with F-hole cutouts. We were not allowed in the den unsupervised. It was my father's private territory," Vicki confides.[18] However, her attraction to the forbidden overcame her. "One day, I snuck into the closet and positioned myself behind the guitar to try it out. It seemed huge in my hands, and the action was set up so high—I remember the strings being a full inch from the fret board. I'm sure they weren't, but that's how it seemed. I literally ended up putting Band-Aids on my fingers because I figured they would provide some padding."[19]

When Santa brought Vicki a plastic guitar from Sears that Christmas, the kindergartener realized two things. First, that her covert visits to her father's lair were not so secret; and second, though pleased to now have her own instrument, what she held in her hands was not a "real" guitar. An upgrade came four years later, when at age nine she received "an actual wood 'folksinger' with a rope strap," another purchase from the illustrious Sears.[20]

It took a third grade talent show, though, for the Peterson parents to fully appreciate the determination and chutzpah their second born had in regard to her blossoming musicianship. "I came home from school and told my mom, 'I'm gonna be in the talent show.' She said, 'That's great. What are you gonna do?' I said, 'I'm going to sing an original song and play guitar.' My mom looks at me like, 'You don't play guitar?' I said, 'I have two weeks. How hard can it be?' I was determined."[21] A last-minute change saw Vicki do an a cappella number instead of unplugged original; however, the grinding work ethic and never-give-up attitude had begun to be set in place. "That was the start of my personal identification," she now says of that initial show. "To be able to play was my goal."[22] By fourth grade, Vicki had talked Milt and Jeanne into buying her an even better instrument. "It was a Japanese Electro guitar," Vicki remembers.[23] "It had the silver case identical to George Harrison's in *A Hard Day's Night*. I kept it through all my teenage years."[24]

Music played a part in forging early friendships as well as forming a sense of self. Toni Kasza met the Petersons when she and Vicki were just six years old in Northridge. "If I went to her house for a sleepover or she came to mine, the guitar came with us," Toni says.[25] At just ten years old, Vicki shared a song she had written with her friend. "I felt like nobody actually wrote songs because music came from the church or were folk songs sprung from the campfire—they had just been around forever. It wasn't something possible for one of *us* to do."[26] This was an early example, Toni says, of "Vicki always being just a step ahead of the curve, of doing something everyone else thought impossible."[27]

Religion also was intertwined with early performances as the girls attended Our Lady of Lourdes Catholic school through eighth grade. "The church had an unbelievable focus on music," Toni recalls.[28] "They would bring in famed conductors and organists…there were a lot of activities in there."[29]

The neighborhood around Our Lady was very insular. "Everyone knew each other; we definitely all grew up with like-minded families," Toni recounts, the church at the center of the community.[30] "It was very wholesome. There was an emphasis on volunteerism, on being kind: you treat people the way you want to be treated. Nobody's parents were divorced."[31] It was "really Catholic," Toni says, so the four kids in Vicki's clan was "not considered a big family."[32]

As she started tenth grade, Vicki found herself uprooted from her life in Northridge as the Petersons moved across Los Angeles County to the aspirational region of Palos Verdes. Gone was the five-bedroom house with a den and swimming pool; Vicki was now bunking in the same room as her sister in a condominium complex. In an effort to assimilate to her surroundings, the sophomore joined the drill team at her new high school. It was there that she first met Julie Cameron. "The drill team at her old school was a big deal," Julie says.[33] "The drill team at my school was rather for the nerds; it wasn't the cool thing to do."[34] Regardless of the disparities, Vicki continued to build a friendship with Julie.

British native Amanda Podany, née Hills, was also a new arrival to Palos Verdes, having started ninth grade at Rolling Hills High School in 1972. Like the Petersons, the Hills placed a similar importance on music. "My parents played records all the time in the house when I was a kid," Amanda says.[35] The Fab Four were a popular choice in the Hills household. "At age three, my mom remembers me singing along to 'She Loves You,'" Amanda laughs.[36] "It was a very music-filled childhood."[37]

Within weeks of starting school in 1973, Amanda found herself at the local outlet of Shakey's Pizza lunching with Vicki and members of the drill team, or as she called them, "the Rah's."[38] Several months after the fated Shakey's meal, Vicki invited Julie and Amanda over to the Petersons' condominium for a slumber party to celebrate her sixteenth birthday. "We discovered that she had an electric guitar, which

I thought was the coolest thing on the planet," Amanda says.[39] Vicki's already blossoming prowess on the instrument also impressed, with talk turning to the idea of forming their own band. A week later, the girls decided to give the notion a trial run. Vicki got out the family cassette recorder, Julie had brought her guitar over to the party, and Amanda had come equipped with a British recorder. It was decided that the trio would have a go at Paul McCartney's "I Am Your Singer" while accompanying themselves on their respective instruments. Amanda met Debbi, Vicki's younger sister, who joined in on the vocals.[*] "I have no idea why we picked that song," Amanda laughs.[40] "We all just sat around the tape player and played and sang. We thought, 'This is great.'"[41] Upon rewinding the tape and listening back, the girls were horrified to admit that what they had created was terrible. Despite not nailing their first attempt at cover song greatness, the fire had been lit to start their own group. "I didn't know how to play at all," Amanda says.[42] "From that moment on, it was my goal. I was fourteen at the time."[43] Spurred on by her new friends, Amanda began listening intently to the basslines provided by McCartney. Looking at her own potential group, Amanda saw an opportunity. "I hadn't realized the parts of a band until we started playing," Amanda admits.[44] "I didn't know bass guitar existed."[45] "If we were going to have a band, I was going to be the bass player," she smiles.[46]

Through 1974, Amanda pursued the bass as she and Vicki simultaneously started writing songs together, aspiring to be the female Simon and Garfunkel. Early tunes included "Can't Buy Me Tequila," "Standing at the Station," "The Fog Song," and the ironically titled "Park It Under a No Parking Sign." In June, less than six months after the despairing attempt at capturing McCartney magic, Amanda, Julie, and Vicki had their first public performance. Looking to expand her instrument repertoire, Vicki had undertaken lessons on the keys, overseen by local instructor Mrs. Harrison. "She somehow talked her teacher into letting

---

[*] Perhaps a temporary casualty of an unsuccessful first go, "Debbi never played with us again until 1977 when she actually joined the band," notes Amanda.

our band play at the piano recital," laughs Amanda. "We were three guitars. I would just play the basslines on the guitar. It was just Julie and Vicki and me. We were so excited to just have an audience."[47]

While the friends tried to find their footing, Vicki continued to look for other avenues that would allow her to perform. Having left the drill team after tenth grade, she tried out and made her high school cheerleading squad. A self-confessed "rebel cheerleader," Vicki found that her love for being in front of a crowd conflicted with the elected position of being on the team. "I remember Vicki feeling mixed about [how cheerleaders are perceived] because we were not popular. We just didn't want to go along with what was expected of girls," Amanda recollects.[48] "She wanted to be a cheerleader because she really loved the performance part of it; but she didn't want to do the whole 'be popular' thing. It's just there was a feeling that she didn't quite match what was to be expected of a cheerleader."[49]

Vicki adds, "I was accepted by the cheerleaders and dance squad, I just didn't go to those parties. Also *big* at this time was the a cappella singing group that Amanda and I were both a part of. It was one of my favorite things about high school! We did Christmas performances with the Madrigals, singing at senior centers and shopping malls. They were our first 'tours'!!"[50]

In a 1984 *LA Weekly* piece, Vicki recalls her experience donning the pom-poms, illustrating how it helped set the foundation for her love of being in front of varied crowds:

Yes, I'll admit it now—I was a cheerleader (rah, rah), which is way out there beyond the valley of the super uncool, I know. But in high school the biggest audience is found at the football games, and uncured ham I am.

Okay, so this is a night game away and we were out there in our tricky little Rolling Hills blue-and-gold uniforms doing all these incredibly soulful dance steps but feeling pretty goddamn Wonder Bread all the same. Somewhere in the middle of the second quarter the lights went out—couldn't see a thing. I went up to the mike, which for some strange and suspicious reason was still working, and started this groove-rap cheer we did (crowd control, they call it) and everyone in the stands picked up the rhythm and echoed everything I shouted/sang at them—just a lot of voices shouting in total darkness.

The moment was a revelation. The next day, Vicki recounts, friends said to her, "You can fuckin' sing rock & roll."[51]

As the summer of 1975 started, Amanda, Julie, and Vicki decided to give the band idea another go at a conveniently close venue that allowed them to be in front of an audience again. "Julie's mom had a flower show at her house where she sold blooms that she had grown. We played at that," Amanda recalls. The trio appeared as Shantih, a moniker acquired via Amanda's passing infatuation with T. S. Eliot. As they started their senior year of high school, the decision was made to "get serious" about being a band. They had an arsenal of tunes penned by the two best friends and they practiced relentlessly for hours on end.

The chance to perform in front of an audience of any size was always quickly snapped up, with any venue fair game. Even Julie's folks finally begrudgingly admitted to the inherent talent of the three girls. "My parents have a picture of us sitting on the stairs of my childhood home. My mom was having a party and the three of us provided background music. At the end of it, my dad came up and said, 'I didn't think you were that bad. That was pretty good.'"[52]

However, there was one problem: the lack of a drummer was becoming acute. "When we started, we were going to be a girl band," says Amanda. "By senior year, it was the three of us [Julie, Vicki, and I]. None of us was a drummer and none of us wanted to be the drummer."[53] With no possibilities for filling the vacancy in sight, the teens accepted that they may have to let go of their all-girl idea and make do with a male addition.

Around this time, Vicki's boyfriend, Joel Ciniero, stepped into the group. Though not a drummer, Joel took over lead guitar, freeing up

Vicki to do rhythm. The addition of Vicki's beau was not "a decision," Amanda says. "It was just he could play guitar so there he was." Things went smoothly at first, with everyone getting along. However, the couple "did a lot of breaking up and getting back together again." "Every time they broke up, he left the band; every time they got back together, he joined the band; he came and went," Amanda says. "I don't think [we] thought that he was a permanent member because we had always had the all-girl thought in our minds, but he was there and he took it seriously."[54]

In March of 1976, the new foursome configuration premiered in public for the first time. Though lacking a drummer, attendees of the Rolling Hills High Hootenanny—the school's talent show—were treated to the group covering the Beatles "Norwegian Wood" and Carly Simon's "Legend in Your Own Time." Three months later, even though everyone graduated from high school, they stayed dedicated to prioritizing the band.

A new determination to fill the drummer spot saw them advertising in every possible location for talent, including a nearby grocery store. "I remember we put up a sign in the local Safeway saying, 'Are you a drummer?' 'Are you a girl, we want you for our band?'" Amanda remembers. Though the ideal was to have a female in the role, the friends thought it was "pretty unlikely." The girls had big dreams, already envisioning themselves as trailblazers. "Right from the beginning, we were ridiculously ambitious," Amanda laughs. "We would talk about how cool it would be for a girl band to get really famous. It was the three of us and then some other unknown girls in the future who would join us."[55]

2.

Jeanne Peterson was giving birth and the stakes were high; after all, there was a bottle of booze on the line. It was 1961, and the Petersons were about to have their third child. Milt and Jeanne had bet the doctor his choice of whiskey that the newest addition to the brood would be a longed-for boy. The Petersons had to hand over a bottle of the good stuff when Debbi arrived. Sister Pam was ecstatic, as she personally had made it known she had hoped for another baby sister.

From the start, the young girl was immersed in sound. "Our house seemed to be constantly filled with music. Between the radio, my parents' albums (Harry Belafonte, musical LPs such as *Sound of Music* and *Mary Poppins*), I had a very good introduction," Debbi recalls.[1] "Pam had an allowance, so she got to go and buy records. She would be playing music all the time. It was the Beatles, Cat Stevens, Mamas and Papas, Joni Mitchell, and folk rock groups," Debbi says. "I think a lot of stuff got internalized by just constantly hearing different musical styles and records; it just gets in your blood."[2] Like her sisters, Debbi attended Our Lady of Lourdes, being a student there first through sixth grade. "We had a principal who was a nun," Debbi tells me. "She was nasty! You certainly didn't want to get called to that office! I did once, but only because they confused me with *another* Debbi Peterson who was an eighth grader!" In the fifth grade, Debbi and a couple other kids got in trouble "for hanging around the nunnery's bathroom." The punishment, she recalled, was "slaps on the wrists with a ruler!...Plus writing 'I will not go in the nuns' bathroom' loads of times on the chalkboard in front of the class."[3]

School became a space for the emerging performer to practice. "We were good Catholic girls who went to mass," Debbi recalls. "We'd be at the pew singing along with the choir. We'd come up with harmonies to what they were doing. It was just a natural thing."[4] Car rides could become a battleground, however, for the siblings. "Our parents liked to drive a lot and do family trips. The radio was always on. I just remember sitting in the back of the car, Vicki and I singing together. We would automatically go to one part or another together," Debbi laughs. "We'd be arguing over which one of us should sing. It became this competition, who's gonna sing which part because we could both hear the different harmonies."[5]*

With Pam collecting albums, Vicki learning guitar and singing with Debbi, youngest sibling Dave asserted himself as the family drummer. "He was the classic little kid in the kitchen banging on the pots and pans," Debbi recalls.[6] "I didn't have any interest in that. I wanted to be a bass or guitar player." However, experience with the rhythm section was attained by "air" drumming in front of the family hi-fi. "I had no idea what I was doing, I was just instinctively connecting to the beat," Debbi says. "I could figure out by listening how to actually do it."[7] Practice also came through having "drum-offs" with Dave "by playing beats with our mouths!" Debbi laughs. "We'd come up with a beat, and we'd have to guess what song it came from."[8]

When the Petersons moved from the Valley to the South Bay of Palos Verdes, tween Debbi was in an awkward phase. "I had these horrible glasses and felt like a huge geek. It was a middle school—sixth, seventh, and eighth grades. I got there in seventh grade, so everybody had already grouped up."[9] One day Debbi struck up a conversation with a girl she had class with. Like Debbi, Marji Banda, née Mize, was equally obsessed with the Beatles. A firm friendship was quickly established on the shared love of all things Fab Four. "We just clicked," Debbi remembers.[10] Activities revolved around the Liverpudlians. "We'd watch Beatles movies

---

* Eventually, the sisters strived for their dual vocalization arrangements to have a "phasing effect...like a musical piece of instrumentation."

together, stay up all night and bake chocolate chip cookies and pretend we were talking to the Beatles on the phone. I felt like I found my Beatle soulmate."[11]

Further Beatles indoctrination occurred after Debbi persuaded Marji to watch *Help!*, which was playing on a local television station. "After that, it was just Beatles everything," Marji laughs. "They [the Petersons] could recite dialogue from *A Hard Day's Night* and *Help!* with British accents. It was so much fun." Debbi's sense of humor was a lifeline to Marji. "Debbi was funny. She used to make me laugh all the time, which I really needed."[12]

Marji and Debbi soon became inseparable. "I was just there all the time; we were attached at the hip," Marji says. The girls would often go into the room shared by the two middle sisters and listen to records, with the Beatles and other '60s music being in high rotation. "There was creativeness everywhere," Marji recalls. "Debbi would draw in a style called rendering. Her and Vicki could make a picture look like it was real, they were just really gifted that way."[13]

Having spent so much time with the siblings during their formative years, Marji had a front row seat to the family dynamic. "Debbi was the third daughter; I think she had to wade through a lot of other people's stuff to be heard, so she kept quiet," Marji diplomatically states, "even though in her head she knew what she was seeing was right." Marji felt she provided a place for Debbi to be herself. "When I showed up, Debbi would let it all out because I was going to listen. When Dave came, he was the wanted son, so maybe Debbi was ignored. She was just trying to find her place in the scheme of things. Pam went to college and she became a CPA. She was very professional. Vicki was the outlier. Vicki would jump in and do things. Debbi, through the years, was more tentative."[14]

Her ability to survey any scene eventually provided Debbi the ability to "read situations" that might take Vicki "a second" to fully comprehend, Marji claims. "Debbi was such a good listener. She was a different kind of person, more subdued. I've never known anyone to tell you straight up the truth of what was really going on [like Debbi]. When it was time to listen, Debbi was right; she was right about a lot of stuff."

As Marji and Debbi became close, Vicki, Amanda, and Julie were embarking further on their band adventure. "It was just interesting [to me] that they were doing music," Debbi recalls. "I remember them rehearsing and playing guitars in the living room. I just wanted to be a part of that. I was seeing it from afar and thinking that I really wanted to be in a band. I could tell that they were serious and were writing songs. I found it fascinating."[15]

The trio of older girls still did not have a drummer. "We thought we were experienced and that we were the shit," Julie smiles.[16] One day during practice at the Peterson house, discussion turned to further advertising ideas for a drummer, and the possibility of even holding auditions, though they "weren't even thinking about Debbi" as she had "never picked up drumsticks in her life."[17] Brother Dave had a kit, "but we were already thinking this is a girl's band."[18] With no other prospects on the horizon, Debbi was given the chance to try out.

The official audition took place twenty miles away in the rehearsal space of a cover band, Life. The group had a drum set and had offered to let the girls use it for Debbi's formal trial. Amanda, Julie, Joel, and Vicki had all brought their own instruments, ready to see how they would work as a possible fivesome. "Their drummer, Jim, just stood behind Debbi and showed her what to do," Amanda remembers. "He said, 'Yes, this is the snare drum, this is the bass drum and this is the kick,' and put her hands in the right places." It was the first time Debbi had ever sat behind a kit.

The older kids started in on the Linda Ronstadt version of "Heatwave." Debbi found herself keeping up without any help from the seasoned Life veteran. "She could just drum, she could just *do it*," Amanda emphasizes. "It was the most uncanny thing I've ever seen. She was the world's most natural drummer you can imagine. It didn't take even a second for her to just get it. I remember looking at Vicki and Julie like,

2.

'Holy crap, this has been here all along. We didn't know.'" For Debbi, it was a revelation. "I initially would have rather been a bass player or even a guitarist. I never thought of myself as a drummer. I guess the air drumming had incorporated itself into my subconscious."[19]

The audition also welcomed in a new band moniker for the teens, a Stevie Wonder–inspired name: Aisha. Named after the famous singer's daughter, Amanda thought "it was just beautiful." When Life's manager asked the newly christened group what they were calling themselves, Amanda proudly proclaimed, "Aisha." Confused, he replied, "I Eat Shit?!" "We had this parallel band name," Amanda smiles. "When we were good we were Aisha and when we were really sloppy, we were I Eat Shit."[20]

Now the girls needed a drum set. Under the guidance of Life's drummer, Jim, an affordable and appropriate rig was picked out at Hogan's House of Music. Vicki paid for the kit, but Debbi had to figure out how to reimburse her sister. "I had no money," she recalls. The way forward was the part-time job rite of passage: "I had to get a summer job in McDonald's." Debbi shivers. From the start, it was a match made in hell for the then fifteen-year-old. "I hated that job," she says. "They had me doing everything: the trash, the cleanup, and the cash register." Determined to part ways with the Golden Arches as soon as possible, Debbi's tenure only lasted six months, after which she was able to pay her sister back in full. The experience cemented a belief in Debbi. "I just thought, I want to be a musician and I never want to do this ever again," she recalls.

Finally in the group, Debbi realized there were few women behind the rig to look to for inspiration. "There were not that many female drummer influences for me at that time," she confides. "I was inspired more by male drummers," she says. "Ringo and Charlie Watts and others from '60s and '70s groups." As she started getting into the live music scene, Debbi began picking up techniques from other percussionists she saw playing out. "I used to go to local clubs in Los Angeles with Vicki and Amanda and see the bands," she tells me. "Bruce Gary from the Knack was a fucking powerhouse; I learned a lot from watching him."

While Debbi honed her drumming skills, Joel decided to quit the group, possibly because of a breakup with Vicki. Now minus Vicki's former beau, the unflappable girls instantly were a unit determined to succeed. "The times when we did have guys in the band, there was definitely a dynamic that we didn't want," Amanda remembers. "They tended to think they could assume control."[21] Underlying stress dissipated upon Joel's exit. "Between Vicki, Amanda, Debbi, and I, if it needed to be done, one of us was going to do it," Julie says. "Joel brought a lot of tension into the band. When he left, that tension went away," she recalls. "I liked Joel. He was friendly but there was always some distance there."[22] With Debbi, there was an instant positive shift. "She never really understood how good she really was," says Julie. "She's a naturally humble person."

From the start, Debbi shared her bandmates' vision of boundless possibility. "Being an all-female band wasn't the main reason we all got together," she says. "We wanted to be on TV. We wanted to be on the radio and be huge stars. We were serious, very single-minded. We liked having the dynamic of all-girls because it felt like a club! The female part was just a bonus."[23]

The Peterson parents were very supportive of their daughters' endeavor. "They went to a lot of their shows, going all the way back to the beginning," Dave recounts. "They were at the very first gig ever and many after."[24]

Not only did Jeanne and Milt go to see their kids perform, but their home was also open to the fledgling band. "They let them practice in the house for years," Dave says. "My parents liked pop music. They liked what was happening." An inclusive atmosphere extended to the band members as well. "When we would go over to play at Vicki's house, we were accepted as if we were part of that family," Julie recalls. "We would go downstairs to the kitchen and eat ice cream. We would stay the night. We'd be playing upstairs. Somebody would say, 'Hey, can you keep it down?' but we could still play, they didn't care. All the parents accepted that the group was the group and everybody belonged in the family."[25]

2.

The members of Aisha were busy, all trying to balance the rigors of academics with substantial band commitment. A sophomore in high school, Debbi was finding it challenging to concentrate on her studies, often feeling like she was leading a double life, "student by day, drummer by night." Upon graduating from high school, "Amanda went directly to UCLA because her parents said, 'You can be in the band all you like but you have to have an education, you have a brain, you're going to UCLA!'" Julie recalls. "There was just no question that that's where she was going to go." Vicki, though always wanting "the classic kind of collegiate experience, the Ivy League,"[26] had only applied to the same school as her best friend. She ended up deferring for a year to save money, instead spending her freshman year at Los Angeles Harbor, a junior college. More focused on band activities than academics, Vicki admits to having "spent my first year not being very attentive to classes, which seemed ridiculously easy."[27] Determined to push herself more, sophomore year saw Vicki joining Amanda at UCLA, becoming part of the English department.

The friends found themselves at an impasse. "We got to a point where Vicki, Debbi, and I were more serious about the band than Julie was," Amanda recalls. The foursome had vowed to never "Pete Best" each other—a reference to the original drummer of the Beatles who was fired right before the band hit it big. With this promise and a close friendship on the line, they all struggled with what to do next.

The girls eventually decided the band was not worth risking losing each other over. By July 1977, the foursome formation of Aisha had broken up.

However, so much work and effort had already gone into the project. By August, Vicki and Amanda found themselves writing and playing new music. "I think we believed it ourselves that we were going to disband," Amanda recounts. "It was very hard emotionally. But we just had to keep going."* Julie eventually enrolled in a music education course at

---

* The incident still haunts Amanda to this day. "There were lots of other band members that came and went but none of them were like Julie. She was the person who had been

Long Beach State University. The original trio remained friends, though now pursuing different musical journeys. "We were still really close," says Julie. "I would go to see them all the time, listening to what they were doing."[28]

Debbi, meanwhile, was finding it harder and harder to relate to her peers. "Debbi was really moving away from high school," Marji recalls. "After Debbi joined the band, it felt like she was gone a lot more. On the weekends, we didn't do anything together because she'd be practicing."

All the practice helped when Aisha reformed, this time as a trio composed of Amanda, Debbi, and Vicki. Rehearsals resumed in the Peterson family home, with preparation for the first gig of the new formation on the agenda. The August 31, 1977, date was at the Sweetwater Cafe, a venue in Redondo Beach. The girls did five or six songs, including "Dreamboat Annie" by Heart and "Don't Stop" by Fleetwood Mac. "We might have done a couple of songs that Vicki wrote in the very early days, but we did mostly covers," the drummer remembers.[29]

Still just sixteen years old, Debbi was legally far too young to even be inside the very clubs at which she was performing. "I'd have to be wherever the backstage area was and stay there because I was underage," Debbi explains. "I was sixteen pretending to be eighteen—but I'm still underage because they were over twenty-one clubs! I wasn't allowed to go out and mingle because I wasn't old enough."[30] Neither Vicki nor Amanda was twenty-one, making the threesome all far below the parameters for setting foot in the establishments. When asked if this made for a stressful atmosphere, Debbi responded, "We always managed to talk our way in. I'd be stuck backstage after the show or in between performances. I couldn't go anywhere. But it was what I really wanted to do. I always wanted to be in a band."[31]

---

there since the very beginning."

3.

While the Beatles remained the foundation upon which Vicki's musical aspirations may have been originally conceived, another band made an indelible mark during a different childhood *Ed Sullivan* viewing. It was December 24, 1967, the episode's musical guest American pop group the Cowsills. Featuring six siblings, ranging from ages eight to eighteen—plus their mother, Barbara—the band would go on to inspire the popular 1970s television show *The Partridge Family*. However, on this Christmas Eve, nine-year-old Vicki saw a framework for structuring a musical outfit. Youngest group member, Susan, was featured up close and center screen; the entire family unit was there, working and harmonizing together. The stylistic singing appealed to Vicki; but more important, the Cowsills illustrated a rarely seen combination of seemingly close-knit ties between members and a girl being a valued and integral part of the group.

The importance of the festive performance over a decade before was still tangible in 1978. The Cowsills had reunited, with a show booked at a local venue, Sweetwater Cafe. Amanda, Debbi, and Vicki attended the gig, and a firm friendship formed between the older performers and the up and comers. It was crucial to the elder Peterson that she be viewed as a peer from the very first interaction. "I was so desperate to be seen as an equal," she tells me. "I made a big point to tell them that we had just played the club. I wanted to make sure that I wasn't coming on as a fan; I was absolutely a fan—but my goal was to be accepted as an artist."[1]

The Cowsills acted as mentors and teachers, taking the threesome seriously. Seeing the difference between the Cowsills in the practice space and the end product at their shows helped further inform the young group's work ethic. "If you see a band live, you see it all pulled together. If you see them rehearse, you see them bringing the pieces into view. It was such a learning experience," Amanda explains. Watching the siblings work together also had a profound if subconscious impact, hypothesizes life-long friend Toni Kasza. "For Vicki, that pull of a musical family was there. I think the fantasy for Vicki to have a family musical situation was huge."

With Vicki having transferred to join Amanda at UCLA, the two decided to get an apartment together in Santa Monica. "Vicki was booking all of our shows," Amanda says. "She was incredible. She would put these packets together for the club owners with pictures of the band and articles that had come out about us with a bio. We jokingly would call ourselves Vicki and the Peterettes, as she was the boss," Amanda laughs.[2] Vicki confirms this, telling me, "Although we operated as a democracy, I was the one who ran rehearsals, wrote, and sang the songs at the shows. It's just worked out that way."[3]

The band kept press kits always on hand in case they might "meet someone." Such an event occurred on August 17 as the threesome stood in line for an audition at the iconic Whisky a Go Go for a forthcoming movie, *Teen Angel*. Performing Dwight Twilley's "I'm on Fire" got them called back three times, though ultimately they were not cast for the film. It gave the girls a taste of what could be. It also provided the chance to brush elbows with music industry royalty in the form of legendary DJ, club owner, and music promoter Rodney Bingenheimer.[*] "He came up to us and he was really nice," Amanda recalls. "It was like, 'Hey, how you doing? Are you a band?' We gave him one of our headshots."[4] When Bingenheimer asked if the girls were playing any time soon, they invited him to an upcoming gig at the Sweetwater Cafe. To their astonishment, he attended. "Rodney came all the way from Hollywood to see

---

[*] In December 2023, five women, including Go-Go's guitarist Jane Wiedlin, told *Rolling Stone* that they were sexually assaulted or molested by the DJ when they were minors in the 1970s and '80s.

us at the Sweetwater in Redondo Beach. He was always cool to us and very supportive," Amanda says.[5]

Bingenheimer was the original trendsetter, an "amplifier"[6] to ground zero of the punk rock scene in Los Angeles. Born in the San Francisco Bay Area, the self-described "ageless" provocateur moved to Los Angeles as a young adult, opening a club in the west end of Sunset Boulevard near a Denny's all-night diner. With up and comers like the New York Dolls and Iggy Pop gracing the stage of Rodney's establishments, he was eventually approached by local radio station KROQ about hosting a slot on-air. The trial grew into mandatory listening, Bingenheimer having four hours of *Rodney on the ROQ*, eight o'clock to midnight on Saturday and Sunday nights. The show was crucial for new groups hoping to break into a bigger audience. A spin from Rodney could alter the entire trajectory of an artist's career. From the first song played in 1976—"Beat on the Brat" by the Ramones—through to now iconic groups like Black Flag, Social Distortion, Circle Jerks, and the Go-Go's, Bingenheimer wanted to get music from local talent "for people to hear."[7]

Often a crucial element to getting onto Rodney's radar was to frequent one of his club nights. The events were awash with women of questionable legal age to be in the venues. "Rodney liked young girls, and his club was full of them....Knowing Rodney or being prepared to interact with Rodney was a prerequisite to going to Rodney's English Disco. [It] was Rodney's storefront, where he did his business," said Angela Bowie, ex-wife of the legendary singer David Bowie. The club was a petri dish illustrating "the stereotype of women in pop [as] 'glorified groupies,'... dilettantes, dabblers, not really serious."[8] At Rodney's, "the groupies were pretty obvious...they were underage girls who wore red sequins and that's about all."[9] Rock photographer Theresa Kereakes recalls a similar vibe, with "cult rock stars" making appearances "because they wanted to meet unchaperoned teenage girls."[10]

Bingenheimer was not the only person outside immediate family and friends starting to take notice of Aisha; Amanda was beginning to field calls from Toby Mamis. Mamis was looking for a new bass player to replace Vicki Blue in the all-girl band the Runaways. It would be the fourth person in the role, following the departure of Blue, Jackie Fox, and founding member Micki (later Michael) Steele.

Formed in 1975 in Los Angeles, the group had put out four studio LPs in as many years as well as a live album before breaking up in 1979. Mamis had been hired the year before, after the group parted ways with original producer Kim Fowley, a man with the self-ascribed power to spot talent. Such a proclamation came to fruition with the Runaways, which the provocateur claimed was his idea. When asked about the process for putting the lineup together, Fowley responded, "I went to find people to be the group...through a series of confusion, luck and design, five girls were selected."[11]

Fowley saw a space in the commercial marketplace for a young, nubile female outfit. "When you get women doing traditional male things," Fowley famously said, "You're gonna have combustion and controversy."[12] "Why couldn't there be a girl Elvis, or a girl Beatles, or a female Little Richard, or a girl Bo Diddley?" he argued. "There's always been that female version of everything in music, but nobody ever recruited five girls and said, 'These five girls are magical, and if they sing songs and look a certain way, the public will buy it.'" According to him, finding the right people for the group was "like casting a movie."[13]

Part of his "selection" process included placing an advertisement in LA-based fanzine *Who Put the Bomp*, stating:

WANTED: FOUR GIRLS
JOB: to play pop music
PURPOSE: To find the female Beatles, Stones, Who, Shangri-las of the '70s.[14]

A young Joan Jett was the first of the soon-to-be lineup to meet Fowley. "I told Kim Fowley I played rhythm guitar and about my idea of forming an all-girl band," Jett recalls. "I just thought people would freak out over an all-girl teenage rock-and-roll band."[15] Jett's aspirations were clear. "I wanted to be a rock star, not to be chasing rock stars for autographs or waiting around hotel lobbies for them," she confesses.[16] Fowley connected Jett with drummer Sandy West. "I took four buses all the way to her parents' house in Huntington Beach so we could jam," Jett recalls of the first meeting. "We got along well. Then we decided to start looking for other people."

The next person to seem a good fit for the burgeoning band was Sue Thomas. A native Los Angeleno, Thomas's family wealth has been likened to that depicted in the 1974 classic movie *Chinatown*, as it came from the powerful and affluent municipal resource of water. "She was older than us; maybe eighteen or nineteen, very nice, very quiet and kind of…strange, I guess, for lack of a better word," Sandy wrote of the initial impression. "She had a deep voice, but she was intelligent and she could play the bass pretty well, even though she didn't seem like a real rocker type."[17]

The power threesome now secured, Fowley went about systematically "reinventing" each of the young women. Joan and Sandy took on new last names (Jett and West, respectively, changing from Larkin and Pesavento), while Fowley "thought of calling the new bass player Micki Steele: an androgynous, hard, metal name."[18*]

Writer, DJ, and scene provocateur "Phast" Phreddie Patterson was privy to an early practice, having been invited to check out the group by Fowley. Writing for *Back Door Man* magazine in 1977, Patterson recounts:

> Once Kim asked them to do a song for us the way they'd do it live. This meant that they'd put on a show—chord after power chord; Sandy kept a solid beat, often twirling her sticks like batons; and Micki sang and danced, her voice dripping with innocence and sensuality, her movements nearly perfect. They were actually very exciting like that.[19]

---

* Vicki Peterson questions the provenance of the moniker "Micki Steele" being a Fowley invention, instead arguing that the bassist created the title herself.

Patterson hosted the first Runaways show in the living room of his family home in Torrance. He describes Micki as "a complicated and sensitive person interested in truth and beauty...young and pretty and talented and perhaps naive, or at least new to the games that Hollywood tends to play on people."[20] Other nights out on the town to see the group are burned into his brain as well. "I remember seeing [Micki] in the band when The Runaways played crappy little bars and discos in Orange County and San Fernando Valley....She was the lead singer and bass player...and a damn fine one. In those days, [Micki] could sing the rock'n'roll stuff quite well."[21]

As great as the singing may have been, things were not going well for the bass player, as Fowley's mental and emotional manipulation began to take its toll. In a later *Mojo* magazine interview, Micki recounted, "Early on this thing started with Kim, this sordid personal angle....He was enamored of me in a way that I found very uncomfortable. I'd been raised in a sheltered manner...and wasn't savvy enough to know I could say, 'C'mon Kim, fuck off.' My performance went down the tubes. I—I started going kind of nuts from it."[22] Micki later added, "Guys like Kim are weird," their actions based on "not having become a pop star themselves. They always try to be the idol maker—they always try to live through their own bands which is weird. He always said, I'm too *tall* to be a rock star. And then he'd turn round and say to me, 'You're too tall to be a rock star. You can never wear high heels. Rock stars are supposed to be 5' 4" or under'—stuff like that. I developed this horrible, round-shouldered posture because I was afraid I was too tall. It was unbelievable."[23]

Bandmate West noted, "Micki had told me that she was thinking about quitting because she couldn't deal with Kim's weirdness. His behavior toward her was abusive. She didn't care for his filthy mouth or when he would come on to her. When Kim would say inappropriate things or yell at us during a rehearsal, Micki never stood up to him, whereas Joan and I would just tell him to fuck off....She was a nice girl who always seemed uncomfortable. At the time it seemed to me that she really lacked that personality that you need to survive in a band situation."[24]

Fowley began spewing disparaging comments about Micki to Jett and West, complaining that the two-year age gap between the girls was "throwing off the jailbait marketing angle," claiming, "She didn't fit in and was bringing the group down," as she lacked the quintessential rock and roll vibe needed to ascend the desired heights of commercial greatness. Fowley later accused Micki of "always having migraine headaches." Her behavior after gigs of sitting "in the kitchen and look[ing] down on the ground…would put a bummer on the rest of the girls," Fowley claimed.

According to Fowley, one night he asked what was wrong, to which she responded:

> This isn't tasteful. We're singing to guys who jack off and girls who fist fuck, and there's all this rock 'n' roll shit, and it's fun, and it's interesting, but I'm older than Joan and Sandy, and I want more. This music has to go somewhere. I can't keep doing this stuff.[25]

Micki recalled Fowley saying to her, "'This is your one chance. You'll never get another chance. Period. I am your one and only chance at rock stardom.' I was really young and really impressionable and he was just a really manipulative, unhappy person and he just tried to make everyone else feel unhappy and under his control and he was horrible. He almost put me off music altogether. I thought, God, if this is what it's like, well, fuck it."[26]

Jett recounted a similarly distraught Micki. "The vibe was that she didn't like the songs," she says. "She seemed very unhappy after shows, almost to the point of tears, like the shows [were] depressing. She just didn't seem to be at all on the same page. It wasn't 'cause she wasn't a nice girl or a talented person; she was a great singer, a really good musician."[27]

Fowley eventually fired Micki from the Runaways after a Halloween show in Laguna Beach. Unsurprisingly, there are two different versions of how the parting of ways went down. According to Fowley, Micki accepted that the age difference and conflicting visions for the group made leaving the band the best decision for everyone. In the *Mojo* article, Micki recalls a much contrasting scenario. "When Kim finally got rid of me, he was out for blood," Micki recounts. "He'd realized I wasn't into it, and I guess he resented my inability to simply tell him to knock it off. But I was just too intimidated. When he pulled the plug he went a little over the top. He said, 'You have no magic. This is the only chance you'll ever have to be a rock star and you've blown it.' Perhaps my musical thing didn't lend itself to his slutty jailbait design, but the way Kim treated me made me depressed for a long time. Then I got angry, and I decided I was gonna show him. It was a harsh experience, but it firmed my resolve," Micki later admitted.[28]

Bomp writer Lisa Fancher confided that she, too, "was disappointed" when Micki left the group. "I didn't see any reason to replace her because she wasn't difficult, she wasn't a bitch. I totally believe that they wanted a blonde chick who would wear a corset, and I don't think Micki would have ever done anything like that. The way Micki was let go, it was extremely unkind how much it traumatized her. I think it probably took her a while to bounce back from that."[29]

Runaways biographer Evelyn McDonnell contextualizes the moment, noting that "[The Runaways] were very young women…putting themselves out there in this powerful way." Fowley, she says, "liked to find women that were on the edge, vulnerable—and prey on them." Micki, she guesses, may have unfortunately fallen into this category. "The fact that she left the band so quickly indicates that something happened and nobody seemed to really know [why]." She concludes, "I feel like [the Runaways] could be a case study of all the ways in which being a woman in a man's world is seriously damaging."[30]

Though the Runaways were already signed to a record label, had a swelling Beatle-like fan base in Japan, and several records under their belts, Amanda was not tempted to join, repeatedly giving Mamis a firm and consistent "No" to his overtures.

Besides regular appearances at the Sweetwater Cafe and the Kerckhoff Coffee House on the UCLA campus, Vicki had succeeded in accomplishing the nearly impossible feat of getting the band into the Los Angeles club circuit, with numerous nights at the Driftwood—a dive bar in Redondo Beach—locked onto the calendar. The new momentum required yet another new name to match. Rechristened the Muze, Amanda, Debbi, and Vicki began mixing with other bands on the burgeoning independent scene.

Joe Nolte of the Last provides a timeline of a changing Los Angeles music scene, coinciding with the Muze venturing out into small venue life. Nolte describes a city "done with music," disco having eliminated the live scene completely. "There weren't any gigs," Nolte recalls, before sharing, "The Whisky had actually shut down for a while." The ability for new groups to build a live performance following was nonexistent, as the club scene "was a closed circuit." Nolte describes a chicken-or-egg quandary that made it nearly impossible for new talent to evolve. "You had to already have played at a club or have a record out in order to play *at a club*. How do you first play in a club where you have to have already played it? They didn't want any new blood, no unsigned bands, no original music." It was not until 1978, Nolte argues, that things started to change, specifically with the opening the year before of a new spot called The Masque. "It was an underground basement, labyrinthian with various rooms underneath the Pussycat Theater on Hollywood Boulevard. Punk Rock Heaven," he smiles.[31]

Though only existing in its original location for a year—1977 to 1978—The Masque was ground zero for much of the early Los Angeles punk scene, and completely different than the places the girls had been frequenting. "We were very middle class living in the South Bay," Vicki recalls. "We have never done the Hollywood scene at that point, hadn't been hanging out at the Whisky. We had not been going to punk rock clubs at all. We were very nice girls who did covers of Heart and obscure '60s tunes. We were not punk rock." The atmosphere of The Masque's dark basement was completely alien to Amanda and Vicki, "fully graffitied, smoky…absolutely a different planet."[32] It was the twosome's "first real exposure to that world," Vicki says. "Amanda was slightly horrified and I was absolutely fascinated," she laughs, explaining, "Amanda was horrified that I was fascinated. We just didn't know it at all before that."

4.

While her peers were "hanging out with their jock friends, going to parties, getting drunk, and throwing up a lot," Debbi was already doing what she wanted to do for the rest of her life: making and performing music. "I would not be thinking about what the teacher was saying in class," Debbi admits. "I'd be playing songs in my head, songs running all day constantly in my brain like an iPod shuffle." She was completely focused on just getting "home to rehearse or go to a show that night." It was all that mattered to the teen.

A typical day would begin as early as 6 a.m. and could run well past midnight. "I'd get up, go to school, somehow get through the day, come back and do homework," Debbi remembers. Then the band part of Debbi's life would begin. "I would go to rehearsal. On the days we had a show, we'd have to pack up all our equipment, load in, and do the gig. We were usually the opening band. By the time we had performed and loaded out, it would be past midnight, sometimes early morning."[1] While parents Milt and Jeanne were not crazy about their teenage daughter being out so late on a school night, they were supportive. They knew the sisters were together, and that Debbi was keeping up with homework. A journal, originally kept as part of an assignment for a psychology class during her senior year, captures the highs and lows of the young girl as she enters the Los Angeles music scene. It also illustrates the heartbreaking awareness the teenage drummer already had about the misogyny inherent in the industry, and the industry's perception that women musicians were inferior to their male counterparts.

Debbi's Journal Entry

I feel as though I'll be able to sing, play and entertain people, even if I'm a girl...I really want to perform. THAT'S where I belong. Although it's not easy, I think me, Vicki and Amanda will stick to it.

"I did not care about being a homecoming queen," Debbi tells me. "I didn't have a lot of friends in high school. I was a bit of a loner. Most of the kids were worried about how they looked or their boyfriend. I didn't care about any of that. I thought, 'I'm going to be a musician. I'm going to be on stage, I'm going to be successful.' That's all I cared about when I was in high school. It was just not the norm."[2]

Performing even came before the sacred college tests. "When I had to take the SATs in my senior year," Debbi laughs, "the night before I had played at a club till two in the morning. I had to get up and be there by eight to take my exams." In her characteristic self-deprecating way, she jokes, "I'm surprised I didn't flunk the whole thing—I did pretty good actually, considering."[3]

Gigs at the Driftwood were happening at least once a week. The venue was not alone in seeing a new fad bubbling up in the local area. Los Angeles bookers were starting to catch on to the small but increasing all-female group phenomena happening in the underground scene. "There were some women in bands but it wasn't common," Henry Rollins recalls when I ask him about the presence of female musicians at the time he was coming up in Los Angeles. "I could be generous and say the scene wasn't a total 'boys club' and women in bands were not seen as an exception but a band with an all-woman lineup, that by comparison was rare and perhaps stained with the term 'girl band' to denote they were somehow not to be taken seriously. They could never just be a band, they had to be considered a 'girl' band if that was the case, then they needed to look good because they weren't being judged by the quality of their music."[4]

For these reasons, the Muze had avoided playing at shows that were marketed as entirely "girl" lineups, instead preferring to be with bands they liked as people and were good as musicians. "If you'd hand them a tape, because that's what you have to do, you're trying to book yourself into a club, then they get the idea of, 'I know! I'll put them on with the other two all-girl bands I just got tapes from and we'll have all-girl band night. The battle of the all-girl bands! Ahh! What an idea! We'll have a wet T-shirt contest and we'll make them all wear T-shirts!'" Vicki recounts of various encounters of trying to get the group shows.[5] However, when Doug Weston, owner of the Troubadour, asked the Muze to submit a demo for consideration to be included in a "girl-group" evening he was putting together, the lure of possibly playing the legendary venue outweighed any aversion to being pigeonholed in the pink ghetto.

Debbi's Journal Entry

Amanda met Doug Weston, the owner of the Troubadour. He said he's planning on having some all-girl groups play there. The two groups he booked are the LA Girls and Backstage Pass. A band who was going to play there, the Go-Go's (or something like that) decided against it. So, he became interested in another local female band—US! He said he wanted a tape of us, so we recorded ourselves playing at the Driftwood. It didn't turn out very good (we didn't play so hot that night...). We tried it again the next night, and it came out a bit better...So, we've picked out 5 specific songs and we're gonna send it to Doug and HOPEFULLY get the job! Ah, but who knows...

Though having only taken on the Muze moniker months earlier, the trio felt it was still not quite right. Out went the Muze, in came the newly agreed title of the Fans. "We just loved that everyone always assumed we were fans, rather than a band ourselves, so it was tongue-in-cheek," Amanda says.

Now playing as a threesome, Vicki had been taking on lead and rhythm guitar duties, as well as singing. "We knew we needed a fourth person because Vicki just didn't like doing both the guitar parts," Amanda remembers. "She really wanted to hand the lead over to someone else." Band manager Vicki placed an ad in a local music trade paper and fielded potential candidates. Playing prowess and dedication to the band's success were crucial characteristics for the new person; gender was not a consideration. "Being female was not on our agenda," Debbi says. "We were playing music. We wanted to be huge, to be big stars. Whether this person was woman or not didn't really matter."[6]

However, as luck would have it, it was a girl who responded. Culver City native Lynn Elkind had been playing guitar since age ten and was currently in another group, Queen of Hearts. "We knew [being an all-female band] was different, visually and musically," Debbi says. "We liked the camaraderie; it was like a girls club. It was an 'all for one' mentality. It was about us girls going out there and invading the men's world."[7]

Amanda's first interaction with Lynn took place at the Santa Monica digs she shared with Vicki and friend Lauri Sing. "We were still at UCLA in our nice two-story apartment," Amanda recalls. "I'm standing at the top of the stairs and Lynn walks in. I'm looking at her and thinking, 'Yes, this is our girl, she has to be good.' She was tiny, had this shock of curly hair, was carrying her guitar, and wearing a striped T-shirt."[8] Debbi was equally impressed upon first laying eyes on the possible bandmate. "We used to make ourselves laugh because she had big boobs and a little waist," Debbi smiles. "We used to think she would fall over, in the nicest way possible. She actually resembled Marc Bolan; she even moved exactly like Marc Bolan meets Keith Richards with breasts."[9] Besides looking the part, Lynn was also the same age as the other Fans. "We had seen a lot of people who were so much older than us," Amanda says. "Debbi was eighteen, I was nineteen, and Vicki was twenty-one. We didn't want somebody who was like twenty-five or twenty-six."[10] She was different from the tightknit sisterhood of the "Peterettes," Amanda says. Lynn, in contrast, "wasn't much like us in terms of somebody we would have necessarily picked out as a best friend."[11]

But none of that mattered. Lynn's guitar prowess won the Fans over. "She had a really cool bluesy sound which added a nice flavor to what we already had," Debbi recalls.[12] Amanda is equally complimentary: "She was a really good guitarist with good musical instinct." Most important, "she just really wanted to play guitar," Amanda says. "It was a time when there really weren't that many women out there playing, let alone lead guitar at our age. She was just such a good fit."[13]

Like the other Fans, Lynn had a day job working for her parents' paper binding company. They were supportive of their daughter's musical endeavors, allowing the band to rehearse for free in their offices. With a gig looming and the prospect of the Troubadour tantalizingly within reach, the new foursome got busy preparing for the show.

Just the notion of playing the legendary venue was cause for anxiety. "I think we were all pretty nervous," Amanda tells me. Yet the girls were in actuality ready for anything. Their determination to get as much live playing experience as possible had provided a cross section of audiences, allowing them to develop the needed chops to endure most audience situations. Some shows could be daunting, but they gave the band valuable interactions with an unpredictable crowd. "I didn't do fraternities, I just played them," Debbi says. "I just remember kegs of beer and big plastic cups. There were people just guzzling beer, drunk off their faces shouting, 'Play something *you* know,' as if they were making fun of us. 'Play "Freebird"!'"[14]

Regardless of audience or venue, with the addition of Lynn, the Fans seemed to have finally found the missing element to their group. "She was great," Amanda says. "The first shows we did with her really felt like we had a band."[15]

Now nothing seemed out of reach for the Fans. They had become friendly with the Knack, who were starting to have international success with the single "My Sharona." "They accepted us for who we were," Debbi explains. "I'm sure at the beginning they thought we were just cute little fans and probably didn't think twice about us," she concedes, "because that's how people saw us. Later on, they started taking us a bit more seriously."[16] Watching the Knack's growing success showed the Fans that their aspirations could come true; it was happening in front of their eyes to a group they knew and respected. "It was a band that was going somewhere and we had connections with them," Debbi explains when I ask of why they were significant to her. "We saw the rise in popularity from the inside. We would go backstage and talk to them. We saw them from the beginning."[17]

In the Los Angeles newspaper the *View*, under the banner "The Fans—All-Girl Band on L. A. Scene," journalist Scott Paul gives one of the most baldly honest critiques of the rock landscape.* "Go to any rock club and the scene is the same," Paul argues. He continues:

> While the boys in the band are busy giving a show on stage, the girls in the audience are giving a show of their own. In the front row are the would-be groupies ogling the guitar players. Farther back in the crowd grinning at the band are the girls that have an in to the rock scene, maybe working for a record company. Still farther back are the real girlfriends of the band looking with disgust at the other females. Then in the back there are The Fans. Four girls who have their own band, one that's better than a lot of the male bands playing in Los Angeles.[18]

Doing gigs was not a money-making opportunity. Compensation for shows was usually very little, barely covering the gas used to get to the venues. "We got paid but it was just a pittance," Amanda recalls. "It wasn't pay to play but it was a very small amount of money."[19] Milo Aukerman, lead singer of Descendents, emphasizes this discrepancy between the myths that have evolved from the time period and what it was actually like. "It was not as big a scene as people may think," he says. "Maybe a top drawing band could get a hundred kids to come to the Whisky, and they'd make enough to cover a month's rent. No one was getting rich off punk rock."[20]

The Fans were an anomaly among their peers in avoiding the seedier side of the scene.† Social Distortion shared bills with the band on

---

* In its every iteration, including that of the Bangles.

† So antidrug was Vicki that she did a painfully earnest public service piece for the nonprofit Rock Against Drugs (RAD) in 1987, https://www.youtube.com/watch?v=2UX6-CwuF00.

4.

various occasions during the early years. When asked how prevalent narcotics were during the late 1970s and early 1980s, group founder Mike Ness replied that the girls "were a complete exception to the rule of that period of time, which is kind of cool. They spared themselves a lot of misery."[21] Steve Barton, a friend of Debbi's from the band Translator, also recalls a dirtier version of Los Angeles. "My favorite place, by far, was Blackie's on La Brea," he says. "It was a total dive and I totally loved it. I have never been a smoker, but in those days people could still smoke indoors. I would come away from there (or from any of the clubs for that matter) with my clothes smelling as if I had smoked three cartons of cigarettes. At Blackie's, I remember a woman who worked there serving drinks, taking overflowing ashtrays from the tables and simply dumping them onto the floor. They'd get swept up at the end of the night. It was that kind of place, with a killer sound system. I once opened the bathroom door, which was right next to the stage, to find someone from one of the other bands having sex. They looked up, said hello, I said hello back, and closed the door. I adored that club, at least at that time of my life!"[22]

Milo Aukerman has equally visceral memories:

Sounds: Poorly EQ'ed guitar, often out of tune
Smells: Uninhabitable bathrooms, toilets often overflowing
Sights: Mohawks, chains, dangerous weapons in the crowd
Visceral feeling: That I was where the action was, that I belonged.[23]

Henry Rollins paints a darker vision of the town. "As I remember, there were a lot of runaway youths, escaping some truly awful family situations. Abuse of all kinds was inflicted on these people. I remember meeting a really nice young woman when I first moved out there. She had homemade tattoos and wrote poems. I'd catch up with her here and there at shows and we'd talk. She was sensitive and kind of sad. While we were on tour she jumped off the top of a building. So there was death, lots of drug use. Like scary go to jail or overdose and die drugs and some people died. Shows could be quite intense. There was sometimes police intervention. They were dependably hostile. The music was often great but there was always a chance of something bad happening at any moment. At shows, I can't say I had a 'good' time, more like a fully aware and intense time. I guess the overall takeaway for me was it was fear-tinged hyper-reality and riding a wave of danger."[24]

However, some people found the city a welcome reprieve from where they originally hailed from. "I drove from Kentucky to Los Angeles in October 1977," Sid Griffin, founding member of iconic bands the Unclaimed and Long Ryders, says over a Zoom call. "It was like your parents had gone away for the weekend and they'd left you the house. The amount of the lessening of restrictions and 'this is the way we do things' was just gone. The sense of freedom was incredible. I was just thrilled to be in Los Angeles. I thought it was heaven. I am stunned when I talked to people from the old days and they said they didn't like it. I find that amazing. Anything you wanted to do, people didn't laugh at it. The possibilities there were endless."[25]

5.

Through a combination of word of mouth, a growing audience, and Vicki's tireless promotion efforts, the roster of venues asking the Fans to play was ever increasing. One club that had been added to the girls' circuit was Pippin's in Santa Monica. Often hosting bands like Black Flag and Redd Kross,* an October lineup had the girls sharing the bill with a group they had not heard of before—the Unclaimed.

Kentucky transplant Sid Griffin had formed the band after moving to Los Angeles in April. "There was no massive movement of 1960s-dominated stuff," Sid tells me.[1] "It was the first time people had taken that sort of Lenny Kaye *Nuggets* to an LP set of '60s garage band music and made that a genre. If you wanted to hear a twelve-string guitar and a Farfisa organ, you went to an Unclaimed gig."[2] A mutual appreciation was sparked between the musicians, seeing them trade shows on a regular basis.

The Fans rounded out the year 1979 by providing the in-house entertainment at the Getty museum Christmas party. Though no pictures were taken, the infamous shindig saw curators "dancing with abandon," with festivities getting wild enough that Lynn had to eventually be carried out to the car when things began to wind down.

Vicki was finding herself at a crossroads. She was juggling part-time work, an academic schedule, and the managing, booking, and performance duties of the Fans. The usually upbeat Vicki found herself being "miserable," frustration coming from feeling that she was doing a lot of

---

* Then going by Red Cross, as the humanitarian organization had not yet forced the name change, which happened sometime around 1982.

things—but none of them [in her estimation] well. "It was hard being a part-time student," she says.[3] "Suddenly, I'm getting B's and C's, and not A's and B's. That was very weird and uncomfortable for me."[4] When she compared how she felt to her roommate's optimistic outlook, the contrast was even more glaring. "[When Amanda became an anthropology major at UCLA], she said she'd found her tribe. I wished that was the way I was feeling but I just couldn't. I felt like I was in the wrong place."[5] It was a difficult time for the high-achieving Vicki, as she tried to work out what to do. It was especially isolating as her closest confidant was having the opposite experience. "I went through a pretty serious depression at that time," she confides.[6] "I was living with Amanda, and when I would tell her what was going on in my head, she would be surprised." Having always enjoyed school, it felt "strange" to be so disengaged, Vicki reflects. "I just didn't have the drive, the energy, or the interest."[7]

Things got so bad that Vicki even "slept through a midterm."[8] Decades later, she still seems a bit horrified at this transgression, saying, "We probably played the night before and I was probably up till four."[9] The usually keen student found herself completely nonplussed at the prospect of more years spent in a classroom, especially at that moment. "I just wanted to be doing what I was doing off campus, which was to book and play shows. I started to feel like at twenty-one that I was old and it had to happen now."[10]

The exam snafu did act to provide necessary clarity. The Fans were touching distance to music stardom. Vicki had been gigging through high school and two years of college, then watched her friends, the Knack, get signed and shoot to international super stardom. If she had been able to put all her energy into the Fans, where would they be? "I felt like it was all happening and I wasn't there. I wasn't doing it to the full extent," she tells me.[11] "Music [was] something I [had] to do. I knew if I'd waited another two years to give my all to the band, it'd have just pushed it back that much further. I didn't know if I could sustain it."[12]

Amanda starting to think about the future as well. "I graduated from college with a BA in anthropology in March of 1980," she says. "I was free to do the band. I loved playing but I was thinking, 'Do I want to do this forever?'"[13]

Having completed her degree, Amanda returned to the UK for a month. Much to her horror, she saw other groups in Britain using the name the Fans. "As it turned out, there were about four or five bands called the Fans, but we didn't know about them," Amanda says.[14] Upon discovery, she wrote to Vicki and Debbi immediately. The search began—again—for yet another original moniker.

Back in Los Angeles, Debbi, Lynn, and Vicki decided to live together, finding a place on Detroit Street in Hollywood. Having recently graduated high school, Debbi had decided not to go to college. "I'd already figured out my career," she tells me. "I was originally going to go to community college for a couple of years just to appease my parents." However, she changed her mind, as "I didn't want them spending any money on school because I knew I wasn't going to be into it."[15] A jubilant Debbi logged the event in her journal.

Debbi's Journal Entry

My parents said I don't have to go to college! I'm just gonna keep working at the Getty Museum for now and work on playing with the band. It's gonna be so weird in Sept when I don't have to go back to school. I love my parents. They're so understanding about the band and our love for it.

The girls were gaining bigger crowds, getting invited back to perform at the Hong Kong Cafe, a former Chinese restaurant turned all-ages venue, in June—this time under their newest name, Those Girls.* Soon after, Vicki finally got the call: Those Girls were booked to play the Troubadour. The West Hollywood nightclub, first opened in 1957, had played host to a multitude of the band's heroes, including Buffalo Springfield, the Byrds, and John Lennon. Amanda confides to being "ridiculously excited," as it marked a huge step up for Those Girls. Rehearsal started

---

* It has been incorrectly claimed that the band was called Hollywood Girls for a short time. This was never a name used nor considered at any time by the band.

in preparation for the August 8 show, Those Girls wanting to ensure their performance would give Weston nothing to doubt his decision. The practice paid off, with the performance going "well enough that we promptly got invited back," Amanda says, though no photographs were taken to capture the show.[16]

Even though Those Girls were getting great gigs and playing out twice a week, Lynn did not seem as committed to the group as she had initially appeared. "Lynn just seemed to be losing interest in the band," Amanda remembers. "She didn't like coming to rehearsals and we were feeling that she was on a different path from us."[17] The direction of Those Girls was also changing; where once Vicki wanted to hand over guitar duties to someone else, Amanda says that the group "sounded better as a power trio with Vicki playing rhythm and lead than with two guitars."[18] Vicki's ability had equaled if not surpassed Lynn's, who did not sing, write, or even enjoy practicing. Lynn was also partaking in alcohol and marijuana to excess, both of which were impacting her participation in Those Girls. "There were times when she couldn't play her parts because she was just too far gone," Amanda recalls. "She would come to rehearsals drunk, get drunk at shows and wouldn't be functional."[19]

While the original three were not tempted to sample the escapist extras, Lynn—arguably like many of the other young people around her—was interested in partaking in the free-flowing alcohol and drugs available in the music scene. "She never expressed any interest in leaving the band at all," Amanda says.[20] However, with the additional time commitment the band demanded and the increased sporadic behavior Lynn exhibited, disparity between the original trio and the newest member started to become a worrisome problem. It was decided that the possibility of Lynn making a poor showing was too great for her to stay in Those Girls. "We all cried the day that we fired her," Amanda recalls. "It was really hard but it was necessary."[21] Once again a threesome, though still living with Lynn, Those Girls soldiered on, playing a multitude of shows, including return dates at the Troubadour.

5.

On December 8, 1980, the world heard the tragic news: John Lennon had been assassinated outside his home in New York. The death of their beloved hero and touchstone shook Amanda, Debbi, and Vicki to the core. More momentous news was going to also forever change the trajectory of the trio's life: Amanda was considering leaving the group she had founded with her best friend. "Right the way through, I was the egghead of the band," Amanda confides. "Vicki's biggest dream was to be in a band, my dream was to be an archaeologist." Though Those Girls were now having substantial local success, the original goal was still there for Amanda. "It hadn't gone away," she says. The bass player had thought she could balance the two passions successfully. "Those dreams were right there next to each other for a long time. I was going to be an archaeologist and bass player."[22] The friends endlessly discussed if the dual career tracks could coexist in harmony. "Vicki and I were just constantly talking about it. She was trying to convince me to stay in very deep and profound ways." For a long time, Amanda fought an inner battle of divided attention and affection.

Vicki says she saw Amanda's departure coming, which was made especially clear after a dinner with Amanda's then paramour, Jerry Podany. "Jerry and I joke now that we fought over her," Vicki says. "He already knew that he was going to ask her to marry him." Vicki explains that her best friend's beau wanted to discuss Amanda, who felt torn. "She adored Jerry. She saw a life with him that was going to be fulfilling and wonderful. Yet she had been with me in this dream journey towards being successful in a band." The conversation was "heartbreaking" for Vicki. "I remember saying to him, 'This is what she wants. This is her dream [about staying in Those Girls].' He looked at me and said, 'No, it isn't.' I realized he was not making this up; it was something that she was afraid to tell me." A conversation between the best friends ensued, with Amanda admitting "she wanted this other life" as a historian and archaeologist.

Amanda explains her departure, clarifying, "What was driving me crazy was that I was torn between staying with the band and pursuing my dream of going to graduate school and becoming an archaeologist. I was passionate about both and hated to have to decide. Jerry wasn't a factor. I had to decide for myself what I wanted to do professionally. He didn't ask me to marry him until he knew that I had absolutely made up my mind about my future."

A week after the friends talked, Jerry and Amanda went to San Francisco and got engaged.

On Christmas Eve, Amanda told Vicki and Debbi that she had decided to apply for graduate school and move to the UK. The relocation across the Atlantic meant she was officially departing Those Girls. "It was clear that if I didn't [leave now] the band was going to get famous and it would be much harder to go," she says.

Amanda's departure forced Vicki to reflect and recalibrate. The young band leader felt she needed to "take a breath" after years of nonstop grind in pursuit of stardom. "I had been so insistent and pushing all the time before that, to get rehearsals in, to book shows, writing, and doing everything. On top of that, I had been going to school and working two jobs."[23]

Though no longer in the band, Lynn was still living with Debbi and Vicki. It was a "cordial" situation, Vicki says, but added to the feeling of uncertainty. "It was down to just me and Debbi," she says. "It was the first moment since probably 1977 that I was taking a break and thinking, 'What the fuck am I going to do now?'"

Then the phone rang.

A young woman named Susanna Hoffs was on the other end of the line.

6.

With low population density, idyllic open green spaces, beautiful architecture, and tree-lined streets, Brentwood is one of the most aspirational areas in Los Angeles County, making it appealing to notable residents past and present, including Joan Crawford, Steve McQueen, and Marilyn Monroe. It was also where Susanna Hoffs's parents decided to relocate after meeting at Yale, where father Joshua started medical school after an undergraduate degree completed at Harvard. With women not allowed to attend the academy in 1953, mother Tamar was instead studying under acclaimed abstract painter Josef Albers, a program she had been handpicked for based upon her artwork. The West Coast was appealing to the unconventional couple. "They went to Los Angeles to get away from their parents, the thing to do in 1959," Susanna explains.[1] "An uprooted liberal East Coast family—a beatnik vibe, into Jackson Pollock and jazz."[2]

While Josh was doing his residency at UCLA, Tamar became immersed in the film scene, after being asked by friend and actor Leonard Nimoy to join the art department on his 1965 independent movie, *Deathwatch*. The Hoffses eventually decided to make more permanent roots, purchasing a residence with a nefarious past in Brentwood. "The dilapidated state of the property as well as its mythology made it possible for the young doctor to afford the posh neighborhood," Susanna explains. "It was a crumbling Spanish house with some crazy lore," she continues. "There was a crime story element to it—it's why we could afford the house because nobody wanted to buy it." The tale passed to Susanna and her two brothers was of a previous owner who had attempted to kill his wife in a murder-suicide gone awry before renting a small jet plane and trying to dive-bomb the aircraft into the ocean in a final attempt of a dual death. "As kids growing up, there was always a sense of the house having a haunted history," she laughs.[3]

The then "crumbling" Spanish-style abode was built in the 1930s on a corner lot, boasting "giant trees, beautiful foliage, and native flowers," Susanna recalls of her childhood home. Some of the original elements were still intact, such as a *Downton Abbey*–style bell system, which could be activated in the formal dining room, striking a chime to ring in other parts of the house, signaling the next course of a meal was ready to be eaten. "From the master bedroom, there was a way to climb out onto the roof with a jerry-rigged staircase," Susanna says. Tamar loved sitting there and taking in the heady afternoon sun. "It was fancy when it was built, but by the time we lived in it was very artsy, cluttered, and bohemian," Susanna describes. "It was a fun house to grow up in. The gardens were all overgrown. There were fruit trees. We had a swing set. My mom's art was all over the place. We had a pool table that was cool and popular with our friend group. It was not posh."[4]

Mary Petrie first met Susanna at Paul Revere Junior High School as they were entering sixth grade. "I remember seeing this girl who was really petite and had long, luscious brown hair that she always had in a braid down her back. She was a beautiful creature. She had these almond eyes and was just a doll," Mary recalls.[5] The two grew up walking distance from each other, surrounded by affluence. "It was kids getting Mercedes for their sixteenth birthdays," Mary explains, "wealthy kids who didn't know that they were privileged in any kind of way." The girls, however, had a different experience.

"Our families weren't like that," Mary tells me. "[They] had their heads screwed on and didn't spoil us." Instead of a brand-new luxury car, at sixteen Mary was "driving a '65 seafoam green Buick LeSabre that was from my grandmother," while "Sue was sharing an old car with John [her older brother]." The down-to-earth values of the family never left

6.

Susanna, though assumptions would be made later about her because of the area she grew up in.

The Hoffses defied expectations of those around them, embracing their own unique parenting style. Though they could afford to privately educate their kids, the Hoffses went to public school, with Susanna later commenting that she was not raised with "a lot of dogma," instead joking that Freud was the "religion" of choice.[6] "They valued intellectual ideas, but also kindness," Susanna says. Joshua's professional practice as a psychoanalyst influenced how he raised his children, with Susanna saying that "nothing could surprise him." "He knows the range of how the human mind works," she explains. "It allowed him to be more forgiving because there wasn't a Christian stamp on everything like, 'You must do this, you must not do that.' He just wanted to raise us to be good human beings, but also to know that all human beings are flawed and they have darker instincts."[7] Tamar and Joshua "rebelled against old-school ways of doing things," Susanna says. "My mom wore miniskirts," while Josh allowed the children to experience the various art and culture happening around them, taking them to cinematic R-rated movies like *Midnight Cowboy* and *Bonnie and Clyde*. "My dad's theory was that children should not be barred from seeing things about life, as long as they're explained to them," Susanna says. Open discussion was encouraged regardless of topic. "After we would watch something together, he would ask, 'Do you guys have questions?'" Susanna recalls. "'Yes, I have a question [Susanna raises her hand]. What were those two people doing in the bed?' 'Oh, that's sex,' he would say, then draw a picture on a napkin in a restaurant. 'This is how sex happens.'"

Joshua believed in telling his children the unbridled truth, rejecting many accepted norms of the era. "He thought it was bullshit to make up fake stories and say that a stork delivered a baby," Susanna says. "Stuff like that drove my father crazy. He wanted to slash hypocrisy." As an adult reflecting back on her childhood, Susanna has obvious respect and admiration for her parents' unique outlooks. "I don't think that the rebel streak of 'I'm going to start a band' or any of those things would have happened had I not been raised by my artsy mom and my free-thinking dad," she says. However, as a child, she admits that the "style of parenting made me feel apart from my friends who were raised in more traditional manners."[8]

The open atmosphere of the Hoffs residence was appealing to Susanna's friends, who saw it as a place where they could openly express themselves. "I would go over to her house all the time," says Mary Petrie, as "her parents were really *hip*." "Her mom was a producer, always writing, her dad a psychiatrist. Nothing was off limits in terms of what you could talk about," she explains. With both Mary's and Susanna's parents working full-time, the girls were granted autonomy. "They didn't know where we were most of the time," says Mary. "It's not like now, where there are cell phones and constant checking in. It just wasn't like that. We were kind of able to get away with murder. I wanted to become her friend because she was so interesting and cool," she continues. "We both loved ballet and reading. Our favorite book was *Jane Eyre*. We had a similar sense of humor. We both loved films and music. We were both a little advanced in that way for our age. We were these young wannabee artists. I wanted to be an actress. We were both into fine art and paintings," Mary explains.[9]

Tamar and Josh realized early on that their daughter "loved everything to do with art," an attitude encouraged within the family. "My mom was always painting and drawing," Susanna says. "My dad—even though he was a psychiatrist—was obsessed with art." Susanna recalls Tamar "always playing music in the house, because she was very young and hip, and an artist herself." Family lore has it that even in the crib, baby Susanna was "rocking and rolling." "My crib would be set up near where [Tamar] was in the kitchen, and she would find that I'd rolled all the way across the room because I was so moved by the music she had on."*

Dr. Hoffs had an affinity for classical music, with Susanna laughing at one memory. "He would stand in his underwear, fake conducting," she says. "It was cute." One band specifically enthralled the household. "The

---

* "Don't worry, it was a safe situation," she assures me.

6.

Beatles were my absolute gods," says Tamar. Early copies of the Liverpudlians' releases would make their way onto the Hoffses' turntable courtesy of a friend who worked at the Fab Four's label, Capitol Records. Susanna has vivid memories of first hearing *Meet the Beatles!* at age five. Susanna and her siblings—elder brother John, born thirteen months before, thus almost her "Irish twin"—and younger brother, Jesse—"would just listen to the records until we wore the vinyl out." A rumored local appearance in the neighborhood only fueled the Hoffs kids' fandom. "Once when I was growing up, there was a party down the street," she recounts. "The Beatles were attending a Hemophilia Foundation charity event within walking distance of our house. I was five and my older brother, John, was six. There were cops all over the place." Susanna sends me a vintage newsreel, capturing that evening from August 1964. Scores of children line the streets, hoping for a glimpse of the foursome. It was a memory that stayed with the young girl decades on.

The spread out topography of Los Angeles provided endless opportunities for car journeys, always with a soundtrack supplied by local DJs. "All through the '60s, growing up in LA, I listened to the radio while being driven around from one place to another," Susanna recalls. The radio, in particular, "was the soundtrack to our early years and influenced our development as children," she says. "I loved singing along to the radio, everyone from Dusty Springfield and Dionne Warwick...to Petula Clark and Linda Ronstadt," she recalls. "There was such a great mix of things on the airwaves. You could hear Bob Dylan's 'Like A Rolling Stone,' then you'd hear Petula Clark doing 'Downtown.'"[10] Harmonizing, folk sounds, and acoustic guitars featured heavily in rotation, influencing the budding artistry of young Susanna. Live music also played a role informing the young artist, with early memories including a Donovan show at the Hollywood Bowl as well as a brush with one of the biggest folk heroines of the era. "We were eating dinner at Dan Tana's next door to the Troubadour," she says. "We walked over [to the venue] and Judy Collins was [performing]. I was the youngest person in the audience. I got to come backstage and meet her."[11]

Eager to encourage the children's interest, guitar lessons were provided by Tamar's younger brother, Carmi. "Carmi is a great musician," Susanna says. "He came out to Los Angeles around the time my mom and dad moved here." Carmi was "a guitar aficionado, both a player and a builder of instruments," Susanna tells me. "He worked at a guitar shop and had a company called the Dulcimer Works in Venice."[12] After landing in town, Carmi began gigging, eventually playing the odd show with Linda Ronstadt, as his friends made up the singer's band.

With the bolstering of her family, by elementary school, the desire to be in a group and perform was an aspiration for the young girl. However, Susanna suffered from stage fright. Tamar and Josh were supportive, trying to help their daughter overcome the crippling fear. A cassette featuring a then eleven-year-old Susanna preparing for an audition in a school play showcases her encouraging father. "There's this hilarious tape that wound up in my possession in which I'm practicing for a middle school audition for *The Sound of Music* but find myself stopping and starting to get it perfect. My dad, sensing I'm nervous, attempts to lighten the mood by saying before each take: 'Susanna Hoffs, ready, and go!' I would inevitably be unsatisfied by my performance and try, try again. I suppose I was a bit of a perfectionist, even then. Thinking back, I was so hard on myself. I did, in fact, get the part. I played Gretl, the youngest of the Von Trapp children."[13]

Singing and playing guitar emboldened the often shy, self-described "nerd." "I was a person who was very careful about everything, very trepidatious," Susanna says. "I was always so much smaller than everybody; back then, it was just horrifying," she admits. "I was kind of a late bloomer. I always looked a lot younger than I was. I could get into movies on the kids tickets, which was great. But I also had this part that was just waiting to be released: the voice, the performer." People often underestimated the petite girl, only to be shocked when they heard her sing, best encapsulated by an old classmate's memory of the then tween

Susanna. "She remembered me being this super quiet girl in middle school—until one day when I surprised her," Susanna laughs. "I had my guitar with me, and I just suddenly started singing and playing." The contrast between the unassuming Susanna and the performer were potent. "She was like, 'Wait. What just happened? What is that sound coming out of this little shy girl's mouth?'" Susanna tells me. "This story sums up who I've always been."[14]

With Carmi providing basic starting pointers, Susanna began practicing guitar on her own, learning most things by ear and continuous, repetitive playing. "I really taught myself to sing by just copying Joni [Mitchell], Linda Ronstadt, and Bonnie Raitt in the '70s," she said. "I remember very clearly where I really focused in and tried to learn all the little riffs and stuff they were doing. It went from there."[15]

Parties her parents held at the Brentwood home provided another opportunity for the emerging musician to practice in front of an audience. "My parents would have their cool 1960s friends over. They hung with the real artsy, hip crowd, all of these cool psychiatrists and people like Frank Gehry, the architect, and Leonard Nimoy and his wife, Sandi." At these gatherings, Susanna "would sometimes just start singing." "There are just some people who have swagger; they can walk into a room and be really confident," she says. "I don't think of myself now as a super shy person, but I was then." The change from reticent to center of attention was an "internalized dualism," Susanna now explains. "It was always like this switch that I would have to flip on inside of me."[16]

When Mary met Susanna, she was already studying with renowned dance instructor Don Hewitt at the International Ballet School West in Santa Monica on Montana Avenue. For Susanna, ballet was just the "first iteration of trying to do something the best possible way you could, in terms of an art format," she reflects. She encouraged Mary to join her, the two often going twice a day to receive tutelage under Hewitt's discerning eye. "We would *en dehors* and throw our ballet shoes to save ourselves space in a place where he would notice us," Mary says.[17] The school provided a foundation of rigorous training and strict expectations for Susanna.

Decades later, Hewitt still fondly remembers the dedicated young girl who religiously attended his classes. "Susanna was very serious. I can remember her eyes: very thoughtful, especially for a child that age. They held back a lot unless she really believed in something," Hewitt describes. At one point, Hewitt assigned the aspiring dancer with a solo. "She was very quietly determined," he says, adding, "she did quite well and practiced a lot." One image especially remains, though. "What I remember most is her face, looking at me, just asking me questions and taking in the answers and processing them."

Hewitt concludes with a description that still accurately encapsulates Susanna. "I thought she was a very deep child," he says. "She listened and worked very hard. I looked forward to working with her all the time because I knew that she would do something or be something. She could not fake sincerity."[18]

As they entered high school, film became an important part of the girls' lives, with spring break spent at the Nuart Theatre on the west side of Los Angeles. "We loved all the French New Wave films," Mary says, "and of course, we were seeing popular American films too. I remember standing in line for two hours to see *Star Wars*," she laughs. Another event in the calendar was a film festival imaginatively called Film X. "It was a twenty-four-hour marathon," Mary explains, "you would bring a blanket and pillow."[19] Each festival would have a theme; Susanna and Mary would stay the entire time, watching movie after movie.

While admitting that they did not get "invited to many parties," Mary assures that she and Susanna did partake in "all the stuff that you did in the '70s." She shares adventures of underage drinking, some "dabbling" in cocaine, and streaking through a Baskin-Robbins 31 Flavors ice cream parlor with Susanna's brother John and neighbor David Roback driving the getaway car. Petty shoplifting was occasionally on the itinerary, with the Santa Monica mall on the hit list. Woolworths was the usual target, with small items like gum being the take.

6.

Living in the rarefied atmosphere of Brentwood, the willowy Mary and diminutive Susanna felt like outsiders compared with their peers. "You have to realize," Mary explains, "We were surrounded by absolutely gorgeous people." She describes classmates as "very well-developed and beautiful" women, the men "surfers, volleyball, and football players." In contrast, Susanna and Mary "got our periods late" and "weren't the girls all the guys would go for." "We never went to the football homecoming; I don't think we went to dances," Mary says. The two did not date or have boyfriends, with Susanna even confessing that she did not get her first kiss until after high school. Susanna went to the prom with her brother John's friend, while Mary's brother "enlisted two of his gay friends to take my sister and me."[20]* "We felt like art birds," Mary tells me. "We sang in Madrigals and concert choirs," she remembers. "We were always in the arty crowd and hanging out with musicians and in the drama circle."[21]

When it came time to choose a college, Susanna decided to head up north and attend the University of California, Berkeley. The town, located less than fifteen miles east of San Francisco, had been an international epicenter less than ten years earlier for student protest, social change, and musical community. The recent history of the area appealed to Susanna. "My older brother got into Yale, and I didn't," she tells me, the result of "going rogue" on the Ivy League interviewer. At the time, Berkeley only asked for an application to be filled out and did not require an interview. "I had really good grades, I was a good student and they took me," Susanna says.[22] Accepted as a dance major, Susanna would eventually change to the all-encompassing degree of "art."

---

* Mary goes on to talk about the first high school reunion that occurred after the girls had graduated and Susanna had become a household name. "I refused to go," Mary said, "but she went. She thought that all those boys that she had a crush on then that wouldn't give her the time of day *would* now because she'd done 'something' in the world. But instead of feeling great, she said she still felt like the short Jewish girl in the corner when she went back. I don't think she feels that way now and I don't think if she went to a reunion now she would feel that way but it was our first one."

While most incoming freshmen could be expected to be accompanied by their parents on move-in day to the dormitories, Susanna flew up to the Bay Area from Los Angeles alone, her luggage consisting of one large duffel hold-all. "I was dragging this big bag down Telegraph Avenue in Berkeley, trying to figure out where the dorm was," Susanna tells me, "when a couple of very hunky guys came up to me and said, 'Oh, can we help you?' My first impression was, 'Oh, my God, they don't know me. They don't know who I am. They didn't know that I was shy, physically small, and a sort of underdeveloped kid in high school who had skipped half of a grade.'" She goes on to describe a program called annual promotion, where parents had to decide whether to hold their children back a grade or push them up ahead. All of the Hoffs children had been pushed forward. "We're all really young for our grade and sort of immature physically—not mentally—childlike, when everyone else was developing into hot adolescent teens," Susanna explains. Susanna says that moment signified "an opportunity, an awakening of this new person." Moving to Berkeley provided her with "a blank slate." "Suddenly these two athletes just helped take my duffel bag into my dorm room. It was a revelation—that I could be whoever I wanted to be. I had a fresh start."[23]

After her first quarter of freshman year at Berkeley, Susanna and Mary were reunited, provided with the chance to be in a film together. Susanna's mother was working on her new film project, *Stony Island*, and enlisted the friends to play minor roles. Written and produced by Tamar with Andrew Davis, the film, set in inner-city Chicago, follows an aspirational funk musician as he tries to carve out a career in the local scene. Both girls were on the crew and had small acting parts in the project, seeing Mary play a friend of the band while Susanna was the farm girl, Lucie. A fifteen-year-old Rae Dawn Chong was also cast as one of the singers in the fictional Stony Island band.

The experience was a coming of age for the Los Angeles duo. "We were still geeks," Mary confides.[24] Susanna concurs, adding, "Mary and I were rooming together and Rae Dawn Chong shows up. She's this teenager—I mean, we're all teenagers. I was eighteen but Rae was fifteen or sixteen—it was 1977." Susanna's eyes glitter as she shares the memory. "She was just a wonderfully festive kid who was also quite a wild child. She was just eclectic and delightful. She was dating lots of interesting men, some of them very famous and who were a lot older than her. She was beautiful." Susanna reminds me, "It was the roaring '70s. Behavior among human beings was just something that was definitely different [than now]."[25]

Though slightly younger than her castmates, "Rae was most definitely way more mature," Mary remembers.[26] "She had all the fanciest skin salves and cream. She would walk around in silk pajama pants and topless," Susanna recalls.[27] Marijuana featured in the after-hours entertainment. "We definitely smoked pot," Mary laughs. "The pot they had back then in the '70s was like, 'stand here and giggle with me.' It was not a paranoid, intense, feeling—it was just a ball." Rae had brought a Thai stick into the hotel room the girls were sharing, only to have a maid steal it, replacing the contraband with a tobacco cigarette in its place. "There was nothing she could do as she had this illegal thing in her suitcase," Mary smiles.[28]

After *Stony Island*, Susanna returned to college. The beatnik hangover from the previous decade permeated the area, an atmosphere that suited Susanna. "I was definitely a Berkeley girl in the truest sense, patched jeans and into poetry," she laughs.[29] "Berkeley in the '70s was still very much the Berkeley of the '60s," she says. "They proudly maintained the sort of '60s zeitgeist with the bookstores, the cafés. You could go and drink espresso and then go over to Shakespeare and Company Books or Moe's Books and browse and commune with other intellectuals." The dorms were also a throwback to the university's halcyon days of yore. "The RAs [resident advisors] were growing weed in their rooms. Everybody was sitting on the floors of the hall and you could smell pot smoke," Susanna says. Film was still a big part of Susanna's life, with plenty of places in the area to see the new and eclectic releases. "We were going to these dinky art house cinemas and watching early Scorsese and Brian De Palma movies. I saw *Eraserhead*, also *Caligula*—it was a movie that was considered very, very racy. It was like art coming at us from every direction. It was a really fertile time for me, as an art lover and aspiring artist myself. I didn't really draw any boundaries."[30]

Also attending the university was David Roback. David was a well-known entity, as the Hoffs and Roback families lived a few blocks away from each other in Brentwood. Both fathers were doctors, and the kids had attended the same schools and Idyllwild Arts Academy together. Susanna's older brother, John, was David's age, and his best friend. Mary and Susanna would often hang out with John and David, the foursome working on numerous creative projects together, from attempting to write a novel to filming their own movies in and around Los Angeles. With John across the country at Yale, romantic sparks flew between Susanna and David.

The couple eventually moved in together, taking up residence in a quirky Victorian house. "It was on the corner of either Haste Street or Dwight Way," Susanna recalls, "a very old place, sort of creepy." In keeping with the area's hippie history, the exterior of the place "had peace signs and flowers," with the two young artists adding their own personal touches, if somewhat accidentally. "One time David and I were trying to drag a bunch of art supplies up the stone steps and things fell. For years, there were still splatters from that era on the cement," Susanna laughs. The residence had other unique features that are still memorable decades on. "It had Murphy beds that would come out and retract," Susanna says. "At the top of the very steep staircase inside, there was a crank with a lever. If someone rang the bell and you were upstairs in the apartment, you could crank open the door at the base with just a lever. You didn't have to run down the steps." The unconventional lodging created a safe enclave for experimentation. "Berkeley was a special environment, and very much informed everything that came after," Susanna tells me, later describing the setting as "a sort of think tank for our burgeoning idea of being artists."[31] When John came for an exchange semester at Berkeley, he added more possibilities to the mix, bringing with him a punk album collection, including Blondie, Talking

Heads, and the Ramones. "It was mind-blowing. It really was an unbelievable turning point," Susanna says of first hearing the LPs.[32]

With a steady diet of live music provided by the vibrant Bay Area, Susanna, David, and John immersed themselves in all that was on offer. "We were very, very into the punk and the new wave scenes," she recounts. "Berkeley couldn't have been a more stimulating environment for a kid like me," she says. Emboldened by their surroundings, David and Susanna decided to start their own informal band, practicing, performing, and recording each other in their living room. "I was in my own little world; this little bohemian art scene with…David. We'd sit around playing guitar—copying Velvet Underground songs," she remembers.[33] Susanna still has a box of the recordings they made. "We always talked about the music we did together as an imaginary band…dreaming up what we were going to do," she says.[34] They named the "project" the Psychiatrists, or the Unconscious, the concept being that the duration of the in-house performances would last just fifty minutes—the same time as a paid psychiatrist appointment. "We didn't ever play a proper show," Susanna confides. "We never performed live for anybody, had a drummer or a bass player, or went to a club and did a gig. We just were more interested in trying to create stuff. We just sat around with electric or acoustic guitars, play[ing] a lot of music, but just for each other."[35] She describes their twosome as "John and Yoko meet the Beach Boys," noting that "being in a band is the ultimate art project."[36] David, she says, was "very mysterious in certain ways, in terms of his public persona. But I knew him as a mischievous child and a friend."[37]

After graduating from college and moving back to Los Angeles, Susanna was determined to immerse herself in the local music community. Initially, David and Susanna were going to work on projects together. However, she quickly realized that it was "really hard to be in a band with someone you've been in a romantic relationship with." Though having never done a show outside the safe confines of her own apartment, Susanna had her mind set on what she would do next. At that point, she decided to strike out on her own and build a group from scratch. Though her brother John claims he was one who "planted the seed" about forming an all-girl band, Susanna tells me, "I knew I wanted to work with women," noting, "the Go-Go's were an inspiration to me and very aspirational."

One night, she stumbled upon a band called the Last, and was bowled over with the vibrant, '60s-tinged, punk folk sound. Lead singer Joe Nolte was living at a church with various members of Black Flag and Redd Kross, though he would frequently crash on his mother's couch. One morning while staying at the parental home, his brother woke him up, giving him the news that someone had left a bottle of whiskey and a note for him. The mystery admirer was Susanna. "I was networking!" she laughs. Eager to connect with like-minded creatives and impressed by Nolte's group, Susanna had found out where he lived from brother John, who was already working on a silent film, documenting the various emerging groups in the city. The project included the Last, thus providing his sister with the perfect entrée. "The note said, 'Joe, I think your group is really fab and you are the best thing to come out of LA and I would really like to talk to you sometime. My brother John is making a film about your group and others. Enjoy the whiskey, Susanna Hoffs,'" Joe reads from the note. "I said, 'I've gotta meet her.' At the very least, she had superb taste," he laughs. Nolte goes on to dispel a rumor that Susanna had eventually tried out to be in the Last but had been rejected. "She did not audition," he says. "We'd had to get rid of my brother Mike [the harmony singer] and so I was trying to replace that voice. If you get rid of somebody, you try to find somebody who sounds just right, because all the songs were written for a particular harmony range," he explains. "[The replacement] needed to be a guy with a middle-range voice; Susanna wouldn't have worked."[38]

Susanna's focus became creating her own "art project." "I have always had a determined mindset. If I decide to do something, I am going to do it. I was being tenacious and scrappy," she says. "When I graduated, I was invited to a reunion of Berkeley girls who had also gotten their degrees around the same time," she tells me. "Several people started talking about going to the jobs office, looking for help as to what to do after university. When it came around the circle of women to me, I thought, Well, I didn't really need to go to the jobs office, because what would I say? Would I have sat down and gone, um, I want to start a rock band, can you help me with that, can you put me together with people? It just doesn't work that way. My version of the jobs office was going around LA with a flyer I made—I still have the original copy of it—saying that I wanted to form an all-girl band."[39]

Featuring a list of all of Susanna's favorite groups, illustrations of guitars she dreamed of owning, and "at the bottom, in the biggest letters on the whole thing, the most important recruitment necessity, 'Must Be Nice,'" she left the handbills in the bathroom at the Whisky. "This is really sad!" she laughs, before confiding, "I kept going into the bathroom to see if anyone had picked any of them up." To her dismay, the stack had been unceremoniously removed—into the trashcan. "I kept going in, and putting them back out on the sink," Susanna recalls. "Finally, whoever hated me for putting those flyers there in the first place, ripped them all up—shredded them. I was really bummed out and depressed."

Undeterred by the vicious destruction of her advertisements at the hands of a fellow Whisky attendee, Susanna carried on, continuing to post her flyers around neighborhood record stores. She received exactly one reply. "It was from Maria McKee's mother," she says. Maria was only sixteen at the time. "I went and met with her and her mom in their apartment," Susanna recalls. "The mom wanted to know who would be the singer of the group. I said, Well, I thought I would be. The mom said, 'No, that won't work because Maria's the singer.' I was like, 'Okay, fine. Well, good luck to you.' We both ended up doing it!"

Susanna was steadfast, regardless of the barriers. "Even with these setbacks, I never gave up hope," she remembers.[40] Her next move: placing an ad in a weekly local newspaper, the *Recycler*. Originally called *E-Z Buy E-Z Sell* upon launching in 1973, the *Recycler* was a classified publication, allowing advertisements to be put in for free and charging readers to purchase the paper. "The *Recycler* was unbelievable," remembers Sid Griffin. "There would be a couple hundred 'musicians wanted' ads in each issue—and it came out every week. The *Recycler* was the unsung hero of LA pop music for twenty-five years."[41*] As she put her own hopes into black and white newsprint, Susanna scanned the same columns for other opportunities, praying that between the various efforts something would happen.

It did, but in the most tragic form.

On December 8, 1980, while coming home from a recording session, former Beatle John Lennon was shot and fatally wounded as he entered the Dakota, his apartment in New York City. The murder sent shock waves of grief around the world. "The night that he died," Susanna recalls, "I had picked up the phone to call David Roback. There was just dead air, no dial tone and the phone had not rung. He was already on the line, as he had spontaneously in the same moment called me. We rang each other because the television networks had stopped the football game that was on TV to announce the tragedy. When the news broke, I heard my brother cry out from the other room, 'What? No!' It still chokes me up just thinking about it." The death further mobilized the already motivated Susanna. "He had always been such an inspiration to me," Susanna says. "I took it as a message, as a signal to get it together, and to do what I had always wanted to do."[42]

---

* The circular has been hailed as a great connector for bands from the late twentieth century, with Guns N' Roses, Hole, Mötley Crüe, and Metallica all citing the paper as helping them found their groups.

PART II
COME TOGETHER

7.

It was a call received by Vicki Peterson before the chiming in of 1981 that changed everything.

The connection was simultaneously serendipitous and arguably expected. Susanna had been actively attempting to form a group since landing back in Los Angeles. Vicki, for her part, had tried various methods in the past to find people to join her myriad undertakings. "We had searched for other band members before over the years," she tells me. "We used to go to a place called Musicians Contact Service on Sunset Boulevard. It was an ordinary storefront space that had a large board where people would post ads for band members, and a big book you could flip through to peruse people who were looking for other bands. It was the analogue version of the internet in a way," she explains. Vicki notes that besides "the binder," the only other methods for finding people were the *Recycler* or simply word of mouth, either through friends or via poaching musicians from other bands. "We had used all of these techniques multiple times," she reflects. "At that moment, that December of 1980, my whole world had been stripped down to just me and Debbi."

By the time the phone rang at the end of 1980, it seemed like "an eternity" since anything positive had happened for Those Girls.[1*]

Though having now been dismissed from the group, Lynn Elkind was still living in amicable harmony with Debbi and Vicki. Looking to kick-start her own new project, Lynn had placed an ad for other

---

[1*] Vicki acknowledges that it was only a matter of weeks between Amanda's news, Lennon's death, and the call from Susanna; she admits it just felt much longer at the time.

63

like-minded musicians in the *Recycler*. Soon after the passing of Lennon, the phone rang, the caller asking for Lynn in reply to her classified. Vicki answered. "I had just started to advertise myself in that pre-Craigslist, pre-internet world," Susanna says. "I just called a phone number that was listed there, someone advertising themselves who was a female musician."[2] Though Susanna did not get Lynn, who had placed the listing, everyone was thinking about Lennon that day. "We found ourselves on the phone for over an hour, sympathizing over Lennon's assassination, and many other things," explained Vicki. "I realized the person I was talking to was intelligent, and completely in synch with what I wanted to do."[3] "Eighty percent of our first conversation was about John Lennon and what he meant to us, what the Beatles had meant to us," Vicki reflects.[4] "It became this incredible bond with this strange person that I'd never met," Susanna says.[5] The loss of their hero and a shared love for the Liverpudlians was the founding "glue" between the girls, according to Susanna. "Grief, I guess is the best word, over this horrific incident was really weirdly part of the [band's] inception," Susanna says. "That, and the obsessive love for the Beatles."[6]

Though feeling invigorated and hopeful after her chat with Susanna, Vicki informed her roommate about the call. "It was sort of like I'd intercepted something very cool, but in order to be ethically correct, I passed on the message to Lynn," she explains.[7] For all the immediate connection felt in the first call between the Berkeley grad and Vicki, Lynn and Susanna did not have any chemistry when they spoke in the following days. Conscience clear, plans were quickly made for Debbi and Vicki to meet Susanna in Brentwood.

Having broken up with David Roback, Susanna was back living at her family home, staying in the garage, which had been converted to a studio apartment. Susanna had turned it into her own, decorating the walls with a Velvet Underground poster and a Debbie Harry cutout. Any worry about awkwardness at the first meeting of the three was immediately assuaged upon seeing each other in the flesh, the rapport almost instantaneous upon the Petersons' arrival. "It could have been weird, like you're on a blind date and the person who opens the door is not the person you're supposed to go out with," Susanna recalls. "But instead it was, 'Oh my god, that's the love of my life.'"[8] Having never performed in front of anyone but David, Susanna was unversed even on the basics of live set up. "She did not know how to sound check a microphone," Debbi says.[9] "I went up to the mic, and I blew on it to see if it was on, and they laughed, which is funny," Susanna recounts. "I laughed at myself for it." Susanna admits to lacking the experience of the club-savvy Petersons. "Even though I had done music with David in that same garage, I was green."[10] Vicki helped her new friend, and the three started jamming, choosing Jefferson Airplane's "White Rabbit" as their first attempt at playing together. Susanna also had the Petersons listen to the tapes she and David had recorded of themselves in Berkeley, giving the sisters a further display of her ability. "It just all came together so fast," Susanna says. "It sounded like such a good fit, so natural."[11] Vicki was equally enthused, thrilled to have found a possible collaborator who shared her taste in music and style of performing. "Susanna knew of the Guess Who, Grass Roots, Arthur Lee, and Love," Vicki says. "We had lots in common. Harmony singing was a breeze. We left that night thinking 'This is it. We got it.'"[12]

A new group was born in one evening. "Me and the Petersons created a band that night," Susanna says.[13] "It was sort of like getting married to someone you met an hour before."[14] Vicki concurs. "Being in this band especially was like a marriage. That was the first date. Debbi and I left that night and said, I think we have a new band."[15]

The initial meeting with Susanna was the first time Debbi had ever been to Brentwood. "We were just like, 'Oh my God,'" Debbi recalls of her and Vicki's reaction. "It was seeing how the other half live." Susanna's house, she says, "was huge, with amazing art on the walls." The entire evening, Debbi recalls, "was an eye-opening experience." "I was just thinking, 'Wow, wouldn't that be nice?'" she reflects.

Debbi's diary shows a similar excitement and awe after the initial visit to the Hoffses' garage.

Debbi's Journal Entry

Hey, can you fucking believe it? Vicki and I finally have a guitarist! Her name is Susanna Hoffs-we call her Sue-and she's a total '60's fanatic! Vicki and I had actually met her before, unofficially at the Hong Kong Café when we went to see Sensible Shoes play. We thought she was kinda cocky and spacey. Months later, she saw Lynn's ad in the Recycler Magazine about looking for a band member.

Too good to be true, I thought. Well, we got talking and not only does she love The Beatles, she's into everything '60's! She loves everything about that decade, just like we do. Well, we all caught on like a house on fire, it was amazing! She plays rhythm guitar and has a Rickenbacker (a black one...cool, cool). She's a real talker. She's very excited about the whole idea of playing together. The vibes were right, man, everything was right! It was incredible. I never thought we'd find someone who would click so well, and we did! We're gonna practice together for the first time tomorrow night. Should be interesting! I hope we get on as well musically as we do personally.

Vicki was exuberant after meeting Susanna. "I felt like I had a partner again, which I hadn't had since Amanda," she tells me. "I was thrilled by [Susanna's] energy."[16] Dave Peterson saw Susanna joining as the sisters finding their missing piece. "She was the magic third ingredient in that lineup," he says. "Just the fact that she was able to write with Vicki, they took off at that point."[17] The Berkeley graduate's attitude, Vicki remembers, was infectious. "She had that energy of, 'Yes, we're going to absolutely take this to the top and we're going to do this.' She had world experience and definitely experience in entertainment."[18]

While Susanna and the Petersons began to rehearse regularly at Susanna's place, teenager Annette Zilinskas was cruising the *Recycler*, looking at the "musician wanted" ads. The product of German and Russian parents, Annette grew up in Van Nuys, another neighborhood located in the San Fernando Valley. Music flowed in the Zilinskas household, with Annette and her sister exposed to a constant rotation of country music and her father's favorite album, Fleetwood Mac's *Rumours*. The radio was omnipresent, with Carole King featuring regularly, spurring Annette's parents to buy the singer's *Tapestry* record for their young daughter. "That is the first album that I learned to sing to when I was ten," she says. Opera lessons followed by the time Annette reached sixteen. Though loving music from a young age, it was not until high school that Annette performed in front of an audience. With friend Jill Roberts—"who was a year younger than me," Annette points out (as those details were important at that age)—she got on stage at her school's Spaghetti Dance, held in the venerable Birmingham High School outdoor cafeteria. The duo did their renditions of the Beatles' "Love Me Do" and "Words of Love," with Annette playing harmonica on the former. "What was so memorable about that was that we were so nervous and we didn't know how our peers would react," she says. The two were thrilled when the school's Black cheerleading squad stood up and started dancing. "The cheerleaders got up on their feet and fucking rocked out," Annette recalls. "The minute they started doing that, Jill and I looked at each other, shocked by the response. We felt like little rock stars." Annette goes on to say, "Jill was African American. Back then, you didn't see many biracial bands in high school."[19] The reception was a turning point for the aspiring artist, showing her that an audience could and would appreciate her talent.

Annette continued to look for opportunities to perform, nurturing an interest in rockabilly sounds and two-part harmonies. A Thursday night event at the local Palomino Club provided a venue for Annette and friend Lisa Reed to play in front of a live crowd when they were picked to do a song in a coveted open mic spot. "It was quite a big deal," she tells me. "We were definitely the youngest ones there. We were teenagers. You had cowboy types that were in their forties and women that were singing 'Desperado.' It was like *America's Got Talent*, but for the country western set." To participate, hopefuls would have to sign up and pray to be chosen; though it was a regional event, the number of applicants far outpaced the available slots for singing. Going on stage around 2 a.m., the twosome did place, bringing them to the attention of Kim Fowley of Runaways fame. "We did a song called 'Black Slacks' by a two-girl band called the Sparkletones," Annette says. "Kim Fowley heard about that and started calling us. He took us out to dinner at this place on Melrose." In a scene ripped from a Bret Easton Ellis novel, Fowley then "brought us to this very '80s nightclub, with a lot of neon lights."

Fowley had the idea of the duo being the "female Everly Brothers," an on-trend idea, Annette recognizes, as rockabilly was "invading the local scene." "We were so young, we didn't really think about it," Annette reflects, "but looking back at it, that probably was a really good idea, because nobody was doing that. Nobody." Unfortunately, it was not to be. Lisa moved to Italy and Annette started college. Looking for her next project, Annette turned to the Los Angeles stalwart—the *Recycler*. "I responded to Susanna's ad looking for a bassist and that's when everything changed," she says.[20]

The first chat was a success. "We got on incredibly well," Annette remembers. "Susanna is so good on the phone, and she did know that I was a vocalist," Annette says. There was one slight snag: in her excitement at seeing the Byrds, Love, and the Monkees listed as key influences, Annette had overlooked the ad's main purpose—the need for a bass player. "I played harmonica and acoustic guitar to accompany myself when I was singing, but that was the extent of it," Annette says. "So she said, 'Would you be open to learning?' And I said, 'Absolutely.'"[21] The first meeting with Debbi, Susanna, and Vicki took place in the Brentwood garage. Debbi's journals reflect the shared synergy of the group:

Debbi's Journal Entry

There's a girl named Annette Zilinskas, who's a guitarist (18), but she might be willing to play bass. She's into the '60's also, but more into Rockabilly. But that's ok. It looks like we'll have a new band together in a couple of months! Who knows?? Things really are changing for the better!!

7.

Annette was excited about the chance to join the band. "I was just delighted to be asked to play an instrument, an electric instrument that I could plug in and perform," she reflects. "My aspirations were to be a vocalist and write my songs, to sing kind of country-ish stuff or what you would call alternative country," Annette says. Though the new prospect on offer was slightly different, Annette was eager to get involved. Susanna was especially important to helping the still-teenage Annette feel at ease. "She made me feel safe if that makes sense. I was a little younger than the other women [in the band], so the fact I was stepping out of my comfort zone, from picking up a new instrument to playing live, she just made me know that I could do it."

Susanna also provided cultural awakening and emotional nurturing for the aspiring musician. "Growing up in the Valley, there weren't a lot of opportunities for me," Annette explains. "Susanna just opened my eyes to French films, Fellini, Jean-Luc Godard, and artful type punk-poetesses like Patti Smith. It's just a way of looking at things through a lens that was transformative for me."

Connecting with Susanna also brought a new personal freedom. With the huge multilane freeways, navigating the often treacherous journeys from one area to another in Los Angeles unchaperoned was a rite of passage. "When I say, 'driving over the hill,' it's kind of a big deal," Annette clarifies. "I'm seventeen, eighteen years old, going to a different neighborhood, getting on the 405 [freeway], which is challenging already, and going to rehearsals and then coming home late at night. It was a huge step forward."

Annette was living in the Valley with her parents, a place that she acknowledges provided a foundation of security that often felt stifling for the young woman while she was trying to carve out her own identity. "It was a place to escape from as a teenager," she says. Hollywood provided the perfect panacea. Rodney Bingenheimer's KROQ show "seeping" through the "Valley barrier" paired with the allure of live music were Annette's entrée to the proliferating Los Angeles music community. "I liked growing up in the Valley because it was safe," she says. Yet that is exactly what made Annette want to leave. "As a teenager, you get bored. That's when you start to want to see what's out there," she explains.

Already interested in the rockabilly scene, Annette began going to see local favorites the Blasters at various venues, including the Hong Kong Cafe and the Starwood. "I would hear them on the radio, Rodney would play them," Annette says. "They were so good." She describes their sound for the uninitiated as "kind of alternative country" that was "not slow" but also not punk. "They had greased-back hair—kind of like when Morrissey went solo—rolled-up jeans, and biker boots." The look, the crowd, and the music especially appealed to Annette, who quickly found herself making friends in the scene.

When Annette joined, Those Girls metamorphosed into the Colours. The origin of the newest moniker is lost in time. "I actually do not remember how we came up with 'The Colours,'" Vicki emails me, "but you will note that we used British spelling, Anglophiles that we are."[22] An interview from 1982 claims the inspiration came from "their tunes [coming] in many shades," thus "they dubbed themselves the Colors [misspelling from original article]."[23]

Several shows commenced with the new recruits as the Colours, according to Debbi's journals. "Susanna was impressed because we were quite knowledgeable about playing live clubs," says Debbi. "We had been doing it since we were so young."

Other gigs followed, though Annette admits they are now "a little bit of a blur." "We played a party for a good friend of Susanna's. He had a really nice place, up on Mulholland Drive." Friends from other bands, such as Sensible Shoes, were in attendance, as well as various local scenesters. "The reason these [shows] are important is that this is before we [played] in front of a real audience that were not just our friends," Annette explains. "We could work out how we sounded [in practice]; but you need an audience to work out if the arrangement works or if the song itself works or if the audience even responds to you as a band." The handful of performances confirmed for the group that they had the talent and chemistry, but most important, Annette notes, "the harmonies."[24] The peer approval was tantamount to building further confidence within the foursome. "We weren't the popular girls in high school," Annette tells me. "We didn't come in with entitlement. We had an idea that we had something here or we wouldn't have gotten together to rehearse," Annette explains, "and the big something was the harmonies."[25]

Even collaborator and former paramour David Roback saw the potential in the group. According to future Rain Parade bandmate Matt Piucci, Roback "nearly broke down" after seeing the Colours play, as they were "so good." "David lost it," Piucci recalls. "He was crying. He couldn't take that his friend was going to be more successful than him right off the bat."[26]

The addition of Susanna and Annette signaled a significant change in the band. "Me and Susanna starting rehearsing and things seemed to be going well," says Annette. Annette began taking bass lessons, determined to become proficient as quickly as possible. While her aspirations still were to write and sing her own songs in the ever-growing alternative country style, she was ecstatic to now be in the group, and she wanted to be as prepared as possible to pull her weight. However, her parents had other plans. Keen for their daughter to continue her college education, Annette was pressured to bow out of the alliance. Once again down a member, the band decided to take a hiatus "because they wanted to recalibrate, rethink strategies, reconfigure, reassess, start a new plan of attack, write new material, and rethink a better name."[27]

The first thing that needed to change was the band moniker. It had come to their attention that a New York band was also going by Colors (no "u"),* making it a matter of timely urgency. Inspiration struck while Vicki and Susanna were thumbing through some old copies of *Esquire* magazine at the Hoffses'. Ed Sullivan graced the cover, donning a bad

---

* Vicki: "I'm gonna go out on a limb here and say that there was another band called the Colours. There was the NY based band and I thought there was one in LA, too." [Personal email to Jennifer Otter Bickerdike, July 23, 2023.]

Beatles wig. Inside, a tongue-in-cheek article on popular hairstyles of the day listed one as "The Supersonic Bangs." The girls loved it as a possible band name and rang Debbi at work to run it by her. The younger Peterson sister thought the moniker too long, immediately striking her as reminiscent of Liverpudlian group the Teardrop Explodes. A compromise was struck, the three agreeing on a shortened version: the Bangs. The new name had a '60s vibe, a sassy double entendre meaning, and an intrinsic power, reflecting the tenacious young women in the group. In solidarity, and as an early branding effort, the trio chopped the front of their hair into bangs, with Debbi especially embracing a '60s-esque pouf. After the fiasco of adopting the Colours moniker, just to find out other groups were also using it, the girls carefully studied numerous club listings and record store flyers to ensure no other band had already taken the Bangs handle. It was the first step in their newest strategy for success.

8.

Determined to be the only Bangs in existence and not repeat the debacles encountered with their short-lived adventures as the Fans and the Colours, the trio was adamant at having full ownership over the new name. Their first step was to make a 45 single using the Bangs title. "I was annoyed by the name change thing," Vicki recalls.[1] "I thought, 'We've got to hold on to this one.'"[2] Vicki had gotten information stating that if an item is produced in a "fixed medium," name protection is assured. The three Bangs pooled money earned from their respective day jobs with an eye to get vinyl made. Many of their friends in punk bands were undertaking the same thing. "Black Flag, the Plugz, and others were doing it...even the first Descendents single was put out by the band," Milo Aukerman tells me.[3] "It was doable, if you were able to find the money for the recording, mastering, pressing, cover art, etcetera."[4] Henry Rollins echoes similar sentiments, saying, "As far as the making of a two-song 7-inch, Los Angeles was a great place to do it as in those days, there were studios for every budget."[5] Having product could transform an artist's career, as it would allow them to hand fans and possible industry gatekeepers their music in a physical format. "Take 'em to Zed Records and see if they'll buy a few," Milo recalls, "or try to sell them at school. That's what Bill did for Descendents."[6] The county had a burgeoning ecosystem for those in the independent scene, with shops and, if a group was lucky, Rodney, who was often willing to support an emerging artist. "There were local pressing plants and... probably enough record stores to take a small amount of your release on consignment or you could sell them at shows," Henry describes.[7]

"If Rodney Bingenheimer liked your record, you could sell a lot."[8] The Bangs shared the ethos of their punk colleagues, inspired and spurred on by what they saw happening around them. "Though we were a pop band, we identified with the punk scene of LA," Susanna says. "We were doing it grassroots. We were fueled by this passion to make it happen and to a sound that was unique to us."[9]

Recording was set to take place in Venice at a place called Radio Tokyo, a small venture operated by Ethan James, a "great guy and a very skilled engineer"[10] who was known for helping new artists. James had substantial credibility, having been a member of a Bay Area–based band called Blue Cheer. "Being in the room with a guy who was in an actual group from the '60s was very tantalizing to us," Susanna explains. James worked out of "a very beautiful craftsman house that had been converted," Susanna remembers, with Vicki noting it "would probably be worth millions today," but at the time "was in a very sketchy neighborhood" known for gang violence. "It was very exciting," said Vicki. "It felt like an adventure."[11] James already had a reputation for turning out high-quality records, with Black Flag, Minutemen, and the Last all gracing the tiny studio. "He was resourceful out of necessity," Henry explains. "Ethan could make a good sounding record for cheap."[12] Cheap it was, Susanna recalls, the price tag coming in at $10 an hour, the total cost start to finish of the single commanding a price tag of $800. Debbi, Vicki, and Susanna laid down the tracks, while Annette, still just learning her instrument and having been dissuaded from being in the group by her parents, did not attend the sessions. Lacking a bass player, Debbi and Vicki alternated playing on the two-track release. The A-side featured "Getting Out of Hand," which was penned by Vicki and sung by Susanna, with the B-side, "Call on Me," cowritten by Susanna and Vicki with David Roback. Henry Rollins rates it as "a really good record...[the] two songs [are]...very well written and the vocals are great and totally together."[13]

The next item of business was to create a company of their own to put out the record. The girls decided on DownKiddie as the name of their new entity, after old jazz slang. When asked to elaborate on why this name was picked, Vicki takes on a Lauren Bacall–esque voice, and says, "She's a DOWNKIDDIE, like a cool woman." The first ambitious run of one thousand copies had differing label colors of blue, yellow, and green. David Roback was once again drafted in to help, this time to snap some quick portraits for use on the sleeve. It was a true and classic DIY effort. "We all went to a coffee spot and got to work," Vicki says. "I put together the design, David literally cut out and pasted the pictures. We xeroxed our creations and folded them up." A succinct but cheeky biography was slipped into each single, completing the package:

Vicki Peterson and Susanna Hoffs come up with fresh, true-life songs and Debbi Peterson supplies them with a back beat that dares you to sit still (try it...) Onstage, the girls are fun and frenetic (frank, fractious, frazzled, friendly...) and if you corner one of them backstage, you'll probably find yourself outtalked and out of breath in no time.

The trio of young women, with David in tow, returned to Susanna's garage and began an ad hoc assembly line, putting all the elements together. The finished "Getting Out of Hand" single was ready to be sold by the start of December 1981. Determined to get their music into as many shops as possible, the girls relentlessly pounded the Los Angeles pavement with their wares, Vicki recalling, "We literally kept taking them to every record store until we found some kind of a distribution situation."[14] One place that took some in stock was Jem Records, where label associate Sid Griffin worked. "They were charming when they brought their first record to me. I took it and played it and loved it. I thought we would only sell a few hundred copies. It was me that got them the first distribution deal for that first single," he remembers. As a wholesaler, Jem was looked to by other distributors to be a tastemaker for fresh talent, turning on shops across the region to bands. "You called up the one stops and the distributors in that part of the country and told them about new records," Sid explains. Business was done by fax. "You'd say, 'We think you guys need to buy copies of this.'

We sold a lot of records for a lot of bands. That's how the [Bangs] got going."[15]

Now with their single in select record stores, the band urgently needed to get some airplay for the song. Susanna took it upon herself to hand deliver the 45s to arbiter of taste Rodney Bingenheimer, in hopes of having him play it on his KROQ show. After figuring out that the radio royalty DJed on a Monday night at the Odyssey, an under-twenty-one club in Hollywood, Susanna donned a miniskirt and presented him with the freshly minted effort.

"I'm sure he was completely charmed by her," Annette says of Rodney's initial exchange with Susanna.[16] "Susanna giving the single to Rodney was an important step in the band's career," she notes. Indeed, the veteran music personality was immediately taken by the tenacious young woman. "She looked so stunning," Rodney says of the audacious meeting with Susanna. "Susanna is definitely the Rock and Roll Audrey Hepburn. She shows up, I go, 'Wow.' Then she hands me the single. I took it home and it is like an '80s Mamas and Papas."[17] Before Christmas, Rodney was spinning "Getting Out of Hand" on his show. "He played it and loved it," Annette says. Rodney giving the group their initial plays dramatically changed the trajectory of everything, with Susanna confirming, "Our audience just doubled, tripled, quadrupled after that."[18]

Vicki was abroad visiting Amanda when Debbi first heard the Bangs on the radio. "I was by myself in our apartment," she says. "I was listening to Rodney because he kept saying he was going to play the 'Bangs.' Eventually he spun 'Getting Out of Hand.' I screamed at the top of my lungs. I was so excited. Somehow I called Vicki. It was really expensive to call overseas, but I talked to her for two seconds. It was the most amazing thing ever."[19] Vicki was in a red pay phone booth in London when she got the news. "I remember just jumping up and down screaming."[20]

Seeing no limit to the possibilities, Vicki had brought copies with her on the trip to visit Amanda in the UK soon after it was pressed, fearlessly asking local record stores to play it, and even cold calling major label Sire Records. "We got a good response," Vicki says of her experience with the music shops. Her pitch to the record company did not have the same outcome. "It was like, 'We're a band from LA and this is our record,'" Vicki recalls of her approach. "It was pretty naive and ballsy." She pauses. "We didn't hear back from anyone."[21]

Susanna was equally unrelenting in the quest to promote the Bangs. When she returned from UC Berkeley, her uncle Carmi employed the new graduate to work in his tiny ceramics factory for minimum wage. Uncle Carmi had also hired Erin Cowley. "Erin was in need of a job after having been sent to live with her aunt Linda in Los Angeles," Susanna explains. Aunt Linda was Linda Ronstadt. Eventually, Susanna asked her friend if she could possibly come over and play "Getting Out of Hand" to the famous relative. "She had this incredible house up the street from where I lived," Susanna remembers. The superstar was "so kind," Susanna says. "Not only was it so cool to work up the courage to ask her to listen to the Bangs' first indie single, but her response was so uplifting. I don't know how I worked up the gumption looking back on it," Susanna now says.[22]

Besides providing networking opportunities, it was while working at Uncle Carmi's that Susanna heard the Simon and Garfunkel track "A Hazy Shade of Winter" for the first time. The duo had succeeded in cracking the top twenty on the *Billboard* charts with the song in December 1966, the year of its release as a single, seeing a peak of number thirteen. Yet in comparison with other familiar hits by the twosome, the Paul Simon–penned cut did not receive as much airplay. "I was sitting alone, listening to a local radio station called K-Earth 101, which was an oldies station in the 1980s," she explains. "'Hazy Shade' came on, and I was like, 'Holy shit, this would be perfect for the Bangs.' I thought I knew every Simon and Garfunkel song, but clearly didn't because I didn't know that one," Susanna laughs. "I went running to rehearsal and I pitched it to the band. Vicki's reaction was, 'Oh yeah, that's a cool song' because she was as hardcore of a Simon and Garfunkel fan as I was. It became a staple of our set."

While Susanna and Vicki fearlessly attempted to bring the Bangs to every conceivable pair of ears that may help further the band, more reserved Debbi was trying to figure out what and where she fit in to the shifting group hierarchy. Susanna, she recounts, "definitely had connections in the movie and music worlds and was not afraid to use them." Finding common ground with others and networking was also a strength for Vicki, an imperative skill in her landing gigs for the group early on. "She was much better at connecting with people than I was," Debbi recalls. "So I let her do it." Susanna too was excellent at becoming fast friends with those around her. Debbi started to feel unsure as to how she could add value—besides drumming and singing—in comparison to her sister and new bandmate. "It began to feel like, 'Okay, what else do I have to offer?' I didn't have anything at the time," she says. "I didn't have the network. I didn't make friends with famous people, so I thought I'd just let them get on with it because it seemed like the right thing to do at the time. Unfortunately, in hindsight, maybe not; but you don't know that then. You just go for it and see what happens."[23]

Class, reflects Vicki, "didn't specifically impact the genesis of the band or even how we functioned." She now sees how "it is a real part of the dynamic on some level." This became especially apparent in how the various band members approached situations. "Sue grew up surrounded by famous, successful people, concrete examples of achieving that lifestyle," Vicki says. "Debbi and I were working jobs to pay rent. There was never any concern with Susanna about money; it was never a part of her brain. That's just a fundamental difference," Vicki explains. Though all of the women came of age in close proximity to Los Angeles proper, the Petersons and Hoffses existed in different orbits, Vicki contends, thus having contrasting outlooks of possibility. "The world that Susanna grew up in was extremely showbiz centric. She lived in a very wealthy neighborhood next to the Nimoys and the Newman music dynasty. She had access to societal levels that we didn't have." In contrast, Vicki underscores, "Debbi and I grew up in the San Fernando Valley; we were middle class, not impoverished by any means. Our parents

8.

worked hard. My dad made decent money, but we were made very aware of the fact that we didn't have everything and that money was scarce, that money was tight. My mom bought the store brands instead of the national brands. My friends in middle school always joked that we had Hydrox, not Oreos. It's that level: you don't get the brand soda, you get the store soda." Over the years, Vicki notes, she has "learned a lot" from Susanna. "I was always kind of amazed and watched with interest how she was encouraged from day one, because she was the princess of a family. The idea that you can do anything that you want was right in front of her, whereas for me, I had to imagine it."

9.

It was a twenty-two-minute two-reel film written and directed by Susanna's mother, Tamar, not a music video, that gave the Bangs their celluloid debut. Tamar had been studying at the American Film Institute's Directing Workshop for Women when the chance to make *The Haircut* came up. Originally, Tamar had tapped family friend Ben Gazzara to star as the music business executive who gets the "haircut of a lifetime." However, when Gazzara was unavailable, the actor enlisted friend John Cassavetes to take his place. Cassavetes was so charmed by the idea of getting to improvise around Tamar's script with veteran thespians like Nick Colasanto—who would go on to be known worldwide as Coach on the hit sitcom *Cheers*—that he agreed to a twenty-four-hour shooting schedule. The Bangs show up at the end of the piece, as the daughters of barber shop owner Bobby Russo. Appearing to be playing a jangly surf guitar instrumental in the beams of the rooftop, the three Bangs of Susanna, Debbi, and Vicki are accompanied by friend Marji. *The Haircut* would go on to be considered a low-budget classic, screened in the Un Certain Regard section at the 1983 Cannes Film Festival before going on to be acquired by Universal Studios and becoming an official selection at both Telluride and Toronto Film Festivals, and, later in 1989, appearing at Sundance. After seeing the finished piece with the Bangs' cameo, Susanna's mother wanted to cut their bit out of the film, thinking it diverted attention from the main story. However, star Cassavetes adored the silly authenticity provided by the group. The girls made the final cut.

It was a foreshadowing of the generational defining influence the band would soon provide across global television stations.

"Getting Out of Hand" was now getting substantial airplay in the Los Angeles area. The single had surged in popularity on KROQ, moving all the way up to number three on Rodney's request list. Local Long Beach radio station KNAC was spinning the record, and it had even made an appearance on the *LA Weekly* local airplay charts. The first batch of four hundred singles of the blue label had sold out, with the second run of yellow and green also vanishing quickly from store shelves. Constant comparisons to sixties sensations like the Mamas & the Papas only fueled the excitement, further validated when Michelle Phillips asked for the group to take a picture with her.[1]

Once Rodney added the track to KROQ, the Bangs "started getting, almost immediately, a serious buzz," Amanda remembers. "That's why it seemed as though they came from nowhere because for months beforehand, they had not been playing. There was a phase where they were without a bass player. They had recorded the single because they wanted to save the name; but at that point, you couldn't go and see them play because there wasn't a live band."[2] Adding to the pressure was another hot all-female act garnering industry attention, also from the Los Angeles area. "The Go-Go's had just gotten signed, and they were a big deal," Amanda recalls. "Then here comes this other 'new' girl band."[3]

Though both being composed entirely of women and coming from the same Los Angeles geography, the two groups were striking in their disparity. "The Go-Go's and the Bangles were from two completely different scenes," explains music journalist Robert Lloyd. "The Go-Go's were of LA punk and the first band that played alternative music in crappy clubs in the wake of the CBGB scene. They had varying musical talent," Lloyd says. Unlike the wholesome and bohemian backgrounds of the Bangs, the Go-Go's "lived in the Canterbury Hotel, a flophouse on the top of Hollywood Boulevard," Lloyd recalls. "It was a dark scene with overtones of heroin…and some very self-destructive characters."

The Bangs, by contrast, "were musicians from a young age looking to be in a band…formed on musical perspectives, whereas many other bands were formed on a whim." Lloyd notes how "they came from fandom and a sort of encyclopedic knowledge of the '60s and '70s music that they turned to their advantage. The songs they picked to cover were ones that music nerds knew about. They weren't done for humorous reasons, as punk rock covers were more ironic. There was no irony in what [the Bangs] did; they played music they loved and they came out of the garage as opposed to the flophouse. The stuff that came before had been inspired by punk on one hand and weird artsy bands, not the things that were coming out of London and New York."[4]

The surge of interest in the Go-Go's, as well as their own building fan base, made shows imperative.

With the group's surging momentum behind her, Annette was allowed to once again join the trio. "Everything happened quickly," Annette says. "I remember driving my Volkswagen Rabbit from the San Fernando Valley where I lived to West Pico, over the hill. We would practice at least two, sometimes three times a week. It was very serious and responsible, we were *rehearsing*!"[5]

After several months of almost continuous preparation, the Bangs were ready to finally make their live debut. The big show was a benefit for *NO MAG*, the artsy fanzine du jour started in 1978 by friends Bruce Kalberg and Michael Gira. "Bruce was an art punk guerilla guy," Robert remembers. He describes the publication as "a little bit transgressive and a bit ironic." "Bruce would ask provocative, left-field questions to get a reaction."[6] Into this dirge, the Bangs were set to headline the March 26 gig, coming on after punk bands Saigon, Channel 3, and Descendents.

Initially, the girls were excited about the show. However, as the time neared, the Bangs became nervous, realizing that they were about to release their three-part harmonies on a punk rock crowd. "I remember sitting in the Buick station wagon in the parking lot, rehearsing and singing through the set list," Vicki recalls. "We were changing into our stage clothes in a bathroom and a bunch of punk guys came in. They were just peeking over the stalls."[7] Things were not made any more welcoming upon the Bangs loading their equipment into the venue. "It was one of those early times where we had to just stiffen our resolve as it were," Vicki remembers. "I had to fight for our position on the bill. We were supposed to play third and this other band wanted to play when we were on. They said, 'Fuck you, this is our slot' and I said, 'This is our slot, we're going on.' I was just adamant and started setting up. He mutters, 'I hate girl bands.' It wasn't the first time I heard that and it cracked me up." The tension may have been sexual on the boys' part, as Susanna later said "that the Descendents [were] always…asking us to go out on dates."[8]

A set composed of Bangs originals and covers of "Pushin' Too Hard" by the Seeds and "Steppin' Out" by Paul Revere and the Raiders was met with both peer and crowd approval. "The Bangs were already professional sounding; I really dug them," recalls Milo, admitting, "I crushed hard on Annette Z."[9] While love may have been almost in the air for some, the show marked a huge turning point in the attitude toward appearing on stage for Susanna. "We were on an all-male punk rock bill," Susanna tells me, "and a light bulb snapped on in my head. I went, 'Oh, I don't have to worry about making sure every chord, every strum, every this, every that is perfect. This is not about being perfect. This is about being expressive.' I remember going, 'Okay. I'm going to let it all hang out,' as they used to say in the '60s."[10] So impressed was Kalberg with the Bangs that he asked them to create a commercial for *NO MAG*, announcing the new issue of the magazine (issue nine, which also featured an interview with the group). Back at Radio Tokyo, the group repurposed "Getting Out of Hand," substituting different *NO MAG*–centric lyrics, even adopting the zine's tagline into the jingle ("Pop trash. Noise music. Nancy Reagan"). Officially released on DownKiddie, the tune, "No Mag Commercial," was distributed to local stations before eventually showing up on a 1983 compilation imaginatively titled *The Radio Tokyo Tapes*.*

    The Bangs also wanted to show their gratitude to Rodney for his support, a thank you for the DJ presented in the form of an exclusive track just for him. Originally written by Susanna and David Roback in their Berkeley digs, and then reworked by the brunette and Vicki—a process that included adding all the guitar lines and the bridge—"Bitchen Summer/Speedway" captures the manic energy of Dick Dale via the Bangs. The single was recorded and mixed by Dave Peterson at the family home with his own improvised setup. It was the first time he had access to a four-track machine to help in his engineering endeavors. "We had this downstairs bonus room in our house that was unfinished," he explains. "I actually moved my bed and speakers down there. We ran wires up to the bedroom and made it into a studio."[11] Years later, Debbi still marvels at her brother's abilities. "Dave played a big role, especially early on," says Debbi. "I don't know how he figured it out [how to tape everything], but he was a fucking genius."[12]

    From playing with David Roback to literally standing center stage between Vicki and Annette was a huge jump forward for Susanna. It also marked a different placement for Vicki from where she had traditionally stood in the previous incarnations of the band. "I was always in the center—or just off-center—when we were a trio because I didn't want to upstage Debbi," Vicki explains. "I was always slightly stage right. When we had Lynn in the band, she was stage right, i.e., in my spot, and, and I was in the middle because I sang most of the leads." Things changed when Susanna joined, with Vicki shifting to "the lead guitar spot," Susanna now in the middle of the stage, thus being thrust into the focal point of attention.

    "There was no delineation and assignment of roles to the point of like, 'Okay, you're going to be the lead singer or the center person and I'm going to stand to your right,'" Vicki says of the switch. "I fell there

---

* "No Mag Commercial" can also be found on the 2014 compilation *Ladies and Gentlemen… The Bangles!*

because it's the traditional place where the lead guitar player stands and I became that by default because nobody else was going to take that role. To her [Susanna's] credit, it might have actually been an unintentional move on her part to say, 'Well, I'm going to be the singer, I'm going to be the center here.' It could easily have been that and maybe I'm not giving her enough credit for being conniving but it was not discussed to my memory at all."[13] Debbi recollects that early on "there was still a conscious effort of Susanna being positioned not exactly in the center, as to not block me." She notes, "I've seen early TV shows and films of us at the clubs and she wasn't directly in front of me."[14] Vicki concludes, "I was more interested in song writing, singing, and just accompanying myself. I was a general guitar player, but I had to play leads when I was playing with Debbi and Amanda because nobody else was doing it. I ended up really enjoying it but often feeling overwhelmed by the role."[15] Susanna, on the other hand, "could play rhythm guitar and was solid." However, "she had no interest or ability to play leads and that's probably because she knew she wanted to be the lead singer. She knew that from day one."[16]

After several years of living together in various apartments in and around Hollywood, Debbi and Vicki decided to move from their place in Hollywood Heights into separate accommodations. Debbi found a room in the house of Sid Griffin. Having left the Unclaimed the year before, Sid had formed a new group called the Long Ryders. With friend John Silva, Sid found a house for the duo to rent. "After three or four nights, he moved out," Sid says of Silva. A bedroom was open and offered to Debbi. "She was a terrific roommate, I adored her," Sid says. "I literally take advice from Debbi. She's a really good person." Sid notes that Debbi often underplays her intelligence and can be quiet. "She's very bright. One time, we had a quiz show on, and I remember she would answer the questions, and frequently be right. I thought, 'You should be at UCLA studying for your doctorate.' She was just a terrific person." Despite being smart, Sid says Debbi often suffers from poor confidence when it comes to herself. "She doesn't have great self-esteem," he says.[17]

Vicki relocated to West Hollywood, renting a room in a house just south of Santa Monica on La Cienega at what came to be dubbed the Spock Hotel. Queen bee of the property was Joanna Dean, "the godmother of Los Angeles punk."[18] With her blunt cut bangs and sculpted eyebrows, Dean had been given the nickname "Spock" by Dave Vanian of the Damned. Having been on the underground scene since the '70s and a member of the short-lived all-girl band Backstage Pass, Spock was a well-respected connoisseur of emerging talent, with a rotating cast of roommates composed of local artists. "I slept on the couch for the first six months because there was no bedroom for me," Vicki says. "I cleaned the bathroom and kept the kitchen neat for my rent." As well as providing shelter for aspiring artists, the Spock Hotel became a crash pad for touring musicians. "You'd come home at three in the morning after going out clubbing and being out with your friends," Vicki recalls. "The [band] Lords of the New Church would be asleep on the floor." Groups even began "booking" into the "hotel," with Vicki occasionally fielding "reservations." "I picked up the phone one day and it was the road manager for the Replacements asking if we may have a place for them to crash."[19]

10.

Native Canadian Mike Gormley had already been crucial in the careers of some of the biggest names in popular music by the time he came to Los Angeles in 1980. "I was based in Chicago with Mercury Records in the 1970s." It was right before Rod Stewart's solo career "broke wide open," Gormley recalls. "I spent the next four or five years with him, doing his publicity from the record company side," Gormley says. "He and I got pretty close and had some fun." Before leaving for the West Coast, Gormley worked with Rush and Bachman-Turner Overdrive. Though grateful for the opportunities, he yearned for more. "I wanted to work hands-on with bands," Gormley explains. "When you're with a label, you may get close to certain artists, or they may get popular enough that you got to give them more time. However, you still have the whole roster to deal with." Gormley wanted to be able to focus his energy, helping specific people attain their creative goals. "I wanted to deal with *a* band," he says. "I wanted to take that group from wherever they were to a higher position in the world."[1]

Gormley first encountered Miles Copeland during the former's stint as vice president and assistant to the chairman of A&M Records while Copeland was steering the career of English rock band the Police. When Miles officially decided to start a management organization, Gormley was the first to be tapped. "He came to me and said, 'Why don't you get out of here and we'll go run this company?' That's what happened." Christened Los Angeles Personal Direction (LAPD), the client list included Wall of Voodoo and Oingo Boingo. "Mike was ready to move on anyway, and he became a valued partner in a growing business,"

Copeland later noted.[2] After moving over to LAPD, Gormley drafted in Spock to assist him on the recommendation of Chas Gray from Wall of Voodoo. "I was the go-to," Spock says. "It was me and Mike Gormley in the office."[3]

As LAPD found its legs, the Bangs were playing more gigs, working to improve their live shows. "We didn't issue a lot of demo tapes to record companies and sit back," Vicki recalls. "We wanted to build up a following from the ground floor, by getting out there and gigging. We played all the dives and have gone on-stage in some really horrible places where nice girls aren't supposed to go."[4]

Tour manager Chris Lamson was impressed when he first saw the Bangs.* Having originally moved to Los Angeles to attend UCLA with the idea of becoming part of the university's theater department, Lamson had a change of heart. "I quickly discovered I couldn't act worth a damn," he admits, "so I started working in the campus events office." After a mutual friend introduced him to Copeland, Lamson eventually joined LAPD.

While at friend Louis Gutierrez's house one night, Lamson came across a headshot of the Bangs. "Louis showed me the picture and said I should check them out," Lamson recalls. "The Go-Go's were happening at the time on I.R.S. [Records] and I loved all-girl bands."[5] The two went to "an underground club in a basement" to see the Bangs. "I was just struck by it," Lamson says. "They had a vocal sound that just screamed Southern California with those harmonies." Lamson then took Copeland to see the girls. The boss did not share the same visceral response. "Miles wasn't totally sold on them," Lamson says. "He basically said, 'Look, I'll sign them, I just want you to do everything. I don't want any of that day-to-day, you'll handle it.' I'm like, 'Okay.'"[6] Lamson became the band's tour manager when they eventually began going on the road.

---

* Lamson does start the interview by saying, "I'm gonna put a caveat on this: these are my memories. Other people may have other memories and that doesn't necessarily mean that my memory is 100 percent accurate."

"Anytime they needed something or something happened, I was there. That's how it began."[7]

Copeland clearly recollects first encountering the Bangs at the Starlight Club* on Santa Monica Boulevard in West Hollywood in 1982. "They were refreshing and fun, and had good songs," he says of the band.[8] Besides managing the Police, Copeland also owned I.R.S. Records. He had recently signed the Go-Go's, who were seeing significant success. "Contrary to what one might assume," Copeland says of [the Bangs], "I did not sign them because they were all girls—it was simply that I really liked them." He affirms, "I was not looking for another Go-Go's, but I was also not avoiding one. But I did realize that, as they were an all-girl band from Los Angeles, and also looked upon as part of the new wave, the danger was that they could be classed as a 'poor person's Go-Go's.'"[9]† What Copeland found appealing about the Bangs was "the vibe of it...It was excitement...It was the stupidity of it in a sense that made it engaging."[10] After approaching the band and suggesting a meeting, not everyone in the group was impressed: Vicki had to explain to Susanna who the industry mogul was. "Susanna asked, 'Does anyone know who is Miles Copeland?' I said, 'You know, I.R.S., he manages The Police.'"[11] Wanting to get his partner's eyes on the prospective signing, Copeland sent Gormley to a follow-up show. The unique style of singing immediately impressed the Canadian. "Of course the harmonies—they had pretty good songs at that time—but mainly the vocals," he said of what got him interested. The crowd's reaction also impressed the music executive. "They got four encores that night," Gormley recounts.[12]

---

* "Starlight Club?" Vicki asks me. "I don't think we ever played a place with that name." Susanna asks if Copeland means the Starwood. Debbi specifically recalls in her journal that it was actually the Cathay de Grande where Copeland first saw the band. "It was a basement club with a low ceiling, a real fire hazard," she says.
† "This is funny because I remember making that very comment to Miles when we first spoke," Vicki tells me.

Still cautious, the four Bangs ventured to the LAPD office to see Copeland, only to be met by Gormley. "Miles was in Egypt with the Police or something," Gormley remembers. "I don't know where he was, but I took them out to lunch."[13] In a follow-up meeting with Copeland, held at I.R.S. headquarters, located within the A&M Records offices, Vicki brought with her a tape recorder, "set it on the desk, turned it on," to make sure that every word was captured.[14] "I don't even think there was a tape in it," Debbi laughs of the device. "I think we just brought it for the effect," she says.[15] "There were batteries," Vicki notes, "alas, not fresh [ones].''[16]

Eventually, Gormley and the band worked out a management deal. "They later told me they thought they were having lunch with me because Miles had a little label," Mike tells me. "He owned I.R.S. Records, but he also had a little other label called Faulty Products. They thought they were meeting with me because we wanted to sign them to Faulty. I said 'No, we want to sign you up for management' and they seemed pleased with that."[17] Vicki made it very clear that the Bangs had to be viewed as a separate, unique entity, not a runner-up to Copeland's other successful all-female group. "I said, 'I'm not interested in taking whatever opportunities you found that didn't fit the Go-Go's and placing them onto us,'" Vicki says. "To me, it was really important that we were not just a plan B. It was one of my sticking points."[18] Though comparisons between the two groups may have seemed inevitable, especially since the Go-Go's were on the rise, Gormley says, "we saw them [the Bangs] not as a pop band but a rock band whose members were women. Our first reaction was: They play better than the Go-Go's, they have a different style than the Go-Go's, yet they are still a rock-pop band."[19] Copeland agreed, noting, "Any artist always looks over his shoulder and sees what somebody else is doing. They want to be taken in their own right; they don't want to be a copy of someone else."[20]

Aligning with Copeland changed the entire trajectory for the band, according to Griffin. "[It] was the difference between life and death, as far as I'm concerned," he says. "He gave them the clout in the industry, the ability to breathe the oxygen of publicity."²¹ Yet it quickly became clear that it would be Gormley—not Copeland—who would be the point of contact for the Bangs at LAPD. "Because of Miles's schedule, I ended up working with them much more than he did," Gormley reflects. "It was beneficial all the way down the line; I enjoyed it a great deal. I think they saw it as Miles was their manager and I was their day-to-day guy, which has some truth to it." The band became "a little more personal than the others" he worked with, Gormley hypothesizes, since he was there from the start. "It was important to me because I'd been in the record industry at that point for thirteen years," he says. "I was working with them from a very early stage to millions of records sold."²²

Part of the LAPD deal was for an EP to be recorded and distributed through the Faulty Products label. This was a relief, according to Vicki. "We didn't send out demo tapes or anything so we weren't subjected to the man in the three-piece suit saying, 'Oh, look, a chick band,'" she says.²³ In June, the girls undertook a three-day recording and mixing marathon at Chateau Recorders in North Hollywood with the guidance of producer Craig Leon. Leon already had a stellar pedigree, having worked on albums by the Ramones and Blondie. Featuring five songs—four with writing credits split among Debbi, Vicki, and Susanna—and one cover, a version of the 1960s single "How Is the Air Up There?" by the New Zealand band the La De Das, the self-titled effort showcased what had become the band's signature sound.

Kicking off with lead single "The Real World," Susanna later remarked that the record was "as representative of who we really are and as authentic as anything the Bangles have ever done."²⁴ The EP also provided a significant accomplishment for Debbi. "I wrote on, 'I'm in Line,' which was my first attempt at writing a song," she says.²⁵ "I like the EP. I liked the fact that we were such a unit when we recorded that. Everybody was very much into the sound of how sonically we wanted it to be, and very much in agreement with the songs. It was just such a great vibe."²⁶ Debbi also valued the sense of solidarity among the bandmates that the session brought to the forefront. "It was enjoyable because it was more of a democracy," she reflects. "Even though Vicki and Sue are more of the songwriters and Sue did a bit more singing on it, we all were a unified group, going in a certain direction—together."[27]

11.

When before they had to go knocking for gigs, now the Bangs were in demand across the aspirational cool club circuit. The girls were frequently asked to play at Club 88 and the Whisky amidst a changing musical tide. Punk rock was fading, hair metal and new wave were rising, guitars cast aside for many chart bands in favor of synthesizers. Theresa Kereakes was responsible for booking the Whisky on Monday nights. After getting a tip from a friend who worked at Rhino Records, she decided to schedule the Bangs to open for the Last and Salvation Army. The show was especially significant, as it was backed with substantial advertising dollars. "That was their first big mainstream gig at a venue that would buy ads in the *Los Angeles Times* and the *Herald Examiner*," Theresa explains. The visibility would be a huge step up for the band, as "the Whisky had a weekly ad in every single periodical," Theresa explains. The extra spend paid off in an increased number of attendees. "When it came time for their show, people were lined up around the block before the doors even opened," Theresa recalls. "I worked in the box office so I asked who they were there to see," she explains. "They were all there for the Bangs."[1]

The show marked the start of what would blossom into its own microscene, based on a shared love for the Byrds, Beatles, and psychedelia with a garage rock blend. "We were all bands who wanted to drag the '60s kicking and screaming into the '80s," Susanna recounts. "Because we didn't quite fit into any of the categories that were happening in LA at the time, we all found each other quickly."[2] It was more about being united in mutual appreciation and difference to the trends surrounding them than a similarity in their own music that brought the groups together, Susanna says.[3] The vibe was "more a scene than a sound," Steve Wynn of the Dream Syndicate agrees. "We didn't fit in with what was happening in L.A. That's what really made it: we had enough in common with each other and almost nothing in common with anybody else. None of us were hearing what we wanted to hear, so we just did it ourselves. It was a very definite and particular movement and an exciting moment in time, but it wasn't like we were all doing the same thing. We were going in different directions."[4]

"Basically, we were all record collectors who played music," says Michael Quercio of the Three O'Clock. "The Beach Boys' *Pet Sounds* was certainly a big deal to us. The Dream Syndicate, the Bangs...and the Salvation Army (which became the Three O'Clock) were all playing gigs around L.A. at funky little places like the Music Machine, Dancing Waters, the Whisky, the Cathay de Grande. After about a year of bumping into one another, I think it was Susanna Hoffs who finally came up with the idea that maybe we should be playing together."[5]

It was a "weird time" in the local music scene, according to Jeff McDonald of Redd Kross. "Everyone coexisted," he tells me. "There was a lot of different things happening at once and everyone was forced to play the same venues, so there was a lot of cross-pollination. It was really fun."[6] The audiences coming to see the shows "included punks, goths...[and] rockabillies," all united in fandom.[7]

Journalists wanted a banner to label the amalgamation of bands; Quercio inadvertently provided the tagline the media had been looking for. "We were being interviewed by the *LA Weekly*, and the writer asked me: 'So what do you call this new scene of you and the Bangs, Rain Parade and the Dream Syndicate?' At that time it was really just those four groups. And I said, 'Oh, it's the Paisley Underground.' I didn't think much of it—it was just an off-the-cuff remark. The piece came out and it wasn't until a couple of months later that other papers started picking up this name and started to write about the scene and call it that."[8] The Long Ryders and Green on Red "got thrown into the Paisley

Underground," says Sid, "because we all lived in the same neighborhood and were friends."[9]

Ground zero for swapping ideas and inspiration became the two-story Green on Red house in East Los Angeles. Sunday gatherings became the unifying place for bands to drink, gab, and socialize. "We'd get together, have barbecues, lots of alcohol and play records till dawn. The great thing was that we all paid a lot of attention to each other and were all simultaneously cheerleaders and competitors.... When each new record came out, we'd try to raise the bar a little," Steve Wynn recalls.[10] Another element of bonding was the lack of individual baggage many of the artists had, a contrast to the cliché stereotype. "This is a horrible thing to appear in print, but most of us had pretty decent backgrounds, so there was no cultural or economic status that on a personal level had stung us so much that we wanted to bite back against society. 'What are you rebelling against?' 'Er, nothing.' Most people had a decent enough background and a few years of university. We didn't like Ronald Reagan, but we were not brick-throwing anarchistic punks."[11]

In June, some of the Paisley Underground decided to undergo an overnight trip to Catalina Island, with members of the Bangs, the Dream Syndicate, the Salvation Army, and other friends all along for the ride. "Michael Quercio had the idea to go on a little vacation," says Wynn. "Catalina is a half-hour boat trip from down in San Pedro. We all went out there and walked around, drinking and talking. We had no money, so when nightfall came someone had the idea of sleeping on the golf course. I think the sprinklers went off about four in the morning, so that was that. It was back to the mainland."[12] "It was like going on a big school trip with all of these amazing bands," Annette explains.[13] "We were so in the moment. I had such a great time just on the boat ride there." The next day "we walked through this abandoned golf course," Annette says. "People coupled off, not romantically but people went into smaller groups," she recalls. "I brought my two best friends with me." Susanna got to know twenty-year-old Louis Gutierrez better that evening. "My little relationship with Louis [Gutierrez, of the Three O'Clock] blossomed on that trip," she laughs. "Our bands had been playing together for a while and then we dated."[14] It marked a hopeful time for all involved. "It was an incredible bonding experience," Annette states. "There was nothing else like this going on," Quercio recounts.

12.

With management, a recorded EP awaiting release, and a steady buzz created by a stream of publicity and shows, the Bangs were poised to take off. Yet every article written about them mentioned "the other girl" band, highlighting the entirely female makeup of the group while comparing them to the Go-Go's. That quintet was riding high; the previous year had seen the Go-Go's get to the top of the *Billboard* chart with their debut album, *Beauty and the Beat*, a first for a band made up entirely of women. While gender, geography, and shared management were where the main likenesses ended, the Bangs could not escape being constantly appraised as the runner-up facsimile to Copeland's other signing. The indulgent repetition of journalists to lazily place the bands side by side repeatedly as a main talking point is rarely seen in pieces focused on male contemporaries. "Even though they *are* girls," writes Jeff Spurrier in the *Los Angeles Times*, "they don't sound *at all* like the Go-Go's."[1] Just being female and from Los Angeles made it a real risk "of being called a cheap Go-Go's knock-off," *Creem* comments, "even if its set consists entirely of Lou Reed, Brian Eno or, hell, Kraftwerk cover tunes. It's just a sad fact of life, like next month's rent check."[2]

Steve McDonald of Redd Kross knew both bands from their earliest stages. "We saw the Go-Go's as early as '79, when they were a couple of years away from their sort of polished breakthrough," he recalls. "At that stage, they were very primitive. They were learning to play their instruments." In contrast, members of the Bangs were already experienced performers. "Both groups had that one thing in common that a lot of the bands in the scene didn't," Steve continues. "Their songwriting was advanced, more advanced than even their ability to play."[3]

The media, however, often seemed incapable of celebrating the groups as separate successful entities with differing sounds and aesthetics, instead endlessly pitting them against each other. "In many respects, they're much better," writes the *Sacramento Bee* of the band. "The Go-Go's may have the beat (and now the bucks), but [the Bangs] clearly have the heart."[4] The journalist then goes on to lambast the Go-Go's, deriding their stereotypical "girlie" attributes of "slumber party stage presence" while likening their musicianship to that off "the back of the cereal box at best." In this equation, the Bangs are said to be able to "play circles around" their peers, thus "perhaps put[ting] a stop to the Go-Go's."[5]

With every interviewer asking the band to justify their existence, one writer—notably a woman—comments that the "[Bangs] seem to expend as much energy dispelling forced comparisons fostered by the local press—telling people what they're not—as they do show[ing] people what they really are. 'We didn't hop on any bandwagon,' asserts the ebullient singer-guitarist Susanna Hoffs. 'We're not a record company's gimmick, and we're not a packaged money-making scheme to cash in on what's happened to them [The Go-Go's]. This has been a dream—to be in a band and to play. And we've all been musicians for years. It just so happens that we're girls.'"[6] The tone of questioning utilized often placed the Bangs on the defensive, justifying their style and substance, reinforcing the idea of limited opportunities for more than one female group to be active and successful at a time. In a *NO MAG* profile, Susanna is asked, "Do the Bangs copy the Go-Go's?" to which she answers in all-caps emphasis, "NO NOT AT ALL."

This begins to be made even more apparent in a later *Rolling Stone* article titled "The Bangles: A Female Fab Four?" with writer Michael Goldberg opening the piece by pondering, "Are the Bangles the new Go-Go's? One can't help but wonder."[7] This immediately creates a dynamic where Vicki must again assert herself, saying, "Anyone who listens to the new

Go-Go's album and the new Bangles album isn't going to say that these two bands sound anything alike. Because we don't."[8] It is difficult to imagine when a pair of all-male bands hailing from the same area would be relentlessly presented with occasion to site the variants between them. The novelty of an all-female dynamic creates a scenario where "girl groups are considered a genre, as they are so rare," according to Joe Nolte.[9] Indeed, a piece in the *Los Angeles Times* surmises this quandary, saying, "The success of the Go-Go's has been a mixed blessing for female bands following in their footsteps. There's now more acceptance of girl rock groups, but these bands also have to deal with the inevitable comparisons to the original Go-girls."[10] An *LA Weekly* piece echoes this sentiment, proclaiming, "The Bangs are in the rather dubious position of being touted as 'the next Go-Go's' for four obvious reasons: they play '60s influenced pop-rock, the members of the band are all female; they live in Los Angeles and people don't know any better."[11] Founding member Vicki is once again put in the position of defending her band, saying, "Being compared to the Go-Go's both helps and hurts us....We don't want to be considered the poor man's Go-Go's....We have something equally valid."[12] Susanna emphasizes the previous years put into the group before her arrival, adding, "A lot of people don't realize that the Bangs have been around, in various forms, as long as the Go-Go's."[13] Susanna backs up her bandmates' experience, saying, "She (Vicki) is the ancient veteran," with bass player Annette chiming in, "It's been the two of them (Vicki and Debbi) with different members."[14]

There is a strange, repeated motif that the Bangs, because they are women, must have as their main influence other all-female bands. Questions and statements asking if the girls align themselves with former '60s groups like the Ronettes, the Crystals, and the Shangri-Las bejewel many articles, along with a seemingly surprised tone taken by the respective authors when the band reveals it is "predominantly male influences—Stones, Yardbirds, Paul Revere & the Raiders, Turtles, Seeds" that inform the group's "melodic...original material...shot through with excellent garage guitar riffing, power chords and crashing, surf-type drumming."[15] Repeatedly, the Bangs have to note the AM radio fodder that infiltrated their musical upbringing, listing again and again "the all-male groups" who inspired them. The continuous fascination with this line of questioning makes it seem unbelievable that young girls could find possibility models in male musicians, as if to be visible, successful, and creative at a rarefied level is only a dream accessible to men. "I felt like how dare I come out and compare ourselves in any way, shape, or form to the [all male bands]," Debbi reflects. "In my head, those are examples of how I envisioned our band could be. We're all singers, we all write, we all play, and we should all be seen as a group like the Beatles. I just liked the concept of the group doing things together."[16] She continues, "We wanted to be number one, wanted to have a hit song. We wanted to be on the top of the charts," she says. "You must be like that when you're in a band. If you aren't, you're gonna fail. You must think beyond your means."[17]

When a writer comments on the musicianship instead of the genitalia, it makes for rarefied reading, such as Mark Leviton's August 1982 *Music Connection* review, where he notes, "While no one solos extensively, it is obvious that all members have tough, imaginative approaches, with Debbi providing often difficult rhythmic changes and Vicki tossing in good counter lines. The Bangs have apparently passed quickly through that amateur stage the Go-Go's overcame and gone straight to a highly professional but never stiff level of performance."[18] An inability to experience the Bangs as their own entity or untethered from unfortunate stereotypes seems deemed impossible for many reviewers, with a *Daily Sundial* writer claiming that the band's "main influence is Josey [sic] and the Pussycats, a group of fictional female rockers brought to life via television, in a Hanna-Barbara [sic] cartoon."[19] Such two-dimensional, inept descriptions made with broad brushstrokes sadly stand as the rule, not the exception, throughout most of the early Bangs and Bangles pieces.

By October 7, 1982, the band was ready to celebrate the release of their official Faulty Products self-titled debut EP at the Lhasa Club in

Hollywood. However, festive feelings were quickly extinguished when a letter from the East Coast crossed Mike Gormley's desk. "We found out about this band in New Jersey called the Bangs," he tells me. "They wanted [something like] $10,000 for us to use the name. Otherwise, we'd be able to be the Bangs everywhere in the world, except Massachusetts, or someplace like that, because that's where they…had some claim to it." Action had to be taken. "We decided we'd have to change the name," Gormley recalls. "I remember them coming into my office at the corner of Melrose and La Brea with a precise idea of finding the name; ideas were being thrown around."[20] It was Susanna who came up with the idea of the new possible moniker Eight Arms to Hold You, inspired by the working title of the Beatles movie *Help!* "For eighteen hours, the band was called that," Mike laughs. "Then we all woke up in the morning." With the new day came a change of heart, with the group discarding the full title. "We then thought it would be cool to be called Eight Arms, as it's just so punchy." However, full group consensus was not to be had, and time was of the essence. The name debacle had momentarily postponed release of the forthcoming EP right as radio was picking up and fans were demanding it in stores. On top of that, Miles had landed the group a spot opening for I.R.S.'s 2 Tone British breakouts the English Beat across the US. With the clock running down, Mike says, "I think it was Vicki who just suggested adding the 'les' on the end and call it Bangles."

There are other memories of when and how the name came to be. As Vicki remembers it, inspiration struck while all key parties were sitting at a table together at the famous Los Angeles Mexican restaurant Lucy's El Adobe Cafe. "[We were] actually writing on napkins, when the 'les' came about, and my memory is that we all liked it well enough, after getting over the loss of the Bangs.[21]

Susanna recalls the name change occurring while the band was staying in a hotel room together. "We were all pitching ideas," she says. "Bangles was the best one. We looked up the definition of *bangle* and found one that said: to hang loose. I liked that. It had a beatnik feel to it."

The new suggestion was still not immediately embraced, Gormley remembers. "They're like, 'But that's just so girly and doesn't have the punch,'" he says, "but it was the best we had so we went with it. That's how that came to be."[22] Vicki later confided to having mixed emotions about the new name. "We were really heartsick about it, because I really liked the Bangs," she said. "I liked the innuendo, and the sound of it—it was explosive, and short—so we just tried to keep the syllable in the word. Even though Bangles is a much softer image, and a much softer sound. We felt like we had already established an identity as the Bangs."[23] Unfortunately, record sleeves for the Faulty Products EP were already printed, forcing a delay in the record's release as the artwork was revised.

The girls played their last show as the Bangs on October 28, 1982, leaving the confines of Southern California to open for British band the Boomtown Rats in San Francisco before departing on their first national tour as the support act for the English Beat.* Flying high on their third successful album, the ska group had already achieved stardom in their homeland, and was garnering traction in the US, driven by the tracks "Mirror in the Bathroom" and "Save It for Later," which featured on the *Billboard* charts and the fledgling music video channel, MTV. Copeland had secured the Bangs (now the Bangles) the supporting slot just five days before the tour began, with Lamson in the role as tour manager and Marji joining the group as girl Friday. "I hadn't any qualms about them going on the road," Mike Gormley says. "The English Beat were on their way up at the time so it was good visibility for the girls."[24] Others though were a bit more tentative as to how the sunny California sounds of the Bangles would mesh with the British boys, with one writer noting before the shows commenced, "The girls are aware they might face a rude awakening when they perform in front of unfamiliar crowds impatiently waiting for the English Beat to come on stage. But, The Bangles have the talent and the determination that

---

* The band is known as the English Beat in the United States and Canada, and as the British Beat in Australia. Everywhere else, they are simply the Beat.

makes success almost inevitable. Vicki summed up the band's attitude and drive for success: 'If they boo at us, we'll boo right back!'"[25]

The astute prediction proved true once the rookie travelers took to the road. Lamson, who went on to do countless shows with the band, almost perceptually shivers when he says, "The roughest tour [we ever did] was certainly the English Beat."[26] Audiences for the shows had come to skank and see their rude boy heroes from abroad. Faced with four women singing upbeat harmonies was an unexpected and, for some, an unwanted surprise. "When I think about it musically, the English Beat are melodic and musical," Lamson reflects, "but the crowd was basically punk ska, super rough. Punk was coming up at the time and so it was very in vogue for the crowds to be super aggressive. These poor girls would go out on stage and it was just trial by fire. They were so tough."[27] Vicki later described the gigs as "forty-five minutes of people donning leather jackets, spitting, and flipping the bird at you as you try to play."[28] For twenty-year-old Annette, "there were some amazing places" that the band went to. However, she remembers, "We did get some audience reaction that was less than favorable. Every once in a while we would get, 'Show us your tits!' or something very sexist like that. People were not used to seeing an all-female lineup. People just wanted us off the stage. There were some places that were just lukewarm, which is hard, but at least they weren't being abusive. Then there were other places where they were pretty rough on us."[29] Debbi concurs, telling me, "Our forty-five-minute set felt like fifteen minutes! We never played so fast! We basically wanted to get the set done before we were the target of too much carnage." Susanna recalled a milk carton hitting her so hard that it cut her head as she was singing. Another time, Lamson found himself scissoring gum out of her hair, as someone had thrown it at the singer during the set. "They had to steel themselves to go out on stage because they just got booed off, virtually every time," Lamson says. "I would say, 'Hey, look, there's maybe five hundred people out there. If you can reach five people and connect with them, those five people will tell five more people who will tell five more people etcetera. It was just kind of like a psychological trick just to find some positive thing in the tour but it was rough." Susanna agrees, saying, "It was literally like vaudeville—people throwing tomatoes at you."[30]

The tour proved to be a chance for the Bangles to tighten their stage show in front of the most challenging of audiences. "We were so concerned about playing every note right and it showed," Annette remembers. "We were just looking at our instruments and [it was getting to the point] where it wasn't natural. One of the members of English Beat told us to just have fun out there and not to worry." The advice proved to be another definitive moment for the foursome. "It was still hit or miss with the audience," Annette says, "but at least we enjoyed the moment and were just having fun up there. That was a big deal."[31]

Susanna smiles when asked about that first trip across the states, noting, "One of my tour names was Major Hive—I don't know why. Another was Mr. Gus. I got those from [bassist] David Steele and [guitarist] Andy Cox. They went on to be the band in Fine Young Cannibals. I hung out with them the most while on the road."[32]

Inside jokes and dalliances between bands and crews were rife. One Beat vocalist had his eye on Susanna from the start of the tour. "She's going to hate me [for telling this story]," "Ranking" Roger Charlery of the English Beat confides. "I had this massive crush on Susannah [sic].... I had the hots for her," he says, going on to describe her as "one of the most beautiful women...there was something about her. She was so cute and innocent, yet she was so talented. I know she fancied me." One evening, things got intimate between the two, but did not go as planned. "It was premature ejaculation," Charlery admits. "It wasn't even in her and everything was bursting. That was how hot the scene was." Despite the failed consummation of shared admiration, Charlery confides that he would have asked Susanna to marry him if they had ever been seriously involved. "I have the upmost respect for her. I've always had a little bit in my heart for Susannah [sic], even more than Madonna [Roger dated Madonna on a couple of occasions]."[33]

12.

Vicki was also having fun, finally seeing her dream of touring across the country come to fruition. "I was thrilled to be on the road," she tells me. "I absolutely loved it. I didn't care that there were five girls in one room, and then Chris got his own room. There were two beds, two girls in each bed, and then poor Marji had a cot. That was our first tour."[34] Per diem for food was approximately "$20 each per day," Vicki says, describing it as "poverty touring." "We had deli trays," she laughs. "If you wanted to eat, you'd make a sandwich. You'd have fruit and meat and cheese and bread. That's about it. Maybe some beer, which we never drank, and some Diet Coke."[35]

Vicki in particular recalls going to New York with the band for the first time, when even the smallest things made for an enchanting stay. "We're having all these great New York experiences, like driving through Central Park West where there was snow. It was dawn and everything was beautiful. I just remember thinking, I love this so much. We were staying in a short-term rental apartment, infested with cockroaches. I was brushing my teeth. I drank water out of the tap and thought, 'Oh my god. This is the most delicious water I've ever tasted.' It shocked me that in this crummy hotel in this crummy place in this big scary city that the tap water was delicious." Annette also has positive memories of the tour. "It was exciting because it was the first time I saw the country through playing in a band," she recounts. "It was very magical."[36] Debbi was similarly wowed by the city, writing in her journal, "All of Central Park was this wonderful blue color. I'll never forget it."

For the younger Peterson, at just twenty-one, having older sister Vicki by her side provided assurance to Milt and Jeanne as their relatively sheltered youngest daughter embarked on a cross-country trip. "I think the only reason I could get away with this is because I was with Vicki," Debbi says. "My parents would never let me go off on my own. I was a younger sister and it's always the older sister going, 'Don't worry, I'll take care of it' and she would. Vicki would always take care of [things].

I'm not putting her down in any way, shape, or form. She was great. She took care of me because Mom and Dad were, 'Oh, God, you're gonna go on the road.' I'm sure that was probably scary for my parents, for us both going on the road. Vicki, bless her heart, she was kind of mother hen and took care of me, which was great, but it was also a little stifling at times." She goes on to confide, "I feel like a bit of a shadow…Vicki's shadow, because she's a lot more outgoing than me and expressive. The band would always listen to Vicki. It was crazy. She was like *the* person, the head honcho."[37]

Adventures abounded during the time period Debbi refers to as "van life," with highlights including "driving in a vehicle overflowing with alcohol (they did a lot of drinking), peeing on the lawn beside a Masonic Temple in Champaign, Illinois (they couldn't always stop at gas stations)…[being] barked at by a dog, [stealing] gas in Iowa, [getting] stopped by a midwestern policeman (he was 'nice'), [getting] trashed in San Francisco…nothing majorly interesting.'"[38] Early on in the tour, Lamson had connected with another young music aficionado, Joe Stella. Stella was working at the mixing board of a club and was keen to get more experience. "He was cheap," Lamson laughs. "We needed a guy that was with the band day to day. You go into these clubs, and you get the house guy [who does not care about the individual band]."[39] Stella appreciated the talent on display, especially that of Debbi. "I remember when I met the girls for the first time, I said, 'Where's the drummer?' Debbi put her hand up, I said, 'You're fucking amazing.' She replied, 'Really?' I said, 'Absolutely, I play drums. I know how hard it is to sing and play drums at the same time."[40] Seeing a possible opportunity, Stella pitched himself to go on the road with the Bangles. "He just said, 'Hey, do you want me to just come out?' and he joined the tour." Travel was not glamorous, with the entourage now composed of the four Bangles, Marji, Lamson, and new addition, Stella. "All of us were in a fifteen-passenger van with all the stuff piled in back," Lamson says. "I think eventually we graduated to a truck for all the luggage and the gear, but we had that same fifteen-passenger van. We took out the back seats and we would put a sleeping area in the back. That was a big upgrade in those days. At least we had a place to crash in the rear."[41]

Lamson took on the lion's share of the driving, with Vicki occasionally taking a turn behind the wheel. "There were no cell phones. There was no GPS. There was nothing. I had one of those big Rand McNally maps to get around the entire country," he laughs. "We had some crazy incidents," Lamson says. "I remember one time we were in Canada going to Quebec City in the winter. I was driving, it was snowing, and it was late. It's a two-lane highway, I'm in the fast lane. I'm a California guy so I don't know about snow or ice. I'm passing all these cars and thinking, 'Oh, maybe I must be going too fast.' I slowed down and hit the brakes. As I'm crossing over into the right lane, I hit black ice. The van goes sideways at fifty miles an hour and we go right off the road. We go right into the snow. The snow is all the way to the back of the van. All the windows are covered. We all just started laughing because it was that nervous laugh—we had just escaped serious harm. It was like, 'How the hell are we supposed to get out of here?' We all had to climb out, open the back doors and go out that way. I had to flag down a guy and tell them, 'Hey, when you get into town, can you send someone out for us?'"[42]

While the tour may have been a trial by fire, it worked to spark nationwide interest in the group, at one point seeing the EP sell more than ten thousand copies in a week.[43]

Inspired by the Beatles, the band had started their own fan club for aficionados. "Me and Vicki wanted to connect with our audience," Debbi says. "We would answer letters and draw things for the fans using old-fashioned snail mail. It was so cool to engage with our fans. We thought it was very important."[44]

They called it Bangles 'N Mash—a take on the British dish of bangers (sausages) and mash (mashed potatoes). Marji was originally put in charge of responding to anything that arrived at the PO Box printed on the back of the EP. "Marji had a section called Mojo's Milieu," Debbi explains. "She was working with us, so it was a way for fans to get insider information about what was going on."

Bangles 'N Mash quickly grew, with the Peterson family being drafted in for reinforcement. "We had the whole family working on Bangles stuff," Debbi laughs. "Pam was helping with the books. Mom and Dad were helping by opening letters and getting things printed. We were on the road so much we couldn't really do it ourselves."[45] The band made Christmas tapes to send to fans, and a regular newsletter began circulating. Everyone from small children inspired by the band to prisoners began to write to the girls. "I got a lot of good stuff," Debbi recalls. "We would get renderings of us through the mail. It was kind of full circle, as I used to do fan art drawings when I was young." Debbi's favorite thing to receive were notes from other girls about being a female drummer. "They'd be like, 'What advice can you give me?' I just said, 'Stick to it. Don't let anybody tell you that you can't do it.'"[46] For a generation reared on MTV, the band provided a glimpse of what could be. The constant rotation of Bangles videos was a snapshot for many girls of women not just doing but excelling on a global level at the previously often unimaginable. "There were many times when I was signing autographs for fans, and girls would say to me that they were learning to play drums because of me," Debbi says. "We were early day influencers, inspiring girls to pick up instruments."

The importance of the group, and Debbi in particular, for younger women was immense, Sid Griffin reflects. "I don't think they realized how impactful they were as role models to their own gender," he reflects, Debbi especially, because she was "a really good drummer." "There were those who thought being a drummer was not ladylike. That it's pounding or sweaty. They had such great success and meant so much to young girls," Griffin notes. "I know that their audience really shifted away from Paisley Underground and indie hipness to a lot of young girls. One of the roadies once told me that he felt that it frustrated them a bit, that they had so many young teenage girls go to their gigs. I said, 'But they're an inspiration for those kind of young girls.' Okay, maybe they don't get this graduate students' intellectual, hipster bohemian audience that they desire. I saw their 1980s incarnation. It was those girls who were just screaming at hit singles and stuff. You had young girls, I feel, seeing an example, seeing how they can be empowered to make their own little statement. They were such a symbol to them. I have had people in England say, 'You lived with the Bangles, wow.' They would reply that they wanted to play the guitar and their father didn't want them to do it and they wanted to be the drummer. That side of the Bangles should be played up."[47]

Besides messages from younger girls looking for advice, their mail regularly included marriage proposals, as well as unusual trinkets of affection. "One time, Vicki got a chicken bone necklace," Marji laughs. "Somebody actually ate a chicken dinner, took the bones and made a necklace out of it, wrapped it up in a fancy box, and sent it to us."[48] Marji even had a fan phone line installed in her house, as the club was so popular. "It just started going crazy," she remembers. "Every year was just more."[49]

Skeletal poultry remains were just one example of darker, disconcerting communications sent to the women. Gracie, who has worked with the band for over two decades, discussed what she refers to as "the toxicity of fame," a specific type of abusive, inappropriate discourse aimed at female stars. "I used to do the snail mail," she says, "and would take showers after [as what was written was so upsetting]. I started wearing gloves while opening their correspondence after I received a little apothecary bottle for Susanna full of cloudy, white viscous liquid. There were some other things in that package as well and they all got burned. Sometimes I would cry before my first job, it was so fucking disturbing [the things they got sent]. There is weird shit out there that these girls had to navigate while being asked about their sex lives, stuff that people don't ask guys."[50]

13.

As 1983 dawned, the newly christened Bangles found themselves back in Los Angeles, fresh off the six-week tour with the English Beat. Faulty Products was finally officially releasing the band's eponymous five-track record after holdups due to the name change in the fall, which had hindered the album hitting stores for its original street date. Composed of five songs—four written by the band and one cover—*Bangles* captured the frenetic, unpolished sound of the band's live shows. However, there was yet another problem: Faulty, which was having organizational issues, folded not long after the vinyl hit stores. This made it difficult for fans to find the EP. Though the EP was eventually picked up by Copeland's bigger label, I.R.S. Records, the initial lack of stock hampered the continued evolution of a sales story, creating another challenge for the band and management. The lack of physical product was noted by keen shoppers and journalists alike, one writer arguing that the demise of Faulty dragged the group "back to square one."[1]

The setback did not stop the band from doing more shows. Their mixed reviews were most heavily adorned with Go-Go's comparisons, illustrating the inability of the almost entirely male reviewers to separate the two bands, fixated as they were on their similarities in terms of geography and gender. "Let's see now: How can I get through this report on the Bangles' Thursday night show at the Roxy without mentioning the Go-Go's? (Oops, that's once)," is how Robert Hilburn kicks off his *Los Angeles Times* piece under the banner of "The Bangles at the Roxy: Do They Measure Up?"[2] Hilburn flaunts a special kind of belittling hatred of women, seemingly incapable of writing a single sentence without including an unflattering comparison between the two groups. One example occurs in the fourth paragraph when he notes, "Measured against the almost irresistible vitality of the Go-Go's…the Bangles appeared almost plodding as they opened with a punchless version of Simon & Garfunkel's 'Hazy Shade of Winter'…after a couple of so-so original numbers."[3]

There are rare examples where writers were able to objectively experience the band as their own entity, without the parameters of previous or contemporary girl-groups informing a majority of their opinion and word count. These are the few occasions when the women seem to be finally seen as artists first instead of being shuffled into the "all-girl group" purgatory lazily utilized by many. "If the Beatles came back as young women, they would be the Bangles," glows the *Sacramento Bee*. "The Bangles, who even grin and cut up on stage, are the closest thing to an early English rock band on the scene today." The review goes on to describe "faultless three-part harmonies, stirring Rickenbacker rhythms, and some neat swipes," as well as "real lyrical maturity and thoroughly assured musicianship."[4*] *Creem* offers up an equally Go-Go's-free article, stating, "It's easy to be charmed by the group's bursts of energy and songs about the ups and downs of love and growing up."[5]

With the newly launched MTV channel not yet having reached Southern California cable networks, *MV3*, a syndicated music video show, shot in Los Angeles, temporarily satiated the teen masses eager to see their favorite new groups on the tube. Featuring bands that were in rotation at KROQ, the Bangles scored a coveted spot in January on the program, lip-syncing performances of the Susanna-led "The Real World," and the Debbi-fronted "I'm in Line." The group also recorded a short, cringeworthy interview with KROQ DJ and show host Richard Blade. Blade kicked

---

* The article does, however, appear under the title "Keeping Up With the Go-Go's: Backstage with The Bangles."

off by introducing the band as "four hot ladies." He then asks who is the lead singer, to which Susanna responds, "There is no one lead singer." Blade then contemptuously replies, "There's three lead singers and you fight over it." The subject changes, and Blade states, "You're more of a pop band—you classify yourselves, right?" To which Susanna fires back, "We're kind of a garage band."[6] The exchange, while seemingly lighthearted, provides a template for countless interviews that follow, with the host/interviewer attempting to create public division between band members while instantaneously categorizing them based on their looks and gender.

The next month saw the girls invited to join Faulty Production clients Wall of Voodoo at a festival in Puerto Rico. Though excited about the date, Annette was less than pleased about the impending flight to the destination. The news had been speckled with reports of plane crashes, with three separate fatal incidents involving DC-10s occurring in rapid succession. Regardless of her anxiety, the bass player boarded the first of two jets necessary to get to the gig. "I remember Susanna sat next to me because she knew I was uncomfortable," Annette recalls. "She always made me feel safe, there was a maternal vibe." The first leg of the trip from Los Angeles to New York was uneventful. The band was on a layover, sleeping on the floor of the airport, waiting for the next part to bring them to Puerto Rico. When the scheduled plane popped up on the monitor, "Susanna pointed out [to comfort me] that there was no DC-10s." Annette nodded off again, having "the weirdest experience of sleep paralysis." When she came to, she saw with horror that another delay had occurred, shuffling the group onto a DC-10. "Susanna says to me, 'Look. Three DC-10s have gone down in the past six months. You don't think that the plane mechanics aren't being hypervigilant right now because there's a bunch of bad PR on DC-10s that they're going to make sure that they're going to be the safest airplanes in the sky.'"[7] Assuaged by her friend's reassurance, Annette boarded the packed aircraft.

Everything was going smoothly until the plane reached "the midpoint over the ocean" of the trip. "All of a sudden, we feel the temperature changing," Annette says. Suddenly the plane started bobbing up and down, with Susanna, still trying to soothe Annette, dismissing the radical movements to "turbulence." "The bumps are now becoming more frequent. I grabbed Susanna's upper arm. She whispers to me, 'If you ever feel really nervous, just look at the stewards, they're always calm, cool, and collected and that will make you feel better.'" Just then, the seatbelt sign went on overhead. "I listened to Susanna," Annette recalls. "I'm looking at the stewardesses: they are calm and they go to their seats and they start buckling up." Then the plane started shaking, out of control. "It was rough." Annette shivers. "It was also going horizontally. It was going back and forth." Still having eyes on the flight attendants, Annette watched a woman unbuckle her seatbelt and start to walk down the aisle on her knees. "She had to kneel because she couldn't stand, it was that rough," she says. "This is very alarming to me," Annette confides. "I'm shaking and I am forgiving all my enemies." Everyone around them was equally terrified. "Some of the Puerto Rican passengers thought the stewardess was on her knees praying, so they got on their knees and started to pray and in Spanish."[8]

Though eventually making a safe landing, the flight was unnerving throughout its entirety. "Usually turbulence don't last that long," Annette comments, "but they just didn't go away. It was consistent. I was so on edge [and kept] thinking we were going to die. We were going to be that rock band that goes in an airplane." Susanna, admittedly not a huge fan of flying, was the steadying influence. "Susanna was great," Annette says. "She held it together. I'm surprised she didn't get a bruise on her arm because I was clutching her so hard." Debbi "had a drink or two," with the thinking that "if you're gonna go down in a plane, you might as well be smashed." Tour manager Chris Lamson, Annette recalled, "was actually very quiet and biting his nails" until the wheels touched down.[9]

Annette was not the only one who had a bumpy ride. "When we finally landed, the captain got on the loudspeaker," Annette tells me. "He said, 'I've been an airline pilot now for twentysomething years, but I've never experienced anything like this. God bless. We're here.' He was shaken up too, I could hear it."[10] Upon returning to the United States after the performance, Annette realized that she should not have been surprised by the terrifying flight, as the route the plane took on that day went through part of the Bermuda Triangle.

Back stateside, the Bangles continued to gig. Milo of the Descendents caught a performance on the same tour. "I saw them for the second time at the Rodeo in La Jolla, while I was going to college at UC San Diego," he says. "This would have been early 1983. I showed up for their sound check, and they invited me to have dinner with them! We ate at El Toritos near the club; the Bangles had margaritas but I was underage and had to order a Coke. It was not a well-attended show, maybe fifty people total. I was amazed people hadn't heard of them. But it was great; they played their cover of '7 and 7 Is' by Love, and all their early classics."[11] Susanna later commented on the Bangles' dedication to slowly building a following organically, even if a payoff of sorts was part of the equation to get bodies to shows. "I remember in the early days, I used to bribe people with, 'I'll buy you a beer if you stand at the front of the stage and dance a little bit.' There would be five people there. I'd end up buying them the beer and then they wouldn't even dance," she laughs. "It took a long time of building building building to get any sort of audience."[12]

When not on tour, Vicki was still bunking at Spock Hotel. However, roommate Steve Wynn had moved out, leaving a vacancy and a need for a new tenant. In moved one Micki Steele. She was a well-known entity in the Los Angeles scene, having started her career in the Runaways. By the time she took up residence with Vicki and Spock, she had already been in several other established local bands, including Slow Children, Toni and the Movers, Nadia Kapiche, and Snakefinger. She could have been part of a major record deal with Arista during her tenure as bassist and backing vocals with power pop group Elton Duck. However, according to former bandmate Paul Reed, "Micki decided not to sign with us. I'm sure it was a matter of intuition—something inside told her to hold back, so she did," he reflects. "I think she was looking for the perfect fit—a situation that would satisfy her on all levels."[13]

Micki was looking for something, if nothing more than an escape from her upbringing. "Micki grew up in a very wealthy family in Orange County," Vicki explains. "Unlike Susanna, Micki wanted to get out of there. It was not a place she wanted to stay. Ideologically, it was not a fit for her. She was happy to leave that area, that lifestyle—but she's always had money."[14]

The privately educated, introverted bright girl did not feel at ease in the wealthy, self-described "WASPy" enclave of Orange County's Newport Beach from where she hailed. "She had a difficult upbringing and a difficult young life," says former manager Maria Corvalan.[15] Micki later described the area as "embarrassing," remarking that "everything was named after John Wayne," a place "where rich kids take drugs and crack up their sports cars." Real-life decadence was illustrated by Micki sharing an anecdote of someone riding a motorcycle into a swimming pool during a high school house party.

Like future housemate Vicki, as a child Micki found herself out of sync with her peers, becoming obsessed with all things related to the Beatles and the British Invasion. By fourteen, she was playing the violin and the guitar, switching over to the flute to join the high school band. At Corona del Mar High School in Eastbluff, surfers and football athletes were at the top of the social hierarchy, with music students at the bottom, making them a frequent target for abuse from the dominant bullies. "They'd fill milk cartons with mud and throw them at the people from the music department. They had a kind of macho mentality," Micki later reflected. Such incidents pushed the teen further into the still-thriving local counterculture of like-minded artists and creatives. Yet it was not until after graduation that the idea to play the bass took root. "Early on, some friends took me to see Carol Kaye in a little nightclub in Hollywood," Micki recalled. "She's a great bass player, she's played on tons of records with everyone who's anyone. When I saw her do it, I wanted to do it too." Micki approached the artist afterwards for advice, noting, "She said, 'I play ballads with fingers, and rock songs with pick,' which was cool, so I learned how to do both."[16]

Soon after, she found herself in the Runaways, carving out a career as a musician, to the chagrin of her parents. Changing her name, while part of Fowley's marketing scheme, also created a clear dividing line between Susan from Newport Beach and Micki the artist. "I guess it's not as normal as 'Pam,'" she told an interviewer in 2007 about her chosen moniker.[17] "I changed my name in 1976, for personal reasons." Micki never spoke specifically about why she decided to switch, joking once "that she thought having a sex change would be the only way to get into a real rock band."[18] Though having a nasty fallout with Fowley at the end of her time in the Runaways, by keeping the name he gave her, Micki chose to assert the new persona, perhaps in an attempt to abandon what she may have seen as the unsavory aspects of her upbringing and be taken seriously as an artist in her own right. "She has family that refuse to accept the fact that she's not Susan," Corvalan says, underscoring the clear break between Susan (pre-band involvement) and Micki (bassist in a group).[19]

Speaking with Micki's friends from the 1980s, certain personality traits—a need for belonging, mental health problems, specifically depression, paired with a great intelligence and wry sense of humor—repeatedly come up to describe the redhead. Sid Griffin was once a romantic paramour of Micki's and remained a friend for many years. "Micki was sensitive, intelligent, and desperately wanted to be accepted as one of the gang," he reflects. "She's not had a great upbringing. It had its pitfalls."[20] Former manager Ian Lloyd-Bisley saw this, noting, "I got on really well with her, but she seemed a bit of a troubled soul."[21]

Various former male band members all admit to having had crushes on the musician, wax poetic about her beauty, and comment on her fast wit. "I just remember her as quiet, introspective, mysterious, and very attractive," Paul Reed recollects. "Sue [Micki's birth name] always dressed in a way one would associate with someone out of the past, think Stevie Nicks, and had a flair for the unconventional."[22] Vicki Peterson's childhood friend Toni Kasza spent time with the bass player. "My perception of Micki was that she was just the coolest chick on the planet," Kasza smiles. "It was always nice when I had conversations with her because I realized she was as insecure about things as any of us."[23]

From feeling like an outsider as a child to having a rough time in the Runaways, the interceding years had changed Micki, noted Phast Phreddie when he reconnected with his friend in the mid-1980s. "Ten years later, she was still young, even more pretty, even more talented, but she showed signs of having been snake-bitten, so to speak," he says. "My impression was that she had gained quite a bit of life-experience in between—some of it not very positive. She wasn't as bubbly and she no longer seemed to trust people she didn't know."[24]

While a shuffle of housemates happened at Spock Hotel, the Bangles were about to make their debut on *American Bandstand*. Originally hitting television sets in 1952 and hosted by eternal teenager Dick Clark from 1956 through to its final season in 1989, *Bandstand* was the template for countdown chart shows around the world, featuring teenagers dancing to top-forty hits and live lip-synced performances of hot artists. To appear on the show was an indicator of success, of having "made it." Though still without a major label deal, the Bangles performed two songs—"The Real World" and "Want You"—for the March 26, 1983, episode. They also spent several minutes being interviewed by Clark. "It was surreal," Annette says of the group's first of what would be five appearances on the iconic program. "It was such a big deal to me, I didn't even know how to process it. I remember driving to the studio at ABC, which is in Silverlake. Jane Wiedlin was also on the show; she was doing her solo stuff, so we got to meet her. That was the first time I met anybody in the Go-Go's. We met Dick Clark. He was so nice."

The entire experience felt "very unnatural" to Annette. "It was all lip-synced. It was weird having to dance and move because everything was filtered and channeled through speakers so we weren't even really playing our instruments," she recalls. "Once you do that a couple of times, you get used to it." When asked about speaking to Clark, Annette grimaces, recalling, "I remember opening my mouth and I was so nervous that my voice just squeaked when I talked." The gravity of the appearance was not lost on the girls, Annette says. "We definitely knew this was a big deal. We did not take it for granted. It was very amazing. We were on our way."[25]

Bandstand was significant for Debbi as well. "We all grew up watching the show and suddenly we're on it," Debbi explains. "We were all cute and kind of grungy looking, with really short hair." It seemed unreal even as it was happening for the younger Peterson. "Just being with Dick Clark was like your childhood dream—and 'I'm there with him!' It was amazing."[26] What stood out for Debbi especially from this first of several *Bandstand* appearances was the attentiveness of Clark. "Dick Clark sweetly interviewed all of us," she explains. "It wasn't, 'Let's interview the people in the front and ignore the drummer,' which usually happens. He put the microphone up to me and I got to talk." Subsequent appearances on the show did not give Debbi as much, if any, airtime with the host. "The third time we were on, he interviewed the people in the front [of our band] and ignored me," she recalls. "It was just like the classic thing that was happening in the '80s," she says. "Ignore the drummer. I'm like, 'But I'm a singing drummer. I'm a little different.'"[27] The bigger the band got, the more Debbi felt excluded. "I remember doing *Solid Gold* and a lot of other TV shows. There would be one shot of me." Even in Europe, where appearances were often mimed, Debbi's frustration grew as she felt her visibility become nonexistent. "That was also part of the paranoia thing, 'I never get in videos and in every shot of the video I sing on, Sue is singing on it.' It just turned into a whole paranoia of being ignored and forgotten."[28] Ironically, that first *Bandstand* interview ends with Clark saying, "You've been left out, Debbi."[29]

The day after *Bandstand*, the Bangles were booked to play the 209-acre amusement destination Magic Mountain. Located thirty-five miles northwest of downtown Los Angeles in Valencia, the park was almost as well-known for hosting shows as for its indomitable number of roller coasters, with bands like R.E.M. and INXS gracing the park's stage the same year. The Bangles were gigging constantly and building an ever-bigger buzz but had only piqued the interest of one label representative: Columbia A&R man Peter Philbin.

It was because of Bruce Springsteen that the former writer and PR man started signing bands. After catching Springsteen's first show in Los Angeles in 1973, Philbin wrote a glowing review. "He liked the article," Philbin laughs. A connection was sparked, with the two swapping numbers. Soon after, Philbin found himself on the East Coast, coincidently working at Springsteen's label, CBS International. They became friends, just as Springsteen's initial albums were released. "Bruce's first album didn't happen, his second album didn't happen, and they were going to let him go," Philbin recalls. "I said, 'Are you guys out of your mind?'"[30] After Philbin convinced label bigwigs to give Springsteen one more chance, he released the chart-topping *Born to Run* in 1975. "The guy who was head of CBS called me and said, 'You were right. And I was wrong. You ought to be signing bands here,'" Philbin recalls. "I never applied to be an A&R. I don't play any instruments and frankly, hate being in studios. I come to songs through the lyrical door."[31]

By 1983, Philbin was on the hunt for a new signing, averaging thirty shows a week in search of a fresh group. "I don't hope I find a great band because that's the wrong way to evaluate talent," he says. "I'm just going out to do the work. I just put myself in an environment. I'd go to two, three, four clubs at night. Maybe I would meet some friends. Maybe I'd find a new girlfriend. I loved it." Philbin was twenty-five years old. "I couldn't believe someone was paying me to do this," he laughs. He'd first seen the Bangles, then still going by the Bangs, at the Cathay de Grande in 1982. "It's one of those rare times where I'm not saying yes, I'm not saying no, I'm saying maybe. I'm not even talking to them, but I'm just in the crowd," he recalls. "I'm looking at them and something's going on. They're not really 'great' but there's something that looks like a real band. I'm going to have to come see this band a couple more times."[32]

When at shows, Philbin would often not make himself known to the artists on the stage. "I always like to stand in the back of venues. People make too much of record-label people. This is the *Wizard of Oz* syndrome where they think I actually have some power. Basically, when I sign them, I'm going to say, 'Bring me the broom of the Wicked Witch.' You're going to do all the work. I'm going to take all the credit. I basically can't put in what they're leaving out." As for the Bangs, Philbin recognized a lack of polish when he first saw them. It's a shine that only appears after a group has been on the road and spent time together. "When you go out and tour, you get a sense of what each other are like. All of sudden, you give off a feeling that it's us against the world, rather than four individuals going, 'I play an instrument, I sing.' They were in sync personality-wise; they weren't totally in sync playing-wise, however. It felt like that was apropos of what was going on in music with a lot of the punk stuff. It wasn't 'correct' music, but there was a bond with the people on stage."[33]

It was rare for Philbin to see a band live multiple times. "If you're doing A&R, and somebody comes in and plays you a tape, you better say yes or no," he says, "because if you say maybe, they will hound you. They want a real answer. So this was one of those rare bands that I was still on 'maybe.'" Philbin connected with the music and thought other people would too. "I actually believe if I find a band that I love, at least a million other people are going to love it as well."[34]

Looking for a second opinion, Philbin decided to enlist a friend for some feedback before deciding if he wanted to offer the Bangles a deal. The Magic Mountain show of 1983 provided the perfect opportunity for him to catch up with buddy Springsteen while garnering a possible stamp of approval. Now a seasoned veteran of the industry, Springsteen was a star, having had two number-one albums; a year later, he would release the biggest LP of his career, *Born in the U.S.A.* An endorsement from Springsteen could change the fate of any band.

"It was a funny little amphitheater on a concrete stage," Susanna recalls of the gig. "Bruce said all the right things." However, Bruce also warned Philbin that "it could be a problem to have more than one lead singer," Vicki recalls. "Of course, I found [this] ridiculous!" she says. "Uhhh...the Beatles?"[35]

With Philbin still on the fence, the girls still did not have a label, and were putting all efforts toward touring. With just a handful of days off between finishing the national English Beat tour and starting their own show dates, along with sharing bills with everyone from Social Distortion to the Greg Kihn Band, the girls' demanding schedule included an increasing amount of press responsibilities. Amid the earnest interviews, fun was had while on the road. Redd Kross opened for the Bangles on several of their first headlining tour dates, and they have clear memories of the band at the time. "Vicki always used to get pissed off at me because I always joked she reminded me of Mary Richards [protagonist of *The Mary Tyler Moore Show*]," Jeff McDonald says, who was dating the guitar player at the time. "To me, that is a huge, huge compliment. Very cool, very poised." Vicki never partook of drugs and rarely of booze, Jeff says. "When we were together, I was a giant pothead and she hated it," he confides. There were a few exceptions, however. "I did one time talk her into taking a quarter of acid with me to see *Rocky III* at a drive-in," he laughs. Debbi "liked to party," the younger Peterson once admitting to drinking eight beers on her birthday before throwing up in a dog dish.[36] But it is Susanna whom he describes as "at the time the extreme, wild one in the band...people don't realize that she was very much on a level with Go-Go's because 'wild' is [associated with] the Go-Go's."[37] Brother Steve concurs. "The Go-Go's have some dark history like that, but Susanna wasn't a druggie. She was mischievous."[38] The mid to late 1980s were "an excessive time," Jeff recalls. "They [the Bangles] were really smart girls, funny and witty, and didn't really need to go through that paradigm [of drugs]."

Even though she was enjoying being in the Bangles, Annette was beginning to feel increasingly torn. "I still fancied myself as a singer and a songwriter and they already had those bases covered before we played live," Annette recalls. "They already had harmonies down and I'm not a particularly strong harmony singer. I can do it, but it's not like a natural thing like what the girls had. I was fine with that. I accepted it." When she was not on the road with the band, Annette had started collaborating with singer-guitarist Greg Davis. The two had originally met at a gig of seminal punk royalty X and began duetting in the style of Johnny Cash and June Carter. Davis had done a turn in New Orleans, picking up bluegrass and traditional country technique. Upon moving back to Los Angeles, he began infusing these genres with punk and elements of sped-up alternative country, a sound that was right up Annette's alley. "We would take my parents' old folk albums and sing over them," Annette recalls. "It was something that I was wanting to do and he was doing it. However, I was on the road with the Bangles so there was a little bit of a tug." Annette now says she could have done both but she was "super young" at the time and the Bangles schedule did not allow for many extra activities. "They were just getting busier and more popular," she says. "I couldn't split my time. At that juncture, we were either touring or writing more songs or rehearsing. We were a very busy band and we were very responsible, work ethic–wise. I couldn't do both." With "Greg's project" starting to gain momentum, Annette felt a "pull at her heart" to write and sing her own songs.

Eventually, Annette felt she had to make a choice between the "Greg project"—now called Blood on the Saddle—or the Bangles. "I wanted to do both," she confides. "It was very much a hard thing for me to have to figure it out." However, doing the groups simultaneously became more and more problematic. "It was a struggle for me to have to do both because I'm an *all-in* person," Annette reflects. The bass player was still a teenager, noting how "raging hormones...can always get a little dramatic." As Blood on the Saddle began to gain traction, Annette felt more drawn to the project as it aligned with her true musical aspirations.

Greg had also become Annette's first boyfriend, adding another layer of tension to the already fraught situation. "He was very competitive and wanted to make it," Annette explains. "His style of music was not their style of music. His writing had to do with, like, social injustices and such. He felt like the pop stuff was inconsequential. Greg's thing was that you had to suffer." Though Annette didn't feel the same, the contrast between the two groups was striking. "The main songwriter in my new project was this tortured artist type and the Bangles were sailing away on their upward trajectory," she says. "What blew my mind is that it happened very quickly with the Bangles." Annette admits to having "a kind of guilt because I felt like it happened really easily for us...It felt like other bands have worked so hard and we did it within a year of getting attention," she recounts. "It was imposter syndrome," she reflects. "I felt like, 'do I deserve this?'"[39]

The Bangles were troubled about their bass player's decision, as they were on the precipice of signing a label deal with Peter Philbin. However, they realized that it was the best thing for their friend. "Annette wasn't a great harmony singer," Vicki recalled, "plus, she was more into rockabilly. We would learn a token rockabilly song or two so that Annette could sing, but it wasn't a great fit. We started to realize that we were not in sync." Said Susanna: "She wanted to sing some leads, on more country-ish sounds. Bass wasn't her passion."[40]

Those close to the Bangles also thought the departure was for the best. "I remember Annette showing more interest in her band with her boyfriend at the time [than the Bangles]," recounts Steve McDonald. "It was difficult for them because she was the lead singer in her own band. I think Annette had been sort of intimidated by trying to jump in there with Vicki, Debbi, and Susanna on the vocals. They [Vicki, Debbi, and Susanna] would have been friendly and encouraging but at the same time, they would have intimidated anybody, because they just were so gifted."[41]

Annette was still learning the instrument, which she had picked up specifically to join the band. Debbi (who always secretly wanted to play bass) gave Annette pointers along the way, including helping her learn the part for "Getting Out of Hand," which she had penned before Annette's arrival. Debbi had known that Annette might leave at some point, as her interests drifted further from those of her bandmates as time went on. "She was already going in that direction. I was a little concerned about who we were going to get next, but it was very amicable because she was already going away from our style of music towards the rockabilly thing," Debbi says. "She was a good worker, a hard worker. Just stylistically the music was changing for her. It was fine, we talked it out and there was no animosity, no bad feelings." Annette's last show with the Bangles took place on May 20 in Reseda, California. "The band was on its way of becoming famous rather quickly at the time I joined," Annette tells me. "I had no idea that band would become so successful as fast as it did." Leaving was a very difficult decision for Annette, and proved a turning point for her own identity. "I came in with an abundance of enthusiasm and strong desire for playing music," she reflects. It was especially hard as Annette had gotten to know the girls as friends, in particular Susanna. "She was delightful," Annette emphasizes.

The Bangles were once again on the hunt for a fourth member. As Annette started making plans for her departure, the band was beginning to draw closer to getting signed to a major label deal, a scenario that did not surprise Vicki's former housemate Steve Wynn in the slightest. "I always tell people who weren't around back then that The Bangles were probably the most rocking and most assured of all the bands," he says. "They had it down."[42] Susanna echoes this sentiment, recalling, "We had this kind of naïve, youthful confidence. It was funny, we never sort of went 'Oh, it's not happening, guess I'll go back to law school.' We just had this odd feeling that it was going to work out."[43] Peter Philbin had been "sniffing around" the band for months by the time he got formally in touch with Miles Copeland in June. "I had been used to banging on the doors of labels to try to get deals myself, so Peter approaching me was a first," Copeland recalled. "I was not aware at the time that he had already seen the band several times, but he convinced me he was keen to have them on Columbia."[44] While both Copeland and Mike

Gormley were "very ready to make a deal that would put the Bangles in the game—and with a really strong company" like Columbia, they worried that the corporate structure of the label might not be a fit for the band. "At the top, it was run by what we might politely call 'suits' who worked more by the numbers than by the gut," Copeland explains. Though Philbin offered an exception, with Copeland remarking that the A&R executive was "an artist guy," "he [still] worked for the suits. Surviving in that world was not easy."[45]

Philbin explains the hierarchy and misconception many artists have about major labels. "When a new band signed with Peter Philbin, an A&R guy at Columbia, they thought that they were signing with the label of Columbia, or CBS," he explains. "But their record may come out in the same week with artists on the label who have sold hundreds of thousands if not millions of albums. A brand new band is rarely [at a major label] a priority. We would have printouts of sales, and they were tens and tens of pages. I always felt a band wasn't recognized as a 'Columbia' artist until they've gone over six figures. That first hundred thousand—which are the hardest albums to sell—that's when they think they're signed to Columbia and I realize they're signed to Peter Philbin at Columbia. Labels are not your partner." He goes on to explain that as a new artist if you are "not selling records" and are competing for the label's attention with a surefire sales winner like Billy Joel, it is up to the band to create enough momentum to warrant efforts being thrown their way that would otherwise go to support a known success. "You need to go out and create a fire and walk out of that theatre and yell, 'Fire!' and the label will take notice," Philbin says. "I learned something very important from my job signing bands, is that you can find someone with the songs and the talent but you don't find out the most important element of this whole thing until you have all your money in the pot. That the most important element is drive."[46] Philbin continues, "The reason I bring that up is because of the Bangles. Susanna and Vicki have equal weight [as leaders]. They both brought different things to the band," he reflects. "Susanna Hoffs in particular does not see walls. I've never met anyone who has more drive than Susanna. It's really both frustrating and a beautiful thing to watch."[47]

Having already seen the band multiple times, Philbin now had to convince the "suits" at the label that the Bangles were worthy of bearing the Columbia name. Upon bringing the EP into a label meeting for feedback, Philbin was met with negative comments. "One of my friends on the A&R staff, as soon as I present the record, he says, 'These girls can't play.' That started the whole thing of doubting their ability. As soon as he said it, I didn't know what to say. I turned around and said, 'That bothers you, right? Because this is rock and roll, what are you worried about? Keith Richards is probably out of tune on the first two or three albums.' Everyone laughed, and we moved on."[48]

Still undeterred, Philbin brought his quandary to the head of the West Coast A&R staff, Ron Oberman. "He said, 'Peter, are you serious about this band?' And I go, 'Yes. Frankly, we better act on this right now because in another three months, there's gonna be a crowd around them.'" The duo then flew up to a show the band had in San Francisco.* The Los Angeles executives had also invited the newest Columbia hire to the gig, a producer by the name of David Kahne. Originally trained as a high school English teacher, Kahne had been making a name for himself as a producer at 415 Records, a San Francisco–based label, where he had worked his way up from answering the phones. After the show, Oberman and Philbin agreed to sign the band. However, some details were inherent in the proposal, and completely out of the Bangles' control, Philbin explains. "David had some enthusiasm after seeing the show and he's going to produce the record. That makes my life easy because I'm signing a band and I already have a producer."[49]

Day-to-day manager Mike Gormley had no idea that Columbia was even interested in the girls until the deal dropped on his desk. "I didn't even know they were looking at the band," he tells me. "They never contacted us. Then one day one of them did: Ron Oberman." Gormley

---

* It is unclear what venue and date this was, but it may have been August 12 at the Keystone in Palo Alto, a city located about an hour south of San Francisco.

knew Oberman, having worked together previously at Mercury Records. Gormley eventually put the final touches on the agreement, bagging the band a $125,000 budget for making their first full-length album. "I got them a nice advance," Gormley says. Gormley also led the charge on securing the details of the agreement, with Copeland literally along for the ride, asking Gormley on the way over to the label offices to sign the paperwork, "'So what is the agreement?' He didn't even know what the deal was," Gormley recalls. "I explained what the advance was and what the percentage was on the way over to sign this thing. I hope he remembers it that way, but that's the way it happened."[50]

Copeland was pleased with Kahne being part of the package for signing to the label. "He knew the group, having remixed 'Real World' for a Faulty mini-CD EP," Copeland says.[51] "It was pure coincidence that he had then taken a job at Columbia." Even though they had used him before, it was the label, not the band, who had final deciding power over who would oversee their debut full-length effort. "Ron Oberman brought David Kahne into the picture," Gormley recounts. "David was incredible, I thought, but in the studio itself, it was rough on the Bangles. He was a taskmaster."[52] Whatever reservations management or the girls had would be imprudent to bring up at the time, Copeland believed. "We felt that it would not be cool to challenge the record company so soon, unless we had a good reason for it—and we didn't," he recalls. "David Kahne had definite ideas about producing, and the band found out too late that he had no problem bringing in a session musician to play a part if he felt one of the Bangles was slow or, in his view, not up to the part. Columbia was paying for this, and the Bangles were not yet famous, so it was a matter of suck it up and try to make it work."[53]

With the impending record deal now in the balance, the Bangles needed to fill the hole left by Annette. Interestingly, having Debbi move from drums onto the bass was never discussed, though the younger Peterson had originally envisioned herself as a guitar player. "Everybody saw me as the drummer," she says. "That's what my position was;

I don't think it [swapping instruments] was ever brought up. I didn't feel good enough to come in and play bass." A solution, however, was literally in Vicki's house, under the same roof at the Spock Hotel. It is unclear exactly how the idea of Micki Steele joining the band originated. "I am the one that told the Bangles to get her in the band," says Sid Griffin. Keyboardist Mark Buchholtz worked with Micki during her turn in Nadia Kapiche and recalls "Micki telling me one time that she had heard…the Bangles were looking for a roommate to share a house. She had also heard they were looking for a new bass player. She told me, 'I did the first calculated thing ever in my life'…and met with them to be a roommate…and to try to get an audition.'"[54]

According to Debbi, Vicki had already been thinking Micki may be a good addition to the band. "Vicki thought we should get Micki to try out. I remember her saying, 'She might be a better fit [for the group than Annette].'"[55] The personalities clicked during the trial, with Vicki describing the bass player as "perfect."[56] Micki told an interviewer later that she had to audition twice for the band, saying the girls had "tortured" her, as she did not know if she was in or not for a while.[57]

Though she wanted in on the band, Micki was still a bit shell-shocked to once again find herself in an entirely female lineup. "It's kind of funny," she says. "After the whole Runaways experience, I was like, 'I will never do a girl band again. Ever.' So never say never."[58] The Bangles, she explained, were fundamentally different than her former group. "The Runaways was like a fake girl band; this was a real band that happened to be women."[59] Along with a new group came the major record deal. "That was so amazing to me," Micki recalls. "Columbia was [Bob] Dylan. The Byrds were on that label."[60] The original trio now brought Micki to meet Gormley and Philbin. "I liked Annette," Gormley says. "I don't know what happened there or whether she didn't want to continue with them." Upon being introduced to the replacement, the once PR guru thought a name change was once again in order. "I said, I'm going to start calling her Michael. She was beautiful, but she wasn't cute. She was a serious musician and 'Micki' just seemed a little too precious so I just said Michael. We put it in the bio, 'Michael'; she said fine. I thought it was good and she went along with it."[61]

Philbin was surprised that Annette would choose to quit the group right as they were on the precipice of getting a deal. "When I signed them, Annette was leaving. I thought 'What the fuck?'" However, when he heard that Michael was joining, his reaction changed. "I thought, 'Fucking great. She's great and a solid player.'" As Philbin got to know Micki more, her background and personality began to emerge. "I believe she does come from money and I don't hold that against her. It's none of my business. I found her delightful."[62]

Now with a four-piece firmly in place, it was time to embark on recording their first full-length album. "It was scary," Debbi recalls, "just thinking we can be a part of such a big machine."[63] Since the Bangs, it had always been "four people working on this project together," she clarifies. Susanna had similar anxieties. "We'd always been a self-contained unit," she says. "All of a sudden, there were these 'guys in suits' listening to us and looking at us. This is serious now."[64]

14.

> I really loved *All Over the Place*. I really had a thing for the bass player. I thought she was fucking hot and I had a thing for the sisters.
>
> —COURTNEY LOVE[1]

Recording of *All Over the Place* commenced in October, the entire process taking three months, though the band was only in the studio for about four weeks. "David Kahne was working with Romeo Void doing their album," Michael explained in an interview. "It was frustrating because we were put on hold a lot," Vicki adds. "But that was our choice, we knew that going into it. We knew David had made a commitment to Romeo Void." The girls actually did *not* have a choice but to wait; Kahne was the only option Columbia had given them to work with, stipulating his involvement as part of the deal. The label, according to Michael, was still unsure how to market or place the Bangles in the wider context of current commercial music. "We're a strange band because we don't really fit in any kind…" She pauses. "We're not heavy metal obviously. We're not soul, we're very white. And in the beginning the people at CBS [Columbia Records] were saying, 'I don't know where you guys are gonna fit in. You're not AOR [album-oriented rock], you're not top forty. Where are you going to fit?'"[2]

14.

The band felt prepared to lay down the tracks, having a repertoire that had already been part of their live sets for a long time. "*All Over the Place* was years in the making, because we played those songs a lot in the clubs," said Debbi. "I felt proud of our performance; we sounded like this great, raw rock band."[3] All but two of the eleven tracks on the album were penned by the band, either solely by Vicki (five) or with Susanna (four). "Many of the songs on *All Over the Place* were written by me," Vicki tells me. "They were from the Fans or Muze eras."[4] Having had ample time to hone the sound and aesthetic of each one, the band felt confident upon going into the studio.

Yet even the best aspirations could not save the band from the critique of Kahne. Almost immediately upon starting to work together, the producer found problems with the girls. No consideration was taken for the lack of experience in a formal corporate setting nor the impressive proficiency of the self-taught musicians. Instead of using his position and expertise to support and bolster the confidence of the new signing, Kahne chose to inflict deriding accusations at the group, taking aim particularly at heart-on-the-sleeve Debbi. By building on the assertion levied against the women in the initial label meeting, Kahne paved the way for any output by the band to be shaped to his vision, not necessarily representative of the group. "The first week that David is working with the band, he comes into my office and shuts the door," Philbin says. "He goes, 'I can't do this album—the drummer can only play a shuffle.[*] When I pointed that out, she begins to cry.' I'm thinking my life is going down in flames. Someone had already said that the girls couldn't play. Now I have our newest A&R producer, the latest and greatest fashion on the staff, saying he is going to quit. I thought this guy was going to help me. I do not have a replacement." Instead of having concern for the group and what challenges they may be facing, Philbin's worries were around watching his own backside. "I've got a headache here," he recalls. "I say, 'Look, David, if you walk off of this project, one of us is going to look

---

[*] Vicki tells me that a shuffle is actually quite hard to play, so if Debbi was using this technique, it would show prowess, not a lack of skill as implied here.

really bad. So you better figure it out because it's not going to be me.' I got out of there and he continued with the album."[5] Philbin obviously knew the clash of characters in the creative configuration. "David is not the most empathetic person you're ever going to want to meet," Philbin chuckles. "I can laugh at this because I'm not a Bangle. I think that the Bangles were very good for David Kahne and I think David was very good for the Bangles."[6]

Though upset by the feedback, Debbi got a drum machine, and dutifully utilized it to perfect her skills. "David wanted Debbi to be a better drummer because he thought that her timing wasn't that great," soundman Joe Stella recounts. "She would play to a click track. It made her one of the best drummers. She would start the song up again and be milliseconds off or dead on time. I told her how amazing her timing was after rehearsal once and she said, 'Really?'"[7]

Next Kahne drafted in mixing engineer Joe Chiccarelli to work on the album. Chiccarelli was already a fan of the band, having seen them live many times and running in the same social circles. He had done projects in the past with other Mike Gormley acts, including Oingo Boingo and Wall of Voodoo. It was an exciting time to be in Los Angeles and involved in music, Chiccarelli recalls. "The music scene in LA was really vibrant," he says. "There was so much going on in terms of new artists, new wave and punk rock. There were loads of clubs filled with great bands." Chiccarelli describes an inclusive community uniting a generation of young people. "Even if there were differences in your upbringing, there was a commonality there. People were excited to be a part of the scene."[8]

Chiccarelli viewed the Bangles as being perched at the precipice of stardom but acknowledges how going into the studio with a seasoned veteran like Kahne may have been scary for the scrappy DIY outfit. "He [Kahne] is going to change something that has been successful up to that point: the LA clubs love you, you got a record deal at a big management company—any artist is going to be protective over that," Chiccarelli explains. "If someone tells you that you have to bring in a producer, you may get worried he may change what is already working so well. There was always this fear."[9] The way to create a successful match between producer and talent he says is "to bond with the band" and "make them feel at ease." Chiccarelli notes, "Although it may be difficult at the moment," he says that "down the line you are going to make a better record out of it. You would have done something you could not do on your own."[10]

Chiccarelli explains the process for approaching *All Over the Place*. "Now you can take a course or look online to gain insight into the steps necessary in production and engineering," he says. But back then, he notes, "I'm sure they [the Bangles] would have spent time with him [David] in a rehearsal situation. Typically when I do records, I spend anywhere between one to two weeks going through songs, working out arrangements, tempos, keys, and overall directions for the song." This is a crucial part of the process, he explains, as "you get to know the people and what they are trying to achieve. You meet a common ground. I would have hoped that happened when they made the record together and a sense of bonding [had happened] before they hit the studio [referring to the Bangles and David]."[11]

Yet this was not the case between Kahne and the group, according to Philbin. "The Bangles fought him every step of the way," he says. "The band made sure they were the personality on that record," he tells me with a laugh.[12]

Having just relocated to Los Angeles from San Francisco, Kahne needed somewhere to temporarily crash while he recorded. "David stayed on the couch at Spock Hotel and we became friends," Joanna "Spock" Dean says. Eventually, he suggested to Columbia that they needed to hire his well-connected roommate to do A&R. Spock had the "ears" for a hit song and brought Kahne the track "Going Down to Liverpool." The song had been penned by English singer-songwriter-guitarist Kimberley Rew. Spock had originally come across the cut when she tried to sign

Rew's band, Katrina and the Waves, to Columbia. However, it was not to be, as the "men in suits" always shot the young female executive down. "With everything I brought them, they went, 'We don't think so.' It was like, 'Yeah, we hired that girl in LA.' I tried to sign the Cult; I tried to sign Bruce Hornsby, and the Replacements. The last person I tried to sign was Lucinda Williams. When I couldn't sign Lou, I left. I was the lowest on the totem pole in the whole department. I was the newest member, but I was the only girl. All the other women were secretaries. Other departments had women: the head of press was a woman and her whole staff were women. But product management were all men. I don't know if they ever hired another woman to do A&R. When I was at the label, there were not many women in A&R, and those that were no one paid attention to."[13] Kahne, however, respected Spock's taste, and brought the track to the Bangles. The girls loved it, and it became part of the album listing.

Vicki admits that although they had been touring and writing a lot as an independent group, when the Bangles first walked into the studio to record *All Over the Place*, "we were pretty green," she says. "Aside from a self-produced 45 and the EP we'd recorded recently, we'd had maybe a few hours' experience in a studio making demos and didn't know a lot about the tricks and disciplines of recording," she confides. "We arrived with our much more relaxed, punk rock, DIY attitudes in contrast with David Kahne, who had the weight of a major label—and its budget—on his head. He had his work cut out for him. I learned a great deal from him, some of which took years to *un*learn."[14]

The atmosphere made a turn for the worse when Debbi went to lay down her lead vocals for "Going Down to Liverpool" ["GDTL"]. "I remember thinking, 'What an incredibly cool song.' I was very much excited about doing it," she says.[15] However, that feeling quickly changed once she started spending significant time with the producer. "Working with David Kahne was rather difficult," she reflects, describing the experience as "torture."[16] "He had pressure from the record company to deliver something successful. He put a lot of pressure on us. I remember singing 'GDTL,' and singing it many, many, many times. I kept thinking,

'This has got to be the take.' He would triple track me, quadruple track me. I had to do it over and over again. It left me in tears. He would just be sitting back in the control room, pressing the button saying, 'Do it again. Do it again.' He didn't give us any kind of feedback. I felt proud of our performance; we sounded like this great, raw rock band. But sonically, at the time, I didn't think the album sounded good enough. It was just so different from what we'd experienced recording before," Debbi continues. The contrast between doing things for themselves and the Kahne way was shocking. "We were taken aback," Debbi recounts. "Oh, my God, what's going on here? Is this what it is like being on a major label? All of this stress?"[17]

Debbi was not the only one who was finding Kahne a challenge. "I'd already been singing [lead on some of the songs] for a while when I brought them into the Bangles," Vicki says. "Kahne made it pretty clear that he preferred Susanna's voice on them, and ultimately I agreed—she sounded great."[18] Capturing the unique harmonic trademark of the band was imperative, according to Chiccarelli. "The balance between all the vocals was really crucial," he says. "David was really keen on getting all layers of harmonies. He was really good at balancing those." Unlike his questionable bedside manner with the band, Chiccarelli found the producer decorous and great to work with. "He knew what he wanted and he gave me a lot of space," Chiccarelli remembers. "It may have been the first record he got an outside engineer to mix on," he says. "David was very gracious and very patient and kind with me, in terms of inviting me in on that project."[19] Mike Gormley also respected the job Kahne delivered on the record but knew that things were less than ideal for the Bangles. "David was incredible," he tells me. "I never saw him be a jerk, but he was a taskmaster. Sue especially was really upset with him."[20] Gormley recalls one specific incident when Susanna "came to my office one day, and was in tears," he says. "We had to hold her and make her feel better." The cause of the upset "was about David," he notes. "I don't know specifically what happened, but it was rough on them. I didn't ask; I just believed them."[21] Susanna has no memory of this episode, noting that in her relationship with Kahne, she was "teacher's pet," trying to make things work as best she could.

However, Kahne's communication style with the band did not facilitate a happy environment. "He made us more aware of what our flaws were than the things that we were good at," Susanna says. "It has a kind of debilitating effect after a period of time. On the one hand, you want to feel inspired, you want to feel confident, but you're around someone who's very vocal about what the shortcomings of the band are. You don't want somebody who's just going to say everything you do is great, but there's a different style of working."[22] Vicki faced similar problems. "There wasn't a joy of creation going on there," Vicki says. "Everything was complicated. As a matter of fact, it was a phrase he was famous for. He would sit with his head in his hands on the board and go 'Damn, this is complicated.' What does that say to the artist? That says OK, this is a mess. You're basically incompetent. I'm at a loss. I'm going to have to fix it."[23] Kahne had a vision for how he wanted the record to sound, with the producer viewing "*All Over the Place* as his record, and the Bangles themselves as obstacles."[24] The garage vibe of jangly guitar and rough edges of the group were quickly being buffed down by Kahne. "We were very basic as a band, and he was hearing symphonies in his head," said Vicki. "He would have all these sort of sonic images he wanted to realize, and were we just, 'Huh? Uh...OK.'"[25] Kahne, says Gormley "wanted to do things his way because he didn't think their way was going to be very good,"[26] even though it was "the way" that had already garnered the girls a large fan base, management, and a record deal.

Though the band found their personal agency mostly ripped away, and the outcome of their record at the mercy of Kahne, some things were still nonnegotiable. "I went toe to toe with [Kahne] over the string arrangement on 'More Than Meets the Eye,'" Vicki says. "I was adamant that there would be *no synthesizers* on this Bangles record (inspired by Queen's declaration on their first album), and although it would stretch the budget, Kahne finally agreed to a string sextet, arranged by himself and the iconic Jimmie Haskell. Sitting in on that string session was one of those I-can't-believe-I'm-here moments for me."[27]

Another issue that arose was the use of studio musicians to play some of the parts on the recordings. Chiccarelli notes that getting other people to come in and play bit parts in the studio was not unusual. "It was a common thing to do," Chiccarelli says. "Not to defend or take any sides, but a producer does what he has to do to get a great record. The measures to make a great record back then were more extreme. It just took more time and money." Aware of the issues between band and Kahne, Philbin did not want to tinker with the process, instead choosing to let the creatives get on with what he thought they did best. "I know that there was some tension because he was bringing in some session guys," recounts Philbin. "Lots of A&R guys want to go into the studio, which means you waste a lot of time selling the A&R guy [on the producer's vision and what he/she is doing]. I always said, 'Make me a cassette, I'll listen in my car.' My job is to find the band, sign the band, go over songs, get a producer, let them do their thing. If you want Picasso to paint you a blue painting, don't stand over them and say, 'That's the wrong blue.'"[28]

Chiccarelli also thought emotions may have run high when Kahne added his own stylings to the album. "I gathered that the girls were upset that David had played some of the guitar parts himself," he recalls. "But back then, before Pro Tools and digital audio, if something was not right, you had to replace it with a human being. You had to go to harsher measures to get things right. I believe David was doing what he felt he had to do to get them the best record for them—and he did."[29]

Despite what the girls remember, Chiccarelli tells me he doesn't "recall there being any drama or uncomfortable moments or anything in the studio at the time. I really don't," he says. "I never witnessed any arguments or bad conversations or tension in the studio."[30] Philbin has a philosophical take. "The Bangles had enough sense of self to fight David Kahne," he says, "and by fighting David Kahne, they got their personality on the record."[31]

Within the band's then inner circle, there are mixed feelings about *All Over the Place*. "Although the Bangles were hurt by the introduction of session musicians, the resulting album, *All Over the Place*, released by CBS in May 1984, was mostly performed by them, and almost all of the songs were written by them—and it was a good album," proclaims Copeland. Chiccarelli is similarly positive. "The album was successful musically and commercially. I was happy to be a part of it," he says. "David was a great record maker and his tracks speak for himself." He then puts *All Over the Place* into context, contrasting modern methods with those of the early 1980s. "If you put it into a historical perspective, anyone trying to get a job done then would be met with a much harsher set of procedures than present times. If there is something missing now, it's somebody sitting there quietly fixing the mistakes or errors and no one says anything about it. Back then, I'm sure it was probably a lot more tension provoking."[32]

For the Petersons, it is a bit more complicated. Brother Dave Peterson, so integral in the early demo sessions of the group, likes *All Over the Place*. "It's got excitement and liveliness," he says. "I don't hear that on their other records." Debbi praises the album, noting, "It has short songs and kind of a *Revolver*-esque sound, which is great. There's some real genius guitar stuff going on. David helped with some of those ideas, too, which made it sound cool." However, she adds, "I wish the drums had sounded better."[33]

Vicki has the most conflicting feelings about the first Bangles offering on Columbia. A 2013 article discussing the album illustrates some of the frustrations:

> I felt the first Bangles LP was too slick for my taste....I fought tooth and nail against having any keyboards on the record, and no synthesisers. If there were going to be strings, they had to be real strings. I was adamant about that. I lost that battle as we went on—my bandmates didn't care and they wanted to change musically. But there was also energy towards: "What's the single?" Which I was never comfortable with. It came from producer and label and my bandmates.[34]

A decade later, in 2023, Vicki's opinions have not changed, though they have slightly mellowed. However, the fraught nature of the production process itself, and the realities of being a commodified major label product, still are apparent forty years on:

> It's interesting to note that although at the time it felt we were being over-produced in the studio, upon listening now I find the guitars are barely in tune and we are still very much ourselves....*All Over the Place* is now my favorite Bangles record of the Columbia/Sony years.[35]

She also says that *All Over the Place* "is the only one [album] that I can listen to and feel like 'Okay, yeah, that was the band that I was in.'"[36] The process of making it, she reflects, "was definitely not what I expected. There was actually quite a bit of pressure," admitting that "I probably suppressed the feelings and didn't really acknowledge that there was a lot of pressure being put on us. Micki or somebody made a comment when David Kahne...made a point of letting us know what the budget was, and how much pressure was on him—therefore on us—to make good for the label. It felt like, 'Why are we talking about that right now?' We should be talking about ten songs that we feel like we could rule the world with and to make the best record we possibly can. Let's make this fun; let's make this great." Instead, Vicki says, "it felt like there was a slant to it that was entirely financial and corporate. It was very foreign to me."[37]

Regardless of how they truly felt, to the press and public the band spoke positively of their time spent under the tutelage of Kahne. "He was like the fifth Bangle...he laughed with us, cried with us," Michael told the *LA Weekly*, with Vicki adding, "It was a very involved experience. The whole thing was really emotional for all of us," and Susanna chiming in that it was "like having a baby."[38]

15.

When *All Over the Place* dropped in May, two songs were flagged as potential singles. The first was the Susanna and Vicki–penned "Hero Takes a Fall" ("HTAF"), reputedly inspired by fellow Paisley Underground friend Steve Wynn of the Dream Syndicate. The lyrics, a "breezy kiss-off to an egotistical dude about to get his comeuppance," at first were a shock to Wynn, who found out about the track while on tour with R.E.M. "I was hurt, of course, because they were my friends," says Wynn. "The song is not the nicest thing in the world." Upon further reflection, the musician acknowledges, "They got a point. I was a little bit cocky. Like anybody at that age who gets lots of success, I had a little bit of an attitude. Once I got past the slight hurt, the slight shock, the slight flattery—'They bothered to write a song about me'—I was like, 'Well, it's a damn good song.'"[1]

The band never confirmed nor denied that the song was based on Vicki's former Spock Hotel roommate, instead noting that she and Susanna were focused on "classic dramatic structures" when putting the piece together. Inspiration struck during a session with the duo pulling a "random book out of a shelf" during a writing session. "It was the intro to *Oedipus Rex*—the hero has a fatal flaw, and his crimes are brought to the light of day and has a tragic fall," Vicki explained.[2] "A personality flaw, a physical flaw, an Achilles' heel. We were playing around with the idea and came up with a composite character of some people we knew. Then the rumors started going that it was about Steve Wynn. Which I never actively denied. And I'm still giving you a non-denial denial [laughs]."[3] Susanna adds, "We were playing on our thighs with our palms and coming up with the rhythm of the lyrics. It was almost like a rap in a way."[4] "'Hero,'" she notes, "was kind of a milestone in terms of our [Vicki and Susanna] collaboration, where we just sat down with an idea in mind to do something that had a good beat and would really be fun to play live. It got a lot of airplay on the college radio circuit."[5] Debbi tells me about when she first heard the track. "I remember when Vicki and Sue wrote the song and said it was about Steve," she smiles. "I said 'No, it can't be.' It's an attitude thing; I guess he was kind of channeling that at the time."[6]

Henry Rollins praises the LP and the Hoffs-Peterson effort. "By 1984, the Bangles were starting to make solid full-length albums," he says. "*All Over the Place* had a really good single called, 'Hero Takes a Fall.' I think KROQ got behind it. I think being all-female certainly made the band stand out, but at the end of the day, I think it was their music that got them the notice. Being an all-woman band will get you so far; but if you don't have the goods musically, then you're probably out of there even faster than if you were a group comprised of men."[7]

Now it was time for the band to shoot the video for the song, "Hero Takes a Fall." For the first time, the group was going to be creating an asset for international use where their aesthetic would potentially be one of the most important aspects for success. "I think having a '60s leaning by sound or by appearance perhaps gave the band some traction," Henry Rollins says, "but ultimately, the boys club will use this against them by treating them as cute."[8] Mike Gormley recalls the styling for "HTAF" as well-done. "The subject came up about what to look like and what to wear," he recounts. "I didn't suggest what the Bangles wore because they had taste and style. They put together a look that in one way or another stuck with them for several years."[9]

Debbi remembers it differently, describing a far less organic process of image building. "I felt like in 'HTAF,' we had someone dress us," she says. "We had CBS/Sony coming in and having their costume designers do it. There's the shot of me playing the drums. I'm wearing this hat and I'm like, 'Why am I wearing that? It was not something I would normally do.' We had [been put into] the Madonna gloves and stuff. We were not feeling ourselves; we were feeling like somebody's trying to put us together."[10]

Day-to-day manager Chris Lamson remembers "creepy stylists" often trying to push their own ideas of how the band should look. Getting the green light on images featuring all band members together could also be a challenge. "You look at those photo sessions, and there are all different pictures because they could never agree on a group picture," Lamson says. "There was all that little jealousy going on." He confides that the cover art for *All Over the Place* is highly edited. "The heads are photoshopped on bodies just to get picture approval," he admits. "We tried to avoid conflict wherever possible."[11*]

With styling sorted to the label's satisfaction, San Francisco–based director David Rathod was picked to film the video. Rathod was hot off a nomination at the second "MTV Video Music Awards" for Best Director, praised for his work on Huey Lewis and the News' "I Want a New Drug" short. Videos were important at that moment, Rathod argues, as it created a new way for experiencing music for a large audience. "Because it was so early in the music video scene, it was all brand new," Rathod says. "Nobody really knew, not the bands or the record companies, a specific method for doing anything. There was no system in place because it was not just how to find filmmakers, but also conceive ideas for videos. It was the Wild West of music videos, the concepts were all so varied."[12]

Rathod convinced the group to come up north from Los Angeles to shoot the video. "The reason I was attracted to San Francisco," Rathod explains, "was that it was a very creative hub for music, fashion, and movies. LA was Hollywood. Big, bloated films. In the Bay Area, everything felt different."[13] The Bangles provided a "visually interesting group, four attractive women that looked independent and strong," Rathod recalls. "They knew what they were doing, they were accomplished musicians and singers…the Bangles had a [gritty] feel. There

---

* On the cover art, Susanna's head is photoshopped, Vicki confides. "My own head is out of focus and I was okay with that."

was something about them that the world wasn't ready for. They were ahead of their time."[14]

The final concept for the video took advantage of the city's local characters, swapping between the band busking on the street for passersby with being in shop windows donning various costumes and taking down mannequin male "heroes." "We were in San Francisco near Union Square shooting that video out in the corner while people are walking back and forth from their offices," says Gormley. "They were very tired. They'd been working hard. It's not as much fun as people think, getting a hit record and carrying on. It's a lot of work and it's a lot of fear of, 'Will we get another one?' That was a pretty tense time." Celebrities were starting to take notice of the band as well, Gormley adding that "Robert Downey Jr. came to the shoot."[15]

While Susanna had lead duties for "HTAF," Debbi was the front woman for the second track, "Going Down to Liverpool." They needed a video with a hook and turned to Susanna's mother for inspiration. Tamar happily took the reins of directing the second output, with Susanna drafting in Hoffs family friend Leonard Nimoy to add some stardust. The premise of this film is the band being driven around to a mystery destination by the *Star Trek* icon, with most of the action taking place in the car. "It was great to work with him because he was such a professional. He very much got into the part and did the eyebrow thing," Debbi laughs, referring to Nimoy's trademark look from the sci-fi series. "It was so much fun." However, excitement was tempered by an on-set appearance by Copeland, Debbi recalls. "While we were making that video, Miles Copeland, our illustrious manager, comes in and says, 'No, girls, you have to be serious. This is about being on the dole and Liverpool. This is about being unemployed.' We were pop stars being driven around by Leonard Nimoy and now we have to look like we're depressed pop stars who are unemployed? Yes, it was very confusing," she notes of the video's premise.[16]

For a band made up of a bunch of self-identified nerds, Bangles fans were a mix of men drooling over the foursome and young girls seeing a possible future version of themselves on the stage. In a *News-Pilot* piece, Vicki tells the reporter, "Most of our club audience is 80 percent male. They're there because they're familiar with our music. It gets pretty wild. We've had some pretty exciting club dates on this tour with people jumping up on the stage."[17] The man-heavy fan base of the Bangles is noted by several concert reviews, described by the *Daily* as "panting male delirium," throwing a fleeting suggestion to the notion that the women may be inducing the same sort of fan mania as their idols the Beatles.[18] Another interviewer asks Susanna if the band "would like to be a pin-up group for boys?" She steers the journalist back to the art, replying, "It's flattering to think that people like our looks but the music always comes first, that's the truth! Actually, it's really fun for us because we were all a bit shy in school so it's quite a turnaround now to have so many male admirers."[19] In the UK press, Michael noted that men in particular were confused when confronted with women unabashedly rocking out on stage. "It's strange y'know," she told *Melody Maker*, "you'll be standing around after the show and you'll see these guys standing 10 feet away, like they're afraid to come up to us or something. We're not really scary people but there's something about what we do that they find intimidating."[20] The band was often made to feel like a strange anomaly, Michael describes. "From talking to people here [in the UK], it seems that it's not that usual this side of the pond to have women who can play, and it's competent and it's fun. It seems like it's more of a novelty. There is a sort of performing-flea aspect to it—'let's go and see these weird girls jump up and down.'"[21]

    Mike Gormley clearly remembers the almost rabid obsession of some crowd members. While the Bangles did their encore, "a wall of boys [was] literally climbing over each other to get to the stage; they were young teenage boys who wanted to get as close to them as possible." Though clearly the combination of musical prowess and good looks could have been a key marketing tool from a management standpoint, Gormley claims, "It's there—you couldn't ignore it—but we didn't push it and we didn't use that in our advertising or anything like that."[22]

When asked by talk show host Joan Rivers in a later interview if the Bangles get male groupies, Michael answers, "Well, we don't really go in for that sort of thing…but, uh, they're around if we want 'em." Vicki added, "They sort of show their affection by tossing their undergarments on stage. You know it's the traditional rock 'n' roll thing. This last tour we did in America, um, it was sort of the jockey-briefs tour."[23]

Chris Lamson also recalls a diverse crowd coming to shows and following the band. "They had an assortment of really bizarre creepy stalker fans and big fans," he says. "But you would go to the shows and there's a lot of mom and daughters and families. I would say their fandom was like seventy [percent] women, thirty [percent] men." There were occasions when the band's privacy was hideously transgressed, he tells me. "You had the guys that were really hot on Susanna that would just show up in hotel rooms. She opened her hotel room door and there'll be a guy standing in there. That happened a couple of times."[24]

Male fans were a rare topic touched on in interviews, however. An often-visited theme by magazines was the questioning of the band's intelligence. *LA Weekly* falls back on such a tired cliché with breathtaking condescension. "This is more the Pillow-Fight Method—leap-frogging enthusiasm escalating towards pop epiphany," the journalist pens. "I mean, they *can* answer the usual questions. They're not stupid. They could probably even get real philosophical if they wanted to."[25]

Remarkably, even in the face of such deplorable treatment, the group remained steadfastly upbeat and professional. "There's a different chemistry," Susanna tells a Fort Lauderdale paper when asked about being in an entirely female band. "It's a statement of control. We're writing, singing and playing on everything. We're in charge of all we do. We're running the show. Even Chrissie Hynde fronts a band and depends on the other (male) members. Gimmicks don't last long. Just making it is tough."[26]

Another favorite media motif was the press manufactured rivalry between the Go-Go's and the Bangles. Indeed, Michael tells a newspaper in Austin, Texas, that the only time the group talks about their fellow Copeland roster residents is when "journalists ask about Go-Go's comparisons."[27] Not accepting the possibility of two female bands thriving simultaneously, reviews of *All Over the Place* often created an equation between the Go-Go's and the Bangles instead of allowing each band to be viewed and experienced individually. In his piece for *Creem*, Craig Zeller begins by praising the single "Going Down to Liverpool." "Everything about it—the propulsive strum of folk-rock guitars, the beautifully wistful harmony vocals, the jingle jangle production, the achingly evocative way drummer-vocalist Debbi Peterson sings the phrase 'all the days of my life'—can be characterized in just one word: irresistible," he gushes. However, the Bangles triumph is placed almost at the cost of the Go-Go's folly, as Zeller adds of the LP overall: "This album does have a hell of a lot more substantial material than something like the incredibly overrated *Talk Show*."[28]

When the Bangles' artistry is complimented, it is often only in contrast with and at the cost of placing them as superior to the Go-Go's. "The Bangles, a four-woman rough-edged rock-and-roll band, are in the strange position of playing second fiddle to another band, namely the Go-Gos [sic], while at the same time they are much better musicians and songwriters," claims the *Record-Journal*. "Rather than the cotton candy pop of Belinda Carlisle and company, the Bangles can play music that rocks with all the gutsy originality of a latter-day Byrds or Buffalo Springfield."[29] This is heralded as a virtue, as, "unlike other all-female rock bands like the Go-Go's, [the Bangles] don't flaunt an apparent musical dumbness as a badge of rock & roll purity."[30]

The fickleness of the music press may be best showcased, however, in the *Michigan Daily*. Noting that the Bangles want to "avoid comparisons" to the Go-Go's, the journalist goes on to argue that "they shouldn't worry, 'cause their first LP…more than stands up to *Beauty and the Beat*, which is nothing really but two great singles…David Kahne's production jumps out at you impressively, capturing the group's blend of guitars, voices, and its rhythm section. Where the Go-Go's first two albums sounded tinny and too girl-groupish, the Bangles have a very listenable, definite sound."

Not even the accomplishment of landing the coveted cover of *Rolling Stone*[*] goes without derision, the *Michigan Daily* concluding, "The Bangles are thankfully free of the space cadet/teen queen image of the early Go-Go's; these women won't pose in their underwear for *Rolling Stone*[;] they're quietly cool."[31]

Though repeatedly grilled about their abilities, acuity, and seemingly "right" to even hold space in the rock pantheon, the only moment where anyone from the Bangles makes a public-facing retort can be found in the "Letters to the Editor" section of *Rolling Stone*. Having been interviewed for a piece in the rock bible earlier in the year, Vicki voices her dismay at the one-dimensional profile curated by author Michael Goldberg in the finished piece:[†]

> Thank you for Michael Goldberg's recent interview with us. ("Bangles: a Female Fab Four?" RS 430). I was disappointed, however, when several hours of conversation were boiled down to include only those remarks and childhood anecdotes concerning our love for the Beatles. Yes, we're Beatles fans, but we're quite happy to be Bangles. Our tongues were—and shall remain—firmly implanted in our cheeks.
>
> Vicki Peterson
> Los Angeles, California[32]

---

[*] The Go-Go's infamously appeared in their underwear for the 1982 cover shoot. Bassist Kathy Valentine later confided that they were "feeling pressured and intimidated" to don the white skivvies provided. To make matters worse, the banner under the image shockingly declared, "Go-Go's Put Out." Two years later, the group made the cover of the magazine again, this time all wearing baggy, colorful sweaters, fists thrust in the air, with the powerful, badass title "Women on Top."

[†] This is the piece where Debbi reveals the ambition to be like the Beatles, a comment that led to decades of derision.

As the videos garnered rotation on MTV, the group toured and undertook countless interviews. The Bangles were connecting with an audience across the country: fans were beginning to queue up to get into their shows, with the hopes of maybe even getting to meet them as they walked into venues. Chris Lamson recalled watching the momentum grow right in front of his eyes. "You'd pull into the gig and there would be kids outside, behind the fence, waiting to get in or wanting to see the band. You go into the radio stations and they'd be all like, 'Whoa, they'll send the limos over to get you here.'" Road manager Lamson would often suggest to the radio DJs that the group "do a little song live, just a cappella." "Those girls could do that just rolling out of bed," he says. "That was always the easiest thing for them. That Bangles harmony sound was their ticket."[33]

Though building momentum, the band was still touring in a large van while continuing traditions started on the English Beat tour. "We'd be laughing and singing and just traveling the country and seeing things and having adventures along the way and getting lost," Lamson recalls. He describes his specific duties at the end of each show. "When we were playing bigger venues, I would go into the office to settle up [get the money owed the band for the evening's performance]," he says. "The deal was 50 percent [of the evening's take] would go to the booking company and 50 percent would be paid in cash, including any 'bonuses.' I had a Halliburton briefcase that all the tour managers had at the time," he laughs. "I would go in on Friday and Saturday night and get paid like twenty-five grand in cash—plus the 'bonus'—which was a big mound of blow. That was my bonus." After accidently misplacing the money and a "bonus"-filled bag one evening, Lamson got a pair of handcuffs in an attempt to never repeat the expensive mishap. "I'd handcuff my briefcase to heavy objects and stuff," he chuckles. "Every day was a different challenge, so it was really a great time," he says. "It was just camaraderie, we were all super young. Those days were really fun."[34]

Rounding off the year, the band was asked to open for Cyndi Lauper on her Fun Tour for a run of dates in October through December.

15.

Lauper was riding high off the success of her debut solo album, 1983's *She's So Unusual*. Having amassed a massive fan base, many of whom were teenage girls, the spot could not have been more ideal for the Bangles. "Cyndi Lauper's audience seemed to be younger than our club audience," Vicki told the *News-Pilot*. "We've been received really well. This makes us feel real good, because these are kids who don't necessarily know who we are."[35] A review of one of the tour dates briefly mentions the group's opening slot, using column space to "nominate [Bangles] lead guitarist Vicki Peterson as rock's latest heartbreaker."[36] Chris Lamson echoes the success of the Lauper-Bangles pairing. "That was a great tour," he recounts. "It was the first time they were playing big rooms. There'd be eight thousand people in the arena just to see them or they came early to see them. We'd go into cities and go do radio and we were getting a lot of attention. The girls were all very happy. They were playing well because they had honed their musicianship from all the small tours. We were just starting to taste real success and the band started to get a name for itself."[37] Lauper was a supportive mentor, taking the burgeoning celebrities under her wing. "One night, Cyndi brought them all into her hotel room and did their hair," Lamson smiles. But the newly minted superstar did more than spontaneous beauty treatments. "She was great," Debbi says of Lauper, who the girls affectionately referred to as "Mrs. Loopner." "She was kind of mumsie to us. She was very sweet. We loved working with her."[38]

Vicki shares a specific tale of Lauper's kindness. One night after a performance, Vicki left the room she shared with Micki and found solace in the stairwell of their hotel. "Micki wanted to go to sleep right after a show and I was too adrenalized," Vicki recalls. The flame-haired Lauper noticed Vicki hunched over her journal. "She had me come to her room where she showed me the beaten old pot that she boiled water in backstage to steam her throat before a show," a technique the Bangles would come to religiously use as well. Conversation turned to tips for touring. "We were talking about surviving the road," Vicki laughs. "'You got a vibrator?' she asked me. I gave her a look and she laughed. She was talking about a massager. 'But the other kind is good, too,' she told me."

Such camaraderie was painfully rare. Some incidents were harsh reminders of the blatant prejudice against the band, based solely on their gender. During a November bout of dates opening for the Psychedelic Furs smashed in between Lauper shows, the girls were deemed unworthy by the headliner's staff of getting a soundcheck before the performance. They were granted only a line check, where all of the gear and instruments are plugged in to make sure they had power. "We heard through our crew members that their crew completely dismissed us," Vicki recalls. "'Who did they fuck to get this gig?' was a quote overheard by one of our crew members. I'll never forget that. I was so innocent, just shocked. How would anyone think that? That was so foreign to my world."

The gig was at Radio City Music Hall. It was the first time that the girls would be performing in front of the East Coast contingent of their record label, making it crucial that they do a great show to impress the very people who were tasked with promoting their album daily at record stores and radio stations. "It felt like there was a lot at stake," Vicki recalls. "We go on stage," she recounts, "and hit the first chords of 'The Real World.'" However, something felt wrong. "This hall is really dry," Vicki remembers thinking. "Normally you hear the sound of the PA coming back at you," she explains, but this night she "wasn't hearing anything." At first, Vicki took the variance to be that the building was simply "just an old hall" with "different" acoustics. Then she turned and saw Chris Lamson frantically waving at her. Being the member of the band who did most of the talking on stage, Vicki immediately stopped playing and talking to the crowd, and made her way to Lamson. "I go over to him and he says, 'They haven't heard a thing you have said or played, except for the amps on stage. Nothing was plugged in; we got it fixed now. Go say something.' I went back to the mic, said, 'Well, that was our acoustic set. Now we're gonna rock' or something along those lines. But I was like, What the hell."

15.

The Bangles later found out that somebody in the Furs entourage had unplugged all of the inputs to the house board, leaving the girls' sound man frantically attempting to reconnect everything for the first two and a half songs of their set. "Who would do that?" I ask Vicki.

"Somebody who is very angry," she solemnly replies. "They did that because we were women; there's no other reason why you would do that to an opening band."

On the road, indulgence was everywhere, whether "bonuses" from venues or offered by friends; the Bangles, especially Vicki, remained staunchly straightlaced compared with their peers. "We've done a couple of tours where we've watched people in other bands just keep going, like coke-alcohol, coke-alcohol, and you get on this real bad sort of downward spiral, and at the end of the tour everyone is out of their minds," she told the *Los Angeles Times*.[39] "We don't work that way." This feeling was underscored after experiencing her first hangover at a show wrap party. "It was at the end of the Cyndi Lauper tour," Vicki tells me. "I said, 'Okay, I'm gonna have some champagne.'" I also took a hit on a joint, then got violently ill. It just didn't appeal. I never bought that it was a way to be cool. And I didn't love what I saw around me, people who are doing it who are spending a lot of money and seemed to be wasting a lot of time and energy."[40]

Back in Los Angeles, Peter Philbin was keeping an eye on how many copies of *All Over the Place* were adding up at cash registers across the country. "The [head honchos at the] label was wondering if the sales department got the Bangles first album in the stores," Philbin remembers. Awareness and visibility were key to motivate shops to bring in an album, something that Mike Gormley had expertly orchestrated, Philbin reflects. "Mike got a ton of early PR, with lots of images of the Bangles," Philbin says. Sony's college marketing representative staff had coordinated Bangle promotions across the country, seeing events held in college dorms, radio stations, and record stores. The band had a lot of "drive," Philbin says, "initiating a ton of press and photos. They were out on the road, meeting the record company sales reps in each city, making sure albums were in the stores. College radio embraced them."[41]

The constant grind and long weeks paid off. "By the time the tours ended, we had gone over one hundred thousand [units sold], which I think of as a magic number," Philbin explains. "I think, 'Okay. They are now a Columbia act.' Next album, if they make the right album, the label will actually take notice from day one, rather than playing catch up later. I thought the first album was very successful, that it got them on the map."[42]

Indeed, the hard work paid off, seeing *All Over the Place* chart in the *Billboard* Top 100 and the music-magazine-buying public showing their staunch support. In *Creem*'s '84 Rock 'n' Roll Readers Poll, the Bangles came in a respectable number five for best new group:

The Winners CREEM's '84 Rock 'n' Roll Readers Poll, March 1985
BEST NEW GROUP:

1. Ratt
2. Frankie Goes to Hollywood
3. Twisted Sister
4. W.A.S.P.
5. The Bangles
6. Bon Jovi
7. Honeydrippers
8. Mötley Crüe
9. Wham!
10. Black 'N Blue[43]

16.

Susanna says that she and Vicki shared "a ferocious energy and a spirit of making this [the band's success] happen." It was with her addition that things came together, she points out, as "in all the other iterations of bands that they had tried to do, they didn't have someone with my level of commitment, drive, and passion. I was a 'go-getter'; I would stop at nothing to help support our group. I would shamelessly try to promote us. I don't mean that in a bad way; I mean it in a tenacious way; that I was ready to rock on behalf of the Bangles."

Susanna tells me that everything she did was in pursuit of garnering success for the band as a whole, a shared ideal forged at the very first meeting with the Petersons. It was not in pursuit, she says, of personally being famous. "That wasn't an important goal for me," she asserts. "When I met the Petersons, I remember thinking that we were testing each other's commitment level to the band, to being successful. We used the expression 'we want to go to the topper most of the popper most,' which was somehow connected to our obsession with the Beatles. That night, those conversations, mattered to me a whole hell of a lot. I was determined for the band to get airplay, for the band to have an audience. I was out there advocating constantly for the band, from my first drive to give Rodney the homemade 45 all the way through every era of the group. None of us were airhead women made by a record company; it couldn't be more erroneous. I had unfaltering commitment to this art project and to take it as far as we could."

Regardless of Susanna's dedication to move the group forward, the sibling dynamic within the band was impossible to ignore, for better or for worse. Since the band's inception, Vicki had been the de facto leader of the group. "Vicki was the woman in charge," Debbi remembers. Though Susanna now says the Bangles were "always a democracy,"[1] things may have felt different at the time, especially for Debbi. Not only was she the youngest member of the group, but she had her actual older sister by her side, undoubtedly adding at least a subconscious layer of sibling pecking order to the already complicated band hierarchy. "Sue would listen to Vicki and then Michael would listen to Vicki. I knew no one would ever listen to me. If I had an idea, I would go to Vick. Vicki would say it to the rest of the band. [Since it was coming from her] they would all say, 'Oh, that's a really good idea.' I did a psychological thing like that because I knew if I went to Vicki, my thoughts would get heard. They'd never really treat me like a separate person. I was just an extension of Vicki."[2]

Even if there was nothing overtly destructive, roles within the band were set and impossible to change. "With any relationship, if you are with them for a long period of time, they see you a certain way and they can't deviate from that," Debbi explains. 'It felt like [everyone] thought, 'This is Vicki's younger sister and her little shadow.' It didn't help that the manager [Miles Copeland] was nowhere to be found and the producers were causing rifts within the band."[3]

Mike Gormley did not see any problems attributed to sibling rivalry but believed that Debbi may have been less than thrilled about her part in the band. "She was pretty unhappy," he says. "She wasn't happy about playing drums. She wanted to be upfront long before any of us met them. She ended up on a drum set while her sister was playing guitar. She wasn't too happy about that aspect." He continues, reflecting, "I never thought of her as being in Vicki's shadow: I really didn't see that. Maybe she felt that way, but I never did. I think she held her own. She was playing drums…she was doing what needed to be done."[4] Yet for Debbi, the feeling of being forgotten occurred in myriad band-related situations. Besides the drums being toward the back of the stage while performing, Debbi often found herself placed behind her bandmates in various press images. "As the tallest in the group, there are so many pictures in the magazines, or photo sessions where they're all in front of me," she says. "That's my position in the Bangles: I was a floating head."[5]

Steve McDonald of Redd Kross understands Debbi's situation. "There are several dynamics [with which] I related to the Bangles," he says. "The younger sibling feels second fiddle. We are the stairs. That lame younger sibling 'never feeling validated, insecure thing.' I don't want to drag Debbi down with me necessarily but I'm guessing some of that might have existed there too."[6] Jeff McDonald, Steve's brother and bandmate, holds a similar view. "Being in the shadow [of Vicki] was definitely a thing," he reflects. However, the brothers also relay the benefits of being in a group with a relative. "There is a really great part of a shared experience, telepathy, and the vocal blends that is just unique to the sibling playing music experience," Steve explains.[7] Jeff agrees, adding, "After all the issues and the dust settles, you're still related to that person so you can eventually start making music again and doing art again. In other relationships, you may just lose touch entirely."[8]

The overall ethos of the band was that everyone involved had equal input and visibility in every area. "They were all for one and one for all," recounts Jeff McDonald. "They were in it to win It. They had a very unified front."[9] Steve agrees. "There was a sincere friendship at the core."[10] This unilateral utopia was rare to find in groups. "Typically the lead singer is the one who is in control of the band," says Joe Chiccarelli. "The one at the forefront is the spokesman and the one making all the decisions." However, when he worked with the Bangles, he noticed an exception. "With them, I didn't feel that was the case," he reflects. "I feel they had equal says in things. I don't remember one person who took charge. Maybe Vicki was more outside the picture than the others. Bands are odd democracies and I feel they interacted like your average rock band."[11] Jeff McDonald has a similar memory of the group. "They tried really hard to run the band equally. That was the goal," he says.

"Sometimes it's difficult because if there isn't a clear-cut leader—as far as the person who runs the band—it can cause problems down the road." The Bangles, he says, "tried not to have a team leader. They were really working as a unit for years before the complications came in."[12]

However, signing to a major label and garnering moderate success, thus becoming a commodity for a bigger machine, may have changed things, Steve McDonald hypothesizes. "Susanna and Vicki were like Lennon and McCartney," he smiles.[13] "Vicki was always confident and an organizer so I could see her being a bit of a leader."[14] While the partnership was successful, it led to the other two band members not getting a lot of writing credits. "It was that same sort of George Harrison vibe," Chris Lamson says. "Vicki and Sue or John and Paul? Then there's, 'Who gets one song on the record?'"[15]

Individual personalities and idiosyncrasies began to show as the group began to amass fame outside of their native Los Angeles. Maybe it was naturally inherent in her personality or perhaps it was partially because she was the newest member, but Micki got a reputation as being, in turn, nice though appreciating her own company. Joe Stella recalls her as being "a bit of a loner." Unperturbed, the engineer "would always try to talk to her." Once they got chatting, he says they would "have fun conversations." "She had a dry sense of humor," he smiles. "She was just so sweet. I would always make time for her."[16]

Peter Philbin describes a slightly flaky Micki, calling her "delightful," but laughing when he says, "I know that when they were on the road, Mike Gormley would often make sure that the road manager Chris Lamson would have someone go with her wherever she went, even to do her laundry; otherwise, she might not make the gig. She's great, but you need to make sure she shows up." For his part, Lamson hypothesizes that Michael "always felt like a bit of an outsider as the last person to join. She was kind of an odd bird but not a bad person. She was just weird in the context of the rest of the girls," he says. "The rest of the girls all wore their heart on their sleeve. Micki was just very reserved."[17]

16.

Time spent in the studio with David Kahne had also disrupted the interpersonal balance of the band. "By the time they started having mainstream success, Susanna had stepped into this role of being viewed by producers as having the most commercial voice, which changed the dynamics," Steve recalls. "Suddenly, there was something for them to reconcile and have to figure out. It began to cause problems."[18]

A&R executive Peter Philbin has a similar view to that of Steve McDonald. "From my vantage point, the forces in this band are Vicki and Susanna. On the first album, Michael was the most experienced player. But Vicki is a band girl, which I say in a good way. She actually wants to be in a rock and roll band. That's her mentality and that's to be celebrated." In Susanna, he argues, there was a unique, steely determination that dictated the trajectory of the group. "Susanna has starry eyes and does not see obstacles. When you're younger, you actually think you can walk through walls. That goes away with any kind of maturity. Susanna hasn't lost that. She's still that girl. I commend that." Vicki, he says, is "more grounded." "The band's influence is Vicki," he says. The two of them, he tells me, "are a good combination." And "both of them are needed," as "the Bangles wouldn't be the Bangles without those two people. Oftentimes, they clash." This is par for the course, Philbin argues. "If there's friction," he notes, "so be it."[19]

However, as Susanna's focus helped push the group forward, it also started to create problems within the foursome. As a classically trained ballerina and film buff, she knew how to move her body, work the camera, and create appealing visuals. "I remember with videos, she really dragged that band into the spotlight," Philbin says of Susanna. "Vicki and Debbi had to come up to par with Susanna. Susanna knew how to look at a camera. She knew how to present herself on film." Having done the main vocals of "Hero Takes a Fall," Susanna was thrust into the focal point for the video and various promotional dates. "People got it wrong as they started thinking Susanna was the lead singer," Joanna "Spock" Dean reflects.[20]

Vicki asserts that Susanna was intentional with the choices she made in marketing assets. "For the 'Hero Takes a Fall' video, Sue picks the French maid costume because she got to be sexy and it worked for her," Vicki says. She then talks about the various appearances the group did to support the albums. "It became Susanna versus the rest of us," she says. "The record label sent us off on a promotional tour for six weeks," she tells me. "It's more exhausting than a traditional tour. When I look at the millions of lip-sync TV performances we did for promotion, I notice that Sue was very canny and smart. Whenever she had lead vocals in a song, she made sure to pitch the performance right to the camera. She didn't move too much. Because of where she stood on stage, the cameras were often in front of her." Ever the self-flagellator, Vicki reflects, "I'm all over the place like a fish, so the camera was never really on me for very long. I was always shot from stage right; profile not being my best attribute, it didn't really work for me."[21]

Vicki tells me that she talked to management in the hope of garnering equal screen time for each member. "We would say, 'Please make sure the director covers everybody. Make sure that everyone gets seen because this is a band and not a singer and a backup. Obviously, we focus on the singer because you want to connect with the lyrics, you want to see the person present the song. But let's just make sure that they shoot Micki and Debbi when she starts the song, and make sure the cameras are on her.'"[22] This request, Vicki says, was "blown up into this oppressive 'we have to have equal time' thing."[23]

"People were calling Sue the lead singer," Mike Gormley says. "Very early on, we would do a TV show and I'd have to sit with the director of the show and say, 'Did you see the Beatles on *The Ed Sullivan Show?*' And a guy would say yes, everybody did. I would say, 'Well, you remember when they showed them individually? They showed the band, but they showed them individually, and they put their name on each one?' And he said, 'Yeah.' I would tell him that we needed to do that here.

We need to make sure every single member of that band is on camera at some point because it was a band." If Gormley did not say this, the TV people would "zoom right in on Sue. I think that just started to wear on the other girls."[24]

Susanna made for excellent television. "She was cute, she knew how to work the camera," Gormley remembers. But there was one feature that made her uniquely appealing. "Those eyes," Gormley states. "People today still ask if Sue still does that with her eyes. They became a trademark." At the time, Susanna was "singing a lot of the lead," Gormley says. "She wasn't the lead singer; it was a band. Sue definitely thought of it as a band but she liked the attention."[25]

Gormley tried his best, he tells me, to be the buffer between the group and the TV teams. "The temptation was to just go with the flow and say to the director, 'shoot whatever you want, the show is your show,' but every director I talked to went along with it. They understood what I was talking about. I don't think the band knew I was doing that and sometimes it may not have worked that well but I would have to sit with the director and make sure everybody got seen. I was a drummer so I know what it's like. You watch yourself on TV and nobody knows you're there. I can understand that particularly for Debbi. I would make sure she got shot a couple of times and then it just became something for the band as a whole."[26] Vicki concurs, observing, "In order for one to 'work' the camera, the camera needs to be on one. I'm thinking mostly about Debbi, who is a wonderful performer, if she is ever seen…"

Time on camera started to be an issue "to some degree," Gormley confesses. Susanna being the focal point of many performances was a recurring motif, despite efforts from management and band alike. "It was happening, but it wasn't bothering them that much," he says, "but who knows what was going on while they traveled across the country."[27]

Chris Lamson was on the road with the group. "There was tension," he remembers. "It grew and grew as the band got bigger." Many different aspects of band life were impacted by this, with Lamson giving the example of stage lighting as just one. "Because their thing was always, 'there's no lead person in the band, there's no lead singer, there's just the four of us,' when they graduated to bigger arenas, in any venue they each got their own spotlight, as there was no lead person: they're all lit. That's just as an example. That was their vibe, and they were all into it." However, such efforts overall were in vain. "The media had to find a lead person. So they start to gravitate towards Sue. That's just what happened. It was not her fault. She did not promote this, in my opinion. She did not cultivate it; it came to her."[28]

Inner band resentment was a "slow build," Gormley says, and felt by those around the group. "From my observation," he recounts, "it was mostly aimed at Sue. To my knowledge, she was getting more attention, thought of as a lead singer, and knew how to work the camera." All of this "brought focus on her more than the others," he remembers. "I think that started it. I don't think she was maliciously doing it. She just knew how to do it." It became a very stressful situation for all involved. "I felt the tension then and it just built like crazy. I felt at times I was holding them together, trying to get to that second album. We'd gone too far for them not to follow it up." Gormley would often get caught in the middle of band relations. "What they didn't realize was that I'd get a phone call from one of them, not complaining about the others, but wanting to discuss something about their situation. Nobody was quitting or anything like that; they just wanted to talk."* The calls were often around the clock. "They didn't realize that…I was trying to balance it. They may not have had any idea I was doing that…but it was tough. It was pressure."[29]

If the band was doing a gig, and not getting along, "Vicki would not go over to Sue's side of the stage, and there'd be backs turned," Lamson remembers. "Most people wouldn't notice it, but I would." Vicki disputes this. "Once we hit the stage, history was erased," she tells me.

---

* Vicki and Debbi both tell me they were not the placers of such calls.

"The actual live performances were the reason we were doing it and went through everything," she says. "The performing was joyful no matter what was going on."

There had been other options for Susanna besides pursuing a career with the Bangles. Right as the band was signing to Columbia, Susanna had been given an audition for the television show based on the hit movie *Fame*. "I sang 'To Sir, with Love' on my guitar for the producers and executives," Susanna says. "I was at a crossroads. The TV people were going to offer me a screen test, which involves them spending some money." However, before a cent would be laid out, Susanna was told she had to choose between possibly being on the show or being in the band. "I had to make a decision at that moment and I chose the band," she tells me. "I so clearly wanted to be a creative force, in a band versus an actor, with a part on a TV show, that it was a clear-cut decision even though it was very flattering to think that they might have wanted to cast me. I definitely wanted to pursue the dream of the band and have that kind of creative empowerment." The appeal of being in a group was irresistible for Susanna. "When you're in a band, you're the architect of your own destiny in a certain way," she says. "Ultimately, bands who get signed have to deal with some input from a record company, [but] there's still a sense of being an artist. That's different from being part of a larger thing, just a cast member on a show that's created by other people. The band is your creation, the group's creation. You have the power in a certain way."[30]

Susanna says the Bangles' "unspoken concept" was to be like the Beatles, crafting a band as a unit, not as solo artists. "I realized that there was animus and envy [because of the perception] that I was getting more attention by the press. I don't even know where the ideas came from," she notes. "It's a band," she says, "and the band has a kind of united front, everybody does their job." However, the very strength of the band also became fraught with challenges, Susanna explains. "With the Bangles, it's exponentially more complex because everybody's singing and writing. You get a certain amount of time to fit an A-side and a B-side on vinyl, which is really what it was then, and a cassette. Everybody's sort of competing to have a really good song, though not necessarily intending to be competing. We're collaborating, we're splitting up or dividing and conquering within the band who's going to write what with what. I think the experience of being in the band was so naturally fraught, in ways that bands are. It's like dysfunctional families, I always use that analogy, because in some ways the friction might add something to it, not always. But behind the scenes, the experience of living the experience, just as a human being, I will say it was stressful." Susanna sighs, concluding, "I just remember trying to survive the experience."[31]

Joanna Dean thinks it may have been inevitable that Susanna was viewed by the media as the front woman. "I think she totally felt she was the lead singer but it's just her personality," Spock says. "I can't see her doing anything else but striving to be that. She wouldn't want to be just the rhythm guitar player. It's just not her character."[32]

There was a price to the record sales, press, and record company support. "Things got very complicated once they became successful," says Jeff McDonald.[33] The more popular the band became, the more existing niggles were aggravated. "In the really early days, it was all fun and games," Chris Lamson tells me, "but when the stakes get higher, and the money gets higher, more people come into your life, trying to direct your career. Now there's a stake in other people's lives. That's when things started to go a little off the rails."[34]

As the year came to a close, the Bangles finally got to return to Los Angeles for a much needed break. Despite a charting album, having the magic number of one hundred thousand copies of *All Over the Place* cross the sales counter at record stores throughout the United States and doing numerous shows and performances, the band had not made a single cent. In a *Melody Maker* interview, Michael laid out the band's current straits:

> Three-quarters of this band is basically homeless. Well, how can you put down $400 when you're not getting a salary? You either sub-let your

apartment when you're touring or you move—and we've moved every single tour. We're always juggling money.[35]

Laughing as she recounts a similar story, Vicki tells me her memories of coming back after a long year on the road promoting an album. Having given up her apartment as she was so infrequently there, the then twenty-six-year-old found herself staying with her twenty-two-year-old boyfriend—Jeff McDonald—at his parents' house. "It was hilarious," she says. Vicki's omnipresent cheery attitude cannot hide the stark reality that hit the young musician of what being in a major-label band entailed. "I remember coming home one night and being in tears," she says. "I just kept saying, 'How does anyone ever make a second record? Does anyone do that again?' It was like childbirth, but the blessings of nature make you forget the pain and go for it again."[36]

17.

There are many different renditions of how Prince first became aware of the Bangles, the circumstances and dates of when they first met and exactly how "Manic Monday" originally got into the band's hands. What is incontrovertible is the impact he had on the group's trajectory. In 1984, the Minneapolis native was arguably at the height of his career, having just scored a box office success with the loosely autobiographical film *Purple Rain*. The eponymous studio album went on to sell thirteen million copies in the US alone, with twenty-four consecutive weeks spent at number one on the *Billboard* 200 chart. With perhaps the exception of peer Michael Jackson, there was no star bigger than the guitar maestro. Any perceived interaction, no matter how tangential, with the rock royalty had the power to instantly bolster a career. "The output was just astounding," reflects Bobby Rifkin of the time period. Rifkin—known professionally as Bobby Z—met Prince at Moon Sound Studios. Rifkin was nineteen, Prince just seventeen. The two struck up a friendship, with Rifkin eventually joining Prince's band, the Revolution. "His songwriting was just the key to it all," Bobby says, "songwriting was the currency of the music business. The power he had was just overwhelming."[1]

It was literally days after first hearing the lead single from the movie's soundtrack, "When Doves Cry," that Susanna found out that Prince had taken an interest in the band after seeing the video for "Hero Takes a Fall." "Somebody came up to me and said, 'Do you know that Prince really likes the Bangles?'" she says. "He'd seen the song on MTV."[2] The timing, she later remarked, provided an "interesting feeling of kismet."[3]

17.

A&R man Peter Philbin credits Susanna's endless chutzpah with making the Prince connection come to fruition. "Susanna heard that I had tried to sign Prince, which I did and had failed," he laughs. Toward the end of the tour in support of the debut album, the Bangles were slated to headline a show in Los Angeles at the Palace on August 4, 1984. "It's on Vine Street, right off of Hollywood Boulevard, right across from Capitol Records," Philbin explains. "It's a nice venue, probably holds a thousand people." Before the performance, Philbin received a call from Susanna. "She asks me to invite Prince to the gig," he says. "So I call Prince's management company and I leave a message with the receptionist: 'The Bangles would like to invite Prince to their show.' I could not believe it: Prince actually showed up," he laughs.[4] "Susanna took it from there and that's how we got 'Manic Monday.'"[5]

Despite having been impressed enough by the album to come to the gig and be spotted by the paparazzi at a celebratory after-party, the media claimed that the band did not actually get the chance to meet their esteemed guest. Susanna, however, tells me that she did get some one-on-one time with the star at the gig, and she shares an example of his witty sense of humor. "Prince and I sat talking after our show," Susanna tells me. "We had been there for a bit when one of his bodyguards said it was getting late. It reminded me of Cinderella. I asked, 'What happens when the clock strikes midnight?' 'The bodyguards turn into rats!' he answered with a smile. He was riffing on a fairy tale."[6] Debbi has a slightly different recollection of the interlude with the Purple One. As she remembers it, a member of the Bangles management team had come backstage to tell the band that "someone special" had come to the show at the Palace and wanted to meet them. "I ran through all of the potential people in my mind but had no idea it would turn out to be Prince," Debbi says. "Because of my height, I didn't see him at first! He was shy, but very nice and complimentary."

Susanna relates another encounter with the Purple One taking place on an international flight. "We were coming to London for a tour and he was coming to accept an award, so we were on the same plane," Susanna related. "I got notified that Prince wanted me to go up into first class and he had an empty seat; maybe he booked two seats because he didn't want to deal with sitting next to someone he didn't know. That is just speculation, but I went up there and hung with him for a big chunk of the flight." The time in the air gave Susanna "the chance to tell him that we were making a record." Upon landing, Susanna was again reminded of their contrasting places at the moment in the hierarchy of pop landscape. "It was so interesting and kind of spoke to the difference between being a Bangle and being Prince," she recalls. "When we arrived at customs, he had these giant duffel bags full of costumes. We just thought, 'Wow, that's amazing. He gets to bring so much stuff with him.' We had our one bag allocation, our one outfit."

The band had a quick spin around Europe in February 1985, with stops including Holland, France, and Germany, along with several shows in England. In an effort to save money, the girls found themselves decamping at the palatial house of manager Copeland in London's tony neighborhood of St John's Wood on Marlborough Road. "I remember we [the whole band] were sleeping in one room upstairs," Vicki tells me. Chez Copeland was also hosting another of his clients simultaneously: none other than Sting, lead singer of the Police, who was "sleeping two floors below" the girls. The striking Brit was already a superstar, having earned multiplatinum global success with his band; now, he was on the cusp of what looked to be an equally triumphant solo career. "It was blowing my mind," Vicki says of being in such close proximity to the front man. "He was very polite, very nice and encouraging," she recalls, yet "possibly hygienically challenged in that British sort of way," earning the blonde the nickname "Stink" among the Bangles.

Though excited to meet him, Vicki could not help taking the opportunity to play a prank on her fellow Faulty-managed artist. "We were on our way out the door," she smiles. "I remember sitting in Miles's parlor, waiting for everyone to get ready. Stink walks by, heading for the telephone in the living room." The singer was repeating numbers to himself, murmuring under his breath, loud enough for Vicki to hear. "He was obviously memorizing, trying to remember a phone number that he was about to dial, saying digits: '437473467.' Under my breath, I started saying: '9123412910' just very quietly. When I got up to leave, I heard from the living room, 'Bugger!' I knew I'd been successful."

Another break for the band came from mentor Cyndi Lauper. Lauper had been tapped by Steven Spielberg to be musical director for the soundtrack of his newest project, the tween action adventure film *The Goonies*. Lauper gave the movie its title song, "The Goonies 'R' Good Enough," which went on to be a *Billboard* top-ten single. Lauper enlisted the Bangles to provide a track, resulting in the Susanna Hoffs–Vicki Peterson–Jules Shear collaboration "I Got Nothing,"* which further strengthened the bond between the artists. "I love the Bangles," Lauper raved to *Creem*. "They sing like angels, so I used them on this real hard track with Nile Rodgers, all these combinations together, and it was killer."[7] The singer was so enthralled that she recruited the girls to costar in the "Good Enough" video, an experience that Debbi fondly recounts. "I loved doing it," she tells me. "I remember [the shoot] was all day long and into the night. We got to dress up as pirates and act like we were swashbuckling and looking for the treasure. I came home at four in the morning. Every time I would blow my nose, blue stuff would come out as they had colored the water around the boat with some sort of toxic neon dye. It was hilarious."[8]

As the Bangles efforts were helping propel them forward, the Go-Go's were falling apart. In May 1985, the band announced that they were officially breaking up. Though the press had consistently tried to pit the groups against one another, endlessly comparing them, they had respect for each other, having played several dates together the previous year. With commercial radio stations having implicit restrictions as to how many female artists could get airplay at any one time, the demise of

---

* Recorded at Sunset Studios in Los Angeles.

their cohorts created opportunity for the Bangles. There were incredibly strict parameters as to how many female artists could be added onto a radio station's rosters and be in rotation simultaneously. This often had a detrimental impact on artists, as it not only created an unnecessarily combative environment between women musicians but could have devastating effect if you were "unlucky" enough to be scheduled for a promotional push the same week as another female on any other label—let alone your own. Vicki clearly remembers this limiting practice causing problems for the Bangles on commercial radio. "We were told by our representative [at the record label], that a lot of stations could not add [us] because they'd already added [another female artist] that week, and you can't do more than one woman at a time. Oh, my God, it was an absolute tokenism format; there was a specific number of female artists that could be added every week, and it was a very low number."[9] The end of the Go-Go's meant one less group to be put in contention with for the already-negligible opportunities.

The Go-Go's disintegration also provided a cautionary tale of the pitfalls of fame and success. "I was kind of disappointed they broke up," Vicki told *Creem*. "We're friends with them but, in talking with several of the girls, I realized it was the best thing for them to do. It's kept them sane and alive."[10] Michael continued, rhetorically asking, "Every time a band that you enjoy falls asunder, you ask yourself, is that going to happen to us? The pressures are the same for all rock groups. Luckily, this is not an outfit that went to #1 with its first album. We're building more gradually. The expectations aren't as severe. We're being allowed to make progress with each record."[11]

Now the pressure was on to begin work on a follow-up album. The band was tired, having been on the road almost nonstop for two years. Columbia was keen to get another release out as soon as possible to capitalize on the burgeoning fan base the girls had worked so hard to build off the back of *All Over the Place*. Even though the band had written a majority of the tracks for the first album, label representatives felt that time was of the essence, speed of turnaround crucial. Feelers began

17.

being put out for possible contributors for the sophomore release to expedite the record-creation process.

Back in 1984, Prince had been working on a new track called "Manic Monday."

"I cowrote 'Manic Monday' with Prince," close friend and *Purple Rain* costar Apollonia Kotero tells me over Zoom. The ageless icon is immediately engaging; within moments of talking, there is an instant rapport. "I've been writing poetry in haikus for years," she explains. "Prince was always interested in reading them. This was in Minnesota, in 1983. In '84, we started writing songs."

It was a transformative moment for the young artist. "I felt like for the first time in my life, I could now put my poetry to music, so it became very exciting," she recalls. Prince encouraged his protégé to keep writing. "He went over to a store called Oz on Sunset Boulevard [in Los Angeles] and bought me, which I still have, a little purple notebook. It was for a kid, really cute, with toys on it. He goes, 'You can start writing your work in here. We will write more songs.'" "Manic Monday" was just one work between the duo, Kotero confides. "There are a lot of my lyrics on other songs [of his] that I'm not credited for."[12]

Inspired by each other, several songs, including "Glamorous Life," recorded by another Prince discovery, drummer Sheila E., came from this fertile period of collaboration, Kotero recalls. "Manic Monday" was the product of Kotero's own verbalizing a wish for an elongated weekend. "There were times when I would say, 'God, I wish there was a day after Sunday before Monday called Smunday. I don't have to run day.' He said, 'What?' I said, 'I wish there was a day after Sunday before Monday, a day called Smunday, my I don't have to run day. We need a day after Sunday to prepare for Monday.' He just laughed. My lyrics were put to music, thanks to Prince. 'Manic Monday' is 50 percent Prince and my lyrics."

The original intention was to give the tune to the newly formed all-girl group Apollonia 6. Featuring Kotero, the original demo had the maestro on lead vocals with 6's Jill Jones and Brenda Bennett singing backup.

Slated to appear on the *Apollonia 6* album, which came out in October 1984, the demo arrangement featured dreamy synthesizers and psychedelic bridges to complement the female "operatic" voices. An alternative version had been done featuring Kotero with Prince, she recalls. "I wanted to put steel guitar on it," she remembers, "because for me it always sounded country and western."[13] She says, "When we first started doing it, we did a really rough demo." However, Kotero was unhappy with the result. "I didn't like my vocals. I don't sing like Beyoncé. I thought, 'Let's just do a rough vocal and then we'll redo it again.' A beautiful song and a fun song. We recorded in February 1984."[14] However, Prince ultimately ended up removing the song from the album's track list.

The encouragement from her friend provided Kotero with confidence, seeing her go on to write songs for the nighttime dishy soap opera *Falcon Crest*. "I always thought that we would continue writing [together]," she says, "but I became very bored with his projects." She describes Prince as being "very chameleon-like," saying that "he had so many different artists [he was working with], like on a conveyor belt," she notes. "That's why I thought, 'I could write songs for them too.' So 'Manic Monday,' to this day, when I hear it, I love the song."[15]

After coming across the Bangles on the radio, Kotero was intrigued to know more about the band. "When I first heard them, I was like, 'Damn it, they sound like the Beatles.' I'm a Beatle fan. I am madly in love with the Beatles." Like the four women in the group, Kotero had grown up with the Liverpudlians as the soundtrack to her life. "My parents listened to them when I was a child," she smiles. "I still have our original *Help!* album that my parents bought for me as a baby." Kotero remembers, "It was around that summer in '84 that I went to go see the Bangles in Hollywood. I was crazy about a song that I heard on the radio called 'Hero Takes a Fall.'" After the show, Kotero connected with the band and was impressed. "We chilled before Prince met the group. It was partly my love for The Beatles and these were all girls in the band, playing hard! Just doing the work!"[16]

17.

Kotero became "crazy" about the band after seeing the Palace performance. "I started to sing 'Hero' to Prince," she laughs. "I go, 'That song is so cool.' He was like, 'Who's is it?' I said, 'It's the Bangles. You got to hear them. You've got to meet them.' I said, 'You're gonna love Susanna Hoffs. She's amazing,' and I knew that he would like her, because I knew that she was his type. He likes little brunettes."[17] She gave Prince a cassette featuring "Hero." "I said, 'Go listen to the song.' And he liked it. I said, 'I think they should do "Manic Monday."' I thought they would make it different because 'Manic Monday' kind of sounded a little bit like 'Purple Rain' to me."[18]*

While Prince was ensconced at the Le Parc hotel in Los Angeles, Kotero continued her campaign, in the hopes of getting her friend to share in the excitement over the band. "He puts the TV on and he's got the video," she remembers. "He's watching her [Susanna] and says, 'I really like her.' I go, 'I know, she's amazing.' I never said like, 'Oh, I knew you would.' I'm watching him watch her." Kotero then jumps to the part in the "Hero" video where Susanna dons a French maid costume. "All of a sudden, she's in that little maid outfit," Apollonia says, "and she's rocking back and forth in a cute little apron." The motion especially caught Prince's attention, with Prince going "wild over her!" Kotero says.[19] "Prince tells me, 'You know what she looks like she's doing.' I was caught off guard. He just gives me this look. He said, 'because it looks like she's sitting on something.' That's where his mind was. I never thought that at all. I just giggled and thought it was cute." Kotero was thrilled as she saw the chance for collaboration. When Prince suggested giving the Bangles "Manic Monday," Kotero responded, "Let them take it. They're amazing."[20] Apollonia elaborates, "I was like, 'Awesome. They're gonna work together and she's going to do my song. It worked and the song was beautiful. Her voice was beautiful. To this day, I'm just so proud that I was able to broker that."[21]

---

* "My biggest dream was that Willie Nelson would do 'Purple Rain' because to me that sounds like a country song," Kotero tells me.

Peter Philbin was simultaneously trying to get Prince's attention through a connection he had made during his time courting the artist. "[Prince and I] didn't hang out with each other [when I was trying to sign him], but I had become friends with this drummer Bobby Z," Peter says.[22] Knowing there was a connection between Philbin and the newly christened superstar, Susanna asked for a copy of the Bangles' *All Over the Place* to be sent over. "I'm thinking, 'Prince won't care about four girls, this is a brand-new band.' But Susanna was an artist of mine and she had asked me to do this."[23] Philbin called on Bobby Z, seeing if he could pass a cassette of the Bangles to Prince. "I don't even know if he'll even give it to Prince," Philbin recalls.[24]

After years of friendship, Rifkin knew precisely how to handle the star. "If you're going to approach Prince, you have to hit him in the right moment," Rifkin advises. The Bangles, though, "had the ingredients," Rifkin thought, to pique his friend's interest. "It was all women and this video was something I could point to so he didn't have to play the record," Rifkin shares. "It was visual." One day, Rifkin saw his chance. "We were watching MTV, and it ['Hero Takes a Fall' video] was on rotation. I said, 'That's the band.' And he said, 'I kind of like that song,' which was a huge development. With Prince, it was pass-fail. It was very difficult to get a pass with Prince."[25]

The Bangles had an intangible quality that connected with both Rifkin and the superstar. "There was a soul to the Bangles and a soul to that song," Rifkin explains. "Peter definitely needed to capitalize on that. Reaching for somebody like Prince was great timing."[26] A month after originally receiving the *All Over the Place* cassette, Z dialed Philbin up. "He tells me that Prince likes the record and I'm shocked," Philbin admits. "At that point, I'm not equating the Bangles with Prince. 'Hero Takes a Fall' is not exactly *Purple Rain*."[27]

Rifkin remembers Prince "dabbling on 'Manic Monday' for quite a while," describing "rehearsals [that were] six-seven-eight hours long." Rifkin tells me that "there were not many songs that he didn't play around with or have the band play." Prince demanded the same grueling dedication from the Revolution that he did of himself. "We had alternative sets," Rifkin says, each set having "twelve or fifteen songs." There was also "the alternative show, show number two," Rifkin recalls. "They weren't really interchangeable songs," Rifkin says, "they were interchangeable shows."

"Manic Monday" had a different feel than other work by Prince, Rifkin reflects. "It was that piano riff," Rifkin says, that showed how Prince "really understand[s] rock and roll." "Everything had an element of funkiness to Prince," Rifkin reflects, "but that piano riff is Beatle-ish with the last note being dissonant in the way it came together."[28]

How exactly the demo with "Manic Monday" came to be in the Bangles' possession is nebulous. One version has word getting to the band via mutual contacts they shared with Prince. "We were working with Peggy and David Leonard, a husband-and-wife engineer team who had done a lot of stuff with Prince," remembers Susanna. "I was told to drive to the iconic Sunset Sound Studios, so I got in my beat-up Toyota with the ripped upholstery and made my way over there. I'm bracing myself to hang out with him, but he was recording when I arrived, so the cassette was left at the front desk for me. I still have that exact cassette."[29]

A slightly different anecdote reports that "Prince sent word that he had written a song for the band. He invited the members to his studio to pick up the cassette and give the first version of 'Manic Monday' a listen."[30] The story takes a slightly different spin in a 2013 *Guardian* article, making the interaction sound very intimate: "At one point he presented us [the Bangles] with a cassette tape of two songs—'Here: do you want to record these?'"[31] Lamson thinks the connection to the iconic song was via Prince's team. "We got a call from the management company at Prince's office," Lamson says. "Prince's person said, 'Prince has two songs he wants to give to the Bangles, primarily Susanna,' and it came on a cassette. Sue came over and picked up the cassette and we listened to it. There was some debate about which song they were going to do or if they were going to do any of them. They were putting together songs for *Different Light* and it wasn't even called that then."[32] Lamson admits to not remembering the exact details, just that the entire transaction "went through Sue because Prince was attracted to her; [they were] the same size."[33]

Susanna describes the experience of listening to the tape for the first time with the band. "We Bangles hovered around the cassette machine—'cause back then, it was tape—and we were smitten with the song."[34] Two songs were included: "Manic Monday" (most likely featuring the Apollonia 6 version) and Prince's 1981 tune "Jealous Girl,"* with him on vocals. Susanna was drawn to "Monday." "It was an instant fit," Susanna recalls. "The minute I started singing it, I was like, 'Oh, this is such an incredible song.'"[35] "The title was really great. It just reminded me of 'Manic Depression' the Hendrix song and had kind of a psychedelic thing. It had these great harmonies, and there were a lot of things about it where I just thought, 'This is a really good fit for the Bangles.'"[36] Vicki says the group picked "Manic" over "Jealous" because it "was closer to something we might write, which is kind of a pretentious thing to say but that's how I felt; it struck me that way."[37]

The band knew it was a big moment. "It was quite a compliment for him to say, 'I think you guys should do the song,'" says Debbi.[38] "He's a guy we respect[ed] and admire[d] a lot. He'[d] written for other people, so we thought 'Why not the Bangles?' We were so flattered that he like[d] us."[39] The group was aware that though *All Over the Place* had been a breakthrough for them, there was still a lot of work to be done; and the value of the Prince association could prove to be a powerful additional boost. "We were getting a lot of good press and our shows were doing well," says Vicki, "but really the idea of getting a single to radio was still a bit of a challenge, and once you have this great hook—'Look! Prince wrote them a song'—it definitely help[ed]."[40]

---

* Prince allegedly had originally penned the track for a 1981 project called the Hookers, a "sexy girl group singing in lingerie." https://princevault.com/index.php?title=Album:_The_Hookers_(1982). When the project did not take off, he supposedly tried to "pawn [it] off to everyone in a skirt." https://princesongs.org/2022/08/15/manic-monday/.

Capturing the interest of one of the biggest celebrities in the world instantly catapulted the Bangles into the media spotlight and put them on an entirely new level. Speculation was constant and insidious, centered particularly around Susanna. Very quickly, the narrative shifted from the hitmaker finding worth in the band as artists and musicians to simply courting the rhythm guitarist. Her bandmates noted special attention being placed upon Susanna. "He sent her a bottle of his cologne, gifts, and things in a seductive way," Vicki remembers.[41] "He was wooing her," Debbi confirms. Prince's inner circle fed the flames of speculation, with one of his own Revolution band members—Wendy—telling *Rolling Stone* "that the connection wasn't that strong [between Prince and the Bangles]. Prince's ears was [sic] pricked up by the Bangles because he thought Susanna was cute."[42]

The appetite seemed insatiable for anything pertaining to Prince, with Susanna becoming an object of fascination. "Prince had seen Sue in the 'Hero Takes a Fall' video where they are busking on the street," Chris Lamson says. "They've got those ridiculous outfits on, the scarves and the hats and all that crap. They were still trying to find their identity in those days and being dressed by label people and stylists."[43]

For better or worse, Prince became an integral part of helping to keep the Bangles in the press between releases. "Prince was already hanging around the band," says Gormley. "I believe he had eyes on Sue. He'd come to their shows. I remember a caravan of limos going to his house in Beverly Hills one night, just all hanging out and getting lost because he forgot where he was living. He was leading the caravan."[44]

The myopic focus on Susanna created more opportunities for the Bangles to garner visibility. However, the founding idea of equality among bandmates was under siege with the interest in the brunette. "It just started to go a little south," Lamson says of relationships within the group. "I think the Prince thing was the first time where Sue got all the attention. There was a time where *Rolling Stone* wanted to put Sue on the cover—that was a big deal. That was a 'No can do.' You've got record company people saying, 'It's publicity, blah, blah, blah.' The band didn't like it. I can see why. There was definitely tension."[45]

Rumors ran rampant, from whispers that Prince was trying to poach Susanna for one of his own band projects to that the duo were having an affair. "The diminutive star has had a thing for Bangle guitarist Susanna Hoffs since he heard her sing 'Hero Takes a Fall,'" proclaimed the *Arizona Daily Star*.[46] "He tried to get her to leave the Bangles and become one of his Princettes, but she refused."[47] *Rolling Stone* echoed this further, trumpeting, "No one could have anticipated that Prince's much-publicized affection for her would vault Susanna into being beyond-Bangles celebrity status." Another of the magazine's blurbs teased, "Los Angeles is buzzing about the heat that Prince has been putting on Bangles guitarist-singer Susanna Hoffs to join his motley band of barely clad players. In between guest appearances at Sheila E.'s dates and rehearsals for his own tour, His Royal Badness has been calling Hoffs constantly at her parents' house."[48]

The band quickly became well-versed at providing a united front to the public in the face of all of the gossip. "Just a rumor," Debbi told the *Chicago Tribune* in a phone interview when asked about Susanna possibly leaving the Bangles to join forces full-time with Prince. "It was somebody's sick idea of having fun."[49]

The hearsay about anything other than professional appreciation between the musicians were untrue, with Q magazine even reporting how "rumours of a dalliance betwixt Hoffs and Prince have, it seems, been grossly exaggerated."[50] Susanna herself provides insight. "They were all unfounded," Susanna says. "I think Prince was interested in a way in me and the band but I always kept a distance from him. This is not hard to do as he is a mysterious person who keeps his distance from everybody. I found it very inspiring and it was very validating for us at the time—for the group and for me personally—for this incredible artist to take such an interest in us."[51]

Yet the press did not seem to care about what actually may have occurred, instead repeatedly choosing to run with the angle that would catch the most attention. "It's so funny when people start writing those

Merry Christmas from the Peterson siblings
(left to right: Vicki, Debbi, Dave, Pam)
Courtesy Vicki Peterson Personal Collection

Susanna Hoffs, 1967
Courtesy Susanna Hoffs Personal Collection

Aisha, August 1978, in the Hillses' family room
(left to right: Vicki, Amanda Hills, Debbi)
Photo by Julian Hills

Those Girls at Sweetwater, September 6, 1980
Courtesy Vicki Peterson Personal Collection

Early show flyer for the Muze, 1979
Courtesy Debbi Peterson Personal Collection

The Fans, circa 1980
(left to right: Lynn Elkind, Amanda, Debbi, Vicki)
Photo by Jerry Podany

Those Girls at the Troubadour, 1980
Courtesy Amanda Podany Personal Collection

Susanna: "My version of the jobs office was going around LA with a flyer I made—I still have the original copy of it—saying that I wanted to form an all-girl band."
Courtesy Susanna Hoffs Personal Collection

The Bangs
(left to right: Susanna, Annette Zilinskas, Debbi, Vicki)
Courtesy Susanna Hoffs Personal Collection

Early Bangs flyer
Courtesy Debbi Peterson Personal Collection

"Getting Out of Hand" single, a completely DIY effort; former Susanna paramour David Roback took the images of the band, with everyone pitching in to assemble the final sellable product.
Courtesy Debbi Peterson Personal Collection

Backstage at the Whisky a Go Go, Los Angeles
"That dress was a thrift store find," Susanna remembers.
Courtesy Susanna Hoffs Personal Collection

"I think this was 1983," Debbi laughs. "It was Halloween; my costume was Goldie Hawn from *Laugh-In*, the old '60's TV show."
Courtesy Vicki Peterson Personal Collection

Vicki and Susanna at the Anti Club
Courtesy Susanna Hoffs Personal Collection

Annette playing the Brian Jones Teardrop Vox bass that Susanna helped her purchase, 1983
Courtesy Annette Zilinskas Personal Collection

Oh so '80s...on the set of the "Hero Takes a Fall" video shoot, where a stylist dressed the band
Courtesy Debbi Peterson Personal Collection

Michael Steele, "Hero Takes a Fall" video shoot in San Francisco, California, 1984
Courtesy Debbi Peterson Personal Collection

Susanna at Les Bains Douches, Paris, France, 1985
Courtesy Susanna Hoffs Personal Collection

Susanna in New York at the Ritz, December 31, 1984
Courtesy Barry Koopersmith

Bangles Polaroid test photo, 1986
Courtesy Vicki Peterson Personal Collection

On the set of the "Walk Like an Egyptian" video shoot
Courtesy Vicki Peterson Personal Collection

"It would get so hot onstage that one time I came off and noticed steam rising from me," Debbi laughs.
Courtesy Debbi Peterson Personal Collection

The girls receive a regal welcome at the Sony offices in Tokyo
Courtesy Vicki Peterson Personal Collection

Vicki strikes a pose in Japan, 1986
Courtesy Debbi Peterson Personal Collection

Debbi: "It was so cold and windy up there on Salisbury Plain, but it was so amazing to see the majestic stones up and close like that."
Courtesy Debbi Peterson Personal Collection

Backstage after winning the BRIT Award for Best International Group, 1987
"My dress was silver," says Vicki. "I looked like a baked potato."
Courtesy Vicki Peterson Personal Collection

Different Light Double Platinum Party; same day as Bangles Day in Los Angeles, February 23, 1987
Courtesy Susanna Hoffs Personal Collection

Happier times: Debbi Christmas shopping in Germany, 1988
Courtesy Debbi Peterson Personal Collection

Real signs of success, according to Vicki Peterson: "We used to joke that you had 'made it' once you had your own washer and dryer in your own apartment. That was pretty much it."
Courtesy Vicki Peterson Personal Collection

Tour bus 1989: "Part of it was just exhaustion because we worked, and were worked, very hard," Michael Steele says. "I remember . . . thinking, 'I'm hating playing music.' That was when I knew the end was near."
Courtesy Vicki Peterson Personal Collection

stories about you," Susanna says. "I get a kick out of it. I think it's funny when I see a picture of me with Michael J. Fox who I met for precisely two seconds and in the two seconds I met him somebody took a picture and it's like suddenly we're not exactly engaged, but we are very good friends."[52*] For Susanna, there was never a question of whether to jeopardize what she saw as her integrity as an artist and as a partner in her current romantic relationship for the possibility of professional gain. "Being true to myself and my boyfriend [at the time] was important," she tells me. "It was a professional relationship [with Prince]. I wasn't like, 'Here's my ticket to fame.'"[53]

Kotero believes that Prince was captivated by Susanna, because of her appearance, but equally for her ability to wield a guitar. "He was probably sexually attracted to her, of course, who wasn't?" Kotero laughs. "I'm sure he was intrigued by her talent. He saw that she was holding the guitar, singing, and cute. He probably even got competitive with her because he was very competitive with all of us, even with me as an actor. Even playing basketball, he was trying to kick my ass."[54] She goes on to describe a very different private man than the Prince most familiar with the music-buying public. "The person that I know and from what I've learned throughout the years is Prince is very sexual, and yes has very explicit lyrics. But in person, he's very shy. Knowing the women that he's dated, he wasn't very sexual that they've admitted to. I was always, like, 'Really?' I think he did really like and respect Susanna."[55]

Bobby "Z" Rifkin agrees that Prince genuinely admired Susanna. "He obviously saw something in her," Rifkin says. "She became whatever their personal relationship became. We know that he transformed her…the eye movements, the makeup, the hair, the earrings: she was Princified. It's not negative. I think it made her a huge star." Rifkin notes that Prince "knew how to make people huge stars…how to make people characters." He points to the "Hero Takes a Fall" video, a pre-Prince effort, where the band was dressed by label-designated personnel.

---

* In 2023, press around the globe ran with a story shouting that "Michael J. Fox didn't remember dating Susanna Hoffs."

"They're a little green around the edges," Rifkin notes of the band. He then contrasts later music videos after the group had become part of Prince's orbit—and had taken control of their appearance and wardrobe. "She's [Susanna] a totally transformed, confident star. He gave people confidence. The power he had to anoint these girls was pretty huge." The Bangles, he says, "benefited greatly from the song."[56]

The shift in the Bangles imagery, Vicki and Susanna both argue, had everything to do with their own evolving sense of style and personal presentation, and nothing to do with Prince. "If we were part of his stable, we'd still be wearing the lacy socks and tons of jewelry," Vicki says. "I think this comment adds to the narrative that we did not control any aspect of our presentation or artistry, which is just not true."[57] Susanna concurs, noting that until hearing "When Doves Cry," she had "never come across [Prince's] music before." "I was so ensconced in studying '60s and '70s records that I just hadn't been doing due diligence on staying up on new music," she confides. Prince being "such a fan of 'Hero Takes a Fall'" was incredibly meaningful to Susanna as "it was a song Vicki and I had written together in the early days of the Bangles."

Regardless of press speculation, neither Susanna nor any of the other band members spent any significant time with Prince. She underlines how she "had an incredible amount of admiration for him" and "was blown away by his talents." Yet there was never a moment, she clarifies, when she or any of the other Bangles were "swept away to some location" and "given clothes that matched his clothes." Indeed, though hugely visible on TV around the world, all of the Bangles confide that they had "very little help in the fashion department...and it showed," let alone being turned into velvet-and-ruffle-bedecked Prince facsimiles.

Regardless of what actual interactions may have taken place between Prince and the Bangles, interviewers shifted away from the Go-Go's diatribe to obsessively grilling the girls about Prince. It seemed to have been deemed impossible by the media that intimate reciprocation had not been an integral part of the exchange between the Purple One and the group, an unspoken accusation that once again belittled and demeaned the foursome as legitimate artists in their own right. "It was torturous having to do all that press at the time," recalls Debbi. "It was those kind of questions like, 'Who slept with Prince?'* Nobody is talking about the music; they're talking about something they heard, or something sexual. It just really frustrated me because we're more than just four girls getting all dolled up for an album cover or whatever. We're musicians, we're songwriters and singers."[58]

The label was trying, Vicki says, to figure out how to position the band, "how to sell it, how to package it and what's the most efficient way to get it done." The "famous Prince connection," with all the titillating though fictional incidents, provided an obvious story and hook. "This is where being in an 'all-girl' band could be quite an asset as well as a curse because now being marketed as a 'hot thing' was probably a part of the process and if maybe one or two of the members fit this ridiculous criteria, they would be put out front in photos, interviews, wherever possible," says Henry Rollins. "Meanwhile the rest of the band is being treated as the help. I think this led to unnecessary tension in an otherwise hardworking group of musicians. In a way, an all-female band had to be so much tougher than an all-male band because even at the label they've been signed to, they're being treated like a 'bandette.' Even when the Bangles were having success they had to deal with pesky journalists. I saw them being interviewed about 'Manic Monday' and the host asked, 'Okay, did any one of you sleep with Prince?' Really? I felt bad for them. That's not right. By asking that, the band is 'kept in their place' and their work and ambition is relegated to girly time. If you put a guy from a band in that same position, he might have decked you. If one of the Bangles decked you, she'd be called a bitch or a dyke."[59]

---

* Such as Joan Rivers on her talk show. Joe Johnson. (2012). "The Bangles on 'Late Night' with Joan Rivers." {November 21, 1986} December 13. Available at https://www.youtube.com/watch?v=Tst4WFxi1lY. Accessed March 28, 2023.

18.

Pressure was on the band to begin recording the follow-up to *All Over the Place*, and to do it quickly. A lack of what the record label perceived as immediate potential "hit" singles also caused concern among Columbia executives and management alike. "They might not like this," admits Mike Gormley, "but one of the reasons Miles and I signed them was the singing and that they did have some good songs—which were used on the first album. They didn't have the tracks for the next album." The grueling, relentless schedule demanded of them to make their first LP a success didn't leave them time to create new material. The band got to work and delivered six possible songs for the still-untitled sophomore effort; but according to Gormley, "they weren't knockouts."[1]

Faith that the women could write their own music seemed to have vanished; that the Bangles-penned "Hero" had been a breakthrough track was a long forgotten fact in the quest to move on to bigger success. Chris Lamson describes there being a "pervasive dismissive attitude that everybody [especially at the record label] had about them." He remembers, "They always had to battle people saying, 'they can't play their instruments, they can't write songs. They can't do this. They can't do that.' Well, they did it all, under arduous conditions. They did it all." Lamson notes, "It was tough for them. There was no support. You were just a second-class citizen when it came to being a [female] musician and being in the arts in general."[2]

In addition, David Kahne was still contractually part of the record deal, giving the Bangles no choice but to once again pair up with the producer. "Somehow, I talked them into going back into the studio with David," says Gormley.[3] "It ended up being a great record but I think they suffered for it. I felt bad for what went on in the studio," he confides, though notes, "I don't know any of the details, I just believe them that it was rough." Regardless of past problems that the band may have communicated to management, Gormley believed that Kahne "was the right guy" for the second album. "I felt we needed David Kahne and so did Columbia Records and we convinced them," Gormley remembers.[4]

The band was not pleased, their rocky experiences in the studio while making the previous album not forgotten. "After we'd done *All Over the Place*, I did not want to work with David Kahne ever again, even though he was part of the Columbia deal. The label told me I had to, otherwise I wouldn't have a hit record," Debbi says. "Honestly, I became suicidal. I don't think Vicki was too happy with it either."[5]

Neither mental health nor personal feelings mattered to those outside of the band. "The God of irony was laughing down upon us," Michael says. "You know you're going to have a huge record but it's going to be the record that you feel the most estranged from as an artist."[6] A sense of horror mixed with stoicism descended upon the group once they realized they did not have a choice but to reunite with the producer. "It was just, 'You are going to work with him again,'" Debbi recalls of conversations. "It was, 'This is your sophomore record, this is a big push, you're gonna have a number one song, this is the big deal. If you guys really are serious about this, you got to work with this guy again. He's really good.' However, I didn't want to work with him."[7] Vicki recounts an incredibly uncomfortable meal between producer and band, meant to assuage any doubts about future collaborations. "Most likely because he was encouraged to, Kahne flew to New Orleans to join us on the road and try and smooth over what he knew to be serious reservations about working with him again," she says. "It was an awkward dinner, but I remember him acknowledging his authoritarian approach and [he] seemed the slightest bit contrite about it."[8]

Kahne's own unhappiness did not help the situation. Recently transplanted from the San Francisco Bay Area, he was in the midst of a painful marriage breakdown. He later recalled that one of his "strongest memories" of the time pertained not to his work, but to the woes he was facing outside the studio. "I was going through a horrible divorce, so I was constantly distracted and depressed," he admits. "My life was completely screwed up."[9]

Conflicting feelings soon began to emerge between band, management, and label. It quickly became clear that there was a chasm between what the band envisioned for their new LP and what Kahne saw as an appropriate follow-up to *All Over the Place*. "I don't think he was the right choice for them on an inspirational basis," remembers Lamson. "It didn't foster an atmosphere of creativity. He was sort of a dictator at the time." Making what would become *Different Light* "was probably the darkest time in Bangle history," he says. "They had all their ingenuity and confidence stolen from them," he remembers. "They were told that they were not playing their instruments anymore and what songs that they were going to do." Regardless of the limits trying to be enforced onto them, Vicki notes that the band soldiered on. "I'm not sure what I was doing for all those hours in the studio plugged in, if I wasn't playing on an album," she says. Yet it was still very hard for Lamson, who was "so close with the girls and so supportive of them," to see this campaign to make them renounce their convictions as a band. Though attending studio sessions at the beginning of recording, Lamson "stopped going," he says. "In the early days, I would go just to hang out," he recalls. "Then I was like, 'I can't go over.' There were tears."[10]

Bobby Rifkin describes the traditional role of music producer as "all-powerful." "The interactions I have had with producers," he reflects, "they're definitely the control freak guy, who are responsible to the record company so there's tremendous pressure."[11] Peter Philbin held such a belief in Kahne, arguing that he "was the man" for the follow-up record. "We get to the second album and they'd been on the road for the first album," Philbin explains. "The benefit of the first album is when you sign a band, they already have an album worth of songs. They didn't have the songs for the second album and they needed more songs, which is not uncommon. They've been on the road and they've been focusing on something else [touring, thus not provided the time and headspace to write]."[12] The hunt quickly began to find more tracks to propagate the LP.

The Prince song was the first one to come into play. Debbi remembers the band feeling happy but anxious about the inclusion of "Manic Monday" on the record. "I think it was like, 'Yeah, the song is great and great for us,'" she says. However, no matter how big a boost it was to garner Prince's attention and accolades, the fear of being overshadowed by their internationally revered patron dogged the band. "We didn't want any attention taken away from the other songs on the record. We didn't want to be seen as not writing our own songs [since we were using the Prince cut]. I felt like ['Manic Monday'] took attention away from the band's material."[13]

Though the Bangles were writing for the album, Debbi remembers feeling "that Sony was pushing songwriters on us."[14] While the group had previously included covers in their live sets, the feeling was different as they prepared to embark on recording. Selecting carefully curated covers that worked with the band's aesthetic and tone was completely different than having external writers pushed upon them by "the men in suits." "From the beginning, we just liked to record other people's songs," explains Debbi, "but cool underground songs you've never heard before, or are not that familiar with and make it our own, which we kind of did from day one, really."[15] Manager Chris Lamson shares similar recollections. "I remember getting songs for the record," he says. "The label was not convinced that the Bangles could do anything, to be quite honest with you. They didn't welcome the band's song writing. That's why they went out and got all those horrible songs that were big hits. They treated them like a commodity and not musicians, in my opinion. It made me mad all the time, every damn day."[16]

Getting the Prince track felt like an opportunity that had to be taken, regardless of possible deviation from former Bangles work. "We just felt like having a Prince song was like, 'Oh, the big single, "Manic Monday,"'" Debbi says. With the inclusion of more outsiders into the formerly tight Bangles circle, band dynamics shifted further. "Suddenly, I felt like we were losing the band," says Debbi. "We were losing that camaraderie, that 'all for one and one for all.' I was worried that things were going to start going in a different direction."[17]

Debbi remembers Susanna coming into the recording studio with the cassette containing the two tracks, "Manic Monday" and "Jealous Girl." "I don't remember why we didn't do the other one," Debbi says. "At that time, the record company was [pushing it on us]. The whole Prince thing was a big deal for the Bangles. I feel like it bit us in the ass because that's the one we got known for, not our songs unlike the Go-Go's, who got known for their tracks. We were trying to be open, telling everyone, 'Oh, sure. A great song is a great song. It doesn't matter if we wrote it, it doesn't matter if Joe Schmo wrote it.'"[18] However, the label did not seem to understand the chasm between the previous carefully considered cover efforts the band included in their repertoire and wholesale having a completely new song written by someone else thrust upon them.

Prince did not officially take ownership of the "Manic" writing credit, listing the track as penned under the nom de plume "Christopher," the name of his character in the 1986 film *Under the Cherry Moon*. Susanna remembers Prince being "a little surprised" that the group wanted to "add their special touch to the track." She confides, "That's one thing that we Bangles decided en masse, and were very unified in this, that we wanted to kind of make it ours—Bangle-fy it, in a sense," she says.[19]

Peter Philbin describes the pressure placed on Kahne to take "Manic" from a rough demo to a Prince-approved hit. "Prince basically sent him the multitracks and wanted the girls to just sing over his version," Philbin laughs. "David went, 'Fuck this' and rerecorded it. That's David Kahne."[20] The brave call to personalize and rerecord the track to become a Bangles belter was actually the band's decision, all three women tell

18.

me, not that of the producer. Yet it is Kahne, not the Bangles, whom kudos are showered upon for the "Banglefied" *Different Light* cut. "He might have had the intention that we would just add our voices to his instrumentation, but that was never really the Bangles' thing," Susanna says. "We wanted to build the track from the ground up. We weren't just adding our voices. So for us, it was very intentional that Debbi would play drums on it, Michael would play bass, I'd play rhythm guitar, and Vicki would play lead guitar. If we wanted to add any bells and whistles with a keyboard or who knows what, we would also throw those on. We always recorded our own tracks in the way we wanted."[21]

Unbeknownst to the band, the cut was not a blank canvas: the producer and group couldn't unabashedly unleash their own touches. This made the choice to bring their own flavor to the single an even bolder move. "Prince had to actually approve every note that was on that song. I don't think he had previously given a song like that to anybody that he wasn't working with," recalled Peggy McCreary, who engineered both the original session with Prince and the one with the Bangles. "I had no idea about this!" Susanna tells me when she hears about the note-for-note approval.

Bobby Rifkin underscores the importance of the song and the alignment with Prince for the band, no matter what the price. "Look, without that song, they wouldn't be who they are," he says of the Bangles. The band, he argues, were not necessarily understanding of the duress Kahne was under from label and the Minneapolis superstar. "[The Bangles] just needed to be musicians and do this for Prince. Ninety percent of the pressure he was putting on at that moment was to take a Prince song and turn it into a record from a demo. That was dangerous to do because [Prince] didn't like anything. The fact that it became something that Prince approved of is a huge accomplishment for David, and the band benefited from that." Rifkin speaks from experience, having suffered the wrath of Prince himself. "Prince was a guy that you wanted to make happy because you knew he knew his musical shit. The hours and the abuse…there's an old expression that the 'pain is temporary, the tape is permanent.'"[22]

Kahne rewarded himself with not just a producer credit, but a keyboard one as well for his contribution to the finished track. The band penned a special word of thanks to "P.R.N."—initials that could just possibly stand for Prince Rogers Nelson—on the final LP, after the man himself had unexpectedly dropped in on a tour rehearsal featuring their arrangement of his song. Prince "really loved" the final version that featured an alternative bridge and a change of chords from his rendition.[23] "He admired the fact that we just did it our own way and changed it," Susanna noted.[24]

"I remember being really apologetic like, 'Well, we don't have the keyboards' and he goes 'You don't need the keyboards.' And then he goes, 'It's gonna go.' And then he walked out," Vicki laughs. "We're like, 'What does that mean[,] It's gonna go?' What did he mean? Who says these words and then leaves?"[25] Susanna laughs, noting, "Prince does."

There were severe time constraints placed upon getting the new album done as quickly as possible, which did not help foster an inspired atmosphere for creativity. Peter Philbin argues that the band was "not generating ten to twelve songs" that could be used for the album, thus was the need for other radio-friendly singles besides "Monday." Perceiving what he sees as the Bangles "not writing all that fast and songs…coming slowly," Philbin "came up with an idea." "I suggested, 'Why don't you guys write with Jules Shear because he's a prolific songwriter,'" Philbin recalls. "I played them a song, 'If She Knew What She Wants.'"[26]

Mike Gormley says he is the one who initially brought the Jules Shear track to the Bangles as a contender for *Different Light*. Either way, the band already knew Shear, having worked with him cowriting the *Goonies* soundtrack song "I Got Nothing." They had also helped him promote his second full-length album, *The Eternal Return*, appearing as his backup band when Shear lip-synced the Cyndi Lauper cowritten single "Steady" on *American Bandstand*. "If She Knew" had been earmarked as the second single from *Return*; but a lack of interest from commercial radio had put the kibosh on label EMI's promotional efforts and a possible tour for Shear. Seeing a chance at a second life for the track with his group, Gormley got a copy of it from Jules's manager to present to the band. "I played it for them in my car," Gormley recalls, "all four of them were in there." While Gormley admits that "they insist Jules gave them the song," the origin of the track getting into the hands of the group is a "small point" that Gormley "never argued."[27]

According to Michael, like Prince, Shear was equally delighted with the Bangles' take on his track, telling *Creem* magazine, "He's even said—and I don't know if we should say this, but it has been quoted elsewhere—of all the people who have done his songs, he likes ours best. And then he went, 'Oh, no, Cyndi's gonna kill me!!'"[28*]

Kahne brought another track to the studio for consideration, Philbin recounts. "David finds the song on a demo that he thinks is great called 'Walk Like an Egyptian.' I'm listening to the demo and it's a funky novelty song I could care less about. David thinks it's great."[29] It was not the Nile, but the English Channel that had inspired the song's inception when Akron, Ohio, native Liam Sternberg encountered choppy currents during a trip across the waters. Watching fellow passengers attempt to awkwardly maintain their balance on the boat's tipping deck, he jotted down the title "Walk Like an Egyptian." Back home in the US, Sternberg penned the lyrics to the tune, originally with singer-choreographer Toni Basil in mind. Basil had scored an international hit single with cheerleader track "Mickey" in 1982, making her a prime target for the emerging songwriter.

---

* Cyndi Lauper included her rendition of the Shear track "All Through the Night" on her 1983 solo debut *She's So Unusual*. It went to number five on the *Billboard* Hot 100.

Keen to get a demo done for Basil to hear, Sternberg drafted in Marti Jones to lay down the vocals on his creation. Jones had performed with her sisters in a folk group and was excited to work with Sternberg, who she later described as "hot shit at the time." Upon presenting the lyrics to Jones for an initial run-through, Jones recalls Sternberg admitting that it was "a total bullshit song, but it's the kind of thing that could work for somebody like her [Basil]."[30] Recorded in one afternoon, Jones found the single "[one of] the dumbest things I'd ever heard in my life." When Basil declined to move forward with the four-track demo, Sternberg got the tape into the hands of Kahne. The cassette had been mislabeled, initially putting Kahne off the track. "The cassette said, 'Rock & Roll Nightmare,'" he recalls. "And I go, 'Huh, well I don't like that title.' But anyway, I listened to it, and I hear [sings main riff] 'Doot-doot-doo-doo.' So I called the publisher and I told her there was this song about an Egyptian on it and she said, 'Oh, they put the wrong song on there. I'll send you it over.' I go, 'No no, I like this one.' That weird, non-linear stuff happens so often doing A&R and the trick is to know if this is the good mistake."[31]

Jones's delivery and the earworm quality of the song made Kahne think it could be a hit. "I wanted to get another single because we had 'Manic Monday' and I didn't feel like there was a strong enough follow-up. There was a song called 'If She Knew What She Wants,' which I love. But I didn't feel if 'Manic Monday' worked that it was the best thing to come right after."[32]

In interviews, the band diplomatically seemed to match Kahne's enthusiasm for the quirky track. Susanna later said her first introduction with the cut took place in Kahne's office. "I was up at Columbia on the A&R floor, talking to David Kahne about songs, and he said, 'God, I've got this crazy song. It's really cool—I don't know what you'll think of it, but…' So now I'm curious. I say, 'Okay, play it for me.' He played me a demo of Marti Jones singing 'Walk Like an Egyptian'.…I was immediately struck by how cool it was.…I loved her cool delivery and the song somehow reminded me of 1960s bossa nova, which I love."[33]

Vicki also connected with Jones's unique singing style, saying, "She's one of those great American voices that just strikes me when I hear her singing anything."[34] On the demo in particular, Vicki recalls, "she had this perfectly droll delivery" that "made it so charming." The group was convinced to ultimately include it on the album, though it was far away from anything the Bangles had recorded or been inspired by previously. "'Walk Like an Egyptian' is a song we never would have written," Vicki says. "But we didn't *not* want to do it. That song came in towards the end of preproduction for that record. Somebody in some office somewhere, or in David Kahne's mind thought, 'Okay, we need something a little different on this record' and that demo came through. He brought it to us. I remember thinking, 'Oh my god, this is the weirdest song I've ever heard.' But because it was so weird, I kind of liked it."[35]

Regardless of any possible misgivings, the band went ahead and recorded the song "on a lark" at the Sound Factory, the rationale, Susanna recalls, being "let's throw it out there and see if anybody likes it." And "when we listened back to it," she says, "it was so bizarrely catchy." Upon playing an early copy for friends, Susanna admits that she was "amazed that so many people were struck by the song. I guess I had gotten familiar with it and had gotten past that first response where it struck me as very quirky but very original, but I never, ever thought it would be a single."[36]

Yet behind closed doors and within the inner circle of the Bangles, feelings were a sharp contrast. "I remember we were in the van talking about 'Walk Like an Egyptian,'" says Lamson. "I was just like, 'We cannot do that song. That song is a total sellout, it doesn't sound like you at all.' David Kahne and the label just super-pushed it and said, 'You're doing it.'" The breakthrough of *All Over the Place*, Lamson explains, made the label think there was a possibility for greater success on further efforts by the band—no matter the cost. Even though sales numbers and show tickets proved there was a solid audience for songs written and performed by the women playing their own instruments, an overwhelming belittling cloud of misogyny hung over the band. "The label was like,

'Well, we got a little nugget here. Let's polish it up ourselves, because they don't know what they're doing, they're girls.' Honestly, that's how it was," Lamson remarks.[37]

As the album began coming together, the girls started feeling that they had lost control over what songs were going to be picked as singles. This was crucial, Debbi points out, as the harmonies and cowriting that were a signature feature of the group were missing on all of the tracks that the record executives had earmarked for promotional purposes. "I wish 'Let It Go' had been a single," she says. "The four of us wrote it and the four of us sang on it. To me, that embodies what the Bangles are. It's very much a group effort. I was very upset at the time. I remember thinking, 'Why aren't there more songs like this? Why is this not getting attention?' Why is it all about 'Manic Monday'? [and the covers]. It was frustrating because I could feel things splintering within the group; Vicki did too."[38]

Vicki, especially, had ideas for how she wanted the album to sound—and they did not match what Kahne was putting together. One element that Kahne introduced was the generous use of keyboards throughout the LP. "I was their first keyboard player," says Walker Igleheart. Igleheart performed with the band for the tour supporting *Different Light*. "I don't think Vicki ever really wanted a keyboard player," he admits. "She really wanted to be just a four-piece rock and roll band. But David Kahne, the producer, forced a bunch of keyboards on their album, so they kind of had to have a keyboard player to reproduce the album live."[39] Kahne, Igleheart says, "left Vicki, especially, just completely demoralized."

Now with three possible label-approved singles, the process of setting the songs to tape could officially begin. The Sound Factory in Los Angeles was picked as the studio of choice, a well-reputed facility legendary for having birthed classic '60s and '70s albums by the Jackson 5, Brian Wilson, and Linda Ronstadt. Much to the dismay of the band, Kahne once again began bringing in session musicians to use on the album, believing that "his" artists could fulfill his vision better and more quickly than the actual band who was making the album. Gormley and Philbin

18.

argue this practice was normal, both pointing to other well-known examples of this technique. "It was pretty common then that other musicians came in and played with the band," Gormley explains. "The Beach Boys hardly ever played on any of the records. It was the Wrecking Crew.* The Beatles had Billy Preston† come in. Prior to that, George [Harrison] had brought Eric Clapton in to play on the record, so even the Beatles had outside help at certain points."[40]

For seasoned veterans Gormley and Kahne, the session players may have been an expected part of the production process. For the Bangles, it was only the second time they had been placed in a professional session setting; nothing had been explained to them nor had they been given much input to what would be on the album or what to expect from the second go around in the studio. "A lot of the bands they [the Bangles] thought was a unit in the studio weren't doing that at all," Gormley argues. "They may not have liked the songs, they may not have played what they wanted," he adds, "and I don't know to the extent of other musicians being in a studio with them, but it was their record and they played."[41] Philbin underscores Gormley's take on the regularity of session players being a part of the recording process. "A lot of what he [Kahne] did is he got other players to play [on the record]," he notes. "This is called recording," he asserts. "David brought musicality to the Bangles. You need the musicality; but if you don't have the personality, you don't have anything. David really helped the Bangles. They have various issues with him as well but he was invaluable."[42]

The band, however, had never been briefed or consulted about the possibility of outsiders contributing to the LP. "I think that Vicki thought it was heresy [using session musicians]," says Philbin. "She wanted everything to be played by the Bangles on the record."[43] "Vicki showed up at a recording session, and somebody else was playing her parts on the guitar," Gormley recalls. "I wasn't there, but evidently she

---

* A group of Los Angeles–based session musicians who became famous for working with Phil Spector, the Mamas & the Papas, and many other iconic 1960s artists.
† Keyboardist and songwriter.

went home, threw up, and was very upset about it."[44] Gormley notes, "they saw themselves as a unit. I think Vicki felt pretty stabbed in the back on occasion. It's possible they just should have talked it out before it happened, but that was very difficult."[45]

When asked about the day Gormley describes, Vicki tells me her side of the story. Vicki abruptly had to leave the studio during a session to attend to a medical emergency with her then boyfriend. Upon returning, she found that "an excellent young guitarist, a David Kahne protégé" named Rusty Anderson "happened to step in right at the moment" that Vicki had been called away. "When I came back from the emergency, the solo was done and everyone was loving it," Vicki says. "Kahne looked at me with this disappointment, frustration, and aggravation on his face. He says in a very dispirited voice, 'What do you want? Do you want to try and do something?' I said 'No, I'm good.' Rusty did a great job." Always the optimist, Vicki adds, "I have a fun time on stage, doing my version of it."[46]

With the inclusion of Anderson—and drummer Carlos Vega, a James Taylor band member—Debbi in particular began to feel a disconnect from the album she was putting together. "I just felt like there was so much bullshit going on with the record company. Too many chefs in the kitchen and too many people trying to come and manipulate the sound and the image. It was sad, because I could really see it happening and I was so frustrated. I felt like this is what we had to do to be successful. I don't know if that's because we were all women. If we were all guys, we would have been like, 'Well, fuck you. I'm not gonna do that.' At that time, it was such a male-dominated industry that trying to do anything as a female musician, or even a female band, was very difficult. We had to work our way into doing things even though that meant giving up a few things just to get success. We had a hard time with the whole gender thing, unfortunately. It just lost all meaning to me," she says, "having the [studio] drummer come in was like a double whammy."[47]

Kahne helped himself to songwriting credits on several more tracks, a misstep that Philbin did not contradict in the name of getting the album finished, though it caused more strain within the walls of the studio. "When I heard that David had taken some songwriting credits, I said, 'I don't think that's a good idea. You're the producer here, so you have influence'...and there was tension. [However,] I'm just trying to get their second album done."[48] Copeland claims the Bangles only told him later why they would never work with Kahne again. "They'd be in the studio and he'd say, 'I don't like the middle bit, so you've got to rewrite it,'" he explained. "They'd go home and rewrite, and he wouldn't like that one. He'd say, 'I wrote one, listen to this.' They'd say they liked theirs better and he'd say, 'let's drop the song, then.'" So, of course, to keep the song, they'd do it Kahne's way. In their view, the reason his middle bit was 'better' [was] because he got a piece of the publishing," Copeland said. "And they were incredibly pissed off about that. They felt that they got raped—that was their word." On *Different Light*, Kahne was credited as a cowriter on the tracks "Walking Down Your Street," "Standing in the Hallway," and "Not Like You." "He wanted to make a hit record and fuck them! That was his view," Copeland said. "And if he wrote a bit of the song, he was going to have his piece of the publishing, fuck them."[49]

Any sort of protest from the band was seen as a lack of dedication and a threat toward further success. "I felt like, 'If I don't go along with this, the song won't end up on the record,'" Debbi recounts. "Now I wish I had stuck to my guns and said, 'Look, I don't want you involved.' But at the time, it was like, 'God, this is your big shot. This is your last chance to really be successful. We have to give up a few things in order to make sure it happens.'"[50]

Though session musicians were considered de rigueur for many established and respected bands, the Bangles had something to prove because of their gender, argues former band member Amanda Hills Podany. "The girls [Bangles] would be determined to play their own instruments," she says. "When David Kahne said, 'We'll bring someone in,' Vicki and Sue were like, 'No, we will play this because we do not want people saying that we can't play.' They're honest enough to put thanks to their session musicians on their albums. I remember when *Different Light* came out, people thought that the presence of the session musicians proved that they really could not play themselves. But they were still playing all the instruments. It was funny because you'd read reviews of live shows and it would say 'They can play.' They had to work harder. They had to prove to everybody that they weren't the dog playing the violin, that they were musicians."[51]

Years later, the band would describe the experience of making *Different Light* as being "tortured by David Kahne."[52] "It was just a really consistent feeling of 'you're not good enough so we're going have to make this work somehow,'" Vicki describes.[53] "We would go in—all four of us in a room—and lay down the song. Then with the guidance of Kahne, we would systematically replace everything we had just done. Every guitar line was replaced with various [cheesy riffs]. It would be like 'Why did we spend a day and a half getting a snare sound and a kick down, and then go in and track for a day and a half to go back and replace everything?'"[54]

Tensions came to a head when recording for "Walk Like an Egyptian" began, with Debbi originally slated to sing the lead. "Ironically, it's our signature song," she says. "It's the song everybody always talks about. Unfortunately, it has a lot of bad memories for me."[55] Instead of Debbi stepping up to the front for vocal duties as originally planned by the band, Kahne asked each girl to individually sing the different parts of the track. "They all wanted to sing and be lead singers," Kahne says. "They used to share."[56]

The clash between band and producer styles of approaching vocal duties became acute. "The nasty part of that was when we were forced to audition for verses," Vicki recalls. "He had us one by one go out to the mic and sing a selected verse."[57] It was, she describes, "a sing-off...with Kahne as head judge. Don't know that I'd ever do it that way again."[58]

There was just one manner in which to do the song, and that was to fulfill Kahne's wishes, according to Michael. "David had one of those minds where he could only see it one way: his way," she says.[59] Debbi admits that she "didn't want [the song] to be successful," as she had "lost the audition," in that she saw Kahne remove her as a voice entirely from the track. To make matters worse, Kahne then utilized a drum machine, though Debbi had programmed it for him. "She played drums over it," Kahne said of Debbi's work with the preprogrammed beats. "I might have fixed them a little bit when she wasn't there [laughs]."[60] For Debbi, there was nothing funny about the situation; she felt completely bereaved of her place on the song and in the band. "I didn't sing on it. I'm not playing on it and I didn't write it," she says. "I felt so distant from that song so I didn't really care if it went to number one. I always was just shaking the tambourine and my ass trying to make do with the fact I wasn't part of the song. It was frustrating."[61]

Even Miles Copeland acknowledged the impact the track had on the youngest member of the band. "That song, as great as I thought it was, had the same effect on Debbi Peterson that 'Every Breath You Take' had on my brother Stewart: there was hardly any drum part, which meant Debbi didn't even play on the song," he notes.[62] As the Police's gargantuan hit showed, sometimes conflict results in an outstanding classic, Kahne later argued. "There was always some tension," David Kahne says today. "But that's not uncommon when producing a band. There's usually tension between the band members and there was in the Bangles.... I always wondered if I hadn't been at the label if they would've decided to get rid of me."[63]

Drum machines became a commonality on *Light*, highlighted in "Walking Down Your Street," a song Susanna wrote with then beau Louis Gutierrez that went on to be the fourth single from *Light*. The recording "was enhanced by a drum machine," Debbi says. "I didn't like that," she remarks, "it just sounded so stiff and computer-like. I don't want to be replaced. I'm a human being and I want to be recorded as such. I felt like we were not a band anymore. We're becoming just a personality or visual thing and not necessarily a group doing our own music. I was worried about that happening."[64]

Not being able to sing or play drums on a key track had a profound impact on Debbi, says family friend Toni Kasza. "I think it's born from being the young one in the band, but also her insecurity," Toni remarks. "What's her worth if she's not doing backup harmonies? What's her worth if she's the drummer and David Kahne took her drums away on the biggest song they had?"[65] Not being allowed to actively participate also made Debbi further question her place in the group and the direction they were going in. "In my mind, we were supposed to be a band," she explains. "It was supposed to be as equal as possible. I always had the vision of the Beatles in my head."[66]

The Bangles' fan club president Marji recalls an afternoon when Debbi shared her mounting frustrations about the Kahne process when she went to the studio to give the girls some of their mail. "Debbi comes out and we sit at a patio table," Marji remembers. "Debbi unloads on me all the things that he's been doing, telling her she couldn't sing, and all this other horrible stuff. I was floored. I just couldn't believe it."[67]

When asked what the main complaint was about the producer, Marji surmises, "His negativity. He was not in a good place. I thought immediately he was a misogynist. I thought he just didn't get the girls; he didn't understand them. I thought he was unprofessional. The girls had worked so hard to get where they were and to be taken seriously as women. He was destroying them."[68]

Debbi's self-worth was shattered by Kahne's critiques. "I had a hard time coming back after making that record," she says. "My confidence was very small. I didn't feel like I was a good drummer anymore. As far as the singing, David Kahne said quite a few things about my voice [that were not very nice]."[69]

At one point, Debbi believed she was at risk of being fired from the group entirely. "I swear to God, I thought I was going to be kicked out of the band. I thought I was going to get the boot," Debbi tells me. "It might not have been the case, but it certainly felt that way. I was getting that vibe from the other band members. That's why I agreed to things and compromised on stuff that I probably shouldn't have."[70] Kahne, Debbi now believes, "used me as a target. The other girls, I felt, were siding with him and questioning me."

18.

The girl-gang unity had fallen apart, at least for Debbi, leaving her feeling isolated and alone. "I was just trying to find somebody who would support and listen to me instead of all this manipulative bullshit that was going on with that producer," Debbi remembers. "It was hard," she confides. "I did not have an ally during the *Different Light* time period. I had nobody behind me. David Kahne was just pecking at me like a bird. It was so frustrating." The more dismissed Debbi felt, the more she was "probably being a pain in the ass," she admits. "I was so insecure," she says. "I know I could do so much better but he just kept pecking away at any confidence I had. It was really sad. It felt like every woman for themselves," Debbi remembers. "There wasn't a lot of support, especially from Sue and Micki. They were like, 'I don't see why you're having such a problem with it. He's fine with me.'"

Debbi found herself continuing to clash with Kahne, as her idea of how the band should be did not match up with his. "There were a couple of drum parts I couldn't play so he would get somebody else in. But I thought, 'Why can't we work the song to a drum part that I *can* play? Why does it have to be black and white? Why can't we just work it out and make it a band effort?' I'll do some kind of drum part that would work for the song in the way I do it instead of having to play a fucking jazz part or something. Somebody else ended up recording the drum part but it didn't sound like the Bangles. It doesn't feel like the band that I had in my head."[71]

Debbi, according to brother Dave, "bore the brunt of a lot of the nonsense" that happened in the studio to a detrimental effect, even though, he argues, she is "easily the most natural singer in our family." He confides, "I don't feel she's had an incredible amount of self-confidence, like me." The Kahne critiques only aided to crumble what little self-worth was there. "He said I physically couldn't sing one of the songs," Debbi recounts. "Physically couldn't sing. It was one of those things where you might as well just stab me right now, just kill me. Cut my throat. Cut out my vocal cords. It was so devastating. It was hard for me to bounce back from that."[72] Even previously unthinkable achievements were becoming meaningless. "It was like, 'You've got to feel so great because you're on TV all the time,' Debbi exclaims. "I didn't even think about how great it was. I thought, 'Oh I've gotta do an interview today' or about losing weight to make a video. It's kind of sad because you're in this moment where you're really successful and you've been working towards this level. Then when it comes, you think about the next thing that you have to do and you don't get to enjoy it."[73]

Debbi even began to think about taking her own life. "It was that bad," she says. "I was thinking of ways of actually doing it. I knew I couldn't. I wouldn't because I'm a chicken; but I really felt like I just don't need to be here anymore. But I was psychologically damaged by that guy. I really was. I don't know why he went for me. He went for Vicki, too. It wasn't just me. Me and Vicki were, for some reason, not worth it and not worthy."[74]

Having her sister in the band added another dimension to the group, occasionally resulting in unintended stress. "Sometimes, Vicki puts on a little protective air," Debbi says. "Maybe it's a sibling superiority thing. She will say, 'Oh, no, Debbi. It's not like that at all. No, it's not like that.' She sometimes would say things to diplomatically work things out with me, instead of saying, 'Oh, fuck David Kahne! He's an asshole' which she did later. She'd always try to make it all work within the band. She was always more confident and better looking, more of a social person. She was always a fixer. I think that's just the way she is. I respect that."[75]

For Vicki, regardless of what was going on, "I felt like we always had each other's backs; but on top of that, and I'm just going to be honest about this, I think I was neglectful of Debbi and her feelings," she admits. "I did the classic older sister thing, which was to sometimes dismiss her, which I later came to see completely differently and really see what a value she is and how incredibly talented she is. I always thought she was talented but I took it for granted. I took *her* for granted. Everything came so easy for her. Musically, I thought she was just a natural. I know she struggled against what I perceived to be her problems with me, because I think she always felt like she was my little sister and she expressed that many times. I was like 'What do you want me to do about that? I can't make you feel differently.' I certainly didn't consider her *just* my little sister, but I didn't give her the props I should have."[76] Keyboard player Walker Igleheart recalled not seeing "a whole lot of interaction between the two sisters during" the tours. But then he admits, "I didn't see a whole lot of interaction between any of them." The Petersons, for the most part that he could make out, "seemed to have a good relationship."[77]

Sibling disparity and a difference of personality played a role, even if not openly acknowledged, within the group, says long-time band associate Gracie. "I think Vicki thought that Debbi was dependent on her a lot," she notes. "Debbi would have preferred to have been up in front singing and playing bass like Paul McCartney, who she loved. She gave that up to play the drums just so she could join Vicki's band. She didn't even want to be a drummer. She just learned to do it, to join the band, so there was always that sort of dependence factor to some degree. I don't think that ever really changed. I think that was just kind of always there."

The elder Peterson may have outwardly put on a cheery face but was dealing with her own personal issues as a result of Kahne. "My will had pretty much been broken successfully by that point. It was really awful," she admits. Susanna adds, "I remember thinking 'Boy, being a producer is a hard job.' I think he made it seem really hard because he was so driven by angst, and kind of perfectionistic. He had been an artist himself and never succeeded as an artist, so I think he was always tormented by 'How would I do this if it was my record?'" And "it was," Michael commented, "sort of an aural version of the casting couch where, well, if I don't do all this stuff, these songs won't be hits. He knew there were going to be some big hits on that album. That album made his career... we were sacrificed on the altar of his career."[78]

Different Light was a huge contrast to past Bangles efforts in every way, Dave Peterson explains. "It got just CBS'd out," he tells me. "I used to call it that when bands that we saw in clubs would get signed to Columbia and then make records that sounded nothing like they did live. They would be really slickly produced and the whole excitement of the band would just be glossed over with this weird sound. The rockiness of it goes away when it gets all polished up like that. That's what happened to them. It happened to the sound, it happened to their look, they're wearing tons of makeup. I didn't even recognize them in some pictures."[79] Dave remembers Kahne's feedback to Vicki being less than positive, saying, "He was brutal with her guitar playing and her singing." He recalls Kahne "wanting to spotlight Susanna, which irked everybody because they all had something to contribute."[80]

But it was not just problems with the producer that were hampering the group, according to Gormley. As recording continued, tensions between members became strained even further. "They were at odds with each other at that point," Gormley tells me. "It was emotional. I'd go to the studio and they were recording. They didn't talk to me about it until after the fact and Sue talked to me about it more than anybody."[81] Open communication had broken down between band members, finding them talking to management instead of each other over various concerns. The idea of everyone having equal time in the spotlight was dramatically shifting—and it seemed completely out of the group's control. "Vicki and I were both, like, 'What's going on? This is very different than the initial band that we had started,'" says Debbi. "It caused friction having Susanna become the lead singer and the focal point of the band, because that wasn't our intention at all. We were trying as much as we could to try to stop it but once the ball started rolling, it was hard to stop."[82]

Steve McDonald also recounts the change within the band. "The music industry pitted them against each other," he says. "Music producers favoring Susanna and things like that caused understandable dynamics that are impossible to avoid."[83] Brother Jeff notes this is unfortunately a common occurrence, explaining, "It's a game played by many producers; it's a divide-and-conquer thing. A producer will get involved when it really should just be the band's decision about everything." The young age of the Bangles also may have been a factor in the shifting relationships within the group. "Take any group that is famous in their twenties and not being able to deal with it on any level," Jeff continues. "I think it's way too much. Your identity is still forming, you're having all this uneven attention and you're dealing with the evils of Hollywood. There are all these wolves in sheep's clothing."[84]

For her part, Susanna was equally uneasy. "It was very challenging because I really wasn't sure what to do," she says. "I was always trying to just be my best." Her way forward was to try to find common ground with those around her and build relationships, she tells me. "I forged a friendship with the label people at Columbia and David Kahne," she explains. "He was the person with his fingers on the dials. There was nothing untoward about it; I just tried to get along with everyone in a situation that was rife with this feeling of tension." However, a divide was starting to become obvious within the foursome. "It was almost like Vicki and Debbi on one side and then Micki and I were kind of over here," Susanna describes.[85]

For Susanna, every day was a test. "I was trying to survive and wondering how to figure out how to make this band function as a family, so to speak, and a creative collective," she explains. "It was difficult. In the Bangles, I felt like I was walking on eggshells a large percentage of the time."[86] Vicki echoes this feeling. "We were a divided force at that point," she admits.[87]

In the midst of the Kahne turmoil, Michael was able to get the producer to agree for her to front two tracks: the first, a cover of the Alex Chilton–penned 1974 Big Star classic "September Gurls." "Gurls" marked Michael's first go at singing lead on an album, an accomplishment that, she confided, filled her with both excitement and anxiety. "I'd wanted to do that song for a long time, ever since I first heard it on a tape a friend made of good, old, weird, unusual songs from the '60s and '70s," she told *Creem*. "I've never sung lead on a record before, but I had to do it. I was nervous. I mean, how can you reproduce that record? The sound of the guitar makes the hair stand up on your arms. I just went in, grit my teeth and did it. I'm pleased with how it turned out. It's a tribute to the art of singing without ever opening your mouth."[88] The second Michael-led track was a song written by the bass player herself, titled "Following," which would go on to be the fifth single from *Different Light* in the UK. It was a miracle the tune got on the album, Michael felt, as she believed Kahne might have "ignored" her because she wasn't one of the group's main songwriters or singers. "He loved Sue's voice, and he loved the way we did harmonies, but everything else [he made us feel] was basically shit and he felt like he had to get rid of it, or try to work around it, or do something to make it palatable," she explained. "She found a way to advocate for herself," Susanna says of Michael's relationship with Kahne, "and that was a good thing."[89]

Ultimately, the time with Kahne, Chris Lamson says, "gave them a very successful hit record." However, there was a steep cost. The experience "broke them." Lamson shivers. "We were never the same after that," he notes.[90]

PART III
FAME

19.

The Bangles second full-length major label LP hit record stores on January 2, 1986. Less than three weeks later, the album's lead single, the "Christopher" penned "Manic Monday," was released, with the Susanna and Vicki–written "In a Different Light" on the B-side. "Manic Monday" debuted at number eighty-six on the *Billboard* chart, with overall positive critical reviews. Even Robert Hilburn of the *Los Angeles Times*, renowned for being notoriously stingy with any positive comments when it came to the Bangles—declared the track should be considered for "song of the year."[1] The accompanying video quickly went into high rotation on MTV. The major label money and pressure dramatically altered the look and feel of the offering as compared with the band's previous efforts. "If you watch the very first video that we did [the independent video for 'The Real World' off the EP] we are all rocking out. Debbi is doing a full-on Ringo, Sue's rocking out, Annette doing that cool bass player thing that she does. We're just playing the music and not miming or posing for the camera," Vicki comments. "That changed pretty quickly for the first Columbia video,"[2] she says, referring to "HTAF." "Manic Monday"—shot in and around the girls' native Los Angeles in one day—showcases stylishly dressed, hip Bangles in a variety of settings, from sun-kissed grassy knolls to romantic embraces with a faceless lover. The frenetic pace of filming, however, reflected the authentic "scrappy" attitude of the band. "Manic Monday" also showcased a return to making their own fashion decisions after the over-accessorized decadence of "HTAF," with the band's own budget chic aesthetic on display. "I am wearing a thrift store miniskirt and fringed suede vest, Sue has on a vintage mohair sweater—this was our 'real' look as far as I was concerned," Vicki says.

As "Manic Monday" rose in the charts, the press perpetually focused on the relationship between Prince and the band—often disregarding all other facets of the new album and the group behind it. The girls were constantly reminded that their newly minted success paralleled the Purple One's stamp of approval. "One of the things that intrigues me about the *Different Light* LP," a Canadian interviewer in 1986 quips, "was the Prince connection that's been made."[3] "The famous Prince connection," Vicki replies. "We met him back in 1945," Debbi retorts.[4] The contribution of "Manic Monday" to the album overrides every other accomplishment, with one journalist after another probing for appropriate reverence and gratitude from the girls. "Okay, here it is. 'When did you last talk to Prince?'" Debbi anticipates in a June 1986 exchange. "Ah, yes. You'll have to explain this," the journalist quips. "You don't ask everyone these questions, do you?" says Vicki. "'When did you last talk to Prince?' You didn't ask George Michael that!" Debbi retorts.[5]

The Bangles were now headlining their own shows, playing larger venues to sold-out crowds. "Just watching them going from those small little van tours, then riding the escalator up to huge singles and buses and big tours—it was just great," smiles Chris Lamson.[6] Moving from the large traveling van to a comparatively luxurious tour bus was a significant step up for the girls, especially as they were relentlessly crisscrossing the US and Europe on nonstop performance dates. "This (tour) is going to be extra special for us because we're going to have a tour bus for the first time in our history," Susanna proclaimed as the dates got underway. "We're out of the van. There'll be no more pit stops at strange gas stations in the middle of the night." Debbi chimes in, bolstering the point: "Yep, we're moving up in the world now, kids!"[7]

While on the road, "Manic Monday" went to number two on the charts—second only to their benefactor, who held on to the top spot with "Kiss." "Of course, we want No. 1," Vicki told a journalist at the time. "We are greedy individuals."[8] The secondary position, however, still propelled the band to dizzying new heights, with fans, media, and even popular television shows of the moment embracing the song. "I remember when Vicki, me, and Susanna were going for a walk in Washington, DC, while we were on tour," Debbi tells me. "We were waiting at a stoplight. Somebody pulls up in a car and the window is slightly down. Their radio is on and playing 'Manic Monday!' We were trying to be cool; but we were like, 'That's us! On the radio!' First of all, you don't recognize it; it sounds familiar. Then you realize it's you."[9]

Being in a hit band, the girls said, felt "like you know a secret, a private joke. It's so weird." Even doing mundane chores took on a new dimension, according to Michael. "[At one point], we went back to L.A. to have jet lag for five days and do our laundry. I was in the store buying some shampoo and 'Manic Monday' came on. I wasn't used to hearing it and I said, 'Oh my God, that's my song.' And the girl who was helping me said, 'Oh, that's my song.' And I didn't say anything for a long time but I had to tell her: 'I'm singing on that, that's me, that's my band.' It took a long time for it to sink in. And it was just really nice that it was somebody's favorite song."[10] The girls were quickly becoming not just a band, but *the* all-girl band that seemingly everyone was aware of. "I think when it really got me," says Michael, "was when we were in the bus outside a hotel somewhere in Texas, and Arnold Palmer was staying in the same hotel....He came out and he was talking to Lamar, our bus driver, and he said, 'So who's in the bus?' and Lamar said, 'It's an all-girl band, you know,' and Arnold goes, 'Is it the Bangles?'"

The headline tour rolled throughout 1986, providing a seemingly endless list of cities to visit and commitments to meet. Walker Igleheart was there from the start. "The beginning of the tour, when *Different Light* took off, everybody was great—so happy and thrilled."[11] The shows were packed, with so many people signing up for the fan club that Marji had to call in reinforcements. "All of the Peterson family wanted to support the group, so they jumped in to help with the fan club," she recounts.[12] At the gigs, audience members exhibited a mix of besotted admiration and standoffishness, according to Vicki and Michael. "There were definitely times when people ran up on stage and tried to kiss us and stuff like that," Vicki tells me. In 1985, she insisted to *Melody Maker* that the girls were "not into the cliched rock n roll bring the 12 year old boys backstage, we'll have a coke party and then have oral sex." After answering a nebulous "Yes and no" when questioned if the band gets male groupies, Vicki contended that the band didn't "indulge."[13]

Walker remembers a specific demographic of fan prevalent in the Bangles audience. "It tended to be awkward guys that were there," he says of the crowd. "I remember Susanna saying, 'Are all our fans just geeks?' I don't think she used that word, though. The idea was why were there so many adolescent boys on the nerdy side. That seemed to be their main clientele. Of course, they appeal to a broad, broad spectrum of the public, for sure. But I think the ones that came to the concert would tend to be on the geek spectrum, a lot of them fantasizing about Susanna."[14]

As the promotional activities continued, Walker recounts that "it wasn't very long before it started deteriorating into, 'Yeah, this hotel sucks,' just bitching about bullshit and driving the road managers crazy." When not in front of a camera, a journalist, or a crowd, Walker says the band "spent most of the time with their headphones on and not talking." Of course, he notes, "this was back in the days when there was no internet, no entertainment, except for a VCR." A favorite movie in constant rotation while on the road was an Al Pacino classic. "One thing I remember is we had a copy of *Scarface* on the bus. Susanna really liked it. We watched that a time or two or three. We all got to be good at saying, 'You stupid fuck!' Somebody would mess up, you'd go, 'You stupid fuck!'" When asked about after-show libations and activities, Walker offers a sedate vision of comfort chain food. "We'd play the gig, then we'd always have a stack of Domino's pizzas waiting for us in the bus."[15] In her *Metal Priestesses Podcast*, stylist Genevieve Schorr's reminisces with Susanna about the time spent on the road with the Bangles. "We weren't like throwing TVs out the window," Schorr says. "Definitely not," Susanna responds. "Every once in a while someone would make a slight mess in the dressing room but not intentionally."[16]

19.

The rare free moments provided down time from the glammed up MTV goddesses that had become familiar to anyone with the cable channel. "On their day off," Igleheart says, "the band would be walking around down the street in their sweatpants and sweatshirts. Nobody would recognize them, not even Sue."[17]

Rebecca Wilson was a sound engineer for the band later in their career, and she describes similarly down-to-earth women from her time spent on the road with the group. "I was terrified to meet them," she confides, "but they put me at ease because they were so professional and just kind people. They seemed very normal, not a lot of flash and circumstance. The music was great and the songs were amazing. Hearing their stuff live was a testament to their skillfulness. People may act trashy as an expectation, [but that was] never the case with the Bangles. They were a class act."[18]

Wilson was on hand for a tour of Japan the band undertook. "All the clubs were underground, super quirky and filled with hipsters," Wilson remembers. "They had a huge, really young audience out there."[19] Fans and press were omnipresent wherever the girls went, Wilson remembers. "They had lots of paparazzi on them," she says. "They handled it like pros, get some shots and get in the car. It was a lot less glamorous than what people thought it was. It was always unexpected, always fans in the weirdest places. Sue was the most notoriously recognizable but each one of them had their own fanbase. It was another thing unique about them. For some people, all they saw was Debbi, or Vicki." Michael confirmed the uptick in celebrity status in a May 1986 *Chicago Tribune* interview, admitting to "noticing a difference in that people are starting to recognize us in strange places. It's not like we can't walk into restaurants. People are really nice about that. But things happen like you walk into a Woolworth's and 'Manic Monday' is playing over the speakers. That's pretty weird."[20]

In contrast to past experiences working with bands who did not provide the sound engineer with instructions for their individual needs, Susanna clearly made her requirements known. "Sue always communicated directness with me," Wilson recalls. "She really had a need to hear herself very loudly, which created issues on stage as all the band heard was Sue sometimes. I had to balance that." Wilson goes on to describe Susanna as "a little of an enigma in the way that she has extrasensory perception." Wilson gives an example. "We were in this hotel and waiting for the elevator," she begins. "Susanna said there was something wrong with the elevator. I thought she was paranoid. I went to go get us coffee. When I came back, there was a sign on it that said 'broken.' She was totally right. She was really intuitive. I've seen her do that about people."[21]

Wilson details the band's live interplay in glowing terms, saying, "I liked the dynamic Sue and Vicki had physically, playing the guitar as women." Debbi was "a master of communication," Wilson says. "She could express herself well. She struggled because, being a drummer, your instrument is so loud and they harmonize so often that when she can't hear the vocals, she feels really paralyzed. But because they all sang lead, they had a unique setup."[22] Debbi, Wilson asserts, "got the raw deal. People (who did the lighting) often forgot that she would sing lead, so sometimes she would be singing the song she wrote in the dark. That sucked for her." Wilson also underscores how multitalented the younger Peterson is. "She played the most instruments, she holds the stage down energetically and in time. She was an anchor back there," she emphasizes.[23] Michael and Debbi "played well together," Wilson says, noting Michael's "feel as a bass player was unique." However, the engineer admits, "I was always quite intimidated by Micki, she was always very quiet and I respected that."[24]

Michael "had a difficult upbringing and a difficult young life," says Maria Corvalan, who worked with the band during a tour of Australia. "She comes from the water wars and boarding schools abroad. She has family that refuse to accept the fact that she's not Susan." She goes on to note the outsider status of Micki in contrast to the original three members, saying, "The other girls had a chemistry that sometimes worked and sometimes didn't."[25]

19.

The subject of exhaustion runs throughout the myriad interviews from the spring and summer of 1986, illustrating a steely determination to do everything necessary to obtain the longed-for success, even if it meant living on little rest with no privacy or down time. "I wish I was asleep," Michael tells the *Washington Post*, "the theme for this tour." Susanna reflects on the predicament faced during composing *Different Light* with a foreshadowing trepidation for creating new material, saying, "You don't have your own room half the time.... The concentration factor isn't there to write new songs. You're more worried about when you're going to eat, when you're going to take a shower, when you're going to do your laundry."[26] The unabated pace is evident in a *Melody Maker* piece, with Vicki saying, "We've seen the inside of a lot of hotels and the inside of a few vehicles, and that's about it. You get worked really hard.... Three hours of sleep a night and that kind of thing, which is fine, we can take that up to a point, but we also worry about 'here I am catching a cold,' y'know..."[27] In a *Creem* article, Susanna shares the "Bangles modus operandi," saying, "It's hard work keeping your sense of humor. Like when you have to get up to do a TV show and you've driven for 12 hours with a cold and snot on your face and there's no water so you can't wash..." Vicki concurs, adding, "You order a Pepsi Lite for $2 and brush your teeth with that." Susanna's conclusion is that "you have to laugh these things off, otherwise you're in big trouble," she says. "You can't take your problems too seriously."[28] However, the band was always quick to be clear that they were "reminiscing, not complaining" about their experiences on the road, repeatedly telling reporters that they were "ready for stardom." "I've been ready for a while," Michael told the *Chicago Tribune*. "Failure I've known like the back of my hand. I've got that down. Success, that's something that'll be interesting."[29]

For her part, Debbi was just thrilled to finally be out of the studio and away from the clutches of David Kahne. "What I liked about [being on tour] was being able to play the songs live. It was just being able to do what I do. I felt like I finally got to fucking play and not deal with the bullshit. There's different bullshit on the road, but it's what I was more comfortable with."

As *Different Light* sold five hundred thousand copies in the US alone, Susanna noted, "It's great seeing those *People* magazine ads on TV (for the issue with The Bangles profile). They play it every 15 minutes it seems like."[30] She goes on to admit it is "endlessly exciting to hear yourself" on the radio.[31] Showcasing her typical droll humor, Vicki confided, "You've really hit mainstream when you are the background music to *One Life to Live*—when they go to a disco and it's 'Manic Monday' playing. That is mainstream. It cracked me up."[32]

While success was starting to be apparent in a variety of forms, longed-for credibility was still proving to be problematic, a situation exacerbated by the widely promoted Prince involvement in the breakout track. "They didn't write the hits; usually that's a huge problem," says Bobby Rifkin. "That would weigh heavy."[33] Industry and press alike would not let the Bangles forget that they had not penned the catchy single. A *Newsday* show review provides a typical example of the disparaging commentary the band received: "The Bangles are reformed Valley Girls…going down, drowning in their own fluff…cover[ing] other songwriters' material."[34] Even the bean counters looking after Prince's business affairs did not believe the Bangles had played their own instruments on "Manic Monday," Mike Gormley remembers. "I got an invoice from Prince's office," he tells me. "I called the person and said, 'What's the invoice for?' They were trying to charge me for Prince's people playing on the record. 'That's the Bangles playing,' I told them. This woman was shocked. A lot of people thought that, by the way; a lot of people thought they didn't play."

Gormley then recalls trying to get the band a publishing deal, and encountering similar disbelief in the Bangles' abilities, even from a female colleague. "I bumped into the woman I was working with to get this deal over the line at the bank," Gormley describes. "We're standing next to each other. She turns to me and says, 'Mike, everyone knows the Bangles don't play. I don't want to do a publishing deal and they can't play.' I said, 'They can play.'" He pauses. "We found another publisher."[35]

A corresponding fallacy pertaining to the songwriting abilities of the Bangles continued to critically dog them as they released a second single, the Jules Shear contribution "If She Knew What She Wants." "Why is it *Different Light*'s best songs are the ones not written by the band?" *Creem* magazine wonders in an album review.[36] An opinion piece in the same magazine further chastises the band, exclaiming, "I'd argue that Madonna, in her own way, is at least as 'manufactured' as the Monkees were. The Bangles just had two big hits with (gasp!) songs they didn't write themselves!"[37]

There are few instances where the Bangles are given the chance to explain why specific songs appeared on their records. In a Canadian interview from 1986, the journalist states with certainty, "Through listening to *Different Light* two stronger songs had been written by other people, Prince and Jules Shear. Do you feel comfortable as songwriters?" He continues, "Or do you feel that you have to go outside for material?" Even though being at the receiving end of a rather withering comment, Vicki still manages to gracefully reply, providing one of the few examples of publicly expressed clarity as to the origin of *Different Light*'s song choices:

> We definitely are comfortable as songwriters. On the *Different Light* album, what happened is that we had been touring right up until we recorded that album. We were trying to pull together our material and [it] came under a time restriction naturally…we've always gone outside for material. Even from the first day, we got together, the first thing we played together was "White Rabbit." We've always grabbed on to good songs from other people. We're not afraid to do that just because, "Okay, I'm a songwriter, I need to feel that I want to be identified as a songwriter. So I'm not gonna sing anyone else's music except for mine." That's fine. But you're also ignoring a lot of great material if you do that.[38]

20.

"Manic Monday" not only made the Bangles stars, but further propelled Prince into global icon status, providing more evidence of his almost magical ability to craft hits. After the track became a worldwide smash, its creator endeavored to deepen the connection between himself and the group who had made it big. "I remember that [Prince] started threatening to come to [Bangles] shows," Lamson recalls. "There were a couple of false alarms that he would say, 'I'm coming to the show,' but not appear."[1]

On May 14, 1986, Lamson was sitting at the light booth at the Warfield Theatre in San Francisco. "Somebody came running over and said, 'Prince is here.' It was nearing the end of the show. I told the lighting guy to take over and I was escorted by security out to an alley behind the venue. I saw these big guys standing there, and said, 'Hey, what's going on?' They said, 'Prince would like to join the band onstage.' I'm thinking, 'Okay, well, I've heard this before, but okay.'

"All of a sudden there's this tiny dude. I mean, really small—and it was Prince! I escorted him in. We go into the green room and he just sits there. He's quiet, super shy, and doesn't say a damn thing, just sits there. I'm like, 'What can we do for you?' He goes, 'Just please tune a guitar to G.' I'm sitting there with them and 'Manic Monday' comes on. The band is playing it and he does his little smirky smile. He's there with just his bodyguard and me. I say, 'Well, I'm gonna go get the stage ready.' It was just awkward."[2]

"We'd find out after we left the stage and before we did the encore: 'Prince is here and he'd like to play with you.' 'OK, here's my guitar,'"

20.

Vicki remembers. Lamson recalls Prince walking up to the girls and a plan being hatched as to what to perform together. "There's a musician conflab about what they're going to do," Lamson smiles.[3] "They go back out. Sue introduces him and says, 'Here's Prince!' I wish we had footage of it. He came out and picked up the guitar and just started shredding; it was just insane. All of a sudden, the Bangles—who was the headliner at that event—became a backing band. They just disappeared into the back as Prince comes out and everyone's going crazy. He did the shredding thing and then they did two songs, 'Manic Monday' and a Big Maybelle cover, 'Whole Lotta Shakin'.' Then, off he goes, hands the guitar to someone, and says, 'Nice meeting everybody!' and walks off."[4]

Susanna remembers things slightly differently, telling me Prince had come to say hello to her in the dark, windowless basement of the San Francisco venue before the show even began. "The Warfield had these concrete, dungeon-like dressing rooms," she recounts. "I hear a knock on the door, and he was just standing there. 'Oh, hi.' He already knew 'Hero,' but this night he played a few covers of classics. He was definitely very nice."[5]

"It was just kind of magical," Hoffs reflects on the Bangles' interaction with Prince. "To have this artist who is so brilliant decide that he wanted to come see the Bangles play, and…perform with us—it was like *the* prince had come to the ball and asked us to dance with him, you know what I mean? There was a fairy tale aspect to it. The truth is, his gift of 'Manic Monday' transformed the Bangles' direction. It changed everything."[6]

Following the show at the Warfield, Lamson recalls, "we started getting messages on the bus" from Prince.

Lamson describes Prince as "floating around" the band, the "threat" of a stage appearance or the desire for an audience with the girls an omnipresent possibility. Michael even came up with a code name for the superstar, "Clint," according to Genevieve Schorr, who was touring with the band during the Paris promotional cycle of "If She Knew What She Wants." "I think our limo drivers were talking to one another. I think he was following us, but it looked like we were following him. At one point, we were in a limo and he was in a limo. We both ended up at the Picasso museum. [We saw him] for five seconds when he jumped out of the car with his big platform [shoes]," she laughs.[7]

Back in Los Angeles, the band was booked to headline a sold-out show at the Greek Theatre. It was a busy day for the Bangles, kicking off with an in-store signing at Tower Records. The performance was next on the agenda, followed by an aftershow party, where the girls would be receiving plaques from their record label to commemorate *Different Light* selling over half a million copies, thus obtaining the aspirational gold status. Julie Cameron and Amanda Hills Podany were on hand for the festivities; but another VIP was also threatening to make an appearance, according to Chris Lamson. "There was a lot of media and press at the event," he recalls. "Prince starts saying he is going to show up and join them on stage [at the Greek]. 'Here we go again,' I keep thinking to myself. It's a repeat [of the Warfield], just at a bigger place."

As Lamson sat waiting for the arrival of the Royal One, he got a call on his walkie-talkie. "Somebody says, 'There are two purple limos, downstairs in the garage. Prince is here.' He wanted to know if he could come up and join them on stage. I am waiting and waiting for his security to make an appearance, but nothing ever happened; he never left the car." After the show ended, Lamson escorted the Bangles out to their waiting limos, ready to take them to the after-party. "We've got two limos," he says, "I'm in the limo with Sue and we're driving along. I look out the back and there's the purple limo behind us, going to the party. Prince followed us. Sue's freaking out: 'He's gonna get out. What's he gonna do?' It was really funny.* We eventually pulled into the parking lot of the party. We get out and it's flashbulbs everywhere. It was like, 'Fuck, this band has really made it.' The purple limo pulls to the curb out front and just sits there. Then the band go in. I come back out and check on everything. The purple limo was gone. That was the kind of thing that went on."[8]

---

* "I doubt I said that," Susanna tells me, but confides, "I'm sure I was excited."

20.

The band had little time to celebrate their sales success or admiration of His Purpleness before being back on the road, first stopping by the *Late Night with David Letterman* show for their second appearance before flying abroad for a smattering of dates and appearances in Europe. At the *Letterman* gig, the building pressures and the exhaustion finally blew up. "There were times when the pot was simmering until finally, the lid blew off," Vicki says of the inner band turmoil. "We were not good at sitting down and confronting things from moment to moment. That was really unfortunate because that could have helped us a lot. We weren't like an all-boy band, who would probably get into fights on stage. I don't want to make that a gender thing because women do that, too. But we didn't do that. It's too bad because there were a lot of things that were happening that we could have worked through, or at least expressed to each other so we would understand what was going on. It's too bad. Sue went one way towards the end of the thing, Debbi was feeling very strongly in a totally different way. I was feeling caught in the middle and trying to make everything okay and none of that was ever said." Michael in particular was "very unhappy" at the *Letterman* appearance, trashing the band's dressing room. "There were words between Micki and Sue," Vicki tells me, "right before we went on to perform."[9]*

Emotions momentarily settled upon crossing the Atlantic, with the anticipation of the band opening for rock gods Queen in front of more than ninety thousand people at the Slane Castle in Ireland. "Another OMYGOD moment was opening for Queen and just walking out on the stage and looking out at the crowd," Susanna recalls.[10] "Despite the rain, despite it being overwhelming and a daunting experience to play in front of thousands of people, it was thrilling," she continues.[11] "To be able to stand in the wings and watch Queen perform and watch Freddie Mercury work a crowd the way he did; I just feel so lucky that I was witness to that."[12] She concludes, "Surreal is the best way to describe it."[13]

---

* Susanna does not remember this incident.

The last part of the summer was spent with the Arizona band Mr. Mister. The group was flying high after scoring back-to-back number one singles "Kyrie" and "Broken Wings" off their second 1985 album, *Welcome to the Real World*. The Bangles, however, seemed to be stalling. Despite the initial Prince-induced publicity of "Manic Monday," the second single, "If She Knew What She Wants," perched at a comparatively disappointing number of twenty-eight on the US charts. After the seismic start of the first single, it was a blow to the band, and the label was nonplussed. "Up to this point, I had had no problem with Columbia—things were going well—but then the US arm of the company said there were no more singles on the album, so they stopped working it," Miles Copeland recounted.[14] With other superstars boasting profitable bottom lines on the release schedule, it would be hard for the conglomerate to justify spending more time and money on the Bangles, a comparatively new group. It would take another otherworldly occurrence for the label to roll the dice on more promotional efforts toward the foursome.

The next song slated to be pushed as the third single from *Different Light* was the Liam Sternberg song "Walk Like an Egyptian." Manager Mike Gormley knew that because "If She Knew" had not performed as well as the label had hoped, he needed to do some work when he met with the head of promotion at Columbia Records in New York City. "He said, 'Look, I like "Walk Like an Egyptian." I'm going to work it. I promise you,'" Gormley recalls of the conversation with the executive. "But then he went on, noting that he had 'a Springsteen coming out, a Streisand coming out.' Often, that's just a brush-off that your record is not going to be a priority. But for some reason, I believed this guy, I believed him that he would work the Bangles." Several months later, the executive called Gormley with a plan: if the Bangles were willing to play two radio events—one in Atlanta and one in Los Angeles—for free, the fate of *Different Light* could be changed dramatically. "He told me [the radio stations would only] pay for transportation. He said, 'If you get into these two stations, I can pretty much promise you the song ['WLAE'] will take off.' These were very powerful stations, like number one and two in the country. I said absolutely, they would be there."[15]

The Los Angeles show was booked in at a regular Bangles haunt, the Palace, for October 20, almost a month after "WLAE" had debuted on the *Billboard* Hot 100 charts at a less than blazing eighty-two. It was at this crucial moment that Prince came through on one of his appearance threats. It could not have come at a better time for the Bangles, according to Gormley. "Prince was the hottest thing in the world and the radio station was impressed that he showed up," the manager recalls. "[Prince] came downstairs into the dressing room and the crowd was going nuts. They went on stage [for the encore] and he came out and played with them. That sealed the deal. That radio station [really pushed] that record so he helped with 'Walk Like an Egyptian' in that sense."[16] As Miles Copeland asserted, "It is hard to believe that a song that to me and others was an obvious hit had until now been blanked by the powers that be at Columbia."[17]

Susanna has a different perspective from the evening. "There was all this whispering in the halls when we were at soundcheck," she recalls. "Word was that Prince was going to come see our performance that night. But it gets even better because we get to the moment in the set where we're playing 'Hero Takes a Fall.' Sure enough, I look over to the side and Prince is coming out onto the stage, already shredding on guitar. I was like everyone in the place, hypnotized by the magic that was happening before our eyes. I mean, never before or since have I ever been witness to someone's otherworldly guitar playing. It was so crazy great."[18] The benefactor's ability was "was truly mind-blowing," remembered Susanna. "I'd never seen anybody play guitar like that. I mean it was almost like his guitar was just part of his body. There was no disconnect, it wasn't like this thing he was holding and playing. He was somehow channeling from the inside out, and it just came through. It was really magnificent on so many levels."[19] "It probably took him like 4.2 seconds to learn 'Hero,'" Vicki asserts in her typically self-deprecating manner.[20] Prince then stepped back to play tambourine on "Manic

Monday." A quick moment of public admiration passed between Prince and Susanna, Debbi remembers. "When we did 'Manic Monday' with him on stage, he sings, 'Come on, honey. Let's go make some noise' to Sue, and he's being sassy."[21]

The elder Peterson understood the importance of the Prince endorsement. "He was just enormously talented," Vicki says. "When he showed up, it was an honor, like being blessed by a holy being. He was a brilliant musician who processed his music so naturally, like breathing."[22] Susanna is equally reverent of the songs performed with the star. "Those moments when Prince jumped on stage and we were watching him be supernaturally brilliant," she says, were "magnificent on so many levels,"[23] a "revelation."[24] Despite all of the overblown rumors to the contrary, Susanna clarifies, "I didn't work with him, apart from having those opportunities to be on stage performing with him," nights that she is genuinely grateful to have had.

The Bangles, according to Revolution drummer Bobby Rifkin, "couldn't have been any more favored" by Prince.[25] "He got on stage with them and performed with them live—it was another endorsement," Rifkin notes.[26] Revolution guitarist and singer Wendy Ann Melvoin was with Prince at the Palace and joined him on stage with the Bangles. "She looked very unhappy," Vicki recounts of the Prince insider. "We found out very soon after that he ended the Revolution, so there was obviously stuff going on. I thought in the back of my head she was looking at me, like she thinks I'm competition. I thought 'That ain't happening, I'm not anywhere near her level of being a player' but that's what I was sensing, and then we found out right afterwards that the Revolution was over."[27]

After the Palace show, the Bangles' presence was requested at Sunset Studios by Prince for an intimate jam session. "He just wanted to play Bangles songs," Vicki tells me. "He knew them all. It was weird to be playing Bangles songs with this guy," she says, though "he was charming and lovely." Prince and the Bangles were both staples of MTV at the time; did Vicki feel she was playing music with a peer? "No, there was no sense of equality, not for me," she admits. "It felt incredible, though it wasn't like we were all hanging out in someone's living room just jamming; it was not that at all."[28]

The atmosphere was anything but relaxed. "Nobody was comfortable," Vicki says. "It was part of his thing…he didn't go out of his way to make people feel comfortable, pretty much the opposite. I think he enjoyed having people on edge at all times because he would do funny things."

The Bangles visit happened around "two in the morning," Debbi tells me, with Susanna put onto vocal duties. "Sue sang mainly because there was no microphone," Debbi recalls. "I think I yelled out because I'm behind the drums. I remember sitting on his drum set," she continues. "The cymbals were really high up and the seat was like almost to the ground because he's got short legs. I'm thinking, 'How the hell am I gonna play this thing?' I thought 'I'll just fucking fake it.' So I just started playing; we were all just trying to figure out what to do."[29] Noodling around in the studio was not familiar territory to the girls, Debbi explains. "The Bangles never really jammed," she confides. "We were not a jam band." A moment of purple approval has stayed with Debbi decades on. "I remember just playing along and him looking over at me like, 'You go, girl.' I felt like I got appreciation from Prince. I got acknowledged by Prince and that felt nice."[30]

"He wouldn't look at you," Debbi reflects on Prince's personality. "I think he was really shy. He wouldn't really do a lot of eye contact, probably because he's a genius and geniuses don't always do that."[31] Susanna echoed these impressions, telling an interviewer, "I think he feels more comfortable as a performer in front of large crowds. [In San Francisco], we really had a chance to see what he is like in action, being a couple feet away from him. It's just astonishing how he can just take over this audience in a second, the minute he gets on stage. But I think he is just very shy. He likes to talk on the phone a lot. He feels comfortable in those kinds of situations."[32] Michael added, "He's weird. He's an amazing talent. Watching him play in the studio is an amazing thing because he's one of those people who has no inhibitions. We watched him sit there and he was just playing guitar. He'd play something good and then he'd play something really bad. And then he'd play drums and it would seem like he had no sense of time, but then, all of a sudden, he'd be playing all this Tony Williams jazz stuff. It's like the guy has no fear of looking like a total fool…"[33]

By the very early hours of the morning, Vicki had to go. "I found out later that Prince had mysteriously left at some point without saying anything and then never came back. Again, making everyone kind of hanging on like, 'What do we do? Should we leave?' According to Peggy McCreary, one of his engineers, he did that kind of thing all the time."[34] Debbi says of the exit, "He suddenly goes, 'My limo's waiting' and then just leaves. We were just sitting there looking at each other. He didn't even say, 'Goodbye.' From then," Debbi laughs, "'My limo's waiting' would be a constant in-joke between me and Micki."

No matter the continent, time of day or occasion, the man from Minneapolis was impeccably turned out, according to both Debbi and Vicki. "He always looked like he looked, perfect from head to toe," Debbi says. "That was his thing. He lived and probably slept in those clothes. He always looked 'that way.'"[35] Vicki shares a similar memory, saying, "We used to joke, 'Do you think he ever walks around in a T-shirt and jeans?' because he's always done up. I couldn't imagine him not walking around in platform shoes and his ruffles."[36]

The girls had had an additional boost of recognition when mentor Cyndi Lauper featured them as backup vocalists on "Change of Heart," the second single from her sophomore album *True Colors*. The recording session took place in New York and saw Billy Joel stopping by to compliment the girls on their harmonizing. "Cyndi was very involved with the arranging and production of that song," Vicki remembers. "I felt that she was always a very hands-on person." "Heart" premiered on November 11, eventually going to number three on the *Billboard* Hot 100, further underpinning the Bangles' growing superstar status.

21.

By the end of 1986, "Walk Like an Egyptian" was an international smash, going to number one on the *Billboard* charts. With the help of the hit single, *Different Light* experienced a huge sales boost, going from number 117 on the charts, where it had been floundering after the promotional cycle of "If She Knew" had finished, to an astounding number two over the Christmas period, only losing the top slot to Bon Jovi's *Slippery When Wet*. Buoyed by the initial airplay from influential radio stations, the accompanying music video for the song provided further impact, as it was in constant rotation on MTV and television shows like *Friday Night Videos* that had sprung up around the US to compete with the hip fledgling channel. Filmed on the streets of New York, the video, with a running time of three minutes, twenty-two seconds, featured a pastiche of elements, from the band performing the song to everyday people on the streets posing and walking in "Egyptian"-inspired shapes. The girls looked intentionally over-the-top glamorous, "cartoonishly so, with the hair getting teased up higher and higher," Vicki says. "I requested three sets of [fake] eyelashes on me because I knew that that's what Twiggy would do," she laughs. Special effects were used on images of well-known entities, including Princess Diana and the Statue of Liberty. The video became its own cultural phenomena, going on to be nominated for Best Group Video at the 1987 "MTV Video Music Awards."

The Bangles enlisted Gary Weis to create the visuals. The band was already fans of Weis from his work on *Saturday Night Live*, where his short films were aired during the show, as well as his spoof film on Beatlemania *All You Need Is Cash*. Because the label had "given up early" on the single seeing any huge success, the stakeholders at Columbia did not "have to do that much" with the ascension of the track, according to Susanna, as it was a "slow build" to success, based on organic listener engagement, as "people [began] calling into radio stations and requesting it. It started developing its own momentum."[1] In another interview, Susanna remarks that the band "knew [the song] was cool, but we had no idea it would take off the way it did. We were really surprised. Columbia stayed with it for a very slow ride up the charts. But once it got to number one, it stayed there."[2] The song ended up being one of the biggest tracks of the year. "It [was just] awesome," Susanna concludes. "It was just completely and utterly unexpected."[3]

Kathryn Ireland was married to Weis and worked with him on the "WLAE" video. "Gary was all about the man on the streets," Ireland says of the video's concept of random people strolling down the pavement or crossing the road while dancing. The most important thing for the video to capture, though, was to make sure the girls "looked fantastic." "That's what we've always done," she notes. "They were all good-looking girls, so it was not hard to do." The band was "fabulous to work with," with Ireland confiding that she "got on best with Sue and Vicki....They were the two driving forces of the band," Ireland remembers. "They were easy and accommodating. The other two were just there. A good time was had by all."[4]

One scene in particular stood out to many viewers and became synonymous not just with the song and video, but with the band and Susanna. At the 2:47 second mark, Susanna trills the title, while moving her eyes from side to side. This lingering look lasts for approximately ten seconds, as the camera is close up, her face filling the screen. It was a tiny segment but it cemented change in the group as well as the public perception of the band. "Yes, she was looking at the camera," Vicki says of the clip of her bandmate, "but the camera was also on her...when we're doing...group vocals [the camera is on her]. Even if you look at the video for 'WLAE,' look at the camera angle: for me they are on the side and there's no close-up. For Sue, it's all close-up. What do you assume when you're on the other end of that?" Vicki asks. "That the directors want to shoot her because they obviously think that she is more appealing and the other ones you shoot a little further away and from the side."[5]

Vicki's approach to videos was "to perform the song like a rocker and not necessarily try and seduce the camera." In contrast, she says, "that's what she was doing and I get that. That was her thing. Her whole thing was wanting to be sexy. She wanted to be Madonna. That was her approach. It worked for her, which is great. It didn't hurt the band. I have no problem with it. It wasn't my approach so there's that. It's just a different approach. But I take exception to the thought that we didn't know how to work a camera, that [the rest of the group is] not skilled at that."[6]

On reflection, Susanna feels in many ways she was practicing for that close-up her entire life. "I grew up doing ballet, being obsessed with movies, and studying performances by actresses like Audrey Hepburn and Natalie Wood. In ballet, it's not just how you're shaping your body into a pose or how you're moving. It's your face as well. There is a lot of work with the eyes, it's all about the expressions," she tells me. The side to side movement was "not something I thought through in the moment," she admits; it was more instinct from years of her own rehearsal in the ballet studio and watching films. "Those early experiences of growing up studying dance and theater and seeing a ton of movies, just being a complete cinephile when I was a kid, and really observing performances—they all came into play when we were making videos. The camera can exaggerate things, but in a good way. It's an opportunity to express, even if you're just lip-synching to a song; it's a whole body experience."

No one asked Susanna to do the particular gesture during the song. She remembers the shot being taken by a "cinematographer way far back" in the room. "We warmed up by actually doing a little mini concert for radio winners," Susanna says. "Gary Weis wanted to have the feeling of us in front of an audience. There might have been multiple cameras, so when the moment of me saying 'Walk Like an Egyptian' at the end of the song, and I was looking somewhat coyly side to side, zoomed in on…

There were multiple cameras, so there's other angles of the footage, but when the edit happened they decided to use that because, yeah, it was a moment of me singing and they were in a close-up.

"Then it became a kind of a 'thing.' It just connected with people. It was just kind of a flirty look. I was always flirting back with the audience. It was like a reciprocal act: they're looking at the stage, we're performing…I think it just was a moment caught on film."[7]

Susanna had "a natural thing for the camera," according to Mike Gormley. "I don't know if she consciously did [the eye movements]. A lot of people thought it was a trademark or something for her. The others actually were pretty good but they weren't into it as much as Sue was. I think Sue enjoyed that stuff. I'm not saying the others didn't. Susanna would just work the camera quite well and guide the directors."[8]

"I was thrilled," Susanna says of the explosion of popularity the song provided for the band. When not on the road, she was still calling her parents' residence her home. "The Bangles already had number one records, and she was still living in that garage," long-time friend and fellow musician Brix Smith Start says.[9] It was a fitting accommodation in many ways for the at-heart garage band. Vicki was also staying in less than glamorous accommodations as her band hit the top of the chart. "I was living in a one-room rental in a large house in Hollywood, but it was literally a converted garage for the most part," she tells me. Debbi, meanwhile, was still in a shared house. Former roommate Sid Griffin remembers sitting around the kitchen table together in December 1986. "Debbi didn't have great self-esteem and she's deserving of high self-esteem," he says. "She was an impressive person in her own sweet, quiet way. I remember she was eating Cap'N Crunch and looked sad. Someone told her to cheer up because she had the number one record in the country, which they did. She looked up at us and sort of gave him a bit of a wince, a bit of a smile and went back to eating Cap'N Crunch. I thought 'Deb, You're so great. You're so terrific. Don't you know?' There weren't any *Yesss* moments, like a scream or holler of excitement. Debbi knew she was in a room with other struggling musicians. The Petersons and Micki would always downplay things. There wasn't champagne being uncorked."[10] Sid recounts getting a glance at a paycheck for Bangles merchandise around the same time period. "My friend said, 'How much do you think it is? Do you think she got a million bucks?'" The payday was "sizable," according to Griffin. "I was so happy for her," he concludes.[11]

For the audience who became fans through *All Over the Place*, the album *Different Light*, and the song "Walk Like an Egyptian" especially, represented a huge deviation from everything the Bangles had been about. "When I first heard that song, I thought, 'This does not sound like the Bangles to me, or anything like I've ever heard.' I got it unfinished. I was like, 'What the hell is this gonna sound like?' And then I heard it finished. I was like, 'Why are they doing this song?'" Dave Peterson says. "My parents liked it and said it could be a dance craze or something, you know 'Walk Like an Egyptian' or something like that. I told my folks, 'Nah, no way.' For people that do not know their music at all, they probably think the Bangles are a one-hit wonder, a one-trick pony. They think that they did 'Walk Like an Egyptian,' and that is it. They won't know there is a whole catalog."[12]

Though the single was bringing the very success that the group had dreamed of, it was also becoming a dreaded part of the repertoire. "They never wanted to play 'Walk Like an Egyptian,'" sound tech Joe Stella says.[13] "Everybody hated it," Chris Lamson remembers. "It was horrible in the fact that it became a hit, which made things even worse because it was a song that has nothing to do with them. It doesn't sound like them and is a total novelty song. For someone who had grown up with them and seen their musical progress and knew what they stood for musically, it was hard to see. Now they're just a circus act. It was a hit and they were making loads of money but it was just so far away from what they were."[14]

Fame, Joe Stella pontificates, impacted members of the band differently. "I think Vicki wanted to be in a freaking garage band and have fun doing it," he says. "All of a sudden, the fame came in and it did change them a bit, I'm not gonna lie. It was tough for some and easier for others."[15] Mike Gormley confides that working on, and then attaining, a number one record, especially at Christmas, had been a childhood dream. "I wanted to enjoy it; an amazing goal had been reached." However, he reflects, "I think we had a day or so to relish the accomplishment because there was so much going on. It was pressure."[16]

With the help of "WLAE," after years of struggle, the band was finally financially beginning to see the benefit of all the relentless grind. But it was a difficult mental switch for Vicki, especially, to make. "It's hard to break out of any kind of childhood indoctrination," she says. "It's something you do carry around into adulthood and you have to be aware of it and to care. It's funny, it does impact your point of view in your life." Even after the band's business manager instructed her to purchase a house with the money that was "finally trickling through the pipeline with a capital P," it was almost impossible for Vicki to pull the trigger. "The manager said, 'You've got to get out of this poverty mentality.' It was the first time it ever occurred to me that perhaps Debbi and I were brought up with this scarcity model, feeling like there was never going to be enough. There was never enough, but not in the way that like 'Oh, I got $100; I'm gonna go buy a satellite dish.' It wasn't that; it was, 'I'm afraid to spend money in case I don't ever make money again.'"[17]

Financial disparity within the foursome began to become more pronounced. The Petersons needed jobs and an income to literally pay for the roof over their heads. Their bandmates were in a different situation, making for an added source of tension. Debbi recounts, "We'd be somewhere shopping and Michael would buy this amazing coat. I'd look at her [Michael] drooling with envy and wish I could afford it."[18]

Susanna was also not overly concerned about income, as she had a free place to stay in the converted studio. "Sue played it down for a while," Debbi says of her family position. "She was very quiet about it. She didn't really flaunt [her affluence]. She was really cool when we were playing clubs in the early '80s. Even during the Beat tour, I used to hang out with her a lot and felt a connection with her. It wasn't really the class thing. [She never acted] like she was super wealthy. It wasn't any of that at all. She would still go and buy trashy clothes and things that were not necessarily super expensive. Sue didn't really flaunt it as far as clothes or jewelry, or any of that kind of thing. She just wanted to be cool, Patti Smith, like Yoko Ono. She kind of played the rich Hollywood person down. That came out more in 1985 since she started getting all the attention. That was one of the things when I noticed a change in her, when the press started paying attention to her, and the management, David Kahne, and everybody started pushing her to the front. She was going into that Hollywood scene a bit more. I never felt like I belonged there. I just don't feel like that kind of person. I don't know how to be; sometimes I wish I did just so I could get more attention or maybe make more money, but I just can't seem to do that. I just, I'm not that person."[19]

Susanna stresses to me on numerous occasions that her father was a doctor, that she did not come from "immense wealth" as Micki did, and that she was "not a trust fund kid." Regardless, money continued to play a part in band relations throughout the years, according to sound tech Rebecca Wilson. "There were dynamics around some [people] needing more money than others because they weren't wealthy," she says. "It was a big thing because Vicki and Debbi did not come from money."[20]

As their profile rose on a global scale, the visual brand of the Bangles became another element that executives attempted to change. Experimenting with how far to push the boundaries of prescribed and expected fashion was all around them; peer Madonna, for example, was creating an entire army of look-alikes with her underwear-as-outerwear look. The Bangles, however, had to constantly work against an industry set on presenting them in an objectified manner, Debbi recounts to me. "We had people telling us to puff our hair up, what to wear and how to look. We had a lot of people try to direct us to appear a certain way. But we would fight against it. It was a constant battle. It was very much like, 'Okay, let's try to make you into this sexy female thing.' We were not into that, although I think Susanna might have slightly gone in that direction."[21] Debbi's former roommate Sid Griffin also tells of pressures placed upon the group that he did not come across as a man in the music industry. "I distinctly remember one time saying, 'I noticed you all really dress up for photoshoots.' Debbi said, 'We just have to Sid, that is the game.' Big hair was a big deal in the '80s. She said, 'Well, ours has been coiffed a certain way and our appearance is a certain way because our looks matter and we are in the spotlight and this is the game.'"[22]

Vicki remembers going "toe-to-toe" with stylists on specific occasions, but overall says the various outfits such as "the ruffled socks with the pumps and four thousand layers of jewelry" was simply the style of the moment. "As far as how we looked, that was just the fashion. Yes, we're gonna pile on more bracelets because we're the Bangles. If you look at what we were wearing in the 'HTAF' video, that was the first time we were 'styled.' It was kind of horrific, but we rolled with it and then didn't do it again. If we were styled again, it was always with either our own clothes or with our direction." Though having virtually no free time, the band continued to source their own clothes for the most part; shockingly, few designers of the time took the opportunity to collaborate with the high-profile group. "We had almost no help on clothes early on," Susanna emphasizes, "that's why we looked so ragtag. We had no brands offering to give us clothes and we were never comfortable with stylists. We wore mostly thrift store finds. I splurged only a few times and shopped at Norma Kamali in NYC and at Betsey Johnson who is a wonderful person. The Bangles never had connections with designers. We weren't sent clothes for our tours." As time went on, the band was able to play around with fashion, Vicki notes, simply "because more was available to us." Despite their international visibility, freebies were not the norm. "I don't ever remember a designer giving us clothes for gratis," Vicki tells me, though she notes, "Boomer Esiason once gave me a pair of cowboy boots."[23]

The crumbling of the insular nature of the band created the change of look, Susanna later reflected. "The glamorization of the Bangles happened because there were more outside people in there messing with us," Susanna says. "We didn't have enough perspective to say no. You want to look good, and you get caught up in 'Oh, let's give you bigger hair!' I remember how big my hair was in 'Walk Like an Egyptian'…and feeling like 'Oh my God! What just happened to me?' You get caught up. A wardrobe person comes and says, 'These are great clothes; put these on.' You're busy on tour. You don't have time to go shop. You look over and the person sitting next to you has got that much makeup on, too. It's just a vicious cycle: fashion faux pas just escalating and getting exponentially worse and worse."[24]

Personal style was expressed when possible, with sporadic bespoke pieces made for band members to wear on stage. Vicki had an established love for bell-bottom jeans, a fetish Susanna regaled a journalist with in a 1986 article, telling him, "Vicki wants to bring back bell bottoms. Not that ruffle flared bell bottoms," she adds hastily, "but bell bottoms like Cher wore."[25] With Mrs. Bono as an inspiration, Vicki had a bespoke velvet pair of her own made to wear on stage. The trousers had Velcro sewed onto the cuffs, allowing her to change the bottom of the legs to a purple ruffle, fringe, or gold lamé, depending on her mood. With so many options for different looks, the pants were omnipresent during performances, so much so that she unknowingly "rotted out the fabric." During a gig at Pier 84 in New York, an unfortunate wardrobe malfunction occurred, revealing Vicki's alfresco vittles. After a quick panic on the side of the stage, Vicki tells me, "I changed into a miniskirt in the wings and ran back out onstage. It was June 18th, Paul McCartney's birthday, so I said I wanted to honor the time Paul McCartney split his pants onstage. I don't know if it's true, but I went with it. I just played it off." Tom Cruise, who was in the audience, told her after the show that he, for one, had "appreciated the costume change."[26]

22.

Though now a chart-topping, stadium-filling, million-album-selling band, the Bangles were still trying to hold on to the idea of parity that had been established when they were playing small punk clubs in Los Angeles with only the Petersons' parents in the audience. "People often compare the Go-Go's and the Bangles, but in fact they were quite different," Miles Copeland notes. "This was especially true in how they treated photography and the general matter of image-making. In the Go-Go's, it was accepted that Belinda would be the front person, the lead singer, and probably get more press coverage because of that. Pretty much like Stewart and Andy's attitude towards Sting in The Police. The Bangles set a rule of 'equality' from the start. That also extended to the stage. The rule was four spotlights, not one. For most road crews, this would not have made any sense, but it was a rule that the group insisted upon, and which sometimes meant no spotlight at all.

"The Bangles' strategy was all based on the group mantra to not single out any member—especially Susanna. There was a fear that [she] would be singled out and eventually leave the others in the dust to go solo. I never felt any push from Susanna herself regarding a solo career—from what I could see, she had resigned herself to the rule as a fact of life in the band—but there seemed to be a real fear in the minds of Debbi and Vicki. Michael was also no pushover, so it really was a group where all parties had to be considered, and each had their quirks and, more to the point, strong opinions. The problem was that many newspapers and magazines wanted front covers showing one person, just like they have done for so many groups in the past, including The Police. Consequently, The Bangles turned down numerous front covers and major articles in the press."[1] The insistence of equality, Copeland said, was "almost an oppressive rule."[2]

By attempting to have identical representation at all times, the band was fighting against the very mechanisms that were giving them success and fame. "When you sign with major labels, they have a lot of power," says friend and vocal teacher Toni Kasza. "When they signed with Sony, that's when they feminized the girls. At that time, everything was much more androgynous and more of a rock look. The label was like, 'No, you girls, we have to glam you up.'"[3]

Similarity of band member representation and opportunity was a motif repeated throughout interviews, as journalists attempted to identify the "true" figurehead of the group. In a 1986 *Creem* piece, the writer asserts, "The question of the band's group image and the confusion as to its 'real' leader is tackled by Vicki, who reaches into history, er, 'her' story, for her comparison: 'When you think of the Mamas & Papas, you might have Mama Cass in mind, but John Phillips did many of the lead vocals.' Doesn't the joint identity ultimately prove frustrating on an ego level? 'Of course, but there's an element of compromise that we all agree to,' offers Michael. 'It's like any relationship. You have to give to get. This is the first band I've been in which is a true democracy.'"[4]

While appearing to the public as a tight-knit group, the seemingly united front was drifting further apart from each other. "In the beginning [of the touring cycle], it was great," Walker recalls. "We'd all get on the bus and chat and have a great time, eating Domino's. Then everybody would put on their headphones and go off into their own space. As time went on, the fun part was less and less and the headphones were more and more."[5] Having a new, impartial person on the road was helpful for some of the group, according to Igleheart. "I remember Micki said to me that I was a calming influence. She was really glad that I was there because she felt like I was keeping them from being at each other's throats. They had such a history; by the time I got in with them, they'd been together for years. I didn't know the backstory when I first got there; it started slowly coming out as I was with them."[6]

Susanna was beginning to feel especially isolated from the rest of the group. "Even though the band is the band, the road can be just long and lonely," she confided.[7] Those close to the group were also aware of the shifting dynamics. "Susanna had a lot of pressure on her," Joe Stella recalled, "and the media does favor her."[8]

The allusion to Susanna as *the* lead singer shows up repeatedly in reviews, interviews, and features about the band. A *Creem* writer in 1986 laments not getting access to Susanna for his piece, disappointment dripping onto the page as he pens, "Whaddya mean I can't talk to Susanna Hoffs?"[9]

That the press would designate one person to be the main focus was inevitable, according to some experienced industry veterans. "Tom Petty said how there is always jockeying for positioning" in any band, Sid Griffin says. "They [the Bangles] certainly jockeyed for position. Everybody has a role and there is always going to be disappointment. Vicki was called the earth mother and a very centered person, while Susanna was understandably the front person that the camera came to. Very photogenic. If Vicki Peterson gave me advice, I would take it every time. There is no Hollywood facade or patina around her. There were those that bad-mouth Susanna because she was obviously pushy. She was forceful. Every band has someone that's doing this. Come on. Someone needed to push on the band. Sometimes resentment can build towards the figurehead. You need that in a band but there will be blowback. That was Sue's role. Democracy doesn't work in rock 'n' roll. If you have a four- or five-piece band, and you give everybody equal vote, it will screw things up. Not everybody has the same amount of chutzpah and business sense and can read the lay of the land as well as the next guy. Some people are better at playing music, and some people are better at helping manipulate the press. Everybody has their role." He continues, "Anytime you had a figurehead, the idea of equality leaves."[10]

For Vicki, it was extremely painful to see the vision she had held since childhood disintegrating before her eyes, powerless to stop the forces outside the group. "For me, it was a struggle, because I saw the band a different way, as a gang, as a democratic institution, which are highly flawed as we know," she tells me. "That was obviously not after the first couple of years; that was no longer Susanna's deal. It's not right or wrong. It's just the truth. At the time, I constantly fought against it and struggled because I am a very stubborn person. I wanted things my way." Susanna's personality, says Peter Philbin, "can cause waves." The Bangles, he argues, would not have gotten as far without her moxie. "Susanna is a force, which I think is to be celebrated," he notes. "She is the 'grab the brass ring' girl."[11]

Susanna asserts that there are "natural tensions within any band," and that the Bangles were no different than any other. "Bands are like families," she tells me. "You don't always get along with your siblings. You add in that there were actual siblings in the group, and there's always going to be a built-in dynamic there. It's also hard being in a band," she continues. "I think that's why it's rare for them to survive past a decade or so."[12]

Balancing personalities and aspirations is part of any group, according to Bobby Rifkin. "I have a theory about bands," he says. "The old joke is by the time you print the poster, there's a different bass player in the band than on the poster. It's just really hard to keep the egos and the musicianship in check. It's a juggling act."[13] Former MTV executive Brian Diamond agrees, noting that inter-band relationships are difficult for anyone to navigate. "Everybody thinks the lead singer *is* the band," he notes. With this model so firmly indoctrinated into the public's mind, the Bangles' style of rotating vocal duties aided in stoking the tensions within the group. "Although Vicki sang songs, Susanna was synonymous with 'Manic Monday' and 'Walk Like an Egyptian,'" Diamond points out. He then uses the example of U2 frontman, Bono, to illustrate his point. "Bono says on stage during the live show, 'Everybody associates me with being the leader of this band; however, everybody in this band thinks *they* are the leader of this band.'"[14]

The band life creates specific situations that are rare not to encounter, according to former Bangles bandmate Amanda Hills Podany. "Bands have this intensity because you haven't chosen to marry these people, you've just chosen to be in a band with them but you're together 24/7," she explains. "I don't think there's any group of personalities where that's going to be easy. Every band has these crises. Even when I was in the band, and we weren't touring, there were these stresses [because] you're together all the time and you're trying to get something done together. You are four very different people. It will be difficult with any band."[15]

The huge difference between being an artist and being a commercial product were shocking for Susanna. "There is something about being an artist, where the focus is just creating art; then suddenly you are working with a company whose business it is to sell the art, so in essence, sell you. When I would walk into the offices of Columbia Records [later Sony], I would face generally a batch of men in suits, who were businessmen. That was their business to sell our music, and other artists' music. There's something nerve-racking about it. It's hard to make art by committee. So not only the committee of the band, but all of these different entities, trying to all come to some agreement on anything, but also the committee of the label, the record label; what are their expectations?

"In many ways, they're the decider. They are like, 'This is the single we're going to release. Oh, really, you're going to release that one?' You as an artist don't necessarily have much say in it. Yes, you have management. But that's just throwing in another batch [of people] in some ways; it makes doing the math exponentially more difficult. This all boils down to *your* life. This is *your* life.

"There's something really intimidating about it, no matter how confident you feel about what you want, or what your goals are; it still can undo even the strongest person. I don't think about the business side of music very often. But at the end of the day, it's like this cage you're forced into. It's this prison because there's so little control you have as an artist. It's very stark to me now, the realization of that. I think the therapy that I was having in the '80s kept me glued together because I couldn't process all of it then. Not only the kind of baked-in drama and complexity of being in a band but add in that you're actually working for a corporation, a company, a conglomerate, whatever. It's Sony Records, you know, it was Columbia, which seems more boutique, but then suddenly this name, Sony, was stamped on top of it. That's when you know: you really are serving this record company in some respect."[16]

Multiplatinum Sananda Maitreya, formerly known as Terence Trent D'Arby, was friends with the Bangles, Susanna in particular, in the 1980s. Maitreya underscores the dehumanization of artists into simply a commercial good, aided and encouraged by a press needing content. "As far as why the media chose to single out the Madam Hoffs, that's more of an agreement between the Record Company and the Machine, for whom the theory has long been that a central figure is easier to promote because it narrows the focus on the 'product,'" he says. "It's also the way of human psychology, even when people themselves are not involved as figures to sell, the eye always goes to whatever image in the frame stabilizes the whole presentation, be it four ladies, a herd of sheep, or a Basquiat painting. The risk is that inevitably, once identified, that person will be singled out to the point & the detriment of the other members of the collective where there will be discussions about 'going solo.' So that the separation is complete & the 'product' easier to manipulate. Bands have no choice but to be tough, because the same forces that exploited their talents, WILL in fact be the exact same forces that will seek to tear them apart. IF MANAGERS, SPOUSES, OR LOVERS DON'T GET THERE FIRST."[17]

When asked what his initial impressions of the Bangles were, Maitreya replied, "As a musician, I responded with respect and admiration. An artist's life is not an easy life, nor a simple road to travel. Triple that degree of difficulty if you're a woman." He then confides, "As someone who has experienced their life as a hetero male, like most sensible bitches, my initial visceral reaction was 'YOWSAH, YOWSAH, YUM, YUM, YUM, Eee Yabba Yabba Doo' like some Fred Flintstones era denizen of Bedrock, as nature did in fact intend. They appealed to BOTH the sensibility AND the senses, which in that blessed age, wasn't yet regarded as a crime against humanity." He goes on to bluntly say, "if I can speak the honest truth, most of us in the 'Dudesphere' wouldn't kick ANY of those ladies out of bed. You also had Madam Michael & 2 blond sisters. It couldn't have gotten more Central Casting if the movie had been made in the Valley."*

Susanna especially, he admits, "at the risk of sounding like I might in fact dare to be authentic & not too programmed by modern mores, as timely and well-intended as some of them may be, SHE WAS A BONAFIDE BABE WHO COULD PLAY HER SHIT! AND she played really cool guitars, so she also had her appropriate 'signifiers' pointing the arrows of homage in the right direction. We in the diehard musical community understand that certain instruments constitute a symbolic 'language' that the insiders speak & understand. HER GAME WAS TIGHT & made all the right moves, as was true of the entire band. And that's not just calculation, but INSTINCT." Susanna, he tells me, "was Kate Moss before the Lady Kate, but with a Rickenbacker around her neck instead of a Tiffany necklace. EVEN STEVIE WONDER could see that. You'd have to have mirrors on the INSIDE of your glasses to miss it."[18]

As *Different Light* soared to multiplatinum status, Vicki grew more conflicted with the direction of the group and her place in it. "I don't know that I ever really acknowledged my lack of power to do anything over it," she says. "I think I always believed something was going to change, which, of course, was completely not true. But I had to believe it

---

* All punctuation, grammar, and notation appears as originally provided by Mr. Maitreya.

because that's what kept me going forward."[19] "Vicki really was the heart and soul of the Bangles," Igleheart reflects. "She was the main leader, really well-respected by everybody. Sue was very driven to be famous, but it was Vicki that really had the vision and the ability to rally the troops around and keep them together."[20] Igleheart concludes, "Vicki is my favorite of the four, as far as somebody I respect and admire. I don't think people realize how much Vicki was the largest part of the Bangles, if you put it down to one person, because she didn't come across that way. Nobody understood that. But on the inside, that was definitely the case. She was the force."[21]

Individual feelings toward what was going on manifested mainly through "grumbling behind the scenes," Igleheart says. "There was never really any fighting that I saw, per se. Nobody ever really jumped down anyone's throat." Debbi, in particular, he says, "was just really jealous [of Susanna]," he explains. "Sue's cool. She doesn't always comprehend how she's being perceived. She could be a little bit of a Jewish American Princess. She was raised by her parents to think that she's wonderful."

Marji Banda thinks Debbi's frustration came from not being heard while the "strong and articulate" Vicki and Susanna were more skilled at getting their points across in specific situations. "People were struggling to see each other's perspectives on things," Marji says. "Debbi held things in, then it percolated up and exploded. It was the third child thing."[22]

Debbi admits that she was jealous of the attention given to her bandmate. However, her youthful naivete may simply have led her to voice what the others in the group were thinking, but not saying aloud. "I was young, trying to find myself, and I wear my heart on my sleeve," she tells me. "I did not know how to articulate my feelings, so I would blurt things out without thinking. Sometimes it was very harsh. I was very emotional and I had a hard time hiding my feelings. I may have come across like I was thoughtless and mean. I am not that at all. I care what other people think—too much. I have a big heart." She goes on to talk about feeling "lost during that time." Lacking mentors or role models to look to for advice and guidance, Debbi's only means to attempt to work out what was happening around her was to verbalize it. "I felt like the band was going in the wrong direction and I felt powerless to stop it," she says. "I realize now that I shouldn't have expressed myself to so many people."

Walker Igleheart hypothesizes that the studio experience for *Different Light* was different for Susanna than for the Petersons, creating a huge chasm within the group. "I don't think she came out of the sessions with David Kahne feeling beat up like Vicki and Debbi were," he says. No matter what, Igleheart says, "Vicki was going to stick with the four piece rock and roll badass thing that she wanted to do." Vicki "was not going to give up her principles of being a rock and roll band." As for Michael, she "was kind of just there," he says. "She respected Vicki a lot," he recounts. Susanna's attitude, he remembers was "What do I have to do to become a star and keep moving forward, keep this rocket going up?"[23]

Susanna disagrees with the personification of her trying to be anything but her best. "Why am I being prosecuted for channeling sex in a performance when rock and roll is *about sex*?" she asks me. "You have to give over to it. I grew up watching Tina Turner, Mick Jagger, and so many others. Most rock and roll is about sex! Is it because I am a woman that this is seen as being offensive or wrong in some way?"

In Susanna, the record label and the media had a complete star package, according to Toni Kasza. "Susanna had the lead voice that was extremely recognizable," she says. "When you have a lead singer, that's where the heat goes, that's just the nature of the bear. So Susanna was going to get more of the attention....I think she wanted it and I think she enjoyed it. I think the other girls enjoyed being in a band. I don't think they were looking to be on the cover of *Vogue* magazine. I think Susanna enjoyed the spotlight. Susanna leaned [into being] sexy just naturally."[24]

22.

Just "being in the band" had not been the plan for either Vicki or Debbi. "The record company and the press were making us into something we were not. The whole 'sexy short skirt' stuff, a lot of that was skewing Sue to the front because she was the cute little one with the tiny skirt and *those eyes*," Debbi says. "I kept feeling like that wasn't us and this is not the band I envisioned from day one. We were becoming something we weren't."[25] Vicki later confided that she "started losing a sense" of who she was.[26] She continues, "I have this ability to have a blind spot about things and it enabled me to carry on. I know it's there but if it wasn't, I don't know what would have happened."[27]

For her part, Michael remained an enigma to most people, with some thinking she "hated everything"[28] and others swearing she was the "coolest chick on the planet."[29] "Michael was going to be miserable no matter what happened, that was her vibe," Igleheart tells me. "I like her, she is a fine person and she was always nice to me. But she is troubled." He gives the example of being on the road, and spending time with the bass player in the band's dressing room. "She was just kind of rocking back and forth, crossing her arms over her body and sighing a lot. It really didn't have anything to do with what was going on. It's just that's what she brings to the party." Igleheart recalls her, "bitch[ing] about Sue a little bit, but I never heard her bitch about Debbi." He remembers her as "very tense, unhappy."[30]

Micki admitted to *Melody Maker* that she had felt "very unattractive" while she was growing up. Being placed on a celebrity pedestal was very uncomfortable for her, as she confided, "I can't quite take it in now though. I can't quite buy it. I don't look at myself first thing in the morning and go 'Michael Steele, international sex symbol.' I see the bags from the jetlag." Known within the band for creating nicknames and catchphrases in the pursuit of breaking on-the-road monotony, Michael had likewise created "a term for people who come back after we've made it." She said, "I call these people 'woodwork people.' A lot of people come out of the woodwork that you wish would stay there. They were there for a good reason to begin with."[31]

Toni Kasza thought Micki's attitude was attributed to her insecurity and shyness. "Micki was not approachable or a people person. Her shyness came across as aloofness and it gave her an aura of cool," she remembers.[32] Long-time tour manager Chris Lamson adds, "She was always the loner in the band. She had a great time, don't get me wrong, but...I think she always felt like a bit of an outsider as the last person to join and really didn't get a lot of writing credits."[33]

Having taken over for Chris Lamson on tour manager duties at the start of 1986, Steve Botting had a front row seat to the band's increasing dysfunction. "Susanna was getting most of the attention. All the singles that were released featured her voice; that didn't sit well with the rest of the band."[34] As Susanna's celebrity grew, the band got more and more visibility, a situation that made it hard to find people who were understanding of their unhappiness. "No one [was] sympathetic," Michael said of the time. "'I'm sorry, you're rich, you're famous.'"[35] For Susanna, "It was just very painful. At a certain point, it is out of your hands. I mean, you can't just change what someone's going write about you."[36]

While the constant touring added to the discombobulated, pressure-cooker atmosphere on the road, there was still fun and moments of awe along the way. During a Bristol stop, all four girls were sitting in their van, parked outside the club they were set to play. "It was after soundcheck and we were chilling out before the show," Vicki remembers. Suddenly, "a mop of curly blonde hair sticks his face into the open door of the van," she laughs. "'Hello,' he says, 'Do you know what time the band goes on?' We all froze." After one of the Bangles replied, "9 p.m.," the man said, "Great!" and walked off. Susanna was the first to speak, Vicki recalls. "'Was that David Coverdale?' she asked. Micki then jumped in, gulping, "Oh my gosh, it was freaking Robert Plant!"

Vicki says the show that evening was "really good," though Plant never came back after the performance to give his regards. The promoter later assured the group that the Led Zeppelin icon had enjoyed the gig, confiding that the flaxen haired singer never hob-knobbed with the acts, instead just showed up sporadically to see live music. "He was the opposite of Prince, who would come in with a huge entourage." Plant, Vicki notes, "would just show up and just leave; he was just an average punter."

Band shorthand also became part of the daily lexicon. Robert Plant was referred to as "St. Bob," while "Heavy Salad" was the expression used in the face of something ponderous or wondrous. "A Doorbell" was "adorable," Vicki explains, while "Full Bangle Regalia" referred to "full stage costumes, hair and makeup done, as opposed to the everyday bag lady look." "Shoe Bag Heaven" entered the vocabulary after Susanna accidentally misplaced some vintage shoes belonging to her grandmother. The term became shorthand for any item or items left behind at a venue or hotel room. Micki was especially guilty of this. "Like clockwork," Vicki laughs, "about half an hour after we had been on the road, she would realize a leather jacket or something else was still in a room now fifty miles away."

Susanna tells me that various *This Is Spinal Tap* references also seeped into their jargon, especially in reference to what backstage catering was (or was not) provided at each tour date. "To a snack or a deli tray in a dressing room, we'd say, 'Who's in here?'—a phrase taken from the Nigel Tufnel character in *Spinal Tap*, when he complained to their tour manager about mysterious snackage," she says.

Debbi emails me one night, recalling another Bangles catchphrase. "I thought of another Bangle-expression," she writes, "Stadium Face." She explains, "We used to watch MTV practically 24/7, and when they showed metal bands, you'd see the lead guitarist shredding...with a slightly pained expression on their faces accompanied by a subtle spreading of the legs as they would rock out. That stance, that look became known as 'Stadium Face,' and we would make fun of each other if we ever did it ourselves."[37]

As the girls contemplated their future, they realized that seemingly the only way they would ever be able to have children or any sort of traditional family life was if they got pregnant and gave birth at the same time, during an unknown, future date. The plan was that this would allow them the minimum downtime from being active musicians, allowing them to "gestate" together before theoretically returning to the frantic pace that their music careers demanded. The envisioned era would be their "Bangle Baby Year," as twelve months would likely be the longest they could fathom ever having time off.

Mike Gormley had become the confidant for each member of the band, taking on the job of mediator. "I'll tell you some things the Bangles may not know or may not agree with," he says. "As they got more popular, the pressure, the schedules, and the things they had to do, were difficult. There were definite problems within the band." He goes on to explain, "I would get a phone call from Sue about something. I get a phone call from Vicki about the same thing but from a different point of view. I'm sitting in the middle. I felt like I was holding them together, hanging on to both sides."[38]

For Susanna, turning to therapy during the brief times she was home from touring or promotional duties was the only way she could deal with the intensity. While being treated, Susanna would see a "Freudian-style" analyst four to five days a week. "You're meant to go that much," she tells me. "You lie on a couch. It was a very specific style of therapy." She confides that she "really needed it" at the time. "It was very stressful in the Bangles," she says. "I've never really spoken of it. I just felt this intense sense of being in a pressure cooker....I'm sure the other girls felt it too. It's very hard to put it into words."[39]

The main "challenges" with the band according to Igleheart were "internal." "They were perpetually unhappy with things," he remembers. There was a general feeling of "things weren't good enough, things could be better, they could've gotten more or better press," he says. "Little stuff just irritated them," he recalls, "and then they started getting irritated with each other."[40]

Despite the band drama, the group was garnering more fans and acclaim than ever. A *Creem* magazine readers poll placed them in the top ten for best album and band of the year, along with bands like the

Smiths, R.E.M., and U2. Susanna was once again singled out, this time for the accolade of "best female singer."

The 1986 Readers Poll
READERS POLL BALLOT FINAL RESULTS
April 1, 1987
Creem Magazine

TOP ALBUM
1. LIFES RICH PAGEANT—R.E.M
2. 5150—VAN HALEN
3. THE QUEEN IS DEAD—THE SMITHS
4. THEN & NOW…THE BEST OF THE MONKEES
5. STANDING ON THE BEACH—THE CURE
6. LISTEN LIKE THIEVES—INXS
7. SO—PETER GABRIEL
8. DIFFERENT LIGHT—THE BANGLES
9. EAT 'EM AND SMILE—DAVID LEE ROTH
10. BRUCE SPRINGSTEEN & THE E STREET BAND LIVE/1975-85—BRUCE SPRINGSTEEN

TOP BAND
1. R.E.M.
2. THE CURE
3. VAN HALEN
4. MONKEES
5. U2
6. INXS
7. TALKING HEADS
8. THE REPLACEMENTS
9. THE BANGLES
10. THE SMITHS

BEST FEMALE SINGER
1. MADONNA
2. SIOUXSIE SIOUX
3. ANNIE LENNOX
4. ANN WILSON
5. SUSANNA HOFFS
6. CYNDI LAUPER
7. CHRISSIE HYNDE
8. WHITNEY HOUSTON
9. KATE BUSH
10. TINA TURNER[41]

23.

After the phenomenal success of "WLAE," Columbia was hot to drop a fourth single from *Different Light*. "Walking Down Your Street," written in 1984 by Susanna and the Three O'Clock's Louis Gutierrez, had a doo-wop, Motown feel while again featuring the brunette on lead vocals.

Notably, it was the first of the band's four US Top 40 hits written by at least one band member. David Kahne shares a credit for the tune on the album's liner notes, perhaps explaining why Debbi called the song especially "torturous" to record.[1] Confiding in an interview that she had "talked to Christopher," aka Prince, about the tune, Susanna explained that the track was originally titled "Desire." When the singer told the "Manic Monday" scribe that in her mind desire could be about just anything—"it could be desire to get an A on your report card to desire for a guy"—Prince fired back, "Oh. I only write about one kind of desire!" Taking the Minnesotan's feedback to heart, the finished track was "about that moment where you've been absolutely infatuated with someone, you're madly in love, you have this incredible burning desire, just like in the Supremes' song," Susanna said. "You've just gotten to the point when you're just walking down the street, and the whole song is in the present tense of why you're walking down the street, to go knock on the door and say, 'Here I am.' You're not gonna wait any more, you're not gonna chicken out anymore, you're just gonna do it. But the whole song takes place while you're walking, so there's a possibility you might change your mind but hopefully—you're willing to sacrifice your pride, even. Just saying, 'Look, I'm completely head over heels in love with you.'"[2]

After the success of "WLAE," the duo of Gary Weis and Kathryn Ireland were again brought in to direct and produce the music video. The premise is of a small-town band winning a local contest to open in Los Angeles for rock and roll legend Little Richard. The "small-town band" is the Love Beats, portrayed by the Bangles.

Several memories from the shoot still make Ireland laugh decades later. The first is from a scene at the start of the video, where the band members are shown in a bedroom. Having just found out they have been the chosen group, a celebratory pillow fight breaks out. "The Bangles were meant to be these kids leaving their suburban homes to go to the big city to play with the huge star [Little Richard]," Ireland recounts. "We had rented a very normal, nice looking tract house for a few days to film the founding parts in." After the take was in the can, feathers that had escaped from the pillows were scattered everywhere in the room. "I told the girls that we had to tidy up," Ireland recalls. "We can't leave this mess, so it was all hands on deck to pick up every last feather." To make sure the job had been thoroughly done, "we had to pull the bed from the wall," Ireland tells me. "Under the bed there was a very good selection of sex toys. We were laughing, saying that the people [who owned the home] looked very unexciting but they must have a good time at night."[3]

The next clip shows a map charting the band starting their cross-country trip from the upper Midwest of the US, in a rusty van driven (appropriately) by Vicki, an homage to a favorite film of Susanna's, Russ Meyer's *Beyond the Valley of the Dolls*. Illustrating the group's simultaneous self-sufficiency and celebrity, while pulled over for a flat tire, then up-and-coming actor Randy Quaid drives up next to them and does the arm movements like those in the "WLAE" video. Upon making it to Los Angeles, the group is chaperoned into a dressing room by a manager, played by then real-life day-to-day guru Mike Gormley. As the girls are getting ready for the show, Little Richard himself comes in to wish them good luck on the performance, donning a fabulous gold lamé jacket. The video cuts to the band on the stage, the vintage vibe continued with their purple fringe dresses.

23.

Weis and Ireland were trying for a wow factor in the "Walking" video to top their efforts from "WLAE." Their first try was with actor Quaid. "We had Randy playing a cameo, but he wasn't quite big enough [of a name yet] though he was an actor and a great friend of ours," Ireland recalls. "I still had not been able to figure out who we were going to be 'opening' for in the video. It was already day two of the shoot, and we still did not have anyone." Time and money were especially tight, as the Bangles were touring; decisions had to be made quickly. Once in Los Angeles, luck struck. A friend of Ireland's told her that Little Richard was staying in town. "He was at a hotel on Sunset Boulevard," she recalls, noting, "it was not the Sunset Marquis." Somehow Ireland found out that the rock 'n' roll pioneer had his eye on a particular gold and silver lamé jacket that was for sale at a local boutique. "My friend told me that if I showed up with that jacket, he would have no qualms about appearing in the Bangles video," Ireland laughs. Ireland went and purchased the garment, using up most of the video's budget. Upon arriving at the singer's accommodation unannounced, Ireland managed to talk her way into going up to the icon's room.

Upon that first encounter, Ireland asked how to address the celebrity. "I said, 'Can I call you Little Richard? Do I call you Little or Richard?' He said, 'I'm Richard.' I showed him the jacket and told him, 'Now, Mr. Richard. This could be yours forever. There is just one thing I need you to do.' Ireland then went on to explain the cameo part for Richard, where he would be the "big star" in the video that the band was opening for. "It was like a dog sitting in front of a big bowl of meat," she says of Richard's desire for the glittery piece. "I couldn't keep his eyes off the jacket." Ireland found herself not only getting Little Richard to swap the sparkly item for a couple seconds screen time, but as a counselor for the distressed star.

The opportunity to appear with a hip band was good for the seemingly washed-up performer. "He was not having a great moment in his mind," she reflects. "He had no career." After agreeing on the exchange of time for clothing, Ireland went on to be regaled by the singer. "I spent the next three hours sitting at the end of his bed, howling with laughter, hearing of his life. It was just fabulous." Richard was the portrait of professionalism, showing up early the next day for his appearance, and being gracious and kind. "He was just fabulous," Ireland declares.[4]

"Walking" would be the last US single from *Different Light*, getting to number eleven on *Billboard* and number sixteen in the UK.

Like their experience while promoting *All Over the Place*, the popularity of *Different Light* meant the Bangles were "permanently on the road."[5] Though touring the globe, the band had little free time to see anything but the inside of a tour bus and the stage. "We go to all these fabulous places....We have all these wonderful romantic meals with...no one. Just the three other girls," Susanna told *Melody Maker*. "We're staying in these picturesque Swiss chalets and there's no one there. I just wish that we could share it sometimes with some guy." "We've been in Paris three times," Michael said. "We're there for 24 hours, we do tons of press, we do the show, pretend to sleep for three hours and then leave."[6]

When Vicki looks back, she describes an exhausting and befuddling existence. "We didn't think that [the time period] was going to be that important in some ways," she says. "It was a matter of daily life. We'd be in Japan, we'd be in Tokyo. I would send our keyboard player or a crew member out with my little Instamatic camera. I'd say, 'Go tell me where I am. Go take pictures.' We had no time to go look at the town or look at the city. We just got stuck in offices or studios or the hotel."[7]

A handful of dates in 1987 filled with promotional tour pandemonium in San Remo, Italy, did prove to be particularly memorable, however. Susanna was going through a rough long-distance relationship. "I had the worst boyfriend in LA at the time," she says. "I remember being in my room, talking to him on the phone. He was just horrid, telling me about all his conquests with these famous movie star women. I was just so tormented."[8] However, the singer was distracted from her romantic woes by the various situations encountered while in Italy. "We had a driver called Alberto Creepa," she laughs. "He would chauffeur us around these crazy winding roads. I was certain we would die."[9]

Things just got more bizarre as the trip progressed. "There was something surreal about it," she says. "I remember at one point we were doing a press tour slash concert tour of Europe, and we were in San Remo with Duran Duran. It was right when 'Walk Like an Egyptian' was number one—we'd done many, many, many tours before that, so it wasn't really an overnight success by any means, but there was one point where we did like [in air quotes] 'a real press conference.' We were brought in to what we thought would be a guy and maybe two photographers. Instead it was blinding flash bulbs. We were just standing there like deers in the headlights." It was not at all expected, Susanna tells me. "We weren't that recognizable when we weren't on stage," she says. "I always described it as a *La Dolce Vita* moment," she laughs.[10]

Vicki recounts the scene, saying, "I have a very specific memory of walking into what we thought was a press conference, which we have done before. But this was the cliché rock experience, the stereotypical blinding explosion of flashbulbs that did not stop and not stop and not stop. It was one of the first times we'd experienced anything to that level. This was us Bangles, going into the room, full of press and journalists, then sitting in front of them at a table. I felt like it was a Beatles moment." When asked if it was scary, Vicki honestly answers. "I found it exhilarating. For me, it was physical enactment of one of my teenage dreams."

The band then had another engagement to go to, having accepted an invitation to dinner with Duran Duran. The night started off with both groups "all crammed into a black cab." "We had too many humans in this car," Vicki laughs, "again, your cliché rock and roll scenario." Hysterical fans surrounded the automobile. "Girls were screaming and crying like Beatlemania, Duran Duran mania," Susanna recalls. "'I love you John! I love you Simon!' And they were climbing on the cars," she says.[11] "I sat on Simon's lap." Vicki was squished in next to the British lead singer. "I remember him saying to me, 'You were in the fringe dress in the "Walk Like an Egyptian" video, right?' I answered, 'Yeah.' He goes, 'Oh, dead sexy, very nice. Very nice. Lovely.'" The meal was equally chaotic. "We went to a restaurant and the girls are pounding on the windows," Susanna recalls. When asked how the Duran Duran boys dealt with the constant barrage of attention, Susanna says, "they tuned it out. They were so used to it. They just conversed as girls were shouting 'John' and 'Simon' repeatedly."[12]

Years later, Susanna reminded her old friends about the Italian madness. "Cut to Rock and Roll Hall of Fame in 2019," she says. "I've inducted the Zombies, and Duran Duran are there as well. I get urged on by my friend to go to the after-party that Stevie Nicks is throwing. I'm schmoozing with Brian May and I'm hanging with John Taylor again. Then I go over somewhere else at the party and I'm talking to Simon. I'm recounting the story of San Remo, and how we all crammed into a car and girls were screaming and rocking it like Beatlemania. I said, 'There was no room for me to sit but on your lap.' He just replied, 'Did I have an erection?' I laughed, 'I don't remember that.' It was one of the cheekiest things and he is so funny. I love Simon Le Bon."[13]

Just days after the bedlam in Italy, the Bangles were in the UK. They had been nominated for the prestigious British Phonographic Industry Award, or BRIT, in the category for International Group. Competition was fierce, with the field consisting of A-ha, Bon Jovi, Cameo, and Huey Lewis and the News. "I didn't want to think they were going to get it," Mike Gormley recounted. "I didn't want to jinx the whole thing. When I heard they were nominated, I didn't want to think about it too much; but it did happen! It was great."[14]

The girls from California found themselves not only recipients of the coveted award, but rubbing shoulders with childhood heroes. "It was a star-spangled night," Gormley smiles. "George Martin came up and talked to us."[15] For Debbi, the evening was a moment of happiness. "Kate Bush and Eric Clapton were there," she remembers. "We were onstage with all these amazing people that we totally respected including Peter Gabriel. It was one of those moments where it was like 'pinch me.' We were presented as being on the same level. I felt like we were accepted. Especially being in England, where the press tend to really knock you down."[16] Former MTV executive Brian Diamond was Vicki's date for the evening. "I remember looking at Vicki and going, 'How fucking cool is this? You just won a BRIT Award.' We were sitting at a table right next to George Harrison."[17] Though her main memories of the evening are of chatting with Martin and having a tête-à-tête with Robert "St. Bob" Plant, Vicki tells me about her gala fashion choice. "I had on a silver foil dress with black edging: I looked like a big baked potato."[18]

After the BRIT award win, Sony executives had decided to attempt to flog one more single from *Different Light* in the British and European markets. Their choice of the Michael Steele–penned "Following" was a departure from the previous four singles, featuring lead vocals from Micki and acoustic guitar. The first original song contributed to the band by Michael did not perform as well as the previous Susanna-featured tracks. However, marketing efforts were nonexistent, and no promotional activities, not even a music video, were made to support its release. It charted at an uninspiring number fifty-five in the UK, a better twenty-two in Ireland, but failed to chart in any other territory.

Back in Los Angeles, on a rare day off, Susanna would attempt to spend time with friends. She had been a fan of the Go-Go's since before she had even met the Peterson sisters. "I never felt competitive with them. It was like a light bulb went off when the Go-Go's started to take off. I really thought that they were like me. I revered them."[19] Having played numerous gigs together and running in the same social circles, she and lead Go-Go Belinda Carlisle had found an easy comradery. One night, the duo decided to make it a mission to find Julian Lennon, who they had heard was in town. "We weren't trying to seduce him," Susanna clarifies, "but we wanted to get eyes on him." Still living in her parents' garage in Brentwood, the two women "got a little crazy" before roaming Los Angeles, on the lookout for Beatle offspring. "The fact that he was somewhere in LA was fascinating," Susanna explains. "We just drove around until we eventually found him at a bar somewhere."[20]

Meanwhile, Debbi had been tapped to star alongside Go-Go's drummer Gina Schock in a commercial for a new soda called Slice, which was coming onto the market. With the catchy jingle of "We got the juice… Slice! Slice!" the ad features flying fruit, splashing liquid, and a lot of big hair on the duo of drummers as they bash away, making huge waves with their sticks on the kits. "It was two days of getting wet constantly," Debbi laughs. "I had four outfits that were the same. The drumsticks had hoses coming through my jacket and holes in the drumsticks, with water spurting out of the drumsticks. There was water all over the drums. I remember just being wet for two days. I had fun doing it because it was 'I'm doing a commercial, how exciting.'"[21]

Though the ad hit television screens in 1987, it was shot at the end of 1986. Debbi was by herself on set; in contrast, she describes Schock having a "crew, friends, and an entire ensemble" with her. "I was alone doing this," she notes. At one point, she remembers Mike Gormley coming to the shoot with Vicki. "I was on a break and they told me it ['WLAE'] had gone to number one. I went 'Oh, really?' and then went back to shooting the commercial. I just wasn't like, 'Wow, fucking great. This is awesome. Oh my god, we're number one.' I was like, 'Oh really? Okay' because I just felt like such a failure. It was just constantly prodding, the failure that I was because I didn't play drums on it. I didn't sing on it. I failed the audition. I just felt like a complete failure."[22]

A better experience was had when Debbi made an appearance on *Late Night with David Letterman* two years later. Host Letterman famously did a regular feature, counting down the top ten list of news stories of each week. The suspense as the numbers descended from ten to one was increased by a drum roll, usually supplied by house drummer Anton Fig of the World's Most Dangerous Band, the show's outfit led by legendary music director Paul Shaffer. Occasionally, other artists would be invited to guest on the show. "I had the honor to be chosen and got to play with Paul Shaffer and his band!" Debbi says. "It was intimidating, but exhilarating!" Things did not go completely smoothly, Debbi confesses. "I did drop a stick and was very concerned that I'd look foolish in front of millions of viewers! Luckily, they shoot the show in the afternoon [I'm sure for censoring purposes and camera angles, etc.], so they had edited the show in a way that made me look good! There was a shot of David [when we were playing Palisades Park and I was in search of another drumstick] jumping off his chair, getting into it!"

To the world outside of the inner Bangles sanctum, the accolades kept coming. On February 23, 1987, Los Angeles mayor Tom Bradley declared it Bangles Day for the city. The proclamation was followed by a shindig in New York City at Tramps, the famed music venue, celebrating *Different Light* going double platinum (selling over two million copies in the US). The event was packed with celebrities, including members of the Beastie Boys, captured in a snap with Susanna. An interview recorded at the party with the girls has them promising the third Bangles album will be packed with "more harmony, more drums, more rock," going so far as to joke of the venture being a "rock opera."[23]

The band was styled in vintage glamour, seeing Vicki donning a cigarette holder and flat black hat tilted jauntily to the side and Debbi rocking elbow length gloves. "I remember getting my hair done," Debbi laughs. "We were like, 'Okay, let's all do a *Breakfast at Tiffany's* vibe with fancy bows and dressing up.' Now I look at myself and I'm like 'What the fuck dress was that?' At the time, we were very excited. It was just amazing to get recognized like that, even if it was that record." It was especially important to Debbi, as parents Milt and Jeanne were in attendance. "They were there for pretty much every monumental landmark experience that we had," she says. "They were amazing, my parents."[24]

The Bangles finally had a bit of a reprieve, taking a much-needed six-week break from touring—and each other. "It probably would have been healthier for us had we allowed each other the room to go off and do whatever it was, however silly, however ridiculous, i.e. going off for six weeks and making a movie," Susanna said. "Or making a solo record. But we were kind of a band which focused on everybody being committed to the band and giving all of their time just to the band; it was part of what created the pressure cooker," she later reflected.[25] Much to her bandmates' surprise, Susanna decided to spend the time off acting in a lighthearted movie called *The Allnighter*, directed, produced, and cowritten by her mother, Tamar. "I think I just needed to...go do something that seemed fun and different and exciting," she reflected. Alongside Susanna, the film featured then up-and-comers Joan Cusack and Michael Ontkean, with iconic Pam Grier as a tough-talking cop. The plot of the film centers on a group of friends graduating from college and facing adulthood:

> Molly, Val and Gina are graduating college, but on their final night, frustrations are aired. Molly is still looking for real love and Val is beginning to doubt if that is what she's found. Gina is too busy videotaping everything to really notice. When the final party at Pacifica College kicks off, things don't go exactly as planned.[26]

"It's certainly not the thing I'm most proud of in my life, but I'm happy I did it. It was something I got to do with my mom,"[27] Susanna later said. Mike Gormley had been asked to help supervise the film's music. "It wasn't the greatest movie on Earth," he explains of the project, "but I know she enjoyed doing it. It wasn't trash: it was good."[28]

Not everyone was excited about Susanna's most recent acting turn, especially her fellow Bangles. "I read the script, and I couldn't believe it was getting made," Vicki says. "It was supposed to be a sort of coming-of-age plot. But it is very cringeworthy where a woman directs her daughter to dance in her underwear."[29] Vicki went to visit Susanna on the film set at Laird Studios in Culver City, her former employer during an early incarnation of the band back when it was her, Debbi, and Amanda. In the typical Susanna fashion of maximum preparation, Vicki recalls her bandmate "reading the classic Actors Studio literature. She was really getting into that whole thing."[30] Susanna later admitted that it was "very hard to watch yourself" on screen. "It doesn't surprise me when actors say, 'I've never seen the movie,'" she admitted. "The scary thing about this job is you kind of put yourself on the line."[31]

Susanna was indeed stepping out from her now-familiar world of music, viewing the movie as a chance to work with and spend time with her mother after years of being away on tour. The elder Hoffs "was such a believer in positive thinking that she and her daughter didn't really see how bad *The Allnighter* really was," according to Vicki. "That's what I was up against," she said. "I wasn't going to look her in the eye and say you know what? It's really, really embarrassing. The only concern of mine was that it was going to reflect on the band."[32] Peers and even the group's inner circle were dubious about the cinematic undertaking. Long-time friend Joanna "Spock" Dean shakes her head at the mention of the film. "I'm not dissing Susanna," she says.[33]

For some, the film perfectly encapsulated 1980s teen cinema. "I thought this movie was great," reads one review. "It is your typical '80s flick, and being a child from the 80s, I loved it. Susanna Hoffs shows us she cannot only sing but act. And where do they get the cute guys.[sic] I just wish it was longer or had a sequel."[34]

However, the critics were quick and fast to pile in on the dual Hoffs effort. The Prince hype had just cooled off; and now the press had a new angle to focus on, again squarely spotlighting Susanna. "Grotesque in the AIDS era," wrote Leonard Maltin. "Though it would be a stinker any time."[35] *Rolling Stone* blasted the movie under the banner "Worst Mother and Child Reunion,"[36] while the *Hollywood Reporter* went so far as to say *The Allnighter* "borders on child abuse."[37] *LA Weekly* ripped the pair apart, calling Tamar a "ruthless stage mom" and the film a "teen-flesh spectacle."[38] The brutal reception left the pair feeling, "misunderstood," according to Tamar.[39] For Susanna, it was another example of trying something different and being harshly judged for straying from public expectation. "I've always felt oversensitive to life," says Susanna. "When does the rite of passage end?"[40]

Former manager Chris Lamson says that the film did not calm inter-band relations for the Bangles, and instead stoked an already nearly explosive strain. "It didn't help at all," he says of *The Allnighter*, "because that was another domino in the 'Sue is getting more attention' game."[41] Miles Copeland concurred. "The Go-Go's accepted the fact that Belinda Carlisle was the front person, and she was going to sing the songs, and get most of the press," he says. "The Bangles were very different. They did not want to see any individual in the group step forward and become the star. You had to have four spotlight operators; each one had to be in the spotlight. There were no solo band members."[42]

The public and the press, though, felt otherwise. Susanna could not control the way the press portrayed her in contrast to her bandmates. For example, in a *Melody Maker* interview, she is described as "a tiny little sparrow with animated dark eyes, an excitable manner and a lot more chatter than patter, twirls her legs round in the chair and looks amused." Vicki, on the other hand, is said to be "a forthright, homely-looking Bangle, talk[ing] discontentedly…"[43] When asked about his favorite bands, even Tom Petty singled out Susanna as a "great vocalist."[44] A *Rolling Stone* feature is quick to point out that Susanna "has the most song writing credits on the new album and gets the lion's share of attention for her petite, slightly pouty glamour and her warm vocals on tunes like 'Manic Monday,'" while also noting how "she co-writes all her songs with other group members and sings less than a third of the leads."[45]

Yet instead of enjoying the hard-earned stardom, Susanna found it incredibly difficult, especially when dealing with her own bandmates. "I guess the best way I can describe it is that it became really uncomfortable for me," Susanna admits. "Because when people would say 'Are you the lead singer?' I would say 'No, actually I'm not.' Then I'm sort of defending the fact that I'm not. It just caused this tension with all of us. In some way, it's obviously flattering if someone likes what you do. But the more tense everybody got about it, the more tense I felt about it."[46]

There seemed to be no solution to what was happening that aligned with the band's basic philosophy of consistency on all fronts. "The 'we're all equal' philosophy became, in a sense, a straitjacket," Copeland mused. "Because obviously Susanna began to move forward a bit, reality-wise. It's a natural thing, a little cute girl in front is going to get more attention."[47] Chris Lamson calls fame a "rough thing." "With fame came more attention to Sue and that didn't fly," he says. "There was nothing they could really do about it because it was like fighting a losing battle. When the main media decides you're the star, what are you going to do? They could have addressed it better internally but this happens in bands a lot. A band that goes from zero to sixty pretty quickly and faces that kind of attention and that kind of fame and that kind of spotlight—it's really tough for people to adapt to it. They just couldn't and they weren't 'All for one, one for all,' anymore. It became a battle for who gets what attention."[48]

Even fellow all-girl band member Kathy Valentine of the Go-Go's felt frustration at the Bangles "sudden" success. She writes about the time in her autobiography, confessing:

> The Bangles were everywhere, too, on tour, on the MTV awards, on the cover of *Rolling Stone*. I read the cover story, incensed about how they gave no credit to the Go-Go's for kicking the fucking door down and making it easier to convince a big label to sign an all-female band. The conflict between being proud and protective of our legacy and yet so bitter and depressed over losing it magnified my frustration and unhappiness.[49]

As the focal point of admiration, lust, frustration, jealousy, and aspiration, Susanna says the time period "was just rife for being challenging on a human level…everyone was doing the best that they could in that moment."[50] With relationships already near breaking point, bonds within the band were further stressed when Susanna alone was asked to be on the cover of *Spin* magazine's July 1987 issue. "I, in no way, called *Spin* magazine and said, 'Hey, put me on the cover,'" Susanna tells me, saying the decision was down to the group's management. "We were like the children and the managers were like the parental figures," she tells me. "I was just told *Spin* wants to do this," she remembers, "it wasn't brought to a negotiation table where the Bangles were brought in to say yes or no. I was just told I was doing it. I didn't have a say in it." Susanna sighs, noting, "I don't think I was singled out. I was just a kid in my twenties, trying to do the best I could."[51]

Though actual feelings were rarely confronted and dealt with head on, Susanna was not immune to the emotional turmoil of her bandmates. Instead of discussing what was going on, issues would manifest in what Susanna describes as "extremely obvious uncomfortable silences."[52] She harkens back to the *Spin* cover, saying the tensions in the band over that cover became unbearable.

Susanna confides, "I understand that everybody wanted to be seen and heard in equal measure and that's a fair thing to want." However, she makes a clear delineation between being an artist or musician in a band and being in the "music *business*," noting, "We had very little power, if any, when it came to which songs would be chosen as singles. Those decisions were entirely in the hands of the executives and marketing team at Sony.

"You start off sitting in a room, attempting to write a song and if you're lucky, you end up with one worthy enough to record. Then, you have to hope the record label will like it too. If they do, that song then becomes a 'product' which a 'product manager' at the label must find a way to sell. The ultimate dream is that your music finds its way to someone who will go on to love that song."

She continues, "I don't know what was in their [her bandmates] heads apart from them obviously being a little upset that somehow I was potentially more visible or making a slightly bigger splash even when everything had to be so perfectly equal."[53]

When I ask Vicki about what she thought Susanna's goals were for the band, she thinks carefully before answering. "She's always been very good at getting people to help her do things, which is not stupid," Vicki diplomatically explains. "That's very smart, and efficient. I don't think that occurred to her that there was any inequality there [in the band]. I think she was perfectly fine to be who she was, getting in the middle [of the stage] and singing the songs. That was perfectly comfortable for her." Vicki pauses. "But do I think that at the beginning, she really wanted to be [in] a band? Yeah, I do believe that; but she also had a more overarching vision. Micki said this to me in the early days, 'You know that this is just a stepping stone for her [Susanna]. Right? She doesn't care about this.' I replied, 'That's not true. I've asked her specifically, she told me specifically she cares about it.' I remember that because it stuck with me."[54]

Discussion turns to another Miles Copeland–managed group, the Police, and the idea that Andy Summers and Stewart Copeland did not mind Sting having the lion's share of the spotlight. "If she's ever said that in front of me, it would have been a different conversation because we probably wouldn't have the band as discussed," Vicki says of such an arrangement. "That would not have flown for me ever. That's not what I wanted. I wanted to be in a group that was a group." If Susanna viewed the Bangles as being in a similar situation, Vicki argues, it "underlines and emphasizes everything that I just said about her overarching goals. While we were in the moment, she would just be like 'I'm not looking for that, they just asked me to be on the cover of *Spin*, I don't know why.'"[55]

While miscommunications were brewing among the band members, there was an external backlash brewing about the validity of the group. As the individuals in the Bangles attempted to capture their own piece of the spotlight through personal style, the media were continuously encouraging them to lean into their sex appeal—not their music—to sell the "product." "The Bangles are fighting the old battle to be seen as a band, not simply a group of chicks," *Rolling Stone* rightly asserted. Michael underpins this idea, adding, "We don't want to make it sound like we always complain, some people—especially photographers—get the idea that because we're women, they can treat us like models, dress us up and give us whatever image comes into their heads. They do stuff with us they'd never think of doing with guys. We want people to realize we're not models, we're not actresses, we're not some sixties act, and we're not a cute novelty. We're a rock and roll band and that's the way we want to be treated."[56]

Michael's commentary, while appropriate for how the band was often viewed and approached, is especially pithy, as it came on the heels of Susanna making both a turn as an actress in a film where she did strip down to her underwear. When I ask Susanna about this, she brings up 1980s contemporary Madonna. "Madonna was so big at the exact same time as we were, though it's not an apples to apples comparison," she admits. "But Madonna was very tapped into the persona and started out like us, thrift store chic, which was a cool part of the '80s. It's part of the zeitgeist and what makes the '80s cool: the scrappiness that we all had to create whatever the persona was."[57] In 1987, Susanna told *Rolling Stone*, "There was one [person] not long ago who wanted us to completely change our look, take off our clothes."[58] Susanna now says, "I don't remember anybody telling me, 'Hike up the skirt another inch or two.' No one ever said that, that I remember, but it's been a long time. Maybe they were murmuring on the sidelines, 'We need to sell the band and make them sexier or make them as sexy as Madonna.' I don't remember that. I just remember trying to survive the experience."[59]

Though ties were eroding within, the Bangles were still a united force to outsiders, though there would be moments where flashes of disgruntlement would show through the facade they firmly had in place for the public. In an appearance on MTV's show *Mouth to Mouth*, the presenter puts a question to the girls, then jovially laughs when the girls scramble among each other for an answer. "There's a bit of a fight developing here!" he laughs, not realizing how close to the surface such feelings were actually lurking.[60] A common query the band was repeatedly asked was what "lessons" they had learned from the Go-Go's, as if only another all-female lineup could offer guidance. "Why should we have to learn from that?" Michael told *Rolling Stone* when confronted with the question, with Vicki agreeing, "They might as well ask if we've learned anything from what happened to The Beatles."[61] Though the target for much of the friction within the group, Susanna also defended the band, telling a journalist that the Bangles had "more staying power" than their peers, and that the "secret" to staying together was "being four music lovers who also love each other." She asserted that, "We're more than good friends," saying, "You give up some individuality for the collective, but if you can learn to agree to disagree then it works great."[62]

Being crowned the current "it" girl-group came with the predictable, repeated ad nauseum criticism. In response to a *Rolling Stone* cover story, several fans had issue with some of the ideas posed in the piece, airing their grievances in the magazine's renowned "Letter to the Editor" column:

> The Go-Go's left behind two great albums (*Beauty and the Beat, Vacation*) and one truly brilliant one (*Talk Show*). Now do you have to denigrate them to get us to take The Bangles seriously. Show me a Bangles hit and I'll show you a song someone else wrote.
> Christopher Hill
> New York, New York

> The Bangles are rock? Give me a break. They're everything a male-dominated music industry and a suppressed public expect from a girl group. They're wimpy, cute, benign, harmless, pouty and stuck in the past. Let's not pretend they're breaking new ground.
> Deborah Galli-Boivin
> Studio City, California[63]

No matter what, the girls did their best to focus on the music, regardless of what else was going on. By June 1987, the band was back on the road, with alternating opening bands Hoodoo Gurus and Cutting Crew. In July, the Bangles appeared at a handful of dates with Duran Duran, even providing some guest voices for some of their friends' hit tracks. Just days before, Michael and Susanna had played as a backup band for Hollywood heartthrob Rob Lowe as he performed "Twist and Shout" at an opening of the Hard Rock Cafe in Hawaii. The events cemented the girls' A-list status. Yet their success had not truly set in, according to

Vicki. "We used to joke that you had 'made it' once you had your own washer and dryer in your own apartment. That was pretty much it."[64] Buying flash cars was not high on the agenda for anyone in the group. "Micki had her manual Volvo," Vicki remembers. "I had a hand-me-down car from my dad for years. I never had a cool car. I finally bought a four-wheel drive Montero from Belinda Carlisle."[65]

Around this time, composer friend Thomas Newman got in touch about a possible project, a screen adaptation of Bret Easton Ellis's best-selling novel, *Less Than Zero*. The book, set in 1980s Los Angeles, follows a group of nihilistic, overindulged but ultimately isolated teenagers. Newman was making a name for himself scoring movies and was flying high off the success of 1985's *Desperately Seeking Susan*. "Tommy says to me, 'I'm doing the score for Bret Easton Ellis's adult film adaptation of *Less Than Zero*. It's going to be wall-to-wall music,'" Susanna remembers. Having already been familiar with the best-selling novel, Susanna suggested the band's version of "Hazy Shade of Winter" as an option for the soundtrack. Newman loved the idea, as the song "encapsulated a moment in time in the '80s."[66]

Rick Rubin was brought in to produce the song, as the movie's soundtrack was being released on Rubin's Def Jam label, and saw the Bangles as being on equal terms with the rising stars of hip-hop. "The whole thing is a departure," Debbi said at the time of the album lineup. "We're alongside people like LL Cool J, Public Enemy and Oran 'Juice' Jones. We haven't gone Def or rap. Rick's just given us a hard rock edge which we needed for the cold season."[67] The band was still bruised from the last experience in the studio making *Different Light*, thus there was trepidation at the new opportunity. "We started working with Rick Rubin on 'Hazy Shade of Winter,'" says Vicki.[68] "Well, he started it with us. It was kind of an interesting progression. What we got was a really good basic track going"—with drums and guitars—before "Rubin split for the nearby Rainbow Room," leaving the girls with assistant producer George Drakoulias to finish the track, and ultimately added two further days of overdubs—keyboards, acoustic guitars, and vocals.[69] Neither Rubin nor

Drakoulias had ever worked with women before, later admitting to being unsure of the arrangement.[70] However, the Bangles had been performing "Hazy Shade" for years as part of their set. Having perfected it over countless shows, they were ready for the moment at hand. "We did the whole lot," says Vicki. "We Bangles knew how to sing together and we knew how to arrange vocals. We had done it for many years."

One specific Bangles addition was a keyboard introduction to the tune. "That little keyboard intro—I love it," says Vicki. "[Rubin] hated it. I think it didn't sound organic enough for him. I understood because I was anti-synth for so long." Added Michael, "One of the greatest things he [Rubin] said was, 'I don't want any of those [sissy] synthesizers on my records.' Here's the guy who [took from] Led Zeppelin, which was one of the first great bands that used huge synthesizer sounds. We had a good time with him, though. Rick is a star." The band was also keen to update their rendition of the track to match the film they were making it for. "We wanted it to fit with the movie better," Vicki explained, "so we put a synthesizer on, just to make it more ethereal. And he [Rubin] said, 'synths are homo—totally homo, dude.'"[71]

Rubin was so repulsed by the band's changes that he told them he did not want his name included on the track's credits. "We softened the edges of the song because we put back more of a folk element that was in the original Simon and Garfunkel version," Vicki explained. Rubin, according to Susanna, "had this original minimalist approach, whereas we wanted it a little more filled out; we just didn't agree." The Bangles also brought in another Mike Gormley–managed band member, Steve Bartek from Oingo Boingo, to provide acoustic guitar layers. Ultimately, the band were "basically the producers."[72]

With Paul Simon being a life-long inspiration, Vicki recalls that recording the song was "a little nerve-racking." "He was one of my childhood idols," she says. "You don't mess with one of his songs—it would be like messing around with a John Lennon tune." The band did remove some of the lyrics from the 1966 track, including the lines "looking over manuscripts / of unpublished rhyme / drinking my vodka and lime." Worried about what he may think, the Bangles sent Simon "a tape of the song, with a bottle of good vodka and a sack of limes, and wrote a note saying: 'Dear Paul, Sorry about the vodka and the limes—here's the replacement!'" The girls were given the stamp of approval from the icon; years later, in 2003, when Simon and Garfunkel reunited for the Old Friends concert, a further accolade was laid at the band's feet as "Hazy Shade of Winter" was included on the duo's set list, done with an arrangement based on the Bangles' version.[73]

At the time, though, the girls had low expectations for the song's reception. "We didn't really think anyone was going to hear it," Susanna confided. "We thought it was just going to be lost on a soundtrack album, lost in the movie." Micki concurred, noting, "We had no idea that people were going to go, 'Single! Single! Video!'" Vicki agreed, admitting that, "It was a surprise that it hit so big because we did the whole project just as a fun thing to do." She continued, "Our priority at that time was writing songs for the new album. We didn't want to take a lot of time out to do anything else. But the project came up, it was interesting. We saw some of the rough footage of the film and it struck me as being sort of…antidrug."[74]

At one point, Susanna even admits that the Bangles considered not releasing the track, as they felt "a little uncomfortable." The group's mind was only changed after everyone who heard it unanimously agreed it was a hit. "What really made me happy was a lot of people who didn't really think of the Bangles as a guitar band and a rock band because they'd heard 'Manic Monday,' which has the keyboard riff featured, and 'Egyptian,' which is like a novelty song to a lot of people," Susanna says. "All these kids who wear tie-dye shirts and only listen to Led Zeppelin…They were buying 'Hazy Shade of Winter' and going 'this is the best thing that the Bangles have ever done.' We're happy about that."[75] Vicki agreed, saying, "when people really responded to it, I think it was a nice little confidence booster."[76]

The success of "Hazy Shade" illustrated how triumphant the band could be when left to their own devices. "In my opinion, they proved everybody wrong when they went and cut 'Hazy Shade of Winter' themselves and it sounded amazing," says Chris Lamson. "That's the one song that truly sounds like the Bangles live. It's their soul and their heart and everything in that recording—and they did it themselves." Lamson adds, "It's the most important song they recorded."[77] "'Hazy Shade' represented a moment where we sounded the most on a record of the way we actually sound live," Michael agreed. The track proved to Vicki that "if we were left alone in a recording studio, we were okay, we could function and we could actually do a pretty good job."[78]

Stephen Rice was the art director for *Less Than Zero*. "Out of all the bands that were in that soundtrack, everybody realized that one song ['Hazy Shade of Winter'] was what they really wanted to emphasize as the musical component of that movie," he says. "Everybody recognized from the get-go that it had that hit factor: It has that really nice hook and feel. It's a song that everybody knows but it's better than the original. The song had a bass but their version of it just put it into a more forward-thinking time and repurposed it for a much bigger audience." The band was special, and significant for the time of changing traditional roles, Rice concludes. "What really made them [the Bangles] unique was that they had the chops, they were good musicians and the harmonies."[79]

Released in November 1987, the single went all the way to number two on the *Billboard* chart in February 1988, prompting Michael to tell an interviewer that fans should try to hear the new material the band was working on, "before some producer gets ahold [sic] of them."[80] If we hadn't been so messed up as a band," Michael later reflected, "perhaps it could have been a turning point."[81]

The third album that was contractually part of the Sony agreement was clearly on everyone's mind, as the Bangles were set to begin recording in July 1987. "The first record you make, you had years to prepare for it," Debbi explains. "The second record is a sophomore effort, which you have to get together really quick because you're still touring on the first record, then you have to tour the second one and then the third one is like, 'Can I just get a break from these people?' Because it was like eat, sleep, and drink Bangles. We just needed a break."[82]

While most bands would be thrilled with so many hits in such a short time, the Bangles were disintegrating, with Susanna feeling ever more uncomfortable under the media glare while the rest of the group felt virtually invisible. "I could tell the way the videos were going very pro-Sue," Debbi recalled. "I could see it all happening."[83]

The constant threat by label and management of possibly "losing their shot" of success if they took a breather created a stifling environment. There seemed no choice but to continue to press on. Though having more stakeholders invested in their career than ever before, not one person advised the girls to take a much-needed break or have frank conversations with each other about how they were feeling. "I would be afraid to say anything to Susanna because I was afraid that would be the end," Vicki confides. "Why did Susanna not come to me and say she wanted to take a year? We did not know we could take a break; there was too much fear over possibly taking a break. If you do not get up at 4 a.m. to do breakfast TV, four million people would not see you. You have to do these things to move your record up the chart. We did every stupid show we were asked to do." Though long proponents of substance over style, the girls found themselves each going shorter with the skirts, higher with the hair, and more outrageous with the makeup, in a bid to literally be seen. "I felt very resentful at the time, and I felt it wasn't a true representation of what we were all about, and what we were all working for," Debbi says.[84]

24.

In July 1987, the band went into the studio to begin work on their third contractually obligated album with Sony. The new project had a budget of $350,000, much larger than their previous albums, meaning the expectation to create chart-topping hits was nonnegotiable. Yet there was a complete absence of discussion as to how the newest Bangle venture would come together or how each member was dealing with the grueling schedule, fame, and nonstop touring. "The problem," Debbi said, "was we really didn't talk about it...it's almost like you're married. None of us actually expressed our true feelings. I would try to do it, and of course my emotions would take over and it would just come out all gobbledegook and go the wrong way." The girls desperately "needed space away from each other," Susanna reflected, noting that everyone was understandably "burned out." The only way to "survive emotionally" and fulfill the legal commitment to the record company was to write new songs with other people outside their foursome. "I knew things were tense but I was just used to it," said Susanna. "We were all used to it. It was just part of the fact that we just didn't know how to talk about things when they didn't feel good. Everyone would just kind of sit there feeling weird and uncomfortable. We didn't have any way to have a group Bangle therapy session."[1]

Though band dynamics may not have been ideal, Debbi describes the writing of their third album, *Everything*, as "weirdly good." "It was stressful but...it was like the *White Album* where nobody was in the same room at the same time. We were starting to really fall apart at that point."[2] Though the group was "becoming very separated," it was a moment of artistic expression and emotional healing for Debbi after the horrors of making *Different Light*. "Oddly enough, I felt more freedom doing that record because I felt like they [the rest of the group] weren't around to pressure me; no one was waiting in the wings to take over because I was away from David Kahne."[3]

For Michael, returning to a less polished sound was also of high importance on the newest outing. "The EP and the first album sounded more like the way we think we sound live. More guitars, more of just a natural feel. With *Different Light,* we got into some pretty heavy production values. We started getting away from the way we think we are in real life. You know, we're basically a guitar band, a garage band. And that's what we're shooting for with this next record—the guitar!"[4]

Though now on their third major label release, having had a multi-platinum album and a number one global hit, press outlets were still unwilling to admit that an all-female group could have such talent and musical aptitude. Instead of celebrating the Bangles' barrier-breaking success in their publications, magazines insisted on featuring astonishingly misogynist texts as their headlines. "Two Big Questions were still unanswered," *Cashbox* reported. "Could these alleged musicians actually play their instruments (it was common knowledge that producer David Kahne had brought in a squad of crack studio musicians to beef up *Different Light*) and were The Bangles capable of writing hit songs for themselves?"[5] Though other iconic all-male groups had utilized the exact techniques criticized, it is difficult to imagine such blasphemous assertions being lobbed against them in such a derogatory fashion. Yet the Bangles still found themselves on the defensive when accosted by ruthless reporters dead set on ignoring the factual talent of the foursome. "We have always played our own instruments," Vicki retorted. "Anybody who knows us knows that. We've always had additional instrumentalists on the records, but so did the Rolling Stones, and nobody says, 'Oh, did Keith Richards play that solo?'"[6] In a *USA Today* television segment, the presenter croons, "The Bangles are now making a mark as songwriters. Every cut on this new record is written by the girls in the band, and it's just one more step on a musical journey that began with a childhood dream."[7] Such poorly researched packages completely omitted the literal decades of combined songwriting experience held within the band for the more socially expected angle of female innocence when it came to the male-dominated world of creating tracks.

One thing the band did agree on was that David Kahne would not be included in the making of the new album. With *Different Light*'s success, the girls had finally attained some autonomy from the label's demands, allowing them to decide how to craft their next project. "We knew we didn't want to work with David Kahne again," says Susanna. "The record company probably thought, 'Hey, this works—let's keep doing it.' But they didn't know what it was for us emotionally."[8] After the experience of *Different Light*, Debbi could not have been more pleased to be moving on. "We talked to several producers, but didn't actually have an easy choice," she says. "We weren't sure what we wanted out of the role," she explained, as the group had "only worked with David Kahne; we didn't know what to expect."[9]

Vicki suggested rock writer and budding producer Davitt Sigerson as an option. The New York–born Sigerson had been educated in Britain, making him a great match for the Anglophile-loving Bangles. He had also recently worked on the album *Boomtown* by Los Angeles studio musicians David & David, which had birthed a top ten hit in the lead single "Welcome to the Boomtown." Sigerson had also recorded Olivia Newton-John and "was better than [someone] coming from the Sue camp," reflected Debbi, meaning any person recommended by Susanna. "We talked to different producers but he just seemed like a really nice guy. He seemed really cool and didn't have an attitude," the drummer recounts.[10]

Like some of the record-buying public, Sigerson had been led to doubt the actual ability of the Bangles to play and write their own material. When he found that he had been short-listed as a possible candidate for producing their next album, he was intrigued but not committed. Like many others, he was unsure what actual talent the band had. He recalls being pleasantly shocked upon attending his first band practice as to how accomplished and underrated the women were. "I went and heard them in rehearsal, not knowing what I thought or 'Are they for real?'" says Sigerson. "Before they even sang, from the first notes they played, I thought, 'Goddammit, this is a band!' What I wanted to do, having spent some time with them in rehearsal and having grown to really love their music, was make a record that would reveal them as they really are. It's quite difficult to make a record that reveals their true nature in a way that is immediately palatable and marketable to the kind of mainstream radio audience that they found themselves with after *Different Light*."

The girls were determined to pen every track on the new record, a process that Sigerson says, "makes a big difference." But he also commended them on their ability to make others' songs their own. "I thought it was great that they could do covers with such credibility, because they personalized them; the ones they picked were so appropriate to their identity. But they were determined to write their own material. It was great for them because that was something they felt they needed to prove."[11]

The first thing Sigerson wanted to do was create a supportive and nurturing atmosphere in the studio, a completely unfamiliar concept for the band, though they were now recording their third album. "With Davitt, I felt a bit more free. Davitt had such a better attitude. When I was drumming, I got to do what I wanted to do. I didn't feel like I had this cloud over me or this threat that somebody else is going to come in and take over. I felt like I'd been accepted again and I haven't been fired. I get to play. I get to sing. I'd written a few songs, and so I felt better about those songs too than I did on *Different Light*," Debbi described of the process.[12] Her bandmates had equally positive experiences with Davitt, starkly contrasting the Kahne epoch. "I wanted to feel like there was somebody that I could really respect, somebody I could groove on," says Susanna. "I was just totally impressed with Davitt's brain," she notes, concluding, "The bottom line is he's great working with people. With David Kahne, I always felt there was a wall of mystery because David is an interior, hard-to-figure-out person. Davitt is much more open. We communicated in a different kind of way. He was perfect."

Michael Steele had similarly flattering words for Sigerson, describing him as "very intelligent...He had a handle on the big picture at all times, where we'd be focusing on the minute points." Sigerson possessed the emotional depth needed to get the best out of the Bangles while giving them back their long-missing confidence and worth. "Davitt had a good mix," Vicki said. "He had humor, hyper-intelligence and a very laid-back way in the studio. I was very tense about doing any guitar playing in the studio because of my bad experiences in the past with Kahne. I just felt like I couldn't play, and I was inept."[13] Getting the band back in touch with their individual artistic abilities was crucial for creating the album, according to Michael. "Davitt was adamant about getting us to trust our own inner instincts about how to sing a song," she says. "As opposed to getting really anal about having every note be on key." The entire process, says Susanna, "was truly cathartic."[14]

A different method than before was decided upon for songwriting. Each band member would individually pen her own tracks, with collaboration for the most part coming not from within the group, but from outside contributors. The decision to open up the process was an effort to broaden the Bangles' abilities as both separate creatives while achieving a more diverse and interesting album. "It was basically to branch out a little more with other people and work with other musicians," says Debbi of the choice, "Just trying to expand our horizons."[15]

The girls undertook finding who they wanted to write with. "I wrote with Debbi, because I realized that the other ones already had their writing partners," Walker Igleheart says of how he came to work with the drummer. What Debbi did not have in experience, Igleheart says, she made up for in natural ability. "I think she has good instincts. She might be the most talented in the group in some ways. She plays drums really well and sings at the same time, which is very difficult. She's got a good ear for harmony. The tunes we came up with turned out to be great songs. It worked out and she got better as time went on."[16]

Michael teamed up with old friend, session keyboardist David White. "Writing is so intimate, and I'm still a baby at this," Michael remarked about the experience. "[When] I was writing by myself, I'd write these droney [sic], folky things. I was thinking, 'I'm resisting the pop thing.' I've known David White for 10 years, and he's a brilliant musical person with a very strong pop sensibility. I thought if I tried to write with David, maybe we could meld the two together," she concludes.[17]

Micki could be challenging to collaborate with, according to Igleheart. "I had heard from David White that writing a song with Micki was like being in a very long painful therapy session with him as the therapist, so I was prepared," Igleheart recalled of his experience crafting tracks with the bass player. "She came over and we talked for a long time, but not really much about writing a song. I don't think we even put two chords together. Eventually we called it a day, and that was it. I didn't pursue writing with her after that because it was obvious to me that her energy and thoughts were a bit scattered. She didn't have the focus or drive necessary to achieve stardom."[18]

Susanna, Igleheart says, "has the drive and the smarts," her choice of Tom Kelly and Billy Steinberg for writing contributors exemplifying this.[19] The twosome had already scored a pair of number one singles together, first with Madonna's 1984 "Like a Virgin" and again in 1986 with Cyndi Lauper's "True Colors." Susanna first met Kelly at a Bangles meet and greet in Los Angeles, allegedly the same one where Prince and Wendy from the Revolution joined the band onstage at the Palace. Steinberg had loved the band ever since hearing *All Over the Place* and was keen to have a crack at working with the group. A first attempt at collaboration did not make the cut for *Different Light*, but Susanna had enjoyed working with the duo. "I'd known Billy and Tom for about three years," Susanna said during the creation of *Everything*. "We just went on a writing spree...a writing orgy." She raved about the shared love of all things '60s music. "It's really easy to write with them...because...we just end up sitting around Billy's living room, and he's got the biggest collection of singles you've ever seen in your life…it's just fun."[20]

For Susanna, there were immediate contrasts between working with bandmate Vicki and collaborating with the duo of Kelly and Steinberg. "One thing I found different from writing with Vicki was that when we would write together, we conceived the music first and then the lyrics would begin to be informed by the sound of the music. Whereas with Billy and Tom—and this was really unusual for me—we would first sit down and talk about ideas for songs and what we wanted.…We would then fairly quickly get the lyrics down and go over to Tom's house because he was extremely proficient with recording equipment and able to whip up demos quickly. That was the process for a song like 'In Your Room,' and it was replicated with 'Eternal Flame.'"[21]

Vicki "was resistant to cowriting outside the band," she tells me. "I wanted to write more with Sue, but she wasn't terribly open to that," she recalls. Instead, she worked with two diverse options, the first was actress and new wave cult singer Rachel Sweet; her other pairing was metal guitarist and former KISS member Vinnie Vincent. Vicki and Susanna had both met Vincent at a party, the trio's shared adoration for the Beatles instigating an instant bond.

As the album was coming together, Vicki told *Rolling Stone*, "I keep thinking, 'Are we insane, or is this good?'" with Susanna adding, "Recording it was one of the most positive experiences we've ever had as a band." Outwardly, things seemed on an upward trajectory. "The success of 'Hazy Shade of Winter' was good for us emotionally," Susanna continued. "It filled us with a certain excitement and confidence about going into this record."[22]

When the various songwriting cells formed by individual members with outside collaborators came together, there were over forty tracks to pick from for album inclusion. "We'd all written more songs," says Debbi. "What I loved about *Everything* was it sounded better, it had a better recording vibe but it was also getting a bit more singular, like, 'Okay, this is Michael's song. This is Sue's song. This is my song, this is Vicki's song.'

Vicki and I tried to write a couple of songs together. We were writing with outside writers more and we lost the band element. When we were recording it, someone would sing their lead and then leave. Before we used to all be together in the control room when somebody else was doing the leads, just as a support system."[23]

Even after all of the issues over the previous few years, the band was determined to hold on to their original vision for the group. "Everybody had to have an equal number of tunes on [the album]," Igleheart recalls. "There was that, the same with the photos and the lighting. That's why Susanna taking off and being the front person was so annoying to them because they did everything in their power to keep that from happening. They wanted to be John, Paul, George, and Ringo and each have their own fan club, which I guess they do. Everybody wanted to be an equal, equal partners and have equal notoriety." Sigerson and the band eventually whittled the material down to fifteen songs for the album, thirteen for the album with two reserved for B-sides. For lead vocals, duties were split, with Susanna and Vicki each having four tracks, Michael and Debbi getting two each.

Of the batch, Susanna's were arguably, for many, the most obvious commercial tracks. According to Igleheart, this was no mistake. Susanna "is focused," he remarks. "She may have thought, 'If I ally myself with some of the best songwriters in the world, I'll probably get a hit.' That's how 'In Your Room' and 'Eternal Flame' came to be. That was smart of Susanna." In contrast, the others chose people with less established chart success but who they thought they would enjoy sharing the process with, he notes. "Debbi wrote with me," he says. "The others did not ally themselves with hit songwriters. That was the problem." Igleheart underscores the different way of thinking of the bandmates, noting, "Vicki wasn't about to go call up Billy Steinberg." In contrast, Igleheart points out, "Susanna said, 'That's where I want to be, that's the guy I want to write with.' But Vicki would not have done that in a million years. Vicki had an anti-pop hit mentality to where she wanted to be like the Pretenders or something, more of a rock and roll, no keyboards

24.

mentality. You know, badass; not 'Close your eyes, give me your hand.' To her it [the pop sentiments] was probably horrific. That was always a bit of a rub with Vicki especially."[24]

The positive recording sessions and supportive Sigerson experience "prove[d] that you don't have to be fucking suicidal to make a worthy album," Michael said.[25] *Everything* hit record store shelves on October 18, 1988, and the band was in a "happier place as far as certain elements," according to Debbi.

Their efforts were rewarded with overall positive reviews, seeing even stalwart tastemaker *Rolling Stone* concede that the group "sound[ed] more comfortable than they have since their 1982 EP *Bangles*." Yet the magazine's choice of words still clings to the horrifically condescending, highlighting that on the former album, "many of the instruments were played by session players," and though *Everything* sees the band writing all the songs, they do not do this "themselves," underscoring how Steinberg and Kelly "helped"—not cowrote or collaborated—with Susanna.[26]

Regardless of their success, interviewers still loved to treat the band as if they were a catty group of sorority girls, with an expected question in many interviews to be about how the band was getting on with each other. Often the women's responses to such inquiries would be followed up with a demeaning comment that infantilized the multiplatinum artists. An example comes from an exchange with popular late night talk show host Arsenio Hall on his nationally televised program:

[*Hall imitates Bangles sarcastically*—'*She thinks she's so smart, she did a movie.*']
Hall: Ever any jealousy in the group because you seem to get along and stay together?
Vicki Peterson: No, we don't fight constantly.
Hall: Really? What kind of stuff do you fight about?
Michael Steele: Actually, we fight mostly about musical matters to tell you the truth.
Hall: So, it's not things like you took my crimping iron![27]

The group had become tired of the constant questions about their validity, even in light of scoring worldwide hits and being touted as "one of the most popular bands ever to emerge from the stenches and trenches of the L.A. club scene."[28] Besides their talent being debated constantly, the women were subject to the "inevitable charges of selling out," as their success some tagged as a betrayal to their club roots. "I'm just not going to read articles anymore," Michael said at the time. "People are projecting all this incredible stuff on us. What can you do?"[29] Vicki concurred, adding, "We try to wear blinders about the amount of sexism there is that goes both ways. Instead of walking around with a major chip on our shoulder and a real defensive attitude, we figure the best way to deal with the situation is be a band and go out there and do our job and not complain about how many people think that women can't do rock 'n' roll. You can't worry about offending people. The feminists should be glad we're out there doing what we're doing." She continued, confiding, "It bothers me that people still don't see us as writers and singers and players, and they still have some fantasy that we're put together and someone thought it was cute and kinda sexy and fun. It's a little insulting that someone would assume that you're not smart or assume that someone else wrote those songs and is giving you a little perk by putting your name on there....I don't think in the reverse people would have that assumption. But maybe they do. Maybe when Jon Bon Jovi writes with Desmond Child or whoever, someone's gonna say: 'Oh, Bon Jovi didn't write it, so-and-so wrote it and just stuck his name on.'"[30]

No matter how much they attempted to have the press and public see them as well-rounded artists, "innuendo and folk legend seem[ed] to gather around the Bangles like moths around an eternal flame," as it made better copy. "The cover versions thing," Vicki sighed, "that's just part of the mistaken public perception of the band. I mean we've always been writers. I've been writing songs since I was nine, and it's important to put that information out [there]."[31] It seemed impossible for an interview or a promotional appearance to not include reference to "the all-girl sound,"[32] or "the stigma of being a girl band and being classified as a novelty act."[33] Even as they garnered a worldwide following, Susanna noted that the group was still being asked by journalists to "have a day shopping with the Bangles," or do photoshoots like a "pajama party…in baby doll pajamas, things like that."[34]

While the productive time making the album and the openly misogynistic treatment by the media could have brought the band closer, it still was not enough to heal the conflict within that was still for the most part not discussed. "There was too much focus on Susanna," Debbi recalls. "Even though we were trying to fight that constantly, it just wasn't enough."[35]

There was seemingly no way to get back to the equal partnership originally envisioned. "All the people who loved me wanted to blame everything on Sue," Vicki says. "It was not all Sue's fault, I say this to this day. Which is why I'm able to play in a band with her, because I don't believe that she was…she was neither a victim, nor was she a perpetrator of this crime. It was partially both. Nothing is that black and white."[36]

Jeff McDonald of Redd Kross has watched the same pattern emerge with other groups. "I see from being an outsider in those scenarios and being friends with people who become famous: they're just put on this treadmill that keeps going and going. Everyone loses their mind. In retrospect, it's always like, 'Wow, you should have jumped off that rat race for a solid year and then come back to it.' All these groups are convinced that if you stop for a second, you're going to dissolve.…From the second they were successful the Bangles…were not off the road." Jeff's brother and bandmate, Steve, points out that there was no motivation for those outside of the band to intervene, as the Bangles were financially a great investment for all other stakeholders, even though the situation was potentially detrimental for the girls themselves. "In this industry, when making money, it's, 'Don't be trying to fix what's not broken,'" he tells me.[37]

Now with a new album in hand, the label quickly picked the first two singles, "In Your Room" and "Eternal Flame." Both contributions came from Susanna's songwriting team and featured her on lead vocals. Upon receiving the news, the choices were not met with a universally favorable reception from the band. Michael summed up the mood, saying, "When Sue was covered as far as all the singles, everybody else sort of grabbed the crumbs as they could. We knew it kind of sucked. It was now 'Paul Revere and the Raiders Featuring Mark Lindsay.'* I always hated what they did to that band." While the overall process of making the album was great, Vicki still was not entirely sold on the direction they were going. "All of a sudden it felt like I could be playing in anybody's band," she recalled. "And that feeling never really went away."[38]

As "In Your Room" entered the *Billboard* Hot 100 the month after it was released—eventually going to number five on the charts—the band once again took to the road to promote their newest record.

The group embarked on some warm-up dates in the lead up to *Everything*'s street date, opening for George Michael. Michael was touring to support his mega-hit 1987 solo debut *Faith*. "I just remember them being huge stadiums," Debbi says of the gigs. "I casually played table tennis backstage with George in Florida. It was only three [shows]; it wasn't a long stint. He was a nice guy."[39] Walker Igleheart also recalls events from the few dates the Bangles played with the British heartthrob. "George was apparently a video game fan and liked the game *Centipede* so much that he brought an arcade-sized version on the road with him," he recounts. "Apparently he had been playing the game and was approaching his all-time best when he had to pause it and go somewhere, planning on returning and attempting to resume his quest for his highest score. Who should come stumbling along but yours truly. Admittedly I can be a bit clumsy, so it was not at all surprising that I stumbled on the power cord, which pulled it out of the wall and completely wiped out his game. I heard later that he was not at all pleased. Luckily I didn't run into him after that so I avoided hearing from him what a dumb fuck I am. I don't know why, but I kinda like that story being part of my legacy."[40]

---

* A reference to the 1960s band where the lead singer felt he needed to be separately highlighted instead of simply a part of the overall group.

24.

As the short run with the *Faith* tour ended, the Bangles embarked on their own dates in support of *Everything*. The band found themselves in New Orleans on October 18, the same day the album was released. As the girls wandered around their accommodation for the evening, they spotted some familiar faces outside, according to Susanna. "I was thinking to myself, 'My God, that's the Grateful Dead, and they're staying at this hotel!' I want[ed] to say something but I [was] feeling shy," she recalled. Susanna figured out who the tour manager was and worked up the nerve to introduce herself, thus bagging an invite for the band to a crawfish boil held at the Neville Brothers' house in honor of the rock royalty from San Francisco.

While there, the girls met Jerry Garcia and the rest of the group. Susanna suggested that the Bangles sing backup for the Dead at their show the following night, garnering her kicks under the table from Debbi and Vicki. After the meal, Susanna and Vicki both recall going for a walk with founding Dead member Bob Weir through the streets of the gothic city. "He wasn't paying much attention to it, but there were just so many kids in tie-dyed Grateful Dead shirts all over New Orleans," Susanna recounted. "At one point I looked behind us, and he was like the Pied Piper. There was like a trail of kids in tie-dyed shirts [following us]."[41] They eventually ended up at Weir's hotel, and said goodnight, but not before noticing an "essential" item parked in his room. "He had a 10-speed bicycle in there," Vicki recalls. "He said he always brought it along with him on tour. We had no idea you could do something like that." The next evening, the girls took to the stage to support the Dead during a song pairing of "Iko Iko" / "Knockin' on Heaven's Door." The girls did their best to follow along with the lyrics, as only the Peterson sisters actually knew the words.

For the Bangles, starting the tour with show dates in support of the former Wham! star, and then doing a fun one-off with heroes the Grateful Dead on the same day that their own new record came out, should have been harbingers of good things to come. Instead, the Bangles once again found their petite singer the main draw for press and fans alike, whether that be interview requests, press pictures, or general lascivious commentary. Susanna, Vicki tells me, "was physically ill. She was painfully aware of the fact that we were all resenting the direction that things were going, and she couldn't handle that."[42] The tour started to go sour, regardless of the positivity at the start. "Towards the end of it, we were just going through the motions," Debbi said. "I think Vicki still felt like, 'This can be saved.' Bless her heart, she was very idealistic about it. But I kept telling her it was going in the wrong direction. I think deep down she knew that, too." Debbi recalls everyone on the verge of ulcers, and "Michael...sleeping a lot because she was so depressed. We were not doing well." Michael recounted, "Part of it was just exhaustion because we worked, and were worked, very hard. I remember falling asleep in one of those plastic chairs that they have in convention rooms. I remember for the first time thinking, 'I'm hating playing music.' That was when I knew the end was near, at least for me." Debbi dreaded going to work. "The whole thing was just too painful," she said. "It had already gone beyond the direction I thought it should have gone. It was such a focus on little sex kitten Susanna Hoffs, and to me that's what we weren't all about. We're a band, we're musicians, we're performers, we're not trying to be little sex girls. But that's what everybody expects."[43]

Desperate to make things better, the Bangles concluded a major change was needed. As their "removal of Kahne had been a success," they decided other shake-ups might help fix the band's problems. "They were looking for somebody to blame," Copeland said. "They made me fire my partner Mike Gormley, then they made me fire my brother as the agent, so I was being forced to use people that weren't really my choices, one by one. The reality was that the group was having such internal troubles," he recounts. "You can't advise people who are dedicated to self-destruction. They knew they made a mistake, they knew they would pay the price for it," Copeland concluded.[44]

Vicki has a different recollection of events. "I don't remember us 'making' Miles fire anyone," she says. "We were unhappy with management,

24.

true; but Miles was never around and that was our primary problem with him." Debbi concurs, citing a lack of physical presence the main reason for parting ways with Copeland and his team. "We just felt that Miles Copeland was not there enough for us," she explained.[45] "We're paying him 20 percent [of everything we earn] and he was always with Sting or somewhere; he never came to anything we did. We need[ed] somebody to take care of all our stuff."[46] Vicki concurs that Copeland was less than ideal for the group, his lack of presence keenly felt by the Bangles. "Miles Copeland...was sort of an absentee manager. We'd had this problem with him all along; at one point earlier, we had—not severed relationships—but told him we weren't happy, and he sort of wooed us back. We got, again, to this point where we realized no, we really need something that feels more supportive, something that feels a little more present for us," Vicki tells me. "Of course, we put ourselves in a very vulnerable position doing that because we were just about to release a record, we were rehearsing for a huge tour—and auditioning managers during rehearsals. We were unhappy."[47] Debbi adds, "I think it was the wrong time."[48] Vicki notes, "We've always had good instincts," though she concedes, "We haven't always followed them."[49]

Mike Gormley felt completely blindsided when he got the news. "Miles called me one day and said they were talking about leaving our management company," Mike Gormley says of the band. "I'm told they were told by their lawyer, they needed a bigger manager. I thought, 'How can they get a bigger manager than Miles Copeland?' particularly at that time. I never asked the lawyer. I've never asked them. Miles called me one day and said, 'We worked it out.' I said, 'So am I still involved?' He told me no. I was absolutely devastated."

Having played such a big role in the band's day-to-day life, the parting of ways was very difficult for Gormley. "I was absolutely devastated for a few years because they were not only friends but it was a very important achievement, for me, working with them. I had the rug pulled out from under me. I don't know if they realize how much it hurt because we didn't talk much." Gormley pauses. "I didn't really see them for a while.

I never had anything against any of them. I was very proud of them and I loved them—not in a physical way or anything like that. I enjoyed what we all achieved together. It was pretty hurtful to be kicked out. There were a lot of good times before that."[50]

With the trusted manager gone, things were more precarious as to how the troubled group would move forward. Instead of Miles and Mike, the band put Arnold Stiefel and Randy Phillips in place to handle their affairs. Michael later described the switch of management as "the biggest mistake the Bangles ever made." The issue with the new team, Michael says, is that "they were interested in Sue as a solo artist." The parting of ways with Copeland and company made no sense to Walker Igleheart. "They fired Miles Copeland, which was a big mistake. Miles was doing a great job for them, and they were top of the world. Why complain about Miles? It was just complaining about everything."[51]

Debbi was also nonplussed with the move. "It was more useless people," she says of the new management team. "These guys didn't care about the Bangles; they cared about Sue. It was all starting to break up by then anyway and we were not really talking to each other much. They came in and split the band in half: Micki and Sue this way and Vicki and me on the other. They wanted Sue, that's all they cared about. It was like, 'She's the only viable member of the band. She's the lead singer.' They just basically helped destroy an already breaking up situation."[52]

Susanna later confided that leaving seemed a viable escape from the constant grip of perturbation she experienced within the confines of the Bangles. "I was already kind of...excited," she said about the notion of going solo. "Maybe in my mind there was the idea that there would be another life where I didn't have to feel like I was in this cauldron of anxiety."[53]

Fan club president Marji grimaces when asked to remember this era of Bangles history. "I wish everybody had taken a step back," she says. "Things were not going well. There were people devoted to the band that were being fired and let go and nobody was saying anything. Someone needed to stop the madness and nobody was talking about important things."[54] In an effort to get some clarity, Debbi says she confronted Susanna to see if the brunette was still committed to being part of the group, asking, "Are you still into this?" On reflection, Debbi says, "She was very positive about it but I didn't feel at that time, that she was telling me the truth."[55]

25.

As 1989 began, the Bangles' second single from *Everything* hit airwaves and music video outlets. The inspiration for the lyrics came after the Bangles had received a behind-the-scenes tour of Elvis Presley's Graceland residence in Memphis, Tennessee. Within the gates of the property is the Meditation Garden, originally created for the singer in 1964 as a space for quiet contemplation. It later became the final resting place for the King as well as other Presley family members.

The day of the band's tour, rain was coming down. As they approached the Presley family graves, the women noticed a plexiglass box half filled with water at the head of Elvis's tombstone. When they asked their guide the purpose of the container, they were told that it usually held a constant light, an "eternal flame" for the icon. Seeing that the fire was extinguished, the staff member noted, "Well, it's not on." Michael joked back, "Well, it's the semi-eternal flame."[1]

In a writing session with Steinberg and Kelly, Susanna related the story. "He goes, 'Oh wow, that's a really cool title for a song, "Eternal Flame."'" Susanna recounted, "We just sat down and…wrote the lyrics and then wrote the song."[2] The session proved to be one of the most important of her life. "I was convinced 'Eternal Flame' was one of the best songs I had ever cowritten, and I was very, very proud of it," Susanna says. When the girls presented all of the tunes they had made to their bandmates for consideration, "Eternal Flame" did not make the cut for LP inclusion. "I was like…what?" Susanna remembers. "I should never liken myself to Bruce Springsteen, but there was this lore about how he recorded *Nebraska* and would go around with a cassette of it in his pocket because he was so proud. I had that feeling about 'Eternal Flame.' I would carry that cassette in my purse and to anyone who wanted to hear it, I'd be like, 'This is the song of my life.'" Other people that Susanna played the track for thought it was a hit; it was "only...the other three girls in the band...who weren't so into it."[3] Though present for the moment that inspired the track, Debbi and Vicki were not enthralled with the tune. "I was feeling emotionally divorced from a lot of the music that was going on [at the time in the band]," Vicki confided. "'Eternal Flame' is a beautiful song. Whitney Houston could have a hit with it. Why are we doing it?" she said. Debbi concurred, confiding, "It was frustrating because you feel this complete loss of control about something that you love so much."[4] As what would become the *Everything* album was nearing completion, producer Sigerson told Susanna he wanted to put it on the record after all. "'You know what, Sue? I really love that song too, and I want to find a way to make it work for the Bangles album.' I asked what he had in mind. And he said, 'I think it should be piano-driven,'" Susanna recounts. "It's funny because Billy and Tom knew the Bangles weren't a piano band, so that's why we did the 'Eternal Flame' demo on a guitar."[5]

While laying down the vocals for the song, Sigerson pulled a prank on Susanna. Having previously worked with actress and singer Olivia Newton-John, Sigerson informed the Bangles that the '70s icon had done some of her best work while naked. In the hopes of capturing similar popstar quicksilver, Susanna doffed her attire to perform her part in the buff. The unorthodox method caught the imagination of the press and public alike, once again thrusting Susanna into the limelight. The lack of clothing became a common question during publicity rounds, much to the consternation of the rest of the group. The notion of Susanna in her birthday suit was incredibly titillating. Similarly to the waves of Prince questions and the fascination with Susanna's turn in *The Allnighter*, the bandmates had to go along with the constant barrage of inquiries related to the track's creation, even as the questioning style undermined their validity as artists while further placing Susanna as an object, such as in this Japanese interview:

> **Interviewer:** I heard from radio people that when you sang you took all the clothes off and turn the lights off. Is that true?
> **Susanna:** Yeah, well we always sing with the lights down, that's pretty common. But I did sing with my clothes off actually because I...[*unintelligible audio*]
> **Vicki:** I take my bra off.
> **Debbi:** I put my clothes on.
> **Susanna:** Davitt basically indulged our fantasies and I'd always had this fantasy of singing naked so I did it but you know, he created that kind of atmosphere.
> **Interviewer:** How did you feel?
> **Susanna:** I keep comparing it to skinny dipping. [*Vicki chimes in—"she was cold."*] I wasn't really that cold.
> **Vicki:** You know I was cold because I like to sing surrounded by butter pecan ice cream.[6]

The song zoomed up the charts around the world, going to number one in nine countries, eclipsing all previous success the band had experienced. Instead of being ecstatic, the global triumph of a track that most of the group felt alienated from only further drove a wedge between the women. While having two back-to-back hit albums should have finally silenced their critics, instead the success of *Everything*—especially with ballad "Eternal Flame" blazing to worldwide dominance—had the opposite effect. Reviewers and writers meeting with the band for content that would surely be a boon to their publications doubled down in many cases on the disparaging comments. Instead of holding up the only "token female ensemble in the REM-inspired American guitar revival" not only still going but dominating the charts on a global level, column inches devoted to the group were littered with descriptions of them as "sucrosed," poking fun at what one *Select* magazine writer deemed their "pop cute-ability," which "for anyone interested in music—tunes and what have you—'Eternal Flame' completed a sad decline from the meaty, beaty Bangles to the Debbie Gibson Experience."[7]

They were ridiculed for being role models and for their success, even by female journalists. In *Rolling Stone*, instead of hailing the number of young women attending a Bangles show, Holly Gleason claimed such audiences prove the band lacked veracity as artists, snidely remarking: "The Bangles have said in interviews that they want to be taken seriously as a rock band, but establishing credibility is no mean feat when many of the concertgoers need to have their moms drop them off—or worse, tag along."

Gleason went on to snark, "But a band usually gets the audience it deserves, and the Bangles, who most closely resemble the human incarnation of Josie and the Pussycats, played it safe and straight up the middle, radio hit following upon radio hit." She then lambasted the women for what she referred to as their "clichéd Moves R Us poses" on stage, completely tone-deaf to the lack of female role models for the band she was gleefully tearing down, nor did she offer an alternative to the admitted "double standard, by which women who are performers are expected to be cute playthings."[8] That the Bangles were "big business," that is, a profitable entity, was set as a negative against their origins as "once a jewel of LA's alternative scene," creating an equation where professional musicianship for a woman on a worldwide level is something to be ashamed of and embarrassed about.[9]

With such commentary ripe in the national press, it was not surprising when a *Chicago Tribune* piece described them as "looking a tad weary" as they sat for yet another interview. "Getting respect and recognition is always tough, particularly when you are all women in what is essentially an all-male world," Vicki noted about the Bangles place in rock 'n' roll. Debbi underpinned the unwinnable dilemma, adding, "When we started, a lot of people treated us like a novelty. It was only when we'd been around for a while that we gained some underground credibility." Susanna followed up, exclaiming, "But then the minute we started having some mainstream success, all those people accused us of selling out. And when...*Different Light* went multi-platinum, naturally they all said we'd never be able to repeat it."[10] However, the one thing the group wanted more than anything still eluded them. "It's not enough," Susanna only half-jokingly laughed. "We want some respect, too."[11]

Yet not even a global number one was deemed sufficient to garner the longed-for artistic admiration of peers and press. On the British chat show *Don't Miss Wax*, host Ruby Wax was as equally demeaning of the band as her print peers:

> **Ruby Wax:** Let's be honest here, music's supposed to express the kind of rebelliousness but in those videos. You do kinda look like bimbos. So what's so rebellious?
> **Vicki:** Yeah, so we studied at the Bimbo Institute Technology in Hollywood, B.I.T. It caters to a lot of the bimbos that come from all over the country to Hollywood to...[*unintelligible audio*].
> **Ruby Wax:** So, you have to learn that?
> **Vicki:** Yeah, you got to learn it and it's really hard work.
> **Ruby Wax:** What do you have to like, learn how to stand there with your lips glossed?[12]

Even the group's hometown shows were viciously annihilated, the women's abilities still in question as the *Los Angeles Times* proclaimed, "If you adjust your expectations properly, you won't be disappointed by a Bangles concert. *Properly* means: Don't expect music that's too complex or challenging, don't expect much virtuosity (or that the four women will even be *playing* their instruments), don't expect the best songs to be Bangles compositions and don't expect the set to be very long...Is the rest of the show live, or is it Memorex?"[13]

Greg "Harpo" Hilfman was on the road with the Bangles for the *Everything* tour, having taken over keyboard duties from Walker

Igleheart. He also accompanied the girls on their international jaunts. "We worked several times in Australia [got to pet a jaguar in a zoo] and Japan. England was a big market…probably most enthusiastic fans… also Germany was keen on the band. France couldn't be bothered and Norway was fantastic. They love heavy metal there, so we fit in perfectly." He smiles. "It was a lot of fun, it was great." Though he was a newcomer, Hilfman could feel that things were stressed within the group. "I knew it wasn't all happy street, you could feel a lot of tension," he notes. "There was a lot of money involved."[14]

So much time on the road gave Hilfman the opportunity to get to know the band members individually. "Each one was distinctly unique," he says of the girls. "Debbi has her heart on her sleeve, the most vulnerable. Vicki…The glue. She had the tools to navigate the constant tensions and be the peacemaker. She had to MC the gigs… especially when Sue didn't feel chatty." Michael, he says, "came from a moneyed clusterfuck of a family. Her mother parked her and brother at a very young age in a boarding school in Switzerland, while she acted out her socialite fantasies in Italy. A lot to unpack. Sue…Naturally, since she became the de facto 'lead singer,' was singled out for the bulk of attention."[15]

Hilfman then describes a "normal" day on the road with the band, providing two particular asides about living on the tour bus with the four women. He notes one incident where "none of us was killed in a late-night rollover." He also shares that there was "surprisingly little flatulence in the sleeping quarters. I guess girls don't fart." Despite the inner turmoil that the women were experiencing, Hilfman says, "There really wasn't much drama. There wasn't much arguing." Indulgence on the road was kept to a minimum, he notes. "I don't remember people smoking weed on the bus, though alcohol was usually in abundance. There wasn't a lot of drug paraphernalia. Probably the occasional bump [of cocaine] but that was unusual…it was relatively sedated and things would wind down pretty early. After a few glasses of wine, things could become emotional but nothing got completely out of control." When asked if the Bangles ever brought men back onto the bus, Hilfman gives a definitive no, adamantly declaring, "They weren't picking dudes up."

Michael, in particular, was not fond of being on the road. "Michael famously hated flying and the actual media," Hilfman remembers. "She would take the train from LA to New York to avoid flying. One time in London, we had to do a couple of things in the press and then we flew back, but there was going to be something there again in six weeks. Instead of returning to the US, she just stayed in the Knightsbridge Hotel. That was a little extreme."[16]

The bass player admitted the stress of being on the road did not mix with the constantly strained dynamic of the band, which sometimes manifested itself in uncontrollable emotional outbursts. On a 1988 trip to Japan, Michael recalled that she "started crying on the plane and I couldn't stop...I didn't realize until years later that I'd had a mini-breakdown. The pressure was so intense that it had to stop otherwise I was going to come down with some horrible disease."[17]

After a stint working with UB40, Ian Lloyd-Bisley had taken on the band's tour manager duties around the same time as Hilfman joined the Bangles team. Lloyd-Bisley's daily tasks would be to "do all the bits and pieces" for the band, he explains. Duties could range from the professional to the personal. "It was always fun, because I would get these phone calls," he laughs. "Micki used to ring me up, and say, 'I've got a flat tire' and didn't know what to do. So I drove all the way over there and changed the wheel on a car for her." Nothing was beyond Lloyd-Bisley's responsibilities. "One day, Micki had to go to the gynecologist, and she wanted me to go with her. I went along and sat in the waiting room with a load of other women and read *Cosmopolitan*." The bassist, he reflects, "seemed a bit of a troubled soul. I got on really well with her. She trusted me. She was always a bit distant; she didn't hang out as much with the others on days off."[18]

While he admits that some tasks "drove you nuts at times," Lloyd-Bisley says he "always had a laugh with the girls." The only time he remembers there being any issues between them was when interview requests would come in. "I'd say, 'Okay, so and so wants to do an interview.' Susanna would be the only one to offer to do it because the others weren't that interested. Then when something came out in the press, and it was a picture of Susanna and they would moan at me a bit. I said, 'You didn't do it!' It was just little bits like that. There was Susanna getting more attention than anybody else. As I say, Susanna would be the one that if nobody else was interested, she'd always do it."[19] Vicki remembers a different evolution of press engagement, however, saying that as time went on, Susanna became "choosier about the press she agreed to do."

Regardless, the media were extremely interested in every move the band made, especially Susanna. An *NME* (*New Musical Express*) writer on the road with the group described the brunette as being "besiege[d]" by paparazzi, to which the Bangles present various levels of despise. The article claims that "Vicki rants, 'What a HORRIBLE way to make a living! What kind of person would want to spend their time stalking people as if they were…I DUNNO…ANIMALS! They just don't seem to care whether people want their photographs taken or not!'" The journalist describes Debbi's reaction to the attention, noting how she "folds her arms and go[es] to sleep," while Michael "yell[s] ingenious obscenities at passing bikers." In contrast, "Susannah [sic] is hard at work flashing a Maximum Molar Count at every opportunity, reciting rhymes about her 'sassy ass' to the smitten Dutch TV interviewer.…No great surprise then that when a boatload of paparazzi are discovered lurking nearby, far from shrinking away with distaste Susannah [sic] sprints TOWARDS the clicking cameras so fast…I look for the wings on her Reeboks…the lips sticky with giggles, the happy arch of Susannah's [sic] body as she dances away from groping tabloid hands, only to dance back towards them again."[20] Arguably, no matter how many films Susanna may have watched as a child, there was no guidance for navigating her ever-growing celebrity. "A lot of my friends are not here anymore because of those pressures of being in the industry," Apollonia Kotero tells me. "Back in the '80s, it was crazy. We were like demigods;

we were the biggest thing that ever happened. It was wild. Nobody ever teaches you or coaches you how to handle fame. How do you determine what to do?" she asks.[21]

In yet another attempt to redress the balance of the band, the third single to be picked was the Debbi penned and sung "Be With You." It would be the first single since 1984's "Going Down to Liverpool" that featured the younger Peterson on lead vocals. The track hit airwaves just as "Eternal Flame" went to number one in the US. However, according to Debbi, "It got buried because we had new management." Unhappy with the song's video, Debbi recalls how it was shot in a single afternoon, adding to the seeming lack of attention given to the release. After the colossal thunder of "Eternal Flame," "Be With You" stalled at number thirty in the *Billboard* charts. "I wish we never had those people," Debbi says of Stiefel and Phillips, "but they were very much, 'Okay, we got Sue now. Let's kill the Bangles.'"[22] To Vicki, the lack of promotion behind the song provided a blaring contrast to the promotional efforts put behind songs led by Susanna. "At that point," Vicki explained, "the label was saying they don't want a single unless it's a Sue vocal. As soon as I heard those words—and I heard it inadvertently—I said OK, now the illness is terminal."[23]

Debbi had reached out to her sister about the state of the group. "She just wanted to keep it together so bad that she wasn't seeing how the rifts were being formed," Debbi explains. Vicki, the self-proclaimed "queen of denial," says she was "determined to keep this thing going." Vicki elaborates on the matter. "My choices at that point were go on stage and play the songs and do it as well as I could—or quit," she tells me. "I'm not a natural quitter. I'm pretty damn tenacious/stubborn about things and I'm not gonna quit; but at that point, quitting seemed my only option because we were not a united front and hadn't been for a while. For every time you've heard somebody say, 'Sue was very determined'—she was very determined to be a star. That is what first attracted me to working with her, the indomitable spirit, the desire that was equal to mine to be unstoppable. But that focus changed over time;

instead of putting all that energy into making the Bangles big, it seemed to me that the vision shifted to Susanna being a star in her own right."

Vicki continues, saying, "The whole narrative of she was getting all the attention so we were all jealous—let's flip that for a second. Anytime there was any other attention that wasn't being paid to her, she had a real hard time with that. I can't blame her for being extremely ambitious for her own world and for what she wanted." The problem, Vicki says, is with what Susanna was telling her bandmates and what her actions were portraying. "The thing is at the time, she was lying to me about it. That's the thing; if I knew the whole time, she just wanted to be a star and it almost didn't matter in what capacity, if she just wanted to be a star singer like Madonna, if that was true the whole time, I would have done things very differently. I would have had the balls to say to her, 'Why don't you go and do a solo record, get [it] out of your system, we'll take six months off or something, we'll do something else, we'll come back.' That would have been a smart thing to do. I was thoroughly dug into this concept, this dream, this ideal of a group."

The lack of open dialogue only intensified the contrast between the long-held idealized dream and the realities of the music business, creating a huge amount of conflict within Vicki. "I wanted so badly to have a unit that would stand up to the label, stand up to reporters, and stand up to the standard of quality for our voice as a band," she says. "A band like R.E.M.: I perceive them to be a band that always had…a lead singer. Yeah, sometimes he got on the cover of the magazine, and they didn't give a shit because they wrote the songs together, they played them and they were a unit. They would stand up to the label as a band. They weren't having secret meetings behind each other's backs. Susanna always told me in the early days, 'Yeah, that's what I want'—but it wasn't. It felt like it was turning into Diana Ross and the Supremes; my whole dream that I had been working for since literally kindergarten was tilting on its axis."[24]

PART IV
BREAKDOWN

26.

As the *Everything* tour continued through the spring of 1989, Debbi was preparing for an approaching personal milestone. She had become engaged to the band's sound man and production manager Steve Botting, with the wedding set to happen in England. "I proposed to Debbi—after I asked her father for his blessing, the way you should do things," Botting laughs, "or the way I was taught in England, anyway." For Debbi, the impending nuptials were "a very good distraction because it was such a positive thing."[1]

As the big day drew closer, Hilfman remembers "things really started to heat up" among the band members, the atmosphere so uneasy "you could feel it." "There were some hurt feelings," he says. "Debbi would be prone to being particularly sensitive. It wouldn't take a lot for her to cry. Vicki was pretty stoic, but I could sense something was really going on. There were talks about wardrobes and benign things; it shouldn't have been [anything serious]." For the seasoned road-savvy musician, it was tour normality. "I was having a lot of fun but I was as low profile as possible," he recalls. "I've spent so much time with musicians that there was always shit that cropped up. If you spend all that time together, then that shit happens."[2]

The root of the problems, Hilfman believed, stemmed back to the time spent in the studio with Kahne. "I think anxiety had been built in because they had been treated so poorly," the keyboardist reflects. "David Kahne brought all these musicians in to play and they had to fight to be them, almost because they were girls; it was like they were only meant to look pretty. He [Kahne] had no diplomacy. They were girls, growing up and trying to do their thing. No appreciation was given for what they did and that definitely scarred them, all of them. I could see the frustration." Not everyone showed their battle wounds openly, he noted. "Sue didn't talk about it much, she held it in," he says. Her way of expressing the pain inflicted on her was through continued uncertainty, he remembers. "It was like, 'Am I doing this right?'"

Press undertaken while on a late spring press junket of the UK, Germany, and the Netherlands shows that the band was no longer able to keep the bubbling cauldron of angst and anger under wraps while in front of the media much to the seeming delight of music journalists who were only too ready to pounce upon every nuance of band tension. Michael joked openly about the inter-band problems in one interview, confiding, "we take a marriage counsellor on the road with us, it's the only way," a not so thinly veiled admission to the outside world of the crumbling dynamics happening within the foursome.[3] While spending several hours with a writer from Britain's *NME* in Amsterdam, the band's once united exterior clearly showed its frayed edges to journalist Barbara Ellen's delight, as she captures her time spent with the "teeth baring Bangirls," an "American All-girl ('60s sugar) band."[4] Yet the individuals she portrays in her piece are anything but sweet. Ellen notes how the success of "Eternal Flame" "plac[es] them firmly in the Big Bucks bracket without spoiling what appears to be a unique position in the international music scene." Ellen notes that upon first being introduced to the group, they are "ratty and mean in that way peculiar to Famous Females who've not had time to slap on their make-up. Three of The Bangles wear shades. All four display a body language that stinks. It says: 'I'm a VIP. I lead a rich and creative life and I refuse to accept I might look rough some mornings…'"*

Such assertions in well-regarded press were taken as true, regardless of the Bangles' actual situation. At the time of the story's publication,

---

* Author note: Knowing three out of four of the people in question here very well, I cannot imagine them acting this way—ever—to anyone, let alone a member of the press, no matter how tired.

Vicki "had just recently moved out of a one room apartment and was still driving a used car." Yet reality did not matter when sensationalism and reliance on overused cliché aided in creating an incorrect and damaging profile of the band.

Ellen describes each woman individually and stereotypically, dehumanizing the weary band to banal, one-dimensional characters:

> Susannah [sic] Hoffs is BEAUTIFUL. A mannered, doe-eyed, china-doll of a woman. You keep expecting her to suddenly jump up and rotate slowly with one wrist in the air to the tune of 'Edelweiss'. She is also the only real 'talker.'
>
> The very nice Vicki comes a close and welcome second. Debbi… keeps her mascara-less eyes lowered…Michael just sits there, occasionally contributing but otherwise exuding Bad Vibes for all she's worth. I don't take it personally until much later when she bursts into tears at the photo-session and blanks me…on her way past in the lobby… Michael was "too busy" to talk and indeed looked it as she sat staring at the ceiling and into space approximately five feet away at a different table.

Ellen then underscores the uncomfortable time spent with the group when she goes to review her recorded conversations with the girls:

> Transcribing the tape from this—the first, short 'official'—interview afterwards was almost impossible. Everybody sounds desperately muffled and surly, as if they're trying to be 'friendly' but the caps keep falling off their teeth.[5]

When Susanna recounted the time, she admits, "No one was connecting. I felt like we were kind of all going through the motions at that point."[6] Debbi had similar memories, adding, "Going on tour…It wasn't like we would shout at each other or yell or punch each other out or anything. The Bangles did things in a different way. It was more manipulation and quiet anger. Just kept it all inside…I think it was ready to explode anyway, it just took a while."[7]

Two of the Bangles got a needed break midway through the year. On June 10, in a quaint English village, Debbi and Steve tied the knot. "We were blessed by having an absolutely wonderful day in England," says Steve. "That doesn't come too often." Debbi describes seeing "bunny rabbits" hopping by before the rings were exchanged; but even the miracle of good weather and furry friends in attendance could not mask two glaring absences: neither Susanna nor Michael were at their bandmate's side as she said, "I do." "We had a great time," Vicki remembers. "It was a fantastic wedding. But it made us feel like they didn't care…the fact that Susanna and Micki did not attend Debbi's wedding should have been a wake-up call to me; I think, in a way it was."[8]

The two missing members did not feel they could physically travel to the event, their mental and physical health having become so precariously bad under the strain of the band. "I just suddenly had started having this whole nervous breakdown and crying," Michael confided. "And [was like], 'I have to go home now.'" Susanna was in an equally poor state. "I just wanted to be home so badly that I didn't end up going to the wedding," she says. "I just felt like physically and emotionally it wasn't really healthy to be walking around with kind of a knot in my stomach and Pepto Bismol in my pocket."[9] For Vicki, watching the band fall further out with each other was "devastating." "This band was my baby," she says. "I started it and now it was…disappearing and I could not change that. It was a really horrible, helpless…feeling."[10]

Even dedicated fan club president Marji was becoming ill from the stress of the situation. "I left [working with the group] because I was getting physically sick," she tells me. "The tension was so bad. No one was listening to each other and we couldn't have a conversation. Debbi had just gotten married. I was sad that the other girls didn't show up and everybody was in their corner doing their own thing."

26.

In her opinion, the relentless schedule imposed by the label was one element that led to constant stress within the group. "I think they were grating on each other," Marji says. "It was write, record, repeat, tour and then repeat it again. It's amazing that they were able to sustain as long as they did, given the pressures that were on them." She also believes the parting of ways with Copeland and Gormley played a factor as well. "The new management was a death knell," she says, "because they started to groom Sue and get in her head that the part was greater than the sum. That is not what was happening with the Bangles. The magic was in that they worked through things together, creatively. I watched long-term, supportive staff get fired and removed from the girls. I was told I would be next." According to Marji, the new management "weren't interested in the group dynamic at all."

The former fan club president doesn't "believe that the whole jealousy issue was a huge thing." Marji goes on to explain. "I think it was definitely there," she says, "but I don't think it was the impetus to breaking up. For me, it was the management coming in because the jealousy could flare up over anything at any time." She describes the situation as being "in a hamster wheel," and "moving in the direction of their own ideas." Susanna, she recounts, "was definitely think[ing] of just herself," but Marji points out, "I'm not saying that she wasn't the only one that did this."[11]

In the midst of the band turmoil, new management had scheduled the band to perform at one of the strangest venues to appear on the itinerary: the opening of a freeway segment in Houston, Texas. The free show was expected to draw just over twenty thousand attendees, mostly comprised of radio station winners.

However, an estimated seventy-five thousand people jammed the Sam Houston Tollway under the scorching July sun. Houston local Jacob Calle was in attendance, and still recounts the impact of his first ever show. "As a child, the Bangles was my favorite band," he says. "This was my first concert and I greatly appreciate that a group of women were the ones who introduced me to rock n' roll." As Calle and the rest of the audience celebrated a chance to see their heroines live in concert, the whole overpass started swaying under the weight of the dancing and stomping crowd, threatening the new construction to collapse on its debut.[12] The press were, however, unimpressed by the band, refusing to take in the literally life-threatening circumstances upon which the band played. Write-ups of the show ranged from dismissive to condescending: "wearing the usual miniskirts and black tights…'Bangles' is now synonymous with fluff and tummy-revealing costumes…rock in name only" (*NY Daily News*); "cheap razzle dazzle performance, nearly devoid of musical soul" (the *Glens Falls Post Star*); "they still posture unnecessarily…Hoffs' preening and arching seemed contrived" (*Akron Beacon-Journal*).[13] Decades later, Mike Gormley is still horrified that the new management booked the girls to perform at this oddball event. "They played some opening of a highway—I mean Jesus Christ this is a band that had sold millions of records!" he shouts. "I hope they got a lot of money for it, but it sounded degrading to me."[14] When I ask Vicki if the dangerous gig helped enhance the band's coffers, she replies, "Who knows what we were paid? We hardly ever saw accounting—especially tour accounting." The band went where they were told to, as it was a mandated part of the job, regardless of the payday or potential hazards.

The US tour dates of *Everything* were due to wrap up on September 2 in Santa Clara, California. Through the summer the band played shows to enthusiastic crowds; yet when not in front of an audience, the tone was markedly downtrodden, the years of unspoken emotions finally unable to be ignored, according to Steve Botting. "All the girls were miserable all the time," he recalled. "It just came to a head."[15] "It was the most insane tour," Debbi says. "There was so much fucking shit going on. The band was falling apart; we were fighting a lot. Steve was with me on that tour; that was the only thing that kept me sane." The weather reflected the mood of the group. Debbi specifically recalls that "there was a lot of weather problems. It was like the thunderstorm tour," which further darkened the already dour atmosphere and overall feeling of the entourage. Botting recalls "watching one gig and I had to sit on top of a flight case because there was a foot of water in the bunker where I was mixing the show. The girls were getting soaked. We had to eventually stop the entire thing." Gormley points out that "six months after Miles and I were gone, they fall apart," he says. "I think by that period, they were hating each other. Frankly, I had a lot to do with keeping them together. They may not realize that, but I was pulling strings and trying to keep it going."[16] Remembering that challenging time period, Vicki says, "I continued my efforts to keep us together, despite diminishing returns. I did not, and do not, hate my Banglemates."

Though shows were selling out and record sales were great, there "was basically just this constant narrowing of focus on Sue, and finally her being identified as the one solo artist that people wanted to invest in," Chris Lamson remembers. The ability to work together had completely broken down, according to Susanna. "We weren't operating like a group, we were operating like four individuals trying to protect their territory," she says. As Debbi had suspected, the new management team were keen to start Susanna on a solo career, leaving behind the band. "Their argument to me was, Why do you want to be in a room with people who are mad and frustrated?" Susanna recalls. With all of the stress, any way out of the current situation sounded appealing, she explains. "I was a basket case emotionally, physically. I was riddled with anxiety." Being on her own seemed like a panacea to the problems. "I thought okay, maybe as a solo artist, I won't have to feel so bad," she says.

Michael was having similar ideas. With the band scheduled to leave for a run of tour dates in Australia, the bass player did not see how continuing on was tenable. "We would have torn each other to pieces if we would have gone on that tour," she says. The stress was manifesting itself in frightening ways, Michael recalls. "I'd hit a point where I was starting to have some scary physical symptoms," she said. "I was like, 'Fuckin' A. The Bangles thing is actually making me physically ill.'"[17] Sensing Susanna was having comparable thoughts, Michael finally opened up to her friend about leaving the group. "Sue, I can't do this anymore right now," Michael recalls of the conversation. Stiefel and Phillips had also been talking to Michael about possibly working with her on a solo deal with Columbia once she felt recovered from her Bangles-induced malady. Susanna was relieved to hear Micki's feelings. "I've always been glad that she was forthright about what was going on—because I was still so worried about being open about how stressful it had become with the Petersons, who had an entrenched view of what the band was and should be," Susanna remembers. "After eight years or so of working together, starting in our early twenties, you have to allow for change—people grow up, priorities move on, too."[18]

One sunny afternoon as they were trying to recuperate between promotional commitments, Vicki and Debbi were summoned to a meeting at Stiefel's Hollywood Hills home to discuss band business. A labor strike had forced the cancellation of the sold-out dates for their forthcoming Australian trip, so the Petersons expected the discussion would be focused on what to do next. "I show up and there gathered in the room are all The Bangles, our manager, his partner, his press agent, our lawyer and our business manager," Vicki recalled. "Micki won't look me in the eye. I'm like,'...W–what's going on?' Very soon after that, our manager cajoled out of Susanna the words, 'I don't think I can make this next Bangles record.'"[19] The Peterson sisters were sitting on one side of the room, Susanna and Michael on the other. "Then it was Sue and Micki...expressing themselves, like 'We're really unhappy with the band and the way things are, and I want to go do more singing' and I was like 'Are you already doing a lot of singing?' It was a strange situation because we felt very much like we were just told that the band was over," Debbi recalls. "No discussion within the band. It was strange. We never had the band talk of sitting down and talking about where we are and how we feel. Our big thing was if somebody's unhappy in the band, then they shouldn't be doing it anymore."[20] Yet there was no discourse. Instead, the Petersons were informed that the band was "breaking up because they [Michael and Susanna] want[ed] to pursue other things. It was crazy."[21]

Debbi was shocked to hear that she and new husband Steve were being held partially accountable for the breakup of the band. "Management actually blamed me and my husband by calling it the 'Debbi and Steve Show.' We were playing larger stages, trying to present a gig with different elements of the performance, so my riser might have been getting taller. Sue was getting frustrated, 'Oh, Debbi's riser's getting taller, and she's closer to the lights. And her hair is blonde. And she's like, she's glowing. And it's all because of Steve.' She was blaming Steve. It wasn't Steve's fault. When the spotlight did go on me, which wasn't very often, the fans would get confused about who the singer was. My head with my blonde hair would turn into a lightbulb. In fact, I've seen video of me having a 'lightbulb head' because my hair was so bright and I was up close to the lights," Debbi says. "They [the management] started pinpointing this fantasy about me trying to be a big star. I still don't even understand it, to this day. If anything, I was just trying to stand up for myself because I didn't feel a lot of support from anybody else. Look at the videos: Hello?! They were definitely dividing and conquering between Vicki and I and Micki and Sue. That was their little plan to break the Bangles up so they could get their Susanna. I couldn't stop crying. It was like, oh, being told that your relationship is breaking up. There was no band talk. I had no control over what was happening. I was being told it was over—that was my point of view, that Vicki and I did not have a say in it."

For Vicki, the gathering was a "total blindside." "At that point," she says, "[the issues and arguments] had been the case for almost a year. We were just on the road constantly; it was pretty unbearable." Yet in her mind, there could have been other solutions besides detonating the group. "If Sue had just come to me and said she was done, that would have been less of a surprise than being called to a meeting, which involved every single person in our team at that point, including our lawyer and our managers. Our lawyer was there and all the fabulous people who wanted nothing more than the band to break up. We were way too much work [to have as a band]." Management later told the Petersons and Michael that it would be "so much easier to sell Susanna" who was "much better at self-promotion." "He [one of the new managers] said as much to me," Vicki said of the person she had formerly entrusted with her career.

Susanna, Vicki recalls, had been "groomed" for the solo outing, though "she was a willing participant." Vicki says the brunette "was very unhappy as well with what was going on." Management had decided to divide and conquer. Knowing the "sisters would stick together," Micki was also dangled a possible solo opportunity outside of the group. "He pulled her aside too," Vicki remembers. "He also told me that he knew that if it was just Susanna [that left the Bangles], the band would be likely to continue on. He had to make sure he had Micki on his side too." The plan "worked perfectly." After having Michael record a demo, management "dumped Micki like a hot potato and had nothing to do with her."[22]

This final episode of the Bangles, Vicki says, was "very much like being taken out to dinner by your fiancé and then having him say before dessert, 'Oh, and by the way, I'm breaking up with you.' You're in a public place so you don't want to make a scene. It felt like it was a total setup, that it was intentional."[23] Vicki attempted to float the idea of freedom for band members to do their own projects, with the intention of eventually reuniting; but minds had already been made up.

"It was very final, and it was like nothing you could say could change it," Debbi said. "We all got in our cars and drove off. And that was it: we had broken up."[24]

EPILOGUE

The Bangles re-formed in 1998 to record a song for the soundtrack of the movie *Austin Powers: The Spy Who Shagged Me*. In 1999, they performed at the Hollywood Bowl in Los Angeles in a Beatles tribute concert conducted by George Martin, alongside other artistic luminaries including Stuart Copeland, Andy Summers, and Adam Duritz. It was their first appearance onstage together in ten years. They were then inducted into the Vocal Group Hall of Fame in 2000 before going into the studio to record their fourth LP, *Doll Revolution*, which was released in 2003.

Finally allowed to function on their own terms, the band created some of the best material of their careers. The Bangles wrote or cowrote almost every track on the LP as well as played all of their own instruments.

Doll was a critical smash, finally garnering the group the accolades they deserved, with one reviewer calling *Doll* "a bracing collection of visceral rock songs, raw, exciting and thoroughly entertaining…an unmistakable success, about as good as comeback albums ever get."[1] *Entertainment Weekly*'s Kristina Feliciano was equally complimentary, gushing that the band's "trademark…woven harmonies…knit themselves into your brain."[2]

After Michael left the band permanently in 2005, the original trio began work in spring of 2009 on what would become 2011's *Sweetheart of the Sun*. Like its predecessor, the band once again wrote, played, and sung on every track, sharing coproducer credits with friend Matthew Sweet. "We really worked as a team on these records," Vicki says of the last two outputs by the group. "We had the ideas and the agency to do what we wanted. It was a joyful experience. The music business has changed and we did not have the Starmaker Machinery behind us, but we made two very fine albums."

Like *Doll*, *Sweetheart* was met with overt enthusiasm, seeing NPR's Ken Tucker raving "it's never necessary to have heard a single Bangles song before right now to appreciate the craft and cleverness of the music they're making. Good pop-rock conquers all time and space."[3] The Bangles "rarely sounded more like a natural, organic band than they do [on *Sweetheart*]," *Slant* magazine reflected, noting that the record showcases the group's "commit[ment] to pushing themselves creatively."[4]

Various tours and appearances have peppered the last decades, including two West Coast engagements that reunited various members of the Paisley Underground for a benefit concert in 2013. Annette officially rejoined the group in 2018 after appearing sporadically as a guest bass player since 2014.

Their last show together was September 15, 2019, when they appeared at the Kaaboo Festival in Del Mar, California.

As of 2024, they are still the only entirely female rock 'n' roll band to sing and play their own instruments on five top ten *Billboard* hits.

LEGACY

Fans, critics, popular culture, and even those who were once part of the Bangles inner circle are reevaluating the group, finally giving them the esteem, admiration, and acknowledgment they deserve. Former manager Miles Copeland admits "there was a method to the madness of the Bangles' 'equality' mantra." He provides insight into this thought process. "The secret of the Bangles' success was the unit," he reflects. "They had a combination that worked....Each was a part of a... puzzle—put them together and you had something special."[1] Esteemed music journalist Ann Powers credits the band for "resurrect[ing]" the "crucial element" of "women's conversation into rock 'n' roll." Powers argues, "Even more than the Go-Go's...the Bangles forged a link between women's history in pop and their future, showing how a girl group could take charge and become not just a girl band but a rock band, no gender appellations needed."[2]

The women who started the group more than forty years ago are equally contemplative and appreciative of their place in music history. "My time in the Bangles taught me to become a better person and musician, and respect those I've worked with throughout the years," Debbi says. "It was a good experience overall." She concludes, "I think we were very lucky because it's very hard to be a successful band. But we also worked very hard to get to where we did."[3] Vicki still wishes more people knew of the group's humble roots as a garage band, as it may help for understanding "on a different level and in a more full way."[4] She says, "After all this time, I still feel a deep love and respect for my bandmates and am grateful to all the people who did believe in us and supported us." "There was something catchy about the music," Susanna recounts, "but also about the idea of this unique set of people coming together and trying to create something. That was the goal: to show up and deliver a kind of magic, whatever we could pull off."[5]

The "difficult dynamic" of the group, Brix Smith Start hypothesizes, "created results." "It may have been uncomfortable, but they all worked harder because of it," she says. "Unhappy bands can make extraordinary music: when everything is breaking up, sometimes that creates great art. It's just important to remember what they were up against making that music."[6] Support among female performers was almost nonexistent, Brix recalls. She describes an industry thick with "jealousy" as the "playing field was so narrow for women...everyone that was there was vying for a spot...the competition was fierce."[7]

Besides competing with their peers for opportunities, women had to fight the inherent misogyny of the music business. "If you look at my hands, they're covered in scars, from punching the glass ceiling," Brix sighs. "All of us have those scars, because we have to work so hard for our credibility and to be taken seriously."[8] Former Vicki and Debbi bandmate Julie Cameron underpins Brix's thoughts, noting of the group, "They were much more than they were allowed to be. The world wanted them to stay in their little Bangles bell jar in little skirts."[9]

Like Brix Smith Start, battles fought by the Bangles provided a possibility model both for peers and those who came after them. "They inspired me to continue writing," says Apollonia Kotero.[10] "The world was crazy about them. They're writing those songs, they're playing their instruments, and they're all fucking professional and amazing." Former Debbi roommate Sid Griffin agrees, noting, "They were role models; there's no question of that. They were engaged in a cultural war whether they knew it or not."[11]

Fellow rockers the Linda Lindas also hold the Bangles up as pioneers. "I can't pinpoint the exact first time I heard of them," seventeen-year-old guitarist-vocalist Lucia de la Garza tells me. "'Manic Monday' was a song we covered at one of the first shows," she says. The group often gets compared to the Bangles, which the younger artist thinks is "cool," adding, "They are a great band with catchy tunes."[12] Yet four decades on, the women of the Linda Lindas find themselves enduring some of the same misogyny as their predecessors. "We still sometimes get people asking us, 'Do you guys write everything yourself?'" mystified twenty-year-old guitarist Bela Salazar exclaims.[13] "A lot of the time when girls go up to play, people doubt that it's going to be good," sixteen-year-old bassist-vocalist Eloise Wong concurs.[14] "It's definitely still a thing. It's weird to profile someone just because they're women and being like, they probably can't play or they probably can't write music." The prejudice endured by the Bangles is unfortunately still evident when talking to the Generation Z musicians. "It's so messed up and just debasing," Lucia concludes. "It's like women have emotions too and write songs and have passions and experiences in life!"[15]

Change is slow, but the Bangles made the seemingly once impossible appear tenable, with bands like the Linda Lindas illustrating the inroads blazed by the group. "Even when the Bangles got big, you still didn't see that many women behind the kit," Debbi says. "I'm happy to see that there are more and more women out there now playing. I've even noticed that recently there seems to be more females on the drum kits in commercials!"[16]

The Bangles, says Toni Kasza, proves what can "happen if you work hard enough." "You can't make it on that level without a shit ton of positivity," she emphasizes. "It's not the negativity that gets you there. It's positivity."[17]

The trio of Debbi, Susanna, and Vicki are irreplaceable and incomparable, according to Joe Stella. "That's the magic," he says. "Those girls can sing like fucking angels and that's just the truth. There's nobody better."[18]

"The Bangles are my big sisters and I love them very much," Sananda Maitreya tells me. "[I] thank them for their sacrifice." "[And] one more thing," he asks: "WHEN will they be added to the roll call of the Rock and Roll Hall of Fame?"[19]

After countless hours of interviews, chats, and conversations about her time in the band, Susanna summarizes the experience. "When I reflect on the Bangles now," she says, "after all these years, the word that comes to mind is, grateful."

ACKNOWLEDGMENTS

Thank-Yous

My main and hugest thank you is to the Bangles: Debbi Peterson, Susanna Hoffs, Vicki Peterson. I have loved you since I can remember. You showed me what was possible and have provided countless others with inspiration and hope. As artists and people, I am in awe of all you have achieved together and individually. I love and adore you all. THANK YOU THANK YOU THANK YOU for believing in me and allowing me to tell your important story.

Thank you, Annette Zilinskas and Amanda Hills Podany, for the seemingly endless calls, emails, interviews, and virtual therapy sessions. You two are so badass, and I am lucky to know you!

Ben Schafer, my editor—THANK YOU will never be enough. It has been an honor to bring this to life under the tutelage of your insanely creative, knowledgeable, and supportive vision.

Ian Kleinert: You have changed my life in all the best ways. Thank you for being the agent I never thought existed. You rule. Big shout out to Richie Kern as well. THANK YOU!

THANK YOU to all the gorgeous, generous humans who took time out of their lives to share memories, thoughts, and sometimes difficult bits of personal history:

Rusty Anderson, Milo Aukerman, Marji Mize Banda, banggothebangles, Steve Barton, Steve Botting, Julie Cameron, Joe Chiccarelli, Maria Corvalan, Jonathan Daniel, Lucia de la Garza, Mila de la Garza, Jo "Spock" Dean, Brian Diamond, Jennifer Finch, Nick Gilhool, Nina Gordon, Gracie, Sid Griffin, Meghan Helsel, Don Hewitt, Greg "Harpo"

Hilfman, Walker Igleheart, Kathryn Ireland, Karl Jenkins, Toni Kasza, Robert Lloyd, Ian Lloyd-Bisley, Courtney Love, Eloy Lugo, Evelyn McDonnell, Kevin Miller, Katie Nelson, Joe Nolte, Dave Peterson, Dan Perri, Phast Phreddie Patterson, Brandon Pinkston, Daniel Rachel, David Rathod, Kimberley Rew, Stephen Rice, Bobby "Z" Rifkin, Bela Salazar, Lesley Schiff, Genevieve Schorr, Brix Smith Start, Joe Stella, Bill Stevenson, Raul Vega, Pam Wertheimer, Rebecca Wilson, Eloise Wong, Debi Zornes.

Mike Gormley: This book sparkles with context and truth because of your generous contributions.

Theresa Kereakes: You inspire us all. THANK YOU for your fabulous interview and for letting us use your great picture.

Apollonia Kotero: You were one of my favorite interviews. Thank you for sharing all of your thoughts and fabulousness.

Chris Lamson: Your ability to describe that moment in the music industry, the band's challenges, and weave in your own anecdotes and memories are some of the best parts of this book. Thank you so very much.

Sananda Maitreya: Your thoughts and ability to describe the reality of the music business are second to none. When are we doing a book together?

Jeff and Steve McDonald: Thank you for some of the best personal insight of Los Angeles, fame, and the ups and downs of being in a band. You are two of my favorite people always since our chat.

Mike Ness: Thank you for letting me bring you into another of my projects. Your humility and honesty are always beautiful and astounding.

Mary Petrie: Thank you for taking the time to share your honest and personal memories of your special friendship with Susanna.

Peter Philbin: Thank you for your awesome stories and descriptions of the life and times of an A&R.

Henry Rollins: I can never, ever thank you enough for the support, generosity, thoughts, memories, and all around brilliance as a human, friend, mentor, and genuine fantastic person. THANK YOU, wonderful YOU!!

Thank you to those who have helped me navigate the last couple years with the hills, valleys, and life tsunamis: Jim Brown at the Santa Cruz Arts Council, BBC Scotland drivetime crew Fiona Stalker and Paul Grey, Kristen Carranza, Iain Clacher, Terry Currier, Karen Edwards, Karen Emanuel, Bill Frith, Alan Gonzales, Jordan Hill, Dawn Holliday, Andreas Kohl, Michael Levine, Leigh Anne Lewis (this exists because of you!!), Shirley Manson, Krystal Macknight, Oregon Music Hall of Fame, Tim Piumarta, Rock's Back Pages, Janeen Rundle, Edith Sarfati, Debbie Sayce, John Service, Tiina Teal.

Thank you to the staff at the British Library for the help getting all kinds of materials, from old *Playgirl* magazines to cassette tapes, out of random storage for my research needs: Giulia Baldorilli, Christina Campbell, Steven Dryden, Bill Emery, John Nyergesp, Vedita Ramdoss.

Thank you to Barry Koopersmith for the use of your fantastic Bangles pictures.

HUGE MAJOR THANK YOU TO DINA ROBINSON for coming in to help with transcribing magic when it was needed the most.

Thank you, Steve Lieberman, for the hard work finding newspapers from forty years ago and making them a needed asset for this book.

Thank you, Luke and Jake Griffiths, for the endless work on the Bangles archive.

Thank you, Caitie Inson, for the fantastic transcribing of billions of interviews.

Hugest gratitude for my ride or die of the last two years, the incredible Mason Pharis. This book would not have happened without you!

To my family of friends: I love you to Santa Cruz and back. I would be lost without you: Margareth Ainley, Alix Brodie-Wray, Nina B Budden, Rich Dawes, Pat Dominowski, Audrey Faine, Julie Foxen, Christina and Mike Joyce, Brian Karo, Stephanie Mandell, Celeste Faraola Perie, Janet

Pucci, Ray Santana, Francesca Shepherd, Ben Smith, Julie Weir, Steve Wengert, Jo Whitty, Jane Wiedlin.

Will Sergeant, thank you for being my rock of humor, memes, and lightheartedness when I have needed it the most. Your friendship is priceless and I love ya to bits.

THANK YOU to Richard Novak and Sheri Siegfried. You two are the best.

Thank you to the two most important women in my life, Lynne Collins and Tami Cady. I love you so very much.

Everything I do is possible because of the unerring faith and support of my husband, James. I love you more than I can ever say.

He will never read this, but thank you to my gorgeous rescue dog Woody for being by my side. Please adopt don't shop.

Thank you to all the Bangles fans around the globe who have supported these amazing women through it all.

REFERENCE LIST

Anft, M. (1988). "The Bangles' Seem to Be Stuck in Place with Songwriting That Lacks Sparkle." In *Evening Sun*. Available at https://www.newspapers.com/image/372253738. Accessed January 26, 2023.

aoitoritori. (2016). "The Bangles Interview (1986 Japan)." April 20. Available at https://www.youtube.com/watch?v=AGV-iAPppoE. Accessed April 13, 2023.

Appleford, S. (1989). "Bangles Can't Get Total Respect." In *Macon Telegraph and News*. Available at https://www.newspapers.com/image/848227214. Accessed January 25, 2023.

Author Unknown. (1985). "The Bangles." In *Creem*. March 1.

Author Unknown. (1987). "Bangles." In *Kansas City Star*. Available at https://www.newspapers.com/image/680325888. Accessed January 26, 2023.

Author Unknown. (1982). "Bangles Look Forward to Touring United States." In *Daily Sundial*. November 5. Page 10.

Author Unknown. (1988). "Bangles Offer 'Everything.'" In *Rolling Stone*. October 20, 1988, issue 357.

Author Unknown. (2000). "Bangles Revival Overcomes 'Cheesy.'" In *Palm Beach Post*. Available at https://palmbeachpost.newspapers.com/image/133531808. Accessed January 26, 2023.

Author Unknown. (1982). "Bangs." In *Flipside*. No. 34.

Author Unknown. (1987). "Close Encounters: The Real Thing." In *Tiger Beat*. September.

Author Unknown. (1986). "'*Different Light*' LP Sparkler from Bangles." In *Arizona Daily Star*. February 9.

Author Unknown. (1986). "Intimate Details: Susanna Hoff." In *No. 1*. October 4.

Author Unknown. (1986). "Michael, 'Walk Like a Bangle.'" In *Look In*. October 18.

Author Unknown. (1986). "One Day in Bangleonia." In *Smash Hits*.

Author Unknown. (2001). "One Nation Underground: The Story of the Paisley Underground." Available at https://magnetmagazine.com/2001/05/18/one-nation-underground-the-story-of-the-paisley-underground. Accessed November 1, 2023.

Author Unknown. (1987). "Rock Lobsters." In *Spin*. July.

AwardShowNetwork. (2011). "Dick Clark Interviews the Bangles—American Bandstand 1983." January 14. Available at https://www.youtube.com/watch?v=mIIexkr_EwU&list=PL7BC7EC808AB39B05&index=8. Accessed March 2, 2023.

Aycock, H. (1986). "Bangles Blend to Make Their Own Kind of Music." In *The News and Observer*. Available at https://www.newspapers.com/image/655407440. Accessed January 26, 2023.

Baker, G. (1986). "Bangles Get a Bead on Superstardom." In *The Miami News*. Available at https://palmbeachpost.newspapers.com/image/302596545. Accessed January 26, 2023.

Baker, G. (1987). "'Late Show' on Rock's Cutting Edge." In *The Miami News*. Available at https://palmbeachpost.newspapers.com/image/302984403. Accessed January 26, 2023.

Balaban, S. (2019). "How Prince Worked His Magic on the Bangles' 'Manic Monday.'" Available at https://www.npr.org/programs/weekend-edition-sunday/2019/06/23/735191049/weekend-edition-sunday-for-june-23-2019. Accessed November 2, 2023.

Baltin, S. (2011). "Susanna Hoffs Riffs on New Bangles Album, Eighties Nostalgia." Available at https://www.rollingstone.com/music/music-news/susanna-hoffs-riffs-on-new-bangles-album-eighties-nostalgia-183536/. Accessed March 3, 2023.

banggothebangles. (2014). "The Bangles | Interchords (1986)." May 3. Available at https://youtu.be/qyVENau0JRE. Accessed April 6, 2023.

banggothebangles. (2021). "The Bangles | Interview | March 1986." May 7. Available at https://www.youtube.com/watch?v=7ccmvLnKI0o&ab_channel=banggothebangles. Accessed March 26, 2023.

banggothebangles. (2014). "The Bangles | Limited Edition Picture Disc Interview." April 12. Available at https://www.youtube.com/watch?v=8aPmKaMXrsE&ab_channel=banggothebangles. Accessed March 15, 2023.

banggothebangles. (2021). "The Bangles | The Old Grey Whistle Test | 12 February 1985." January 23. Available at https://www.youtube.com/watch?v=P9gwos1icgc&list=PLGp3HEH8K0yHDGMR1smOzqouoQoA9lewe&index=5. Accessed March 20, 2023.

banggothebangles. (2021). "The Bangles | Pop 'N' Rocker Show | 4 February 1984." Available at https://www.youtube.com/watch?v=Av_3gH_wsVU. Accessed November 21, 2023.

banggothebangles. (2021). "The Bangles | Razzmatazz | June 1986." September 4. Available at https://www.youtube.com/watch?v=iwqzW3PeGAw&list=PLGp3HEH8K0yHDGMR1smOzqouoQoA9lewe&index=4. Accessed March 27, 2023.

banggothebangles. (2020). "The Bangles | Rock Over Europe Interview | 3 May 1989." July 17. Available at https://www.youtube.com/watch?v=BnYHxHU7l1Y&list=PLGp3HEH8K0yHDGMR1smOzqouoQoA9lewe&index=33. Accessed April 5, 2023.

banggothebangles. (2014). "The Bangles | Rodney on the ROQ (KROQ) | 25 August 1985." March 10. Available at https://www.youtube.com/watch?v=soUdA3cqKDI&list=PLGp3HEH8K0yHDGMR1smOzqouoQoA9lewe&index=27&ab_channel=banggothebangles. Accessed March 16, 2023.

banggothebangles. (2021). "The Bangles | Ruck Zuck Interview | 14 June 1986." August 14. Available at https://www.youtube.com/watch?v=0NpErMw9yhU&list=PLGp3HEH8K0yHDGMR1smOzqouoQoA9lewe&index=8. Accessed April 6, 2023.

banggothebangles. (2017). "The Bangles Story (1989)." {June 23–25, 1989}. October 22. Available at https://www.youtube.com/watch?v=e-jvyXJ6Hnw&list=PLGp3HEH8K0yHDGMR1smOzq0u0Q0A9lewe&index=22. Accessed April 8, 2023.

banggothebangles. (2022). "The Bangles | USA Today | October 1988." February 19. Available at https://youtu.be/oALusQMo6ac. Accessed May 4, 2023.

banggothebangles. (2018). "The Bangles | Vicki Peterson and Susanna Hoffs 1982/1983 Radio Interview." January 6. Available at https://www.youtube.com/watch?v=KsMO7IUcGZg&list=PLGp3HEH8K0yHDGMR1smOzq0u0Q0A9lewe&index=31. Accessed March 13, 2023.

banggothebangles. (2021). "The Bangles | The Wide Awake Club | June 1986." August 7. Available at https://www.youtube.com/watch?v=XVFE9jiKl6Q&ab_channel=banggothebangles. Accessed March 27, 2023.

Bangles SVMD. (2020). "The Bangles (The Ritz 1985)—P1." September 7. Available at https://www.youtube.com/watch?v=GAfic7u4R2g&t=1s. Accessed March 21, 2023.

Barnes, K. (1985). "45 Revelations." In *Creem*. April.

Bauder, D. (1988). "Bangles' Maturity Beginning to Show." In *Arizona Daily Star*. Available at https://www.newspapers.com/image/165426070. Accessed January 25, 2023.

Baxton, K. (1987). "'Allnighter' Pulls Few Laughs from Tired Antics." In *Palm Beach Post*. Available at https://palmbeachpost.newspapers.com/image/130234248. Accessed January 26, 2023.

Bearchell, C. A. (1989). *San Fernando Valley: Then and Now: An Illustrated History*. Albany: Windsor Publishing.

Bell, J. D. (1989). "The Bangles Sing Bye-Bye Blues, Hello Bliss." In *Times Leader*. Available at https://www.newspapers.com/image/410652755. Accessed January 26, 2023.

Bell, M. (1988). "It's Those Hazy Crazy Bangles!!" Available at https://www.rocksbackpages.com/Library/Article/its-those-hazy-crazy-bangles. Accessed January 20, 2023.

Benarde, S. (1984). "Bangles Pay Dues—Now Ready to Roll." In *Fort Lauderdale News*. Available at https://www.newspapers.com/image/233164265. Accessed January 25, 2023.

Bessman, J. (1983). "Bangles." In *Cashbox*. May 21.

Best of the Tube. Available at http://cadensa.bl.uk/uhtbin/cgisirsi/?ps=P60H8nngUx/WORKS-FILE/60120051/9. Accessed March 1, 2023.

bjo bjo. (2018). "The Bangles—On the Tube—Jun 6, 1985." Available at https://www.youtube.com/watch?v=VYW-pizEziQ. Accessed November 21, 2023.

Black, J. (2014). *The Girls in the Band: The Worlds Greatest All Girl Rock Band...EVER! The Runaways*. CreateSpace Independent Publishing Platform.

Blair, I. (1989). "A DIFFERENT BANGLES." Available at https://www.chicagotribune.com/news/ct-xpm-1989-04-02-8903310983-story.html. Accessed November 2, 2023.

Blistein, J. (2020). "Billie Joe Armstrong to Release Quarantine Covers Album 'No Fun Mondays.'" Available at https://www.rollingstone.com/music/music-news/green-day-billie-joe-armstrong-covers-album-no-fun-mondays-1071412/. Accessed March 3, 2023.

Bohen, J. (1983). "Bangles—Faulty Records." In *Daily Record*.

Branst, L. (1984). "Bangles' Beat Is '80s Sound." In *News-Pilot*. December 14.

Brantley, M. (1990). "Greatest Hits Album Brings Bangles' Beatback…Sort Of." In *Anniston Star*. Available at https://www.newspapers.com/image/106780131. Accessed January 25, 2023.

Bream, J. (1986). "Just Another Somber Sunday for Bangles' Fair Concert." In *Star Tribune*. Available at https://www.newspapers.com/image/191104389. Accessed January 25, 2023.

Breathnach, C. (2023). "'Everybody Wanted to Sign the Next 1975, Arctic Monkeys and Biffy Clyro. No One Gave a Shit About a Band Like Us!': Cherym Talk Being 'Real' Punk Band (and If That Even Means Anything Anymore)." Available at https://guitar.com/features/interviews/everybody-wanted-to-sign-the-next-1975-arctic-monkeys-and-biffy-clyro-no-one-gave-a-shit-about-a-band-like-us-cherym-talk-being-real-punk-band-and-if-that-even/. Accessed February 3, 2023.

Browne, D. (1989). "Bangles' Rock: The Hollow Sound of Fluff." In *Daily News*. March 27.

Buchberger, J. (1986). "Bangles Play on Beatles Influence." In *Journal-Press*. Available at https://www.newspapers.com/image/821856462. Accessed January 25, 2023.

Buxton, K. (1987). "Allnighter Pulls a Few Laughs." In *Palm Beach Post*.

Caro, M. (2023). "Debbi Peterson (The Bangles)." *Caropop*. S01 E73. Available at https://rss.com/podcasts/thecaropopcast/848495/. Accessed August 1, 2023.

Carson, M.; Lewis, T.; and Shaw, S. M. (2004). *Girls Rock!: Fifty Years of Women Making Music*. Lexington: University Press of Kentucky.

Catlin, R. (1991). "Ex-Bangle Branches Out." In *Palm Beach Post*. Available at https://palmbeachpost.newspapers.com/image/132759473. Accessed January 26, 2023.

Cavanagh, D. (1990). "The Bangles: *Greatest Hits*." Available at https://www.rocksbackpages.com/Library/Article/the-bangles-igreatest-hitsi-. Accessed November 21, 2023.

Challis, H. (2015). *Women in Pop Music*. Kent, UK: Crescent Moon Publishing.

Chicago Tribune. (1986). "Bangles Hit It Big." In *Chicago Tribune*.

Christgau, R. (1985). "Bangles; Kurtis Blow; Talking Heads; The Replacements." In *Creem*. January.

Clerc, B. (2022). *Prince: All the Songs: The Story Behind Every Track*. London: Mitchell Beazley.

Clerk, C. (1987). "The Bangles: Globe Trotters." Available at https://www.rocksbackpages.com/Library/Article/the-bangles-globe-trotters. Accessed January 20, 2023.

Cohen, M. (2018). "The Other Side of '80s L.A. Rock." Available at https://www.rocksbackpages.com/Library/Article/the-other-side-of-80s-la-rock. Accessed November 21, 2022.

col1234. (2021). "6. The Bangles." *64 Quartets*. Available at https://64quartets.wordpress.com/2021/03/19/6-the-bangles/. Accessed November 3, 2023.

Coley, B. (1982). "The Bangles: Big Bangle Theory." Available at https://www.rocksbackpages.com/Library/Article/the-bangles-big-bangle-theory. Accessed January 20, 2023.

Considine, J. D. (1989). "Bangles Do Everything on 'Everything.'" In *Charlotte Observer*. Available at https://www.newspapers.com/image/625635666. Accessed January 26, 2023.

Considine, J. D. (1989). "Bangles Do Things the Hard Way." In *Palm Beach Post*. Available at https://palmbeachpost.newspapers.com/image/130230799. Accessed January 26, 2023.

Copeland, M. (2021). *Two Steps Forward, One Step Back: My Life in the Music Business*. London: Jawbone.

Corcoran, M. (1988). "LA Women." In *Spin*. December.

Cost, J. (2009). "A Conversation with Susanna Hoffs and Matthew Sweet." Available at https://magnetmagazine.com/2009/07/20/qa-with-susanna-hoffs-and-matthew-sweet/. Accessed November 1, 2023.

Court, J. (2018). *Prince: The Life The Genius The Legend*. Nashville: New Haven Publishing Ltd.

crashsite000. (2006). "MV3—The Bangles—I'm in Line." Available https://www.youtube.com/watch?v=HOYI_A8dUAs. Accessed November 21, 2023.

Creem. (1987). "LETTERS." *Creem*. January.

Cromelin, R. (1986). "The Bangles: Local Girls Make Good." Available at https://www.rocksbackpages.com/Library/Article/the-bangles-local-girls-make-good. Accessed January 20, 2023.

Cromelin, R. (1985). "Griffin, Long Ryders Set to Go the Distance." Available at https://www.rocksbackpages.com/Library/Article/griffin-long-ryders-set-to-go-the-distance. Accessed January 20, 2023.

Dammett, B. and Weeden, C. (2013). *Lords of the Sunset Strip*. The Spencer Company.

Dave (2021). "June 2—Michael Had Runaway Success with Bangles." Available at https://soundday.wordpress.com/2021/06/02/june-2-michael-had-runaway-success-with-bangles/. Accessed September 4, 2023.

Dawson, A. and Mortimer, B. (2016). "Athletico Mince Episode 14—The Susanna Hoffs Motorbike Incident." Available at https://explore.bl.uk/primo_library/libweb/action/search.do?fn=search&ct=search&initialSearch=true&mode=Basic&tab=local_tab&indx=1&dum=true&srt=rank&vid=BLVU1&frbg=&tb=t&vl%28freeText0%29=DD00025222&scp.scps=scope%3A%28BLCONTENT%29&vl%2829789 1280UI0%29=any&vl%2829789 1280UI0%29=title&vl%2829789 1280UI0%29=any. Accessed February 6, 2023.

Day Dreamer. (2008). "The Bangles—Be With You & Eternal Flame (Live '89)." Available at https://www.youtube.com/watch?v=fZ4lVegV1NQ. Accessed November 21, 2023.

Deevoy, J. and Puterbaugh, P. (1986). "The Bangle Angle." Available at http://www.muzines.co.uk/mags/im/86/06/932. Accessed November 21, 2023.

Deggans, E. (1989). "The Bangles Turn Out Gutsy Pop-Rock." In *Pittsburgh Press*. Available at https://www.newspapers.com/image/145725072. Accessed January 26, 2023.

DeRogatis, J. (2003). *Turn On Your Mind: Four Decades of Great Psychedelic Rock*. Milwaukee: Hal Leonard.

DeSavia, T. and Doe, J. (2021). *Under the Big Black Sun: A Personal History of L.A. Punk.* New York: Da Capo.

DeVault, R. (1989). "Bangles Trying to Shake Off 'Cute' Persona." In *Atlanta Constitution.*

DeYoung, B. (2000). "Bangles in Harmony Again." In *Star Bulletin.*

DeYoung, B. (2019). *I Need to Know: The Lost Music Interviews.* St. Petersburg, FL: St. Petersburg Press.

DeYoung, B. (2000). "VH1 Goes 'Behind' Bangles Story." In *Cincinnati Enquirer.* Available at https://www.newspapers.com/image/103105517. Accessed January 26, 2023.

DeYoung, B. (2000). "VH1 Series to Tell Tale of Bangles." In *Johnson City Press.* Available at https://www.newspapers.com/image/593052143. January 25, 2023.

Doggett, P. and Murdoch, L. (1987). "The Bangles." In *Record Collector.* March (vol. 91).

Donohue, M. (1987). "Bangles' Susanna Hoffs Likes 'Manic' Musicmaking." In *Miami News.* Available at https://palmbeachpost.newspapers.com/image/302344768. Accessed January 26, 2023.

Doyle, P. et al. (2020). "15 Great Prince Songs That Were Hits for Other Artists." Available at https://www.rollingstone.com/music/music-lists/15-great-prince-songs-that-were-hits-for-other-artists-72421/stevie-nicks-stand-back-1983-171532/. Accessed March 3, 2023.

Doyle, T. (2021). "Classic Tracks: The Bangles 'Walk Like an Egyptian.'" Available at https://www.soundonsound.com/techniques/classic-tracks-bangles-walk-egyptian. Accessed November 2, 2023.

Draper, J. (2017). *Prince: Life and Times: Revised and Updated.* New York: Chartwell Books.

drumsoloterror. (2010). "The Bangles Interviewed on UK TV Circa 1989: Ruby Wax." January 24. Available at https://www.youtube.com/watch?v=zmyvJW0Eh2k. Accessed March 29, 2023.

DVDGuy2012. (2011). "The Bangles Canadian TV Interview 1986 Part #1." January 4. Available at https://youtu.be/GFntqkReyTc. Accessed April 4, 2023.

DVDGuy2012. (2011). "The Bangles Canadian TV Interview 1986 Part #2." January 4. Available at https://youtu.be/JV-Ilo3Mq2o. Accessed April 5, 2023.

Earley, J. and Stone, C. (2016). *What They Said About Prince Rogers Nelson.* BJH Publications.

Ellen, B. (1989). "No Sex Please, We're Bangles." Available at https://www.rocksbackpages.com/Library/Article/no-sex-please-were-bangles. Accessed January 20, 2023.

Ensminger, D. A. (2021). *Punk Women: 40 Years of Musicians Who Built Punk Rock (Punx).* Microcosm Publishing.

Erskine, E. (1984). "All-Girl Band Gets Its Big Break." In *Ottawa Citizen.* Available at https://www.newspapers.com/image/464208104. Accessed January 26, 2023.

Everett, K. (between 1973 and 1994). "[Be bop bonanza, tape 16, medley 6]." Available at https://explore.bl.uk/primo_library/libweb/action/display.do?tabs=moreTab&ct=display&fn=search&doc=BLLSA8443228&indx=7&recIds=BLLSA8443228&recIdxs=6&elementId=6&renderMode=poppedOut&displayMode=full&frbrVersion=&frbg=&&dscnt=0&scp.scps=scope%3A%28BLCONTENT%29&tb=t&vid=BLVU1&mode=Basic&vl(297891280UI0)=any&srt=rank&tab=local

_tab&dum=true&vl(freeText0)=c723%2F114&dstmp=1675706696808. Accessed February 6, 2023.

Everett, K. (between 1973 and 1994). "[Be bop bonanza, tape 17, medley 9]." Available at https://explore.bl.uk/primo_library/libweb/action/search.do?fn=search&ct=search&initialSearch=true&mode=Basic&tab=local_tab&indx=7&dum=true&srt=rank&vid=BLVU1&frbg=&tb=t&vl%28freeText0%29=7.%09C723%2F115+&scp.scps=scope%3A%28BLCONTENT%29&vl%28297891280UI0%29=any&vl%28297891280UI0%29=title&vl%28297891280UI0%29=any. Accessed February 6, 2023.

Farber, J. (1986). "So Fine." In *Creem*. October.

Feldman, C. (2000). *The Billboard Book of Number Two Singles*. New York: Billboard Books.

Ferrar, A. (1987). "The Bangles." In *Stereo Review*. January.

Fertig, B. and Jurrjens, J. (1987). "Hoodoo Gurus: Live in Ann Arbor." In *The Michigan Daily*. March 11 (vol. 97, iss. 109).

Fissinger, L. (1986). "The Bangles: *Different Light* (Columbia)." Available at https://www.rocksbackpages.com/Library/Article/the-bangles-idifferent-lighti-columbia. Accessed January 20, 2023.

Ford, L. (2017). *Living Like a Runaway: A Memoir*. New York: Dey Street Books.

Fowley, K. (1988). "Music." In *LA Weekly*. Available at https://www.newspapers.com/image/578639252. Accessed January 4, 2023.

Frazier, T. (1987). "Bangles Put on Good Concert, But It Wasn't Their Best Night." Available at https://eu.oklahoman.com/story/news/1987/06/13/bangles-put-on-good-concert-but-it-wasnt-their-best-night/62687043007/. Accessed November 22, 2023.

Frazier, T. (1987). "Ever-Busy Bangles to Appear at Frontier City." In *The Daily Oklahoman*. Available at https://www.newspapers.com/image/452458461. Accessed January 26, 2023.

Gaar, G. G. (2002). *She's a Rebel: The History of Women in Rock and Roll* (Live Girls). Cypress, CA: Seal Press.

Gail, L. (2021). *Extraordinary Women in History: 70 Remarkable Women Who Made a Difference, Inspired & Broke Barriers*. Independently Published.

Garrratt, S. and Steward, S. (1984). *Signed, Sealed and Delivered: True Life Stories of Women in Pop*. London: Pluto.

Geffen, S.; Hopper, J.; and Pelly, J. (2019). "Building a Mystery: An Oral History of Lilith Fair." Available at https://www.vanityfair.com/style/2019/09/an-oral-history-of-lilith-fair. Accessed February 5, 2023.

Gepps, F. (1986). "Everything She Wants." In *No. 1*. May 3.

Germann, R. K. (1984). "The Bangles Are a Rock Band!" In *Tennessean*. Available at https://www.newspapers.com/image/112210597. Accessed January 26, 2023.

Gilmore, K. (1986). "The Bangles Sound Recalls 1966." In *Spokane Chronicle*. Available at https://www.newspapers.com/image/569473309. Accessed January 25, 2023.

Ginsberg, M. (1986). "All-Female Rock Band Mixes with 'Royal' Visitor." In *Palm Beach Post*. Available at https://palmbeachpost.newspapers.com/image/129559724. Accessed January 26, 2023.

Gleason, H. (1986). "The Bangles Discover Fame Creates One Manic Day After Another." In *Palm Beach Post*. Available at https://palmbeachpost.newspapers.com/image/130455819. Accessed January 26, 2023.

Gleason, H. (1989). "The Bangles: Santa Monica Civic Auditorium, Los Angeles CA." Available at https://www.rocksbackpages.com/Library/Article/the-bangles-santa-monica-civic-auditorium-los-angeles-ca. Accessed January 20, 2023.

Gleeson, S.; and Gordon, K. (2022). *This Woman's Work: Essays on Music*. London: White Rabbit.

Gnerre, S. (1988). "Everything Hits More Than It Misses." In *News-Pilot*.

Goldberg, M. (1984). "Bangles: A Female Beatles?" In *St. Louis Post-Dispatch*. Available at https://www.newspapers.com/image/140831939. Accessed January 25, 2023.

Goldberg, M. (1984). "The Bangles: A Female Fab Four?" Available at https://www.rocksbackpages.com/Library/Article/the-bangles-a-female-fab-four. Accessed November 21, 2023.

Goldstein, P. (1987). "Lewd Parody of Hit Pop Song Sparks Anger, Criticism." In *Palm Beach Post*. Available at https://palmbeachpost.newspapers.com/image/130193425. Accessed January 26, 2023.

Gordinier, J. and Weingarten, M. (eds). (2016). *Here She Comes Now: Women in Music Who Have Changed Our Lives*. London: Icon Books.

Gordon, G. (1983). "Bangles: Seductive and Something Special." In *The California Aggie*. February 2 (vol. 101, no. 81).

Graff, G. (1989). "Bangles Get 'Everything' with New LP." In *Sun Herald*. Available https://www.newspapers.com/image/743829579. Accessed January 25, 2023.

Graff, G. (2014). "The Bangles Song Premiere: Hear 'The Real World' from Their New Compilation." Available at https://www.billboard.com/music/music-news/the-bangles-song-premiere-the-real-world-interview-6327650/. Accessed November 1, 2023.

Graham, A. (2001). "Second Time Around." In *Desert Sun*. Available at https://www.newspapers.com/image/244195471. Accessed January 26, 2023.

Green, M. (1986). "With a Little Help from Friend Prince, the Bangles Have Become the Queens of Post-Psychedelic Pop." Available at https://people.com/archive/with-a-little-help-from-friend-prince-the-bangles-have-become-the-queens-of-post-psychedelic-pop-vol-25-no-17/. Accessed February 17, 2023.

Gregg, B. (1986). "Busting MS Could Bring MTV to Campus." Available at *Daily Kent Stater*. December 4 (vol. LXI, no. 51).

Grow, K. (2019). "Prince's Unearthed 'Originals': Collaborators Look Back on the Hits He Passed Along." Available at https://www.rollingstone.com/music/music-features/prince-originals-interview-842940/. Accessed November 2, 2023.

Guest Editor. (2009). "Under the Covers with Matthew Sweet and Susanna Hoffs: Go-Go Dancing in the 1960s." Available at https://magnetmagazine.com/2009/07/26/under-the-covers-with-matthew-sweet-and-susanna-hoffs-go-go-dancing-in-the-1960s/. Accessed October 18, 2023.

Guterman, J. (1988). "'*A Different Light*' the Bangles." In *Rolling Stone*, issue 540, page 86.

Hall, M. (1984). "All-Girls Bangles Brings '60s Sound into '80s with Style." Available at *Austin American-Statesman*.

Hamilton, R. (2021). *The Death of the Sunset Strip*. No publisher.

Hann, M. (2013). "The Paisley Underground: Los Angeles's 1980s Psychedelic Explosion." Available at https://www.theguardian.com/music/2013/may/16/paisley-underground-history-80s-los-angeles-psychedelia. Accessed November 1, 2023.

Harrington, R. (1986). "The Bangles: Baubles & a Beat." Available at https://www.washingtonpost.com/archive/lifestyle/1986/04/08/the-bangles-baubles-38/f32f9c2e-d7b5-4028-9e6a-baf001289159/. Accessed October 6, 2023.

Harris, W. (2011). "Susanna Hoffs of the Bangles." Available at https://www.avclub.com/susanna-hoffs-of-the-bangles-1798228045. Accessed October 5, 2023.

Harron, M. (1986). "Albums by Eno, Rosanne Cash *et al*." Available at https://www.rocksbackpages.com/Library/Article/albums-by-eno-rosanne-cash-iet-ali. Accessed January 20, 2023.

Harvey, D. (1984). "Bangles: Guitar Heroines." In *The Michigan Daily*. October 26.

Harvey, D. (1984). "Bangles Make Detroit Their Own." In *Michigan Daily*. October 26.

Heath, C. (1989). "De La Soul: 'Chicken sandwich! Hyapheheehe hyupaheehee who ha ha!'" Available at https://www.rocksbackpages.com/Library/Article/de-la-soul-chicken-sandwich-hyaphehehe-hyupaheehee-who-ha-ha. Accessed January 20, 2023.

Heywood, M. (No Date). *A History of Orange County: 1889 to 2020*. No publisher.

Hibbert, T. (1986). "The Bangles." Available at https://www.rocksbackpages.com/Library/Article/the-bangles-2. Accessed January 20, 2023.

Hibbert, T. (1986). "The Bangles." In *Smash Hits*.

Hibbert, T. (1987). "The Bangles: Girls on Top." Available at https://www.rocksbackpages.com/Library/Article/the-bangles-girls-on-top. Accessed January 20, 2023.

Higham, W. (2001). "Skinny Tie Heaven! The RBP Power Pop Top 100, Part Two! (50—1)." Available at https://www.rocksbackpages.com/Library/Article/skinny-tie-heaven-the-rbp-power-pop-top-100-part-two-50—1. Accessed January 20, 2023.

Hilburn, R. (1983). "The Bangles at the Roxy: Do They Measure Up?" In *Los Angeles Times*. Available at https://www.newspapers.com/image/633647168. Accessed January 26, 2023.

Hilburn, R. (1986). "Robert Hilburn Summer Pop Has Arrived on Airwaves." In *Los Angeles Times*. Accessed October 5, 2023.

Himmelsbach, E. (1994). "The Go-Go's: The Beat and How to Get It (Again)." Available at https://www.rocksbackpages.com/Library/Article/the-go-gos-the-beat-and-how-to-get-it-again-. Accessed November 21, 2023.

Hirshey, G. (2001). *We Gotta Get out of This Place: The True, Tough Story of Women in Rock*. New York: Grove Press / Atlantic Monthly Press.

Hoad, C.; Stahl, G.; and Wilson, O. (eds). (2022). *Mixing Pop and Politics: Political Dimensions of Popular Music in the 21st Century*. London: Routledge.

Hoffs, S. (1983). "Are the Beatles Really Here?" Available at https://explore.bl.uk/primo_library/libweb/action/search.do?fn=search&ct=search&initialSearch=true&

mode=Basic&tab=local_tab&indx=1&dum=true&srt=rank&vid=BLVU1&frbg=&tb=t&vl%28freeText0%29=ARE+THE+BEATLES+REALLY+HERE%3F&scp.scps=scope%3A%28BLCONTENT%29&vl%28297891280UI0%29=any&vl%28297891280UI0%29=title&vl%28297891280UI0%29=any. Accessed February 6, 2023.

Hoffs, S.; Peterson, D.; Peterson, V.; and Steele, M. (1985). "Interview with Mambo." *Mambo Sounds und Trends 85*. February 17. Available at https://www.youtube.com/watch?v=CEfgF-OUDcM&list=PLGp3HEH8K0yHDGMR1smOzqouoQ0A9lewe&index=16. Accessed January 2, 2024.

Hogan, P. (1989). *The Bangles*. London: Omnibus.

Holden, S. (1984). "Pop: Bangles at the Ritz." Available at https://www.nytimes.com/1984/10/01/arts/pop-bangles-at-the-ritz.html?searchResultPosition=1. Accessed February 17, 2023.

Holden, S. (1989). "The Pop Life." Available at https://www.nytimes.com/1989/03/22/arts/the-pop-life-658089.html. Accessed November 22, 2023.

Holdship, B. (1986). "I Like the Monkees." In *Creem*. December. Available at https://monkees.coolcherrycream.com/articles/1987/04/creem-presents. Accessed October 6, 2023.

Hoskins, Z. (2022). "Dance / Music / Sex / Romance." Available at https://princesongs.org/author/dmsradmin/. Accessed October 3, 2023.

Hoskyns, B. (2009). *Waiting for the Sun: A Rock 'N' Roll History of Los Angeles*. London: Backbeat.

Hoyem, M. (1987). "Busy Bangles Say Success Means Having to Say 'Sorry.'" In *Green Bay Press-Gazette*. Available https://www.newspapers.com/image/189503027. Accessed January 25, 2023.

Hughes, R. (2016). "Emitt Rhodes: *Rainbow Ends*." Available at https://www.rocksbackpages.com/Library/Article/emitt-rhodes-irainbow-endsi. Accessed January 20, 2023.

Hunt, D. (1988). "Going a Round with Miles Copeland." In *Los Angeles Times*. July 5.

Infusisio, D. (1986). "Bangles Add New Sparkle to Music of the Mid-'60s." In *Times-Press-Recorder*. Available at https://www.newspapers.com/image/579796999. Accessed January 25, 2023.

Isaacs, B. (1989). "The Bangles Are About Rock Music, Not About Bracelets." In *Daily Argus*. Available at https://www.newspapers.com/image/896570371. Accessed January 26, 2023.

Isaacs, B. (1989). "Star-Spangled Bangles." In *Democrat and Chronicle*. Accessed January 25, 2023.

Jensen, D. (1986). "Capitol Radio Interviews: Susanna Hoffs, Debbi Peterson." Available at http://cadensa.bl.uk/uhtbin/cgisirsi/?ps=JuCwT4x0Vm/WORKS-FILE/104820018/9. Accessed February 4, 2023.

Johnson, D. (1985). "They Just Want to Be Bangles." In *St. Louis Post-Dispatch*. Available at https://www.newspapers.com/image/140920122. Accessed January 25, 2023.

Johnson, J. (2012). "The Bangles on 'Late Night' with Joan Rivers." {November 21, 1986}. December 12. Available at https://www.youtube.com/watch?v=Tst4WFxi1lY. Accessed March 28, 2023.

Jones, C. (2006). *Hit Girls: Women of Punk in the USA, 1975-1983*. Port Townsend, WA: Feral House.

Jones, C. (2006). *Tell Me When It's Over: Notes from the Paisley Underground*. [No Publication Place Given]: Rainfall.

Jones, J. (2016). "The Bangles—American Bandstand—March 26, 1983." Available at https://www.youtube.com/watch?v=sQrqfFr9Dss. Accessed November 21, 2023.

Jones, J. (2020). "The Bangles—MTV Guest VJ." Available at https://www.youtube.com/watch?v=1w6PGHchyzo. Accessed November 21, 2023.

Jurrjens, J. (1986). "Bangles: Different Light." In *Michigan Daily*. March 3.

Kalberg, B. (1983). "AN ALL-GIRL BAND FROM L.A. & IT'S NOT THE??—??'S!'" In *NOMAG*.

Kalberg, B. (1983). "The Bangs." *NOMAG*.

Kaminski, S. (1984). "All Over the Place: The Bangles." In *Michigan Daily*. September 14.

Karlen, N. (2020). *This Thing Called Life: Prince's Odyssey, On and Off the Record*. New York: St. Martin's Press.

Kaye, R. (1984). "All-Female Bangles Slay the Music of Their Youth." In *Fort Worth Star-Telegram*. Available at https://www.newspapers.com/image/638422707. Accessed January 25, 2023.

Kaye, R. (1987). "Bangles Turn On the Speed for Rawer Brand of Rock." In *Fort Worth Star*. Available https://www.newspapers.com/image/640404488. Accessed January 25, 2023.

Kaye, R. (1987). "Weekend Concerts." In *Fort Worth Star-Telegram*. Available at https://www.newspapers.com/image/639902887. Accessed January 25, 2023.

Klisuric, L. (1986). "The Bangles: All-Girl Group Offers '60s Magic." In *Asbury Park Press*. Available https://www.newspapers.com/image/145123748. Accessed January 25, 2023.

Kolson, A. (1986). "The Bangles." In *Daily Press*. Available at https://www.newspapers.com/image/234825018. Accessed January 25, 2023.

Kolson, A. (1987). "The Bangles: Talent + Pluck = Musical success." In *Macon Telegraph and News*. Available at https://www.newspapers.com/image/848098932. Accessed January 25, 2023.

Kolson, A. (1991). "Ex-Bangle Hoffs Tried for Individual Success." Available https://www.newspapers.com/image/664136472. Accessed January 25, 2023.

Kordosh, J. (1986). "Belinda Carlisle: Be Lovely, Be Lucky, Belinda." Available at https://www.rocksbackpages.com/Library/Article/belinda-carlisle-be-lovely-be-lucky-belinda. Accessed November 21, 2023.

Kordosh, J. (1987). "Even More of the Monkees!" In *Creem*. November.

Kreps, D. (2020). "See John Legend, Common, St. Vincent Cover Prince at Grammy Tribute." Available at https://www.rollingstone.com/music/music-news/john-legend-common-st-vincent-prince-grammy-tribute-988041/. Accessed March 3, 2023.

Kupa, E. and McGhee, A. (No Date). "Eternal Flame." Available at https://explore.bl.uk/primo_library/libweb/action/display.do?frbrVersion=73&tabs=moreTab&ct=display&fn=search&doc=BLLSA8877908&indx=24&recIds=BLLSA8877908

&recIdxs=3&elementId=3&renderMode=poppedOut&displayMode=full&frbrVersion=73&frbg=&dscnt=0&scp.scps=scope%3A%28BLCONTENT%29&tb=t&mode=Basic&vid=BLVU1&vl(297891280UI0)=any&srt=rank&tab=local_tab&dum=true&vl(freeText0)=DD00040540&dstmp=1675707389670. Accessed February 6, 2023.

La Femme Makita. (2008). "The Bangles Arsenio Hal 1989 Part 1." December 13. Available at https://www.youtube.com/watch?v=qEpvTelKOAM. Accessed March 29, 2023.

La Femme Makita. (2009). "The Bangles Interview & Manic Monday (Live)." {1983}. August 3. Available at https://www.youtube.com/watch?v=ibFYFazwZEM. Accessed March 2, 2023.

Lababedi, I. (1986). "Bananarama: These Charming Girls." Available at https://www.rocksbackpages.com/Library/Article/bananarama-these-charming-girls. Accessed November 22, 2023.

Lababedi, I. (1985). "Bangles for Sale." Available at https://www.rocksbackpages.com/Library/Article/bangles-for-sale. Accessed January 20, 2023.

Lankford, R. D., Jr. (2010). *Women Singer-Songwriters in Rock: A Populist Rebellion in the 1990s*. Lanham, MD: Scarecrow Press.

Larson, J. B. (2023). *Hit Girls: Women of Punk in the USA, 1975-1983*. Port Townsend, WA: Feral House.

Lee, C. (1986). "The Bangles: Humble but Perfect." In *LA Weekly*. Available at https://www.newspapers.com/image/578487639. Accessed January 25, 2023.

Lee, C. (1982). "Bangs Ignite Rock Audience." In *Los Angeles Times*.

Lee, C. (1982). "The Newest Music: A Look at Ten Bands to Watch Out For." In *LA Weekly*.

Lee, C. (1983). "One's Tight, the Other Isn't: The Bangles, the Three O'Clock at the Roxy." In *LA Weekly*, February 10.

Lee, E. (1989). "Bangles Taunt & Tease." In *Atlanta Constitution*.

Leibetseder, D. (2016). *Queer Tracks: Subversive Strategies in Rock and Pop Music*. Abingdon, UK: Routledge.

Leighton, K. (1984). "An All-Girl Band That Wants More than Fun." In *Times-Advocate*. Available at https://www.newspapers.com/image/570604449. Accessed January 26, 2023.

Leonard, G. (2017). *Gender in the Music Industry: Rock, Discourse and Girl Power*. London: Routledge, Taylor & Francis Group.

Leonard, G. and Snowden, D. (1997). *Make the Music Go Bang: The Early L.A. Punk Scene*. Brighton, UK: Griffin Publishing.

Lev, M. (1986). "Girl Group's Prince Has Come." In *News-Pilot*. Available at https://www.newspapers.com/image/607002219. Accessed January 25, 2023.

Lev, M. (1986). "Impressive Sound Dresses Up Bangles." In *News-Pilot*.

Leviton, M. (1982). "The Bangs: Al's Bar, Los Angeles CA." Available at https://www.rocksbackpages.com/Library/Article/the-bangs-als-bar-los-angeles-ca. Accessed November 21, 2023.

Leviton, M. (1983). "The Long Ryders Shoot 'Em Up." Available at https://www.rocksbackpages.com/Library/Article/the-long-ryders-shoot-em-up. Accessed January 20, 2023.

Lexington Herald Leader. (1986). "Bangles Shining in Music World." In *Lexington Herald Leader*.

Lillard, M. (1986). "Bangles Inspired by Musical Sounds of '60s." In *The Daily Journal*. Available at https://www.newspapers.com/image/155158464. Accessed January 26, 2023.

Lillard, M. (1986). "Bangles Like '60s Comparisons." In *Republic*. Available at https://www.newspapers.com/image/139224297. Accessed January 26, 2023.

Lillard, M. (1986). "Bangles Turn Influences of '60s into an '80s Sound." In *Fort Lauderdale News*. Available at https://www.newspapers.com/image/236655280. Accessed January 25, 2023.

Live Nation Clubs and Theaters. (2016). "The Bangles | Green Room Tales | House of Blues." June 14. Available at https://youtu.be/8Xgo1iY7_hU. Accessed May 17, 2023.

Lizie, A. (2022). *Prince on Prince: Interviews and Encounters with Prince: 22 (Musicians in Their Own Words)*. London: Welbeck.

Lli ylsuo ires. (2007). "MV3 Bangles Interview 1983." February 20. Available at https://www.youtube.com/watch?v=VqdXF9RWUTk. Accessed February 28, 2023.

Lloyd, R. (1984). "The Bangles Bright, Shiny Beats." Available at *LA Weekly*.

Longwood University. "Rotunda—Vol 66, No 5—Oct 22, 1986" (1986). *Rotunda*. 941.

Lounges, T. (1988). "Bangles Cut a Path in Music Industry." In *Times*.

Lynskey, D. (2003). "We're the Mrs. Robinsons of Rock." In *Guardian*. Available at https://www.newspapers.com/image/260905630. Accessed January 26, 2023.

Macari, R. (2018). "There's More Than Meets the Eye to the Bangles and You Should Know Why." Available at https://rachel-macari.medium.com/theres-more-than-meets-the-eye-to-the-bangles-9bfdb968ec2e. Accessed November 21, 2023.

Marlowe, J. (1984). "Lauper Proves She's So Unusual." In *Miami News*. Available at https://palmbeachpost.newspapers.com/image/302713577. Accessed January 26, 2023.

Martin, M. J. and Morgan, S. M. (2016). *Prince Rogers Nelson*. No publisher listed.

Martoccio, A. (2020). "The Zombies Announce New Album, Map Spring Tour." Available at https://www.rollingstone.com/music/music-news/the-zombies-announce-new-album-spring-tour-952214/. Accessed March 3, 2023.

Mawn, R. (1986). "Let's Do the Time Warp." In *Observer*. March 5.

McDonnell, E. (2013). *Queens of Noise: The Real Story of the Runaways*. London: Hachette Books.

Meltzer, M. (2010). *Girl Power: The Nineties Revolution in Music*. London: Faber & Faber.

Mercer-Taylor, P. (1998). "Songs from the Bell Jar: Autonomy and Resistance in the Music of the Bangles." In *Popular Music*. (vol. 17/2).

Metal Priestesses Podcast. (2021). "Episode 10: Linda Ronstadt and Susanna Hoffs!" Available at https://www.youtube.com/watch?v=SxQXyddJqCY. Accessed May 19, 2023.

Metal Priestesses Podcast. (2021). "Season 2 Episode 3: Debbi and Vicki Peterson of the Bangles." Available at https://www.youtube.com/watch?v=GgKIB0aSZfM. Accessed May 19, 2023.

Michael Steele FanChannel. (2014). "Interview with the Bangles—Amsterdam 1989." July 28. Available at https://youtu.be/9baxuCzDsno. Accessed April 20, 2023.

Miles, J. (1986). "The Bangles at the Town and Country Club." Available at https://explore.bl.uk/primo_library/libweb/action/display.do?tabs=moreTab&ct=display&fn=search&doc=BLLSA5023860&indx=1&recIds=BLLSA5023860&recIdxs=0&elementId=0&renderMode=poppedOut&displayMode=full&frbrVersion=&frbg=&&dscnt=0&scp.scps=scope%3A%28BLCONTENT%29&tb=t&vid=BLVU1&mode=Basic&vl(297891280UI0)=any&srt=rank&tab=local_tab&dum=true&vl(freeText0)=the%20bangles%20%2B%20town%20and%20country&dstmp=1675623147397. Accessed February 5, 2023.

Millaa1971. (2010). "The Bangles—Manic Monday and Let It Go—The Tube 1986." Available at https://www.youtube.com/@millaa1971. Accessed November 21, 2023.

Miller, M. (1995). "Continental Drifters 'Predestined.'" In *State*. Available at https://www.newspapers.com/image/752781072. Accessed January 25, 2023.

miscellaneous publication #15. (2021). "The Bangles on Mouth to Mouth." March 18. Available at https://youtu.be/T_i_ZglDU1Y. Accessed May 10, 2023.

miscellaneous publication #15. (2021). "The Bangles on MTV News." {July 3, 1988}. Available at https://youtu.be/rBcKGzH_Rio. Accessed April 12, 2023.

Mojo. (2022). "MOJO Time Machine: The Bangles Walk Like an Egyptian to Number One." Available at https://www.mojo4music.com/time-machine/1980s/mojo-time-machine-the-bangles-walk-like-an-egyptian-to-number-one/. Accessed October 5, 2023.

Mora, A. (1980). "Openers: MEET THE GIRL GROUPS—Those Girls." In *Oui*. (vol. 10).

Morton, R. (1988). "Bring on the Dancing Dogs?" In *Record Mirror*. February 13.

Moser, J. J. (2011). "The Bangles Recapture '70s Spirit on 'Sweetheart.'" In *Morning Call*. Available at https://www.newspapers.com/image/273201651. Accessed January 26, 2023.

Munro, H. (1986). "The Bangles Concert Will Bring '60s Sound to Hanover." In *Valley News*. Available at https://www.newspapers.com/image/833475418. Accessed January 26, 2023.

Murray, T. (2023). "Michael J Fox Says He Doesn't Remember Dating the Bangles Star Susanna Hoffs in the Eighties." Available at https://www.independent.co.uk/arts-entertainment/films/news/michael-j-fox-susanna-hoffs-the-bangles-members-b2334340.html. Accessed November 21, 2023.

Nault, C. (2017). *Queercore: Queer Punk Media Subculture*. Place of publication not given: Routledge.

Nehring, N. (1997). *Popular Music, Gender and Post-modernism: Anger Is an Energy*. Thousand Oaks, CA: SAGE Publications, Inc.

New York Times Service. (2000). "Bangles Announce Reunion, Stressing Union." In *Springfield News-Sun*. Available at https://www.newspapers.com/image/827095007. Accessed January 25, 2023.

N.I.R. (1983). "Bangles." In *Nashville Intelligence Report*. No. 13, May.

No Author. (1989). "*The Allnighter.*" In *LA Weekly*. April 20.

No Author. (1986). "Bangles Are Manic About Their Music." In *Spokane Chronicle*. Available at https://www.newspapers.com/image/570614066. Accessed January 25, 2023.

No Author. (1986). "The Bangles Make Noise at the Beacon." In *Newsday* (Suffolk Edition).

No Author. (1989). "Elvis' Eternal Flame." In *Palm Beach Post*. Available at https://palmbeachpost.newspapers.com/image/132725764. Accessed January 26, 2023.

Noftsinger, K. (2010). "Is Lilith Fair Feminist? Sarah McLachlan's Not Sure." In *Ms*. Available at https://msmagazine.com/2010/07/15/is-lilith-fair-feminist-sarah-mclachlans-not-sure/. Accessed February 6, 2023.

O'Brien, L. (2013). *She Bop: The Definitive History of Women in Popular Music*. Revised Third Edition. London: Jawbone.

O'Brien, L. (2003). *She-Bop II (Bayou Press Series): The Definitive History of Women in Rock, Pop and Soul*. New York: Continuum International Publishing Group.

O'Dair, B. (1997). *The Rolling Stone Book of Women in Rock: Trouble Girls*. New York: Random House.

Oermann, R. (1984). "The Bangles Are a Rock Band." Available at *Tennessean*.

O'Neill, B. and Walsh, R. (2020). *The Great Book of Badass Women: 15 Fearless and Inspirational Women That Changed History*. Sheridan: LAK Publishing.

Orleans, S. (1987). "The Bangles: California Girls." In *Rolling Stone*. March 26.

Out Of Order 2. (2022). "The Bangles—American Bandstand, May 10, 1986." Available at https://www.youtube.com/watch?v=HYxHJywjYwk&list=PLCv4g4XToAo9tSY1L1zafou_6DUZ10UN5&index=42. Accessed November 21, 2023.

Out of Order 2. (2022). "The Bangles—'Backstage Pass' Interview 1986." May 1986. Available at https://youtu.be/_uou_9b5c44. Accessed April 16, 2023.

Out Of Order 2. (2022). "The Bangles—'Going Down to Liverpool' November 23, 1984." Available at https://www.youtube.com/watch?v=QVs8yt. DYucg&list=PLCv4g4XToAo9tSY1L1zafou_6DUZ10UN5&index=33. Accessed November 21, 2023.

Out Of Order 2. (2022). "The Bangles—'Hero Takes a Fall,' February 18, 1985." Available at https://www.youtube.com/watch?v=vfe8sFpZ7Io&list=PLCv4g4XToAo9tSY1L1zafou_6DUZ10UN5&index=25. Accessed November 21, 2023.

Out Of Order 2. (2022). "The Bangles—'Manic Monday,' Villa Tempo, February 24, 1986." Available at https://www.youtube.com/watch?v=O9blaUtNULI.

Ove, T. (1986). "Bangles in Exclusive CMU Show." In *Pittsburgh Press*. Available at https://www.newspapers.com/image/146302834. Accessed January 26, 2023.

Page, B. (1991). "Susanna Hoffs: *When You're a Boy*." Available at https://www.rocksbackpages.com/Library/Article/susanna-hoffs-iwhen-youre-a-boyi-. Accessed November 21, 2021.

Palm Beach Post. (1986). "The Bangles Discover Fame Creates One Manic Day." In *Palm Beach Post*.

Palm Beach Post. (1989). "Elvis' Eternal Flame." In *Palm Beach Post*. March 31.

Palm Beach Post Wire Services. (1989). "Ode to the Bangles." In *Palm Beach Post*. Available at https://palmbeachpost.newspapers.com/image/132699166. Accessed January 26, 2023.

Panizzi, R. G. (2022). *Prince: The Sign of My Times.* Independently published.

Pareles, J. (1989). "Review/Rock; Guitar and Harmony by the Bangles." Available at https://www.nytimes.com/1989/03/26/arts/review-rock-guitar-and-harmony-by-the-bangles.html. Accessed November 22, 2023.

Partiridge, K. (2018). "Why the Bangles, Dream Syndicate & Others Want the Paisley Underground to Rise Again." Available at https://www.billboard.com/music/rock/bangles-dream-syndicate-three-oclock-paisley-underground-8484948/. Accessed November 1, 2023.

Parwati, A. (2021). "The Bangles 'CBS Overnight News' Interview 04/06/1986." May 7. Available at https://www.youtube.com/watch?v=QcLaM3c5_a8&t=93s. Accessed March 23, 2023.

Parwati, A. (2022). "The Bangles on CNN Showbiz Today 05/29/1986." August 28. Available at https://www.youtube.com/watch?v=c8Q1SfDXWVw&list=PL5k-iPKEy545cL9De8JBsqNMlTBzZ0YZW&index=132. Accessed March 27, 2023.

Parwati, A. (2022). "The Bangles ET Inside Music October 1988." May 30. Available at https://youtu.be/mC0a_mplXr8. Accessed April 12, 2023.

Parwati, A. (2021). "The Bangles' Live at Five WNBC Interview 1986." May 18. Available at https://www.youtube.com/watch?v=vXQ7ZzphrjQ. Accessed April 14, 2023.

Parwati, A. (2021). "The Bangles Live @Syria Mosque ('Students Against MS'), Pittsburgh, PA 10/29/1986." Available at https://www.youtube.com/watch?v=MO_rduYBIhs. Accessed November 20, 2023.

Parwati, A. (2021). "The Bangles MTV Interview Recording 11/02/1988." Available at https://youtu.be/BC4nkvh8XnI. Accessed April 13, 2023.

Parwati, A. (No Date). "MTV Reportage 1987—February 23, 1987 Officially Declared as Bangles Day." Available at https://www.youtube.com/watch?v=1qOhiLvFHf8. Accessed October 25, 2023.

Patterson, R. (1983). "Bangles." In *Scrantonian Sun*.

Paul, O. (1986). "Owen Paul + The Bangles—Early Show Concert." Available at https://explore.bl.uk/primo_library/libweb/action/display.do?tabs=moreTab&ct=display&fn=search&doc=BLLSA1815765&indx=3&recIds=BLLSA1815765&recIdxs=2&elementId=2&renderMode=poppedOut&displayMode=full&frbrVersion=&frbg=&&dscnt=0&scp.scps=scope%3A%28BLCONTENT%29&tb=t&vid=BLVU1&mode=Basic&vl(297891280UI0)=any&srt=rank&tab=local_tab&dum=true&vl(freeText0)=C628%2F438%20&dstmp=1675707083157. Accessed February 6, 2023.

Paul, S. (1979). "The Fans All-Girl Band on L.A. Scene." Unknown publisher.

Pearson, M. (2010). *One Step Beyond a Teenage Odyssey in 1980s Los Angeles.* CreateSpace.

Pendle, K. (2016). *Women in Music: A Research and Information Guide.* Place of publication not given: Routledge.

Pescovit, D. (2023). "Prince's Original Version of 'Manic Monday,' Unheard Until Recently (Video)." Available at https://boingboing.net/2023/01/23/princes-original-version-of-manic-monday-unheard-until-recently-video.html. Accessed January 25, 2023.

Peterson, V. (1984). "Class of '77 Vicki Peterson: Bangle." In *LA Weekly.* September 20. Page 38.

Philadelphia Inquirer. (1986). "Bangles Are Not Typical Girl Group." In *Philadelphia Inquirer.*

Playgirl. (1987). "The Bangles." In *Playgirl.* April.

Pollack, B. (2012). "Susanna Hoffs—'Eternal Flame.'" Available at https://www.songfacts.com/blog/playingmysong/susanna-hoffs-eternal-flame. Accessed November 2, 2023.

Polly, S. (2017). "Bangles—Hero Take a Fall/Going Down to Liverpool live—Letterman (1984)." Available at https://www.youtube.com/watch?v=PMdvPYw0hA4. Accessed November 21, 2023.

PopMatters Staff. (2002). "Tell Me When It's Over: The Paisley Underground Reconsidered." Available at https://www.popmatters.com/020430-paisleyunderground-2496101827.html. Accessed November 21, 2023.

Popson, T. (1986). "The Bangles Are All Over the Place." In *Morning Call.* Available at https://www.newspapers.com/image/276250112. Accessed January 26, 2023.

Pouncey, E. (1985). "The Bangles: Yesterday and Today." Available at https://www.rocksbackpages.com/Library/Article/the-bangles-yesterday-and-today. Accessed January 20, 2023.

Prince. (2018). *Prince: The Last Interview: And Other Conversations.* Hoboken, NJ: Melville House Publishing.

Priore, D. (2015). *Riot on Sunset Strip: Rock 'n' Roll's Last Stand in Hollywood.* London: Jawbone.

Quantick, D. (1991). "A *Boy Named Sue.*" In *New Musical Express.* March 16.

Quisling, E.; Rollins, H.; and Wiliams, A. (2003). *Straight Whisky: A Living History of Sex, Drugs & Rock 'n' Roll on the Sunset Strip.* Los Angeles: Bonus Books Inc.

Rachel, D. and Ranking, R. (2021). *I Just Can't Stop It: My Life in The Beat.* London: Omnibus.

Rad Universe. (2012). "The Bangles—A Hazy Shade of Winter (Top of the Pops, 1987)." Available at https://www.youtube.com/watch?v=JH634us5iY8. Accessed November 21, 2023.

Rader, S. (1996). "Peterson Sisters Find Post-Bangles Harmonies." In *News Tribune.* Available at https://www.newspapers.com/image/739336795. Accessed January 26, 2023.

Rapido. (1991). Contributor: Hoffs, Susanna (speaker, female). Identifier: ISRC: CKEY1304972. V224/1 RAPIDO.

Rea, S. X. (1983). "The Bangles: *Bangles* (Faulty FEP 1302 Five-Song EP)." Available at https://www.rocksbackpages.com/Library/Article/the-bangles-ibanglesi-faulty-fep-1302-five-song-ep. Accessed January 20, 2023.

Reader, S. (1996). "New Angle for Two Bangles." In *Santa Cruz Sentinel*. Available at https://www.newspapers.com/image/81146474. Accessed January 25, 2023.

RealInspectorShane. (2011). "An Interview with Joe Iaquinto—February 2011." In *micki-steele-net*. Available at https://micki-steele-net.tumblr.com/post/640011697323753472/an-interview-with-joe-iaquinto-february-2011. Accessed November 21, 2023.

RealInspectorShane. (2015). "An Interview with Paul Reed—March 2015." In *micki-steele-net*. Available at https://micki-steele-net.tumblr.com/post/640018125250822144/the-corona-del-mar-high-school-band-1972. Accessed September 4, 2023.

RealInspectorShane. (2010). "An Interview with Phast Phreddie, July 2010." In *micki-steele-net*. Available at https://micki-steele-net.tumblr.com/post/640017480091353088/runaways-concert-poster-september-28-1975-an?fbclid=IwAR0KRke5XIm71uCFU4EZUmhCBtAbmCrtn0YAJ10JG_kFnPaR8tbNgftIoFw. Accessed August 10, 2023.

reclaimerReclaimer. (1986). "The Bangles Interview 1986." Interviewed by Peter Illmann. Available at https://www.youtube.com/watch?v=h2qQGh2H1Gk. Accessed June 15, 2023.

Record Collector. (2019). "The Paisley Underground." In *Record Collector*. Available at https://recordcollectormag.com/articles/paisley-underground. Accessed November 2, 2023.

Record Mirror. (1988). "Gang Bangs." In *Record Mirror*. December.

ReelinInTheYears66. (2017). "The Bangles—'In Your Room' on Countdown 1988." Available at https://www.youtube.com/watch?v=7sYMYQNNDI4. Accessed November 21, 2023.

RETROVISOR. (2019). "The Bangles Manic Monday 1986 HQ, Top of the Pops." Available at https://www.youtube.com/watch?v=0TlcZ8BuAWs. Accessed November 21, 2023.

Robert, R. (2020). "Susanna Hoffs and Friends Remember David Roback, Who Stayed Creative, and Enigmatic, to the End." In *Los Angeles Times*. Available at https://www.latimes.com/entertainment-arts/music/story/2020-03-06/david-roback-mazzy-star-susanna-hoffs-opal-cancer. Accessed November 1, 2023.

Robincheau, P. (1989). "Momentum Carries Bangles Beyond Poses." In *Boston Globe*. Available at https://www.newspapers.com/image/439099267. Accessed January 25, 2023.

Robins, W. (1987). "Climbing out of the Paisley Underground." In *New York Newsday*. Available at https://www.newspapers.com/image/704676572. Accessed May 3, 2023.

Robinson, L. (1987). "Bangles Feel Like They Are an Exclusive Club." In *News-Pilot*.

Rockportraits. (2014). "The Bangles." In *Rockportraits*. Available at https://rockportraits.wordpress.com/2014/09/24/the-bangles/. Accessed October 25, 2023.

Rolling Stone. (1988). "Bangles Camp Out in the Studio." In *Random Notes*. Issue 527. In *Rolling Stone*. New York: Rolling Stone Licensing LLC.

Rolling Stone. (1987). Double Issue. December 17.

Rolling Stone. (1984). "Letters to the Editor." In *Rolling Stone*. Issue 436. New York: Rolling Stone Licensing LLC.

Rolling Stone. (1986). "Letters to the Editor." In *Rolling Stone*. Issue 472. New York: Rolling Stone Licensing LLC.

Rolling Stone. (1987). "Letters to the Editor." In *Rolling Stone*. Issue 499. New York: Rolling Stone Licensing LLC.

Rolling Stone. (1988). "Letters to the Editor." In *Rolling Stone*. Issue 540. New York: Rolling Stone Licensing LLC.

Rolling Stone. (1987). "Music-Biz Kids." In *Rolling Stone*. Issue 496. New York: Rolling Stone Licensing LLC.

Rolling Stone. (1986). "Musicians Fear Violence in Europe." In *Rolling Stone*. Issue 475. New York: Rolling Stone Licensing LLC.

Rolling Stone. (1984). "Notable News." In *Rolling Stone*. Issue 434.

Rolling Stone. (1987). "Women in Rock." In *Rolling Stone*. Issue 493. New York: Rolling Stone Licensing LLC.

Rolling Stone. (1987). "Worst Mother and Child Reunion." In *Random Notes*. Issue 515–16. In *Rolling Stone*. New York: Rolling Stone Licensing LLC.

Rosen, S. R. (2006). "Revisiting *Rainy Day*: Matthew Sweet and Susanna Hoffs Get Under the Covers." Available at https://www.rocksbackpages.com/Library/Article/revisiting-rainy-day-matthew-sweet-and-susanna-hoffs-get-under-the-covers. Accessed January 20, 2023.

Rosenbluth, J. (1992). "Vega Brilliant on 4th Album." In *Palm Beach Post*. Available at https://palmbeachpost.newspapers.com/image/132851604. Accessed January 26, 2023.

Rosenthal, G. (2000). *Behind the Music: The Bangles*. IMDb, S3, E40.

Rowland, M. (1986). "The Bangles Nobody's Retread." In *Leader-Post*. Available at https://www.newspapers.com/image/497086664. Accessed January 26, 2023.

sab67d. (2001). "Review of *The Allnighter*." Available at https://www.imdb.com/review/rw0240830/. Accessed October 25, 2023.

San Francisco Examiner. (1987). "Bangles." In *San Francisco Examiner*.

Santelli, R. (1986). "Debbi Peterson Knows What She Wants." In *Modern Drummer*.

Scaggs, A. (2000). "Bangles Unite for Club Tour." In *Rolling Stone*. Issue 848. New York: Rolling Stone Licensing LLC.

Schippers, M. (2002). *Rockin' out of the Box: Gender Maneuvering in Alternative Hard Rock*. New Brunswick, NJ; London: Rutgers University Press.

Schneider, M. (1983). "The Big Bangles Theory." In *Creem*. May.

Schock, G. (2021). *Made in Hollywood: All Access with the Go-Go's*. New York: Black Dog & Leventhal.

Scoppa, B. (1988). "Bangles Do the Loosen Up." In *Cashbox*. November 19.

Scoppa, B. (1987). "Tom Petty: Less Is More, More or Less." Available at https://www.rocksbackpages.com/Library/Article/tom-petty-less-is-more-more-or-less. Accessed November 21, 2023.

ScottishTeeVee. (2020). "The Bangles—In Your Room—London 1988." Available at https://www.youtube.com/watch?v=EZjjBAcbKdU&list=PLMe0CUMuSN6HRSjve9TAiVATSMTAIzpkc&index=9. Accessed November 21, 2023.

ScottishTeeVee. (2020). "The Bangles—Interview England 1988." Available at https://www.youtube.com/watch?v=B09YpVL_wSw. Accessed April 20, 2023.

ScottishTeeVee. (2020). "The Bangles—Talking About George Michael." {1988}. September 4. Available at https://www.youtube.com/watch?v=xhN2Pbr84wo&list=PLMe0CUMuSN6HRSjve9TAiVATSMTAIzpkc. Accessed May 1, 2023.

ScottishTeeVee. (2019). "The Bangles—Walking Down Your Street—Germany 1987." {February 9, 1987}. February 2. Available at https://www.youtube.com/watch?v=qslrvExocFk&list=PLMe0CUMuSN6HRSjve9TAiVATSMTAIzpkc&index=7. Accessed April 6, 2023.

ScottishTeeVee. (2018). "The Bangles—Walking Down Your Street—1988 & Interview." December 5. Available at https://www.youtube.com/watch?v=c76LiN74FC4&ab_channel=ScottishTeeVee. Accessed March 28, 2023.

ScottishTeeVee. (2020). "The Bangles—Yokohama Japan 1988." Available at https://youtu.be/Cn7Ylak5xrQ. Accessed May 11, 2023.

Sendejas, J., Jr. (2016). "I Was There: The Day the Bangles Played on Beltway 8." In *HoustonPress*. Available at https://www.houstonpress.com/music/i-was-there-the-day-the-bangles-played-on-beltway-8-9012727. Accessed November 5, 2023.

Senior, J. (1989). "Another Cocktail, Girls?" In *Number One*. April.

Sexton, P. (2021). *Prince: A Portrait of the Artist in Memories & Memorabilia*. Chicago: Chicago Review Press.

Sheehan, T. (1985). "Americans in Paris." In *Melody Maker*. March 2.

Sherman, D. (2000). *20th Century Rock and Roll: Women in Rock (20th Century Rock & Roll)*. Burlington, ON: Collector's Guide Publishing; First Edition.

Silverman, S. M. (1997). "Bangles Bounce Back." Available at https://people.com/celebrity/bangles-bounce-back/. Accessed February 17, 2023.

Simmons, S. (1987). "Cyndi Lauper: Doing That Primitive Thing." Available at https://www.rocksbackpages.com/Library/Article/cyndi-lauper-doing-that-primitive-thing. Accessed January 20, 2023.

Simpson, D. (2004). "Atomic Kitten: Manchester Arena." Available at https://www.rocksbackpages.com/Library/Article/atomic-kitten-manchester-arena. Accessed November 21, 2023.

SiriusXM Entertainment. (2019). "Susanna Hoffs on How Bruce Springsteen Helped the Bangles Get Signed." Available at https://soundcloud.com/siriusxmentertainment/susanna-hoffs-on-how-bruce?utm_source=estreetshuffle.com&utm_campaign=wtshare&utm_medium=widget&utm_content=https%253A%252F%252Fsoundcloud.com%252Fsiriusxmentertainment%252Fsusanna-hoffs-on-how-bruce. Accessed June 25, 2023.

Skinner, M. S. (1986). "'Different Light' LP a Sparkler from Bangles." In *Arizona Daily Star*. Available at https://www.newspapers.com/image/165421772. Accessed January 25, 2023.

Smash Hits. (1986). "Susanna Hoffs, the Bangles, Personal File." In *Smash Hits*. July 28, 1986 (vol. 8, no. 15).

Smith, R. (1985). "Bangles." In *Record Mirror*. March 16.

Snow, M. (1986). "The Bangles: Manic Impressives." Available at https://www.rocksbackpages.com/Library/Article/the-bangles-manic-impressives. Accessed January 20, 2023.

Snyder, G. (1986). "Bangles Are Not Baubles of Rock." In *Fort Worth Star-Telegram*. Available at https://www.newspapers.com/image/639402297. January 25, 2023.

Sollenberger, K. (2004). "The Bangles: Yesterday and Today." In *Vintage Guitar*.

Spatz, D. J. (2007). "Back and Better Than Ever." In *Record*. Available at https://www.newspapers.com/image/505538125. Accessed January 26, 2023.

Spitz, M. and Mullen, B. (2001). *We Got the Neutron Bomb: The Untold Story of L.A. Punk*. New York: Three Rivers.

Spotnitz, F. (1984). "The Bangles: An All-Female Lineup Rooted in Sound of the Early Beatles." Available at https://www.upi.com/Archives/1984/11/30/The-Bangles-An-all-female-lineup-rooted-in-sound-of-the-early-Beatles/5454470638800/. Accessed February 17, 2023.

Spurrier, J. (1982). "How the Bangs Rang a Bell." In *Los Angeles Times*. September 26.

St. Nicholas, R. (2019). *My Name Is Prince*. New York: Amistad.

Staunton, T. (2010). "Unsung Heroes: The Rain Parade." Available at https://www.rocksbackpages.com/Library/Article/unsung-heroes-the-rain-parade. Accessed November 21, 2023.

Strauss, D. (1989). "Lightweight Bangles Don't Dazzle or Disappoint." In *Los Angeles Times*. September 2.

Streeter, L. G. (2014). "Group's Secret? 'Yummy' Voices." In *Palm Beach Post*. Available at https://palmbeachpost.newspapers.com/image/163864235. Accessed January 26, 2023.

Sullivan, J. (1986). "The Bangles: A '60s Sound for the '80s." In *Boston Globe*. Available at https://www.newspapers.com/image/437576544. Accessed January 25, 2023.

Sweeting, A. (1985). "The Bangles." Available at https://www.rocksbackpages.com/Library/Article/the-bangles. Accessed January 20, 2023.

Sweeting, A. (1985). "The Bangles: Dingwalls, London." Available at https://www.rocksbackpages.com/Library/Article/the-bangles-dingwalls-london. Accessed January 20, 2023.

Sylva, B. (1983). "Backstage with the Bangles." In *Sacramento Bee*. Available at https://www.newspapers.com/image/622221843. Accessed January 26, 2023.

Tapatalk. (2003). "GREETINGS INTREPID RP'ERS AND FRIENDS!" Available at https://www.tapatalk.com/groups/returnpost/greetings-intrepid-rp-ers-and-friends-t643.html. Accessed November 2, 2023.

Taylor, J. (1986). "Bangles Have Arrived—via Bus: Now Pit Stops Are High on the Charts." In *Daily Times-Advocate* (Escondido, California). March 6. Page 84. Available at https://www.newspapers.com/image/569983405. Accessed January 26, 2023.

Taylor, L. (1986). "Bangles Jangle Their Way up the Charts." In *Messenger-Inquirer*. Available at https://www.newspapers.com/image/378790201. Accessed January 25, 2023.

Teicholz, T. (2006). "Susanna Hoffs Walks Like a—Rockstar No, a Mom—Rockstar/Mom." Available at https://web.archive.org/web/20061018205847/http://www.jewishjournal.com/home/preview.php?id=16541. Accessed November 1, 2023.

Thaapa1. (2013). "The Bangles—Eternal Flame (Live in 1989—The Arsenio Hall TV-Show)." Available at https://www.youtube.com/watch?v=MLQ98yq1cq4. Accessed November 21, 2023.

The Paisley Underground. (2019). "The Paisley Underground." Available at https://recordcollectormag.com/articles/paisley-underground. Accessed November 1, 2023.

thepopculturefiend. (2011). "The Bangles—If She Knew What She Wants (1987)." Available at https://www.youtube.com/watch?v=8jeZtxB_pGI. Accessed November 21, 2023.

TheProfRobin. (2010). "The Bangles: Walk Like an Egyptian." Available at https://www.youtube.com/watch?v=ZkR1cvLWCZ0. Accessed November 21, 2023.

Thomas, P. (1984). "Sussana Hoffs of the Bangles Intimate Details Article, Picture & Songwords." Publication unknown.

Thompson, D. (2011). *Bad Reputation: The Unauthorized Biography of Joan Jett*. London: Backbeat Books.

Thomson, L. (1982). *New Women in Rock*. London: Omnibus.

Thorne, M. (2012). *Prince*. London: Faber & Faber.

Thorne, M. (2023). *Prince: The Man and His Music*. Evanston, IL: Agate Bolden.

TopPop. (2015). "The Bangles—Walk Like an Egyptian (1987)• TopPop." Available at https://www.youtube.com/watch?v=JA0VfqtIK_A. Accessed November 21, 2023.

Toure. (2021). *Nothing Compares 2 U: An Oral History of Prince*. Nashville: Permuted Press.

Trakin, R. (1986). "The Bangles: Making Pop Her-Story or It's a Girl's, Girl's, Girl's World." Available at https://www.rocksbackpages.com/Library/Article/the-bangles-making-pop-her-story-or-its-a-girls-girls-girls-world. Accessed January 20, 2023.

Trakin, R. (1986). "Honking Off Dudes." In *Creem*. May.

Trebor TV. (2001). "1989 International Rock Awards Seg #2—The Bangles." Available at https://www.youtube.com/watch?v=lASYsN8vO98. Accessed November 21, 2023.

Triplett, G. (2009). "Susanna Hoffs Strolling Down Memory Lane." Available at https://eu.oklahoman.com/story/entertainment/music/2009/08/07/susanna-hoffs-strolling-down-memory-lane/61375860007/. Accessed October 25, 2023.

Tucker, K. (1986). "The Bangles Know How to Rock 'n' Roll." In *Corpus Christi Caller-Times*. Available at https://www.newspapers.com/image/758664191. Accessed January 26, 2023.

Tucker, K. (1986). "Bangles Prove They're More Than a Girl Group." In *Spokesman-Review*. Available at https://www.newspapers.com/image/572504399. Accessed January 26, 2023.

Tudahl, D. (2022). *Prince and the Parade and Sign O' The Times Era Studio Sessions: 1985 and 1986 (Prince Studio Sessions)*. Lanham, MD: Rowman & Littlefield Publishers.

Tysongreer. (2013). "The Bangles—Walk Like an Egyptian—Live Performance." Available at https://www.youtube.com/watch?v=LgpCU39VvH8. Accessed November 21, 2023.

United Press International. (1986). "Impressive Sound Dresses Up Bangles." In *Knoxville News Sentinel*.

United Press International. (1986). "Parental Influence Gives Bangles Band a Sound Background." In *Knoxville News-Sentinel*. Available at https://www.newspapers.com/image/774612709. Accessed January 26, 2023.

Valentine, K. (2020). *All I Ever Wanted: A Rock 'n' Roll Memoir*. Austin: University of Texas Press.

Vallance, J. (2009). "MTV's the Cutting Edge with Jeffrey Vallance: The Bangles." {1983}. Available at https://www.youtube.com/watch?v=X3P2bBLg_bI. Accessed March 2, 2023.

Voland, J. (1986). "The World's Disharmony Is Affecting Music Group's Tours." In *Palm Beach Post*. Available at https://palmbeachpost.newspapers.com/image/129800794. Accessed January 26, 2023.

Walsh, S. (2023). "*Daisy Jones & the Six*'s Costume Designer Has Tips for Your Halloween Looks." Available at https://www.vanityfair.com/hollywood/2023/03/daisy-jones-and-the-six-costume-designer-tips-halloween-looks. Accessed March 13, 2023.

Wells, A. (2008). "Images of Popular Music Artists: Do Male and Female Audiences Have Different Views?" In *Popular Music and Society*. 1988 (vol. 12, iss. 3).

Wheeler, S. P. (1991). "Her 'Boy' May Go Far." In *Daily News*. Available at https://www.newspapers.com/image/466928815. Accessed January 25, 2023.

Whiteley, S. (2000). *Women and Popular Music: Sexuality, Identity and Subjectivity*. Abingdon, UK: Routledge.

Wiedenhoeft, J. (2007). "Talk Like a Bangle." In *Wisconsin State Journal*. Available at https://www.newspapers.com/image/407460311. Accessed January 26, 2023.

Wild, D. (1990). "Record Reviews." In *Palm Beach Post*. Available at https://palmbeachpost.newspapers.com/image/132448692. Accessed January 26, 2023.

Williams, C. (1989). "High-Flying Bangles Take on Rumors, Criticism." In *Leader-Telegram*. Available at https://www.newspapers.com/image/361023772. Accessed January 25, 2023.

Williams, S. (1986). "The Bangles Make Noise at the Beacon." In *Newsday*. Available at https://www.newspapers.com/image/722212182. Accessed January 25, 2023.

Williams, S. (1989). "In Harmony with the Bangles." In *Newsday*. Available at https://www.newspapers.com/image/723611246. Accessed January 25, 2023.

Willman, C. (1989). "Facts and / or Fables About the Bangles." In *Los Angeles Times*. April 9. Page 348. Available at https://www.newspapers.com/image/405383398. Accessed January 26, 2023.

Winwood, I. (2002). "The Violence. The Drugs. The Death. From Black Flag and Social Distortion to Bad Religion and The Offspring, This Is the Story of 20 Years of LA Punk." Available at https://www.rocksbackpages.com/Library/Article/the-violence-the-drugs-the-death-from-black-flag-and-social-distortion-to-bad-religion-and-the-offspring-this-is-the-story-of-20-years-of-la-punk. Accessed January 20, 2023.

Wolfe, P. (2017). *Women in the Studio: Creativity, Control and Gender in Popular Music Sound Production*. Abingdon, UK; New York: Routledge.

Wolff, C. (1989). "Bangles Never Gather Momentum." In *Akron*.

Wolgamott, L. K. (1986). "Bangles, Pandoras Win Audiences." In *Lincoln Journal Star*. Available at https://www.newspapers.com/image/312716069. Accessed January 25, 2023.

Young, J. (1987). "Who's the Boss?" In *Creem*. December.

Zebora, J. (1984). "Gutsy All-Girl Bangles Pack a Punch in Their Rock." In the *Record-Journal*. Available at https://www.newspapers.com/image/676321836. Accessed January 25, 2023.

Zeller, C. (1984). "The Bangles: *All Over the Place* (Columbia)." Available at https://www.rocksbackpages.com/Library/Article/the-bangles-iall-over-the-placei-columbia. Accessed November 21, 2023.

Interviews

Aukerman, M. (2023). Personal interview with Jennifer Otter Bickerdike.
Banda, M. (2023). Personal interview with Jennifer Otter Bickerdike.
Barton, S. (2023). Personal interview with Jennifer Otter Bickerdike.
Cameron, J. (2023). Personal interview with Jennifer Otter Bickerdike.
Chiccarelli, J. (2023). Personal interview with Jennifer Otter Bickerdike.
Corvalan, M. (2023). Personal interview with Jennifer Otter Bickerdike.
Dean, J. (2023). Personal interview with Jennifer Otter Bickerdike.
Diamond, B. (2023). Personal interview with Jennifer Otter Bickerdike.
Gormley, M. (2023). Personal interview with Jennifer Otter Bickerdike.
Gracie. (2023). Personal interview with Jennifer Otter Bickerdike.
Griffin, S. (2023). Personal interview with Jennifer Otter Bickerdike.
Hewitt, D. (2023). Personal interview with Jennifer Otter Bickerdike.
Hilfman, G. (2023). Personal interview with Jennifer Otter Bickerdike.
Hoffs, S. (2023). Personal interview with Jennifer Otter Bickerdike.
Igleheart, W. (2023). Personal interview with Jennifer Otter Bickerdike.
Ireland, K. (2023). Personal interview with Jennifer Otter Bickerdike.
Kasza, T. (2023). Personal interview with Jennifer Otter Bickerdike.
Kereakes, T. (2023). Personal interview with Jennifer Otter Bickerdike.
Kotero, A. (2023). Personal interview with Jennifer Otter Bickerdike.
Lamson, C. (2023). Personal interview with Jennifer Otter Bickerdike.
Lloyd, R. (2023). Personal interview with Jennifer Otter Bickerdike.
Lloyd-Bisley, I. (2023). Personal interview with Jennifer Otter Bickerdike.
Maitreya, S. (2023). Personal interview with Jennifer Otter Bickerdike.
McDonald, J. (2023). Personal interview with Jennifer Otter Bickerdike.
McDonald, S. (2023). Personal interview with Jennifer Otter Bickerdike.
McDonnell, E. (2023). Personal interview with Jennifer Otter Bickerdike.
Ness, M. (2023). Personal interview with Jennifer Otter Bickerdike.
Nolte, J. (2023). Personal interview with Jennifer Otter Bickerdike.
Peterson, D. (2023). Personal interview with Jennifer Otter Bickerdike.
Peterson, V. (2023). Personal interview with Jennifer Otter Bickerdike.
Petrie, M. (2023). Personal interview with Jennifer Otter Bickerdike.
Philbin, P. (2023). Personal interview with Jennifer Otter Bickerdike.

Podany, A. (2023). Personal interview with Jennifer Otter Bickerdike.
Rathod, D. (2023). Personal interview with Jennifer Otter Bickerdike.
Rifkin, B. (2023). Personal interview with Jennifer Otter Bickerdike.
Rollins, H. (2023). Personal interview with Jennifer Otter Bickerdike.
Schorr, G. (2023). Personal interview with Jennifer Otter Bickerdike.
Stella, J. (2023). Personal interview with Jennifer Otter Bickerdike.
Wilson, R. (2023). Personal interview with Jennifer Otter Bickerdike.
Zilinskas, A. (2023). Personal interview with Jennifer Otter Bickerdike.

Personal Journal
Debbi Peterson personal journals, 1979–1980.

Emails
Email from Vicki Peterson to Jennifer Otter Bickerdike. July 28, 2023.
Email from Vicki Peterson. August 1, 2023.

Music Videos
The Bangles. (2013). "Be with You." Available at https://www.youtube.com/watch?v=1VAe_gCBDmI. Accessed November 21, 2023.
The Bangles. (2013). "Going Down to Liverpool." Available at https://www.youtube.com/watch?v=Zj7OJeyhq2Q. Accessed November 21, 2023.
The Bangles. (2013). "Hazy Shade of Winter." Available at https://www.youtube.com/watch?v=TxrwImCJCqk. Accessed November 21, 2023.
The Bangles. (2013). "In Your Room." Available at https://www.youtube.com/watch?v=04HSg0YZi9E. Accessed November 21, 2023.
The Bangles. (2013). "Manic Monday." Available at https://www.youtube.com/watch?v=SsmVgoXDq2w. Accessed November 21, 2023.
The Bangles. (2013). "Walk Like an Egyptian." Available at https://www.youtube.com/watch?v=Cv6tuzHUuuk. Accessed November 21, 2023.
The Bangles. (2013). "Walking Down Your Street." Available at https://www.youtube.com/watch?v=HvnV2jFeWNQ. Accessed November 21, 2023.

NOTES

Foreword

1. Cromelin, R. (1986). "The Bangles: Local Girls Make Good." *Los Angeles Times*. Available at http://www.rocksbackpages.com/Library/Article/the-bangles-local-girls-make-good. Accessed September 7, 2022.

Preface

1. Goldberg, M. (1984). "The Bangles: A Female Fab Four?" *Rolling Stone*. Available at http://www.rocksbackpages.com/Library/Article/the-bangles-a-female-fab-four. Accessed September 7, 2022.
2. McDonnell, E. (2019). "The Manhandling of Rock 'N' Roll History." Available at https://longreads.com/2019/03/29/the-manhandling-of-rock-n-roll-history. Accessed June 9, 2023.
3. McDonnell, E. "The Manhandling of Rock 'N' Roll History."
4. Weingarten, M. (1997). "Prince: The Purple Gang." Available at https://www.rocksbackpages.com/Library/Article/prince-the-purple-gang. Accessed June 22, 2023.
5. McDonnell, E. "The Manhandling of Rock 'N' Roll History."
6. Geffen, S.; Hopper, J.; and Pelly, J. (2019). "Building a Mystery: An Oral History of Lilith Fair." Available at https://www.vanityfair.com/style/2019/09/an-oral-history-of-lilith-fair. Accessed February 5, 2023.
7. Geffen, S. "Building a Mystery."
8. Geffen, S. "Building a Mystery."
9. Geffen, S. "Building a Mystery."
10. Lamson, C. (2023). Personal interview with Jennifer Otter Bickerdike.
11. Rollins, H. (2023). Personal interview with Jennifer Otter Bickerdike.
12. Rollins, H. (2023). Personal interview with Jennifer Otter Bickerdike.
13. *Metal Priestesses Podcast*. (2021). "Season 2 Episode 3: Debbi and Vicki Peterson of the Bangles." Available at https://www.youtube.com/watch?v=GgKIB0aSZfM. Accessed May 19, 2023.
14. *Metal Priestesses Podcast*. "Season 2 Episode 3: Debbi and Vicki Peterson."
15. col1234. (2021). "6. The Bangles." *64 Quartets*. Available at https://64quartets.wordpress.com/2021/03/19/6-the-bangles/. Accessed June 2, 2023.

Chapter 1.

1. Peterson, D. (2023). Personal interview with Jennifer Otter Bickerdike.
2. Zilinskas, A. (2023). Personal interview with Jennifer Otter Bickerdike.
3. Peterson, V. (2023). Personal interview with Jennifer Otter Bickerdike.
4. Peterson, V. (2023). Personal interview with Jennifer Otter Bickerdike.
5. Peterson, D. (2023). Personal interview with Jennifer Otter Bickerdike.
6. Peterson, V. (2023). Personal interview with Jennifer Otter Bickerdike.
7. Peterson, V. (2023). Personal interview with Jennifer Otter Bickerdike.
8. Peterson, V. (2023). Personal interview with Jennifer Otter Bickerdike.
9. Peterson, V. (2023). Personal interview with Jennifer Otter Bickerdike.
10. Peterson, V. (2023). Personal interview with Jennifer Otter Bickerdike.
11. Peterson, V. (2023). Personal interview with Jennifer Otter Bickerdike.
12. Peterson, V. (2023). Personal interview with Jennifer Otter Bickerdike.
13. Peterson, V. (2023). Personal interview with Jennifer Otter Bickerdike.
14. Peterson, V. (2023). Personal interview with Jennifer Otter Bickerdike.
15. Peterson, V. (2023). Personal interview with Jennifer Otter Bickerdike.
16. Peterson, V. (2023). Personal interview with Jennifer Otter Bickerdike.
17. Peterson, V. (2023). Personal interview with Jennifer Otter Bickerdike.
18. Peterson, V. (2023). Personal interview with Jennifer Otter Bickerdike.
19. Peterson, V. (2023). Personal interview with Jennifer Otter Bickerdike.
20. Peterson, V. (2023). Personal interview with Jennifer Otter Bickerdike.
21. Peterson, V. (2023). Personal interview with Jennifer Otter Bickerdike.
22. Peterson, V. (2023). Personal interview with Jennifer Otter Bickerdike.
23. Peterson, V. (2023). Personal interview with Jennifer Otter Bickerdike.
24. Peterson, V. (2023). Personal interview with Jennifer Otter Bickerdike.
25. Kasza, T. (2023). Personal interview with Jennifer Otter Bickerdike.
26. Kasza, T. (2023). Personal interview with Jennifer Otter Bickerdike.
27. Kasza, T. (2023). Personal interview with Jennifer Otter Bickerdike.
28. Kasza, T. (2023). Personal interview with Jennifer Otter Bickerdike.
29. Kasza, T. (2023). Personal interview with Jennifer Otter Bickerdike.
30. Kasza, T. (2023). Personal interview with Jennifer Otter Bickerdike.
31. Kasza, T. (2023). Personal interview with Jennifer Otter Bickerdike.
32. Kasza, T. (2023). Personal interview with Jennifer Otter Bickerdike.
33. Cameron, J. (2023). Personal interview with Jennifer Otter Bickerdike.
34. Cameron, J. (2023). Personal interview with Jennifer Otter Bickerdike.
35. Podany, A. (2023). Personal interview with Jennifer Otter Bickerdike.
36. Podany, A. (2023). Personal interview with Jennifer Otter Bickerdike.
37. Podany, A. (2023). Personal interview with Jennifer Otter Bickerdike.
38. Podany, A. (2023). Personal interview with Jennifer Otter Bickerdike.
39. Podany, A. (2023). Personal interview with Jennifer Otter Bickerdike.
40. Podany, A. (2023). Personal interview with Jennifer Otter Bickerdike.
41. Podany, A. (2023). Personal interview with Jennifer Otter Bickerdike.
42. Podany, A. (2023). Personal interview with Jennifer Otter Bickerdike.

43. Podany, A. (2023). Personal interview with Jennifer Otter Bickerdike.
44. Podany, A. (2023). Personal interview with Jennifer Otter Bickerdike.
45. Podany, A. (2023). Personal interview with Jennifer Otter Bickerdike.
46. Podany, A. (2023). Personal interview with Jennifer Otter Bickerdike.
47. Podany, A. (2023). Personal interview with Jennifer Otter Bickerdike.
48. Podany, A. (2023). Personal interview with Jennifer Otter Bickerdike.
49. Podany, A. (2023). Personal interview with Jennifer Otter Bickerdike.
50. Peterson, V. (2024). Personal interview with Jennifer Otter Bickerdike.
51. Peterson, V. (1984). "Class of '77 Vicki Peterson: Bangle." In *LA Weekly*, September 20, page 38.
52. Cameron, J. (2023). Personal interview with Jennifer Otter Bickerdike.
53. Podany, A. (2023). Personal interview with Jennifer Otter Bickerdike.
54. Podany, A. (2023). Personal interview with Jennifer Otter Bickerdike.
55. Podany, A. (2023). Personal interview with Jennifer Otter Bickerdike.

Chapter 2.

1. Caro, M. (2023). "Debbi Peterson (The Bangles)." *Caropop* podcast. S01 E73. Available at https://rss.com/podcasts/thecaropopcast/848495/. Accessed August 1, 2023.
2. Caro, M. "Debbi Peterson (The Bangles)."
3. Peterson, D. (2022). Personal interview with Jennifer Otter Bickerdike.
4. Caro, M. "Debbi Peterson (The Bangles)."
5. Caro, M. "Debbi Peterson (The Bangles)."
6. Peterson, D. (2022). Personal interview with Jennifer Otter Bickerdike.
7. Caro, M. "Debbi Peterson (The Bangles)."
8. Peterson, D. (2022). Personal interview with Jennifer Otter Bickerdike.
9. Peterson, D. (2022). Personal interview with Jennifer Otter Bickerdike.
10. Peterson, D. (2022). Personal interview with Jennifer Otter Bickerdike.
11. Peterson, D. (2022). Personal interview with Jennifer Otter Bickerdike.
12. Banda, M. (2023). Personal interview with Jennifer Otter Bickerdike.
13. Banda, M. (2023). Personal interview with Jennifer Otter Bickerdike.
14. Banda, M. (2023). Personal interview with Jennifer Otter Bickerdike.
15. Peterson, D. (2022). Personal interview with Jennifer Otter Bickerdike.
16. Cameron, J. (2023). Personal interview with Jennifer Otter Bickerdike.
17. Podany, A. (2023). Personal interview with Jennifer Otter Bickerdike.
18. Podany, A. (2023). Personal interview with Jennifer Otter Bickerdike.
19. Peterson, D. (2022). Personal interview with Jennifer Otter Bickerdike.
20. Podany, A. (2023). Personal interview with Jennifer Otter Bickerdike.
21. Podany, A. (2023). Personal interview with Jennifer Otter Bickerdike.
22. Cameron, J. (2023). Personal interview with Jennifer Otter Bickerdike.
23. Peterson, D. (2022). Personal interview with Jennifer Otter Bickerdike.
24. Peterson, Dave. (2022). Personal interview with Jennifer Otter Bickerdike.
25. Cameron, J. (2023). Personal interview with Jennifer Otter Bickerdike.
26. Peterson, V. (2022). Personal interview with Jennifer Otter Bickerdike.

27. Peterson, V. (2022). Personal interview with Jennifer Otter Bickerdike.
28. Cameron, J. (2023). Personal interview with Jennifer Otter Bickerdike.
29. Peterson, D. (2022). Personal interview with Jennifer Otter Bickerdike.
30. Peterson, D. (2022). Personal interview with Jennifer Otter Bickerdike.
31. Peterson, D. (2022). Personal interview with Jennifer Otter Bickerdike.

Chapter 3.

1. Peterson, V. (2023). Personal interview with Jennifer Otter Bickerdike.
2. Podany, A. (2023). Personal interview with Jennifer Otter Bickerdike.
3. Peterson, V. (2023). Personal interview with Jennifer Otter Bickerdike.
4. Podany, A. (2023). Personal interview with Jennifer Otter Bickerdike.
5. Podany, A. (2023). Personal interview with Jennifer Otter Bickerdike.
6. Winwood, I. (2002). "The Violence. The Drugs. The Death. From Black Flag and Social Distortion to Bad Religion and The Offspring, This Is the Story of 20 Years of LA Punk." Available at https://www.rocksbackpages.com/Library/Article/the-violence-the-drugs-the-death-from-black-flag-and-social-distortion-to-bad-religion-and-the-offspring-this-is-the-story-of-20-years-of-la-punk. Accessed August 1, 2023.
7. Winwood, I. "The Violence. The Drugs."
8. Challis, H. (2015). *Women in Pop Music*. Kent, UK: Crescent Moon Publishing.
9. Spitz, M. and Mullen, B. (2001). *We Got the Neutron Bomb*. New York: Three Rivers.
10. Kereakes, T. (2023). Personal interview with Jennifer Otter Bickerdike.
11. Spitz, M. *We Got the Neutron Bomb*.
12. Spitz, M. *We Got the Neutron Bomb*.
13. Spitz, M. *We Got the Neutron Bomb*.
14. McDonnell, E. (2013). *Queens of Noise: The Real Story of the Runaways*. New York: Hachette Books.
15. Spitz, M. *We Got the Neutron Bomb*.
16. Spitz, M. *We Got the Neutron Bomb*.
17. McDonnell, E. *Queens of Noise*.
18. McDonnell, E. *Queens of Noise*.
19. McDonnell, E. *Queens of Noise*.
20. Phreddie, P. (2010). "An Interview with Phast Phreddie." Available at https://micki-steele-net.tumblr.com/post/640017480091353088/runaways-concert-poster-september-28-1975-an?fbclid=IwAR0KRke5XIm71uCFU4EZUmhCBtAbmCrtn0YAJ10JG_kFnPaR8tbNgftIoFw. Accessed August 10, 2023.
21. Phreddie, P. "An Interview with Phast Phreddie."
22. McDonnell, E. *Queens of Noise*.
23. Hibbert, T. (1987). "The Bangles: Girls on Top." Available at https://www.rocksbackpages.com/Library/Article/the-bangles-girls-on-top. Accessed March 1, 2023.
24. McDonnell, E. *Queens of Noise*.
25. McDonnell, E. *Queens of Noise*.
26. Hibbert, T. "The Bangles: Girls on Top."
27. McDonnell, E. *Queens of Noise*.

28. Spitz, M. *We Got the Neutron Bomb.*
29. McDonnell, E. *Queens of Noise.*
30. McDonnell, E. (2023). Personal interview with Jennifer Otter Bickerdike.
31. Nolte, J. (2023). Personal interview with Jennifer Otter Bickerdike.
32. Peterson, V. (2023). Personal interview with Jennifer Otter Bickerdike.

Chapter 4.

1. Peterson, D. (2023). Personal interview with Jennifer Otter Bickerdike.
2. Peterson, D. (2023). Personal interview with Jennifer Otter Bickerdike.
3. Peterson, D. (2023). Personal interview with Jennifer Otter Bickerdike.
4. Rollins, H. (2023). Personal interview with Jennifer Otter Bickerdike.
5. Spotnitz, F. (1984). "The Bangles: An All-Female Lineup Rooted in Sound of the Early Beatles." Available at https://www.upi.com/Archives/1984/11/30/The-Bangles-An-all-female-lineup-rooted-in-sound-of-the-early-Beatles/5454470638800/. Accessed February 17, 2023.
6. Peterson, D. (2023). Personal interview with Jennifer Otter Bickerdike.
7. Peterson, D. (2023). Personal interview with Jennifer Otter Bickerdike.
8. Podany, A. (2023). Personal interview with Jennifer Otter Bickerdike.
9. Peterson, D. (2023). Personal interview with Jennifer Otter Bickerdike.
10. Podany, A. (2023). Personal interview with Jennifer Otter Bickerdike.
11. Podany, A. (2023). Personal interview with Jennifer Otter Bickerdike.
12. Peterson, D. (2023). Personal interview with Jennifer Otter Bickerdike.
13. Podany, A. (2023). Personal interview with Jennifer Otter Bickerdike.
14. Peterson, D. (2023). Personal interview with Jennifer Otter Bickerdike.
15. Podany, A. (2023). Personal interview with Jennifer Otter Bickerdike.
16. Peterson, D. (2023). Personal interview with Jennifer Otter Bickerdike.
17. Peterson, D. (2023). Personal interview with Jennifer Otter Bickerdike.
18. Paul, S. (1979). "The Fans-All-Girl Band on L. A. Scene." In *View.*
19. Podany, A. (2023). Personal interview with Jennifer Otter Bickerdike.
20. Aukerman, M. (2023). Personal interview with Jennifer Otter Bickerdike.
21. Ness, M. (2023). Personal interview with Jennifer Otter Bickerdike.
22. Barton, S. (2023). Personal interview with Jennifer Otter Bickerdike.
23. Aukerman, M. (2023). Personal interview with Jennifer Otter Bickerdike.
24. Rollins, H. (2023). Personal interview with Jennifer Otter Bickerdike.
25. Griffin, S. (2023). Personal interview with Jennifer Otter Bickerdike.

Chapter 5.

1. Griffin, S. (2023). Personal interview with Jennifer Otter Bickerdike.
2. Griffin, S. (2023). Personal interview with Jennifer Otter Bickerdike.
3. Peterson, V. (2023). Personal interview with Jennifer Otter Bickerdike.
4. Peterson, V. (2023). Personal interview with Jennifer Otter Bickerdike.
5. Peterson, V. (2023). Personal interview with Jennifer Otter Bickerdike.
6. Peterson, V. (2023). Personal interview with Jennifer Otter Bickerdike.
7. Peterson, V. (2023). Personal interview with Jennifer Otter Bickerdike.

8. Peterson, V. (2023). Personal interview with Jennifer Otter Bickerdike.
9. Peterson, V. (2023). Personal interview with Jennifer Otter Bickerdike.
10. Peterson, V. (2023). Personal interview with Jennifer Otter Bickerdike.
11. Peterson, V. (2023). Personal interview with Jennifer Otter Bickerdike.
12. Lababedi, I. (June 1985). "Bangles for Sale." In *Creem*. Available at https://www.rocksbackpages.com/Library/Article/bangles-for-sale. Accessed November 1, 2023.
13. Podany, A. (2023). Personal interview with Jennifer Otter Bickerdike.
14. Podany, A. (2023). Personal interview with Jennifer Otter Bickerdike.
15. Peterson, D. (2023). Personal interview with Jennifer Otter Bickerdike.
16. Podany, A. (2023). Personal interview with Jennifer Otter Bickerdike.
17. Podany, A. (2023). Personal interview with Jennifer Otter Bickerdike.
18. Podany, A. (2023). Personal interview with Jennifer Otter Bickerdike.
19. Podany, A. (2023). Personal interview with Jennifer Otter Bickerdike.
20. Podany, A. (2023). Personal interview with Jennifer Otter Bickerdike.
21. Podany, A. (2023). Personal interview with Jennifer Otter Bickerdike.
22. Podany, A. (2023). Personal interview with Jennifer Otter Bickerdike.
23. Peterson, V. (2023). Personal interview with Jennifer Otter Bickerdike.

Chapter 6.

1. Lababedi, I. (June 1985). "Bangles for Sale." In *Creem*. Available at https://www.rocksbackpages.com/Library/Article/bangles-for-sale. Accessed November 1, 2023.
2. Lababedi, I. "Bangles for Sale."
3. Hoffs, S. (2023). Personal interview with Jennifer Otter Bickerdike.
4. Hoffs, S. (2023). Personal interview with Jennifer Otter Bickerdike.
5. Petrie, M. (2023). Personal interview with Jennifer Otter Bickerdike.
6. Lababedi, I. "Bangles for Sale."
7. Hoffs, S. (2023). Personal interview with Jennifer Otter Bickerdike.
8. Hoffs, S. (2023). Personal interview with Jennifer Otter Bickerdike.
9. Petrie, M. (2023). Personal interview with Jennifer Otter Bickerdike.
10. Cost, J. (2009). "A Conversation with Susanna Hoffs and Matthew Sweet." Available at https://magnetmagazine.com/2009/07/20/qa-with-susanna-hoffs-and-matthew-sweet/. Accessed November 1, 2023.
11. Cost, J. "A Conversation with Susanna Hoffs and Matthew Sweet."
12. Hoffs, S. (2023). Personal interview with Jennifer Otter Bickerdike.
13. Hoffs, S. (2023). Personal interview with Jennifer Otter Bickerdike.
14. Hoffs, S. (2023). Personal interview with Jennifer Otter Bickerdike.
15. DeYoung, B. (2019). *I Need to Know: The Lost Music Interviews*. St. Petersburg, FL: St. Petersburg Press.
16. Hoffs, S. (2023). Personal interview with Jennifer Otter Bickerdike.
17. Petrie, M. (2023). Personal interview with Jennifer Otter Bickerdike.
18. Hewitt, D. (2023). Personal interview with Jennifer Otter Bickerdike.
19. Petrie, M. (2023). Personal interview with Jennifer Otter Bickerdike.
20. Petrie, M. (2023). Personal interview with Jennifer Otter Bickerdike.
21. Petrie, M. (2023). Personal interview with Jennifer Otter Bickerdike.

22. Hoffs, S. (2023). Personal interview with Jennifer Otter Bickerdike.
23. Hoffs, S. (2023). Personal interview with Jennifer Otter Bickerdike.
24. Petrie, M. (2023). Personal interview with Jennifer Otter Bickerdike.
25. Hoffs, S. (2023). Personal interview with Jennifer Otter Bickerdike.
26. Petrie, M. (2023). Personal interview with Jennifer Otter Bickerdike.
27. Hoffs, S. (2023). Personal interview with Jennifer Otter Bickerdike.
28. Petrie, M. (2023). Personal interview with Jennifer Otter Bickerdike.
29. Cost, J. (2009). "A Conversation with Susanna Hoffs and Matthew Sweet." Available at https://magnetmagazine.com/2009/07/20/qa-with-susanna-hoffs-and-matthew-sweet/. Accessed November 1, 2023.
30. Hoffs, S. (2023). Personal interview with Jennifer Otter Bickerdike.
31. Robert, R. (2020) "Susanna Hoffs and Friends Remember David Roback, Who Stayed Creative, and Enigmatic, to the End." Available at https://www.latimes.com/entertainment-arts/music/story/2020-03-06/david-roback-mazzy-star-susanna-hoffs-opal-cancer. Accessed November 1, 2023.
32. DeYoung, B. *I Need to Know*.
33. Lababedi, I. "Bangles for Sale."
34. Cost, J. "A Conversation with Susanna Hoffs and Matthew Sweet."
35. Hoffs, S. (2023). Personal interview with Jennifer Otter Bickerdike.
36. Teicholz, T. (2006). "Susanna Hoffs Walks Like a—Rockstar No, a Mom—Rockstar/Mom." Available at https://web.archive.org/web/20061018205847/http://www.jewishjournal.com/home/preview.php?id=16541. Accessed November 1, 2023.
37. Robert, R. "Susanna Hoffs and Friends Remember David Roback."
38. Nolte, J. (2003). Personal interview with Jennifer Otter Bickerdike.
39. Hoffs, S. (2023). Personal interview with Jennifer Otter Bickerdike.
40. Hoffs, S. (2023). Personal interview with Jennifer Otter Bickerdike.
41. Griffin, S. (2023). Personal interview with Jennifer Otter Bickerdike.
42. Hoffs, S. (2023). Personal interview with Jennifer Otter Bickerdike.

Chapter 7.

1. Peterson, V. (2023). Personal interview with Jennifer Otter Bickerdike.
2. Hoffs, S. (2023). Personal interview with Jennifer Otter Bickerdike.
3. DeYoung, B. (2019). *I Need to Know: The Lost Music Interviews*. St. Petersburg, FL: St. Petersburg Press.
4. Rosenthal, G. (2000). *Behind the Music: The Bangles*. IMDb, S3, E40.
5. Rosenthal, G. *Behind the Music*.
6. Hoffs, S. (2023). Personal interview with Jennifer Otter Bickerdike.
7. DeYoung, B. *I Need to Know*.
8. Rosenthal, G. *Behind the Music*.
9. Peterson, D. (2023). Personal interview with Jennifer Otter Bickerdike.
10. Hoffs, S. (2023). Personal interview with Jennifer Otter Bickerdike.
11. Hoffs, S. (2023). Personal interview with Jennifer Otter Bickerdike.
12. DeYoung, B. *I Need to Know*.
13. Hoffs, S. (2023). Personal interview with Jennifer Otter Bickerdike.

14. Rosenthal, G. *Behind the Music.*
15. Rosenthal, G. *Behind the Music.*
16. Peterson, V. (2023). Personal interview with Jennifer Otter Bickerdike.
17. Peterson, Dave. (2023). Personal interview with Jennifer Otter Bickerdike.
18. Peterson, V. (2023). Personal interview with Jennifer Otter Bickerdike.
19. Zilinskas, A. (2023). Personal interview with Jennifer Otter Bickerdike.
20. Zilinskas, A. (2023). Personal interview with Jennifer Otter Bickerdike.
21. Zilinskas, A. (2023). Personal interview with Jennifer Otter Bickerdike.
22. Email from Vicki Peterson to Jennifer Otter Bickerdike, July 28, 2023.
23. Coley, B. (1982). "The Bangles: Big Bangle Theory." Available at https://www.rocksbackpages.com/Library/Article/the-bangles-big-bangle-theory. Accessed November 1, 2023.
24. Zilinskas, A. (2023). Personal interview with Jennifer Otter Bickerdike.
25. Zilinskas, A. (2023). Personal interview with Jennifer Otter Bickerdike.
26. Roberts, R. (2020). "Susanna Hoffs and Friends Remember David Roback, Who Stayed Creative, and Enigmatic, to the End." Available at https://www.latimes.com/entertainment-arts/music/story/2020-03-06/david-roback-mazzy-star-susanna-hoffs-opal-cancer. Accessed November 1, 2023.
27. Zilinskas, A. (2023). Personal interview with Jennifer Otter Bickerdike.

Chapter 8.

1. Peterson, V. (2023). Personal interview with Jennifer Otter Bickerdike.
2. Peterson, V. (2023). Personal interview with Jennifer Otter Bickerdike.
3. Aukerman, M. (2023). Personal interview with Jennifer Otter Bickerdike.
4. Aukerman, M. (2023). Personal interview with Jennifer Otter Bickerdike.
5. Rollins, H. (2023). Personal interview with Jennifer Otter Bickerdike.
6. Aukerman, M. (2023). Personal interview with Jennifer Otter Bickerdike.
7. Rollins, H. (2023). Personal interview with Jennifer Otter Bickerdike.
8. Rollins, H. (2023). Personal interview with Jennifer Otter Bickerdike.
9. Hoffs, S. (2023). Personal interview with Jennifer Otter Bickerdike.
10. Rollins, H. (2023). Personal interview with Jennifer Otter Bickerdike.
11. Peterson, V. (2023). Personal interview with Jennifer Otter Bickerdike.
12. Rollins, H. (2023). Personal interview with Jennifer Otter Bickerdike.
13. Rollins, H. (2023). Personal interview with Jennifer Otter Bickerdike.
14. Peterson, V. (2023). Personal interview with Jennifer Otter Bickerdike.
15. Griffin, S. (2023). Personal interview with Jennifer Otter Bickerdike.
16. Zilinskas, A. (2023). Personal interview with Jennifer Otter Bickerdike.
17. Rosenthal, G. (2000). *Behind the Music: The Bangles.* IMDb, S3, E40.
18. Rosenthal, G. *Behind the Music.*
19. Peterson, D. (2023). Personal interview with Jennifer Otter Bickerdike.
20. Peterson, V. (2023). Personal interview with Jennifer Otter Bickerdike.
21. Peterson, V. (2023). Personal interview with Jennifer Otter Bickerdike.
22. Hoffs, S. (2023). Personal interview with Jennifer Otter Bickerdike.
23. Peterson, D. (2023). Personal interview with Jennifer Otter Bickerdike.

Chapter 9.

1. Coley, B. (1982). "The Bangles: Big Bangle Theory." Available at https://www.rocksbackpages.com/Library/Article/the-bangles-big-bangle-theory. Accessed November 1, 2023.
2. Podany, A. (2023). Personal interview with Jennifer Otter Bickerdike.
3. Podany, A. (2023). Personal interview with Jennifer Otter Bickerdike.
4. Lloyd, R. (2023). Personal interview with Jennifer Otter Bickerdike.
5. Podany, A. (2023). Personal interview with Jennifer Otter Bickerdike.
6. Lloyd, R. (2023). Personal interview with Jennifer Otter Bickerdike.
7. Peterson, V. (2023). Personal interview with Jennifer Otter Bickerdike.
8. Author Unknown. (1982). "Bangs." In *Flipside*. Issue 34.
9. Aukerman, M. (2023). Personal interview with Jennifer Otter Bickerdike.
10. Hoffs, S. (2023). Personal interview with Jennifer Otter Bickerdike.
11. Peterson, Dave. (2023). Personal interview with Jennifer Otter Bickerdike.
12. Peterson, D. (2023). Personal interview with Jennifer Otter Bickerdike.
13. Peterson, V. (2023). Personal interview with Jennifer Otter Bickerdike.
14. Peterson, D. (2024). Personal interview with Jennifer Otter Bickerdike.
15. Peterson, V. (2023). Personal interview with Jennifer Otter Bickerdike.
16. Peterson, V. (2023). Personal interview with Jennifer Otter Bickerdike.
17. Griffin, S. (2023). Personal interview with Jennifer Otter Bickerdike.
18. Peterson, V. (2023). Personal interview with Jennifer Otter Bickerdike.
19. Peterson, V. (2023). Personal interview with Jennifer Otter Bickerdike.

Chapter 10.

1. Gormley, M. (2023). Personal interview with Jennifer Otter Bickerdike.
2. Copeland, M. (2021). *Two Steps Forward, One Step Back: My Life in the Music Business*. London: Jawbone Press.
3. Dean, J. (2023). Personal interview with Jennifer Otter Bickerdike.
4. Hogan, P. (1989). *The Bangles*. London: Omnibus.
5. Lamson, C. (2023). Personal interview with Jennifer Otter Bickerdike.
6. Lamson, C. (2023). Personal interview with Jennifer Otter Bickerdike.
7. Lamson, C. (2023). Personal interview with Jennifer Otter Bickerdike.
8. Copeland, M. *Two Steps Forward, One Step Back*.
9. Copeland, M. *Two Steps Forward, One Step Back*.
10. Rosenthal, G. (2000). *Behind the Music: The Bangles*. IMDb, S3, E40.
11. Rosenthal, G. *Behind the Music*.
12. Gormley, M. (2023). Personal interview with Jennifer Otter Bickerdike.
13. Gormley, M. (2023). Personal interview with Jennifer Otter Bickerdike.
14. Rosenthal, G. *Behind the Music*.
15. Rosenthal, G. *Behind the Music*.
16. Peterson, V. (2023). Personal interview with Jennifer Otter Bickerdike.
17. Gormley, M. (2023). Personal interview with Jennifer Otter Bickerdike.
18. Peterson, V. (2023). Personal interview with Jennifer Otter Bickerdike.

19. Gormley, M. (2023). Personal interview with Jennifer Otter Bickerdike.

20. Rosenthal, G. *Behind the Music.*

21. Hann, M. (2013). "The Paisley Underground: Los Angeles's 1980s Psychedelic Explosion." Available at https://www.theguardian.com/music/2013/may/16/paisley-underground-history-80s-los-angeles-psychedelia. Accessed November 1, 2023.

22. Griffin, S. (2023). Personal interview with Jennifer Otter Bickerdike.

23. Spotnitz, F. (1984). "The Bangles: An All-Female Lineup Rooted in Sound of the Early Beatles." Available at https://www.upi.com/Archives/1984/11/30/The-Bangles-An-all-female-lineup-rooted-in-sound-of-the-early-Beatles/5454470638800/. Accessed February 17, 2023.

24. Graff, G. (2014). "The Bangles Song Premiere: Hear 'The Real World' from Their New Compilation." Available at https://www.billboard.com/music/music-news/the-bangles-song-premiere-the-real-world-interview-6327650/. Accessed November 1, 2023.

25. Caro, M. (2023). "Debbi Peterson (The Bangles)." *Caropop* podcast. S01 E73. Available at https://rss.com/podcasts/thecaropopcast/848495/. Accessed October 5, 2023.

26. Caro, M. "Debbi Peterson (The Bangles)."

27. Peterson, D. (2023). Personal interview with Jennifer Otter Bickerdike.

Chapter 11.

1. Kereakes, T. (2023). Personal interview with Jennifer Otter Bickerdike.

2. Record Collector. (2019). "The Paisley Underground." Available at https://recordcollectormag.com/articles/paisley-underground. Accessed November 1, 2023.

3. Hogan, P. (1989). *The Bangles.* London: Omnibus.

4. Record Collector. "The Paisley Underground."

5. Author Unknown. (2001). "One Nation Underground: The Story of the Paisley Underground." Magnet. Available at https://magnetmagazine.com/2001/05/18/one-nation-underground-the-story-of-the-paisley-underground. Accessed November 1, 2023.

6. McDonald, J. (2023). Personal interview with Jennifer Otter Bickerdike.

7. Partridge, K. (2018). "Why the Bangles, Dream Syndicate & Others Want the Paisley Underground to Rise Again." Available at https://www.billboard.com/music/rock/bangles-dream-syndicate-three-oclock-paisley-underground-8484948/. Accessed November 1, 2023.

8. Hann, M. (2013). "The Paisley Underground: Los Angeles's 1980s Psychedelic Explosion." Available at https://www.theguardian.com/music/2013/may/16/paisley-underground-history-80s-los-angeles-psychedelia. Accessed November 1, 2023.

9. Hann, M. "The Paisley Underground."

10. Record Collector. "The Paisley Underground."

11. Hann, M. "The Paisley Underground."

12. Record Collector. "The Paisley Underground."

13. Zilinskas, A. (2023). Personal interview with Jennifer Otter Bickerdike.

14. Record Collector. "The Paisley Underground."

Chapter 12.

1. Spurrier, J. (1982). "How the Bangs Rang a Bell." In *Los Angeles Times*. September 26.
2. Schneider, M. (1983). "The Big Bangles Theory." In *Creem*. May.
3. McDonald, S. (2023). Personal interview with Jennifer Otter Bickerdike.
4. Sylva, B. (1983). "Backstage with the Bangles." In *Sacramento Bee*. February 12.
5. Sylva, B. "Backstage with the Bangles."
6. Gordon, G. (1983). "Bangles: Seductive and Something Special." In *California Aggie*. February 2. (vol. 101, no. 81).
7. Goldberg, M. (1984). "The Bangles: A Female Fab Four?" Available at https://www.rocksbackpages.com/Library/Article/the-bangles-a-female-fab-four. Accessed November 1, 2023.
8. Goldberg, M. "The Bangles: A Female Fab Four?"
9. Nolte, J. (2023). Personal interview with Jennifer Otter Bickerdike.
10. Author Unknown. (1982). "Bangs Ignites Rock Music Audience." In *Los Angeles Times*. May 8.
11. Lee, C. (1982). "The Newest Music: A Look at Ten Bands to Watch Out For." In *LA Weekly*. August 26.
12. Lee, C. "The Newest Music."
13. Lee, C. "The Newest Music."
14. Author Unknown. (1982). "Bangs." In *Flipside*. Issue 34.
15. Lee, C. "The Newest Music."
16. Peterson, D. (2023). Personal interview with Jennifer Otter Bickerdike.
17. Peterson, D. (2023). Personal interview with Jennifer Otter Bickerdike.
18. Leviton, M. (1982). "The Bangs: Al's Bar, Los Angeles CA." In *Music Connection*, August 5.
19. Author Unknown. (1982). "Bangles Look Forward to Touring United States." In *Sundial*. November 5.
20. Gormley, M. (2023). Personal interview with Jennifer Otter Bickerdike.
21. Peterson, V. (2023). Personal interview with Jennifer Otter Bickerdike.
22. Gormley, M. (2023). Personal interview with Jennifer Otter Bickerdike.
23. DeYoung, B. (2019). *I Need to Know*. St. Petersburg, FL: St. Petersburg Press.
24. Gormley, M. (2023). Personal interview with Jennifer Otter Bickerdike.
25. Spurrier, J. "How the Bangs Rang a Bell."
26. Lamson, C. (2023). Personal interview with Jennifer Otter Bickerdike.
27. Lamson, C. (2023). Personal interview with Jennifer Otter Bickerdike.
28. Rosenthal, G. (2000). *Behind the Music: The Bangles*. IMDb, S3, E40.
29. Zilinskas, A. (2023). Personal interview with Jennifer Otter Bickerdike.
30. Rosenthal, G. *Behind the Music*.
31. Zilinskas, A. (2023). Personal interview with Jennifer Otter Bickerdike.
32. Hoffs, S. (2023). Personal interview with Jennifer Otter Bickerdike.
33. Rachel, D. and Ranking, R. (2021). *I Just Can't Stop It: My Life in The Beat*. London: Omnibus.

34. Peterson, V. (2023). Personal interview with Jennifer Otter Bickerdike.
35. Peterson, V. (2023). Personal interview with Jennifer Otter Bickerdike.
36. Zilinskas, A. (2023). Personal interview with Jennifer Otter Bickerdike.
37. Peterson, D. (2023). Personal interview with Jennifer Otter Bickerdike.
38. Gordon, G. "Bangles: Seductive and Something Special."
39. Lamson, C. (2023). Personal interview with Jennifer Otter Bickerdike.
40. Stella, J. (2023). Personal interview with Jennifer Otter Bickerdike.
41. Lamson, C. (2023). Personal interview with Jennifer Otter Bickerdike.
42. Lamson, C. (2023). Personal interview with Jennifer Otter Bickerdike.
43. Gordon, G. "Bangles: Seductive and Something Special."
44. Peterson, D. (2023). Personal interview with Jennifer Otter Bickerdike.
45. Peterson, D. (2023). Personal interview with Jennifer Otter Bickerdike.
46. Peterson, D. (2023). Personal interview with Jennifer Otter Bickerdike.
47. Griffin, S. (2023). Personal interview with Jennifer Otter Bickerdike.
48. Banda, M. (2023). Personal interview with Jennifer Otter Bickerdike.
49. Banda, M. (2023). Personal interview with Jennifer Otter Bickerdike.
50. Gracie. (2023). Personal interview with Jennifer Otter Bickerdike.

Chapter 13.

1. Bohen, J. (1983). "Bangles—Faulty Records." In *Daily Record* (Morristown, New Jersey.)
2. Hilburn, R. (1983). "The Bangles at the Roxy: Do They Measure Up?" In *Los Angeles Times*. January 29.
3. Hilburn, R. "The Bangles at the Roxy?"
4. Sylva, B. (1983). "Keeping Up with the Go-Go's: Backstage with the Bangles." In *Sacramento Bee*. February 13.
5. Schneider, M. (1983). "The Big Bangles Theory." In *Creem*. May.
6. Lli ylsuo ires. (2007). *MV3 Bangles Interview 1983*. February 21. Available at https://www.youtube.com/watch?v=VqdXF9RWUTk. Accessed February 28, 2023.
7. Zilinskas, A. (2023). Personal interview with Jennifer Otter Bickerdike.
8. Zilinskas, A. (2023). Personal interview with Jennifer Otter Bickerdike.
9. Zilinskas, A. (2023.) Personal interview with Jennifer Otter Bickerdike.
10. Zilinskas, A. (2023). Personal interview with Jennifer Otter Bickerdike.
11. Aukerman, M. (2023). Personal interview with Jennifer Otter Bickerdike.
12. banggothebangles. (2017). "The Bangles Story June 23–25, 1989." October 22. Available at https://www.youtube.com/watch?v=e-jvyXJ6Hnw&list=PLGp3HEH8K0yHDGMR1smOzq0u0Q0A9lewe&index=22. Accessed April 8, 2023.
13. Reed, P. (2015). "An Interview with Paul Reed—March 2015." Available at https://micki-steele-net.tumblr.com/post/640018125250822144/the-corona-del-mar-high-school-band-1972. Accessed September 4, 2023.
14. Peterson, V. (2023). Personal interview with Jennifer Otter Bickerdike.
15. Corvalan, M. (2023). Personal interview with Jennifer Otter Bickerdike.
16. Spitz, M. and Mullen, B. (2001). *We Got the Neutron Bomb: The Untold Story of L.A. Punk*. New York: Three Rivers.

17. Dave. (2021). "June 2—Michael Had Runaway Success with Bangles." Available at https://soundday.wordpress.com/2021/06/02/june-2-michael-had-runaway-success-with-bangles/. Accessed September 4, 2023.

18. Dave. "June 2—Michael Had Runaway Success with Bangles."

19. Corvalan, M. (2023). Personal interview with Jennifer Otter Bickerdike.

20. Griffin, S. (2023). Personal interview with Jennifer Otter Bickerdike.

21. Lloyd-Bisley, I. (2023). Personal interview with Jennifer Otter Bickerdike.

22. Reed, P. "An Interview with Paul Reed—March 2015."

23. Kasza, T. (2023). Personal interview with Jennifer Otter Bickerdike.

24. Phreddie, P. (2010). "An Interview with Phast Phreddie, July 2010." Available on https://micki-steele-net.tumblr.com/post/640017480091353088/runaways-concert-poster-september-28-1975-an?fbclid=IwAR0KRke5XIm71uCFU4EZUmhCBtAbmCrtn0YAJ10JG_kFnPaR8tbNgftIoFw. Accessed September 4, 2023.

25. Zilinskas, A. (2023). Personal interview with Jennifer Otter Bickerdike.

26. Peterson, D. (2023). Personal interview with Jennifer Otter Bickerdike.

27. Peterson, D. (2023). Personal interview with Jennifer Otter Bickerdike.

28. Peterson, D. (2023). Personal interview with Jennifer Otter Bickerdike.

29. Awards Show Network. (2011). "Dick Clark Interviews the Bangles—American Bandstand 1983." January 14. Available at https://www.youtube.com/watch?v=mIIexk_EwU&list=PL7BC7EC808AB39B05&index=8. Accessed March 2, 2023.

30. Philbin, P. (2023). Personal interview with Jennifer Otter Bickerdike.

31. Philbin, P. (2023). Personal interview with Jennifer Otter Bickerdike.

32. Philbin, P. (2023). Personal interview with Jennifer Otter Bickerdike.

33. Philbin, P. (2023). Personal interview with Jennifer Otter Bickerdike.

34. Philbin, P. (2023). Personal interview with Jennifer Otter Bickerdike.

35. Peterson, V. (2023). Personal interview with Jennifer Otter Bickerdike.

36. Senior, J. (1989). "Another Cocktail, Girls?" In *Number One*. April.

37. McDonald, J. (2023). Personal interview with Jennifer Otter Bickerdike.

38. McDonald, S. (2023). Personal interview with Jennifer Otter Bickerdike.

39. Zilinskas, A. (2023). Personal interview with Jennifer Otter Bickerdike.

40. DeYoung, B. (2019). *I Need to Know: The Lost Music Interviews*. St. Petersburg, FL: St. Petersburg Press.

41. McDonald, S. (2023). Personal interview with Jennifer Otter Bickerdike.

42. Partridge, K. (2018). "Why the Bangles, Dream Syndicate & Others Want the Paisley Underground to Rise Again." Available at https://www.billboard.com/music/rock/bangles-dream-syndicate-three-oclock-paisley-underground-8484948/. Accessed November 1, 2023.

43. DeYoung, B. *I Need to Know*.

44. Copeland, M. (2021). *Two Steps Forward, One Step Back: My Life in the Music Business*. London: Jawbone Press.

45. DeYoung, B. *I Need to Know*.

46. Philbin, P. (2023). Personal Interview with Jennifer Otter Bickerdike.

47. Philbin, P. (2023). Personal interview with Jennifer Otter Bickerdike.

48. Philbin, P. (2023). Personal interview with Jennifer Otter Bickerdike.

49. Philbin, P. (2023). Personal interview with Jennifer Otter Bickerdike.

50. Gormley, M. (2023). Personal interview with Jennifer Otter Bickerdike.

51. Copeland, M. *Two Steps Forward, One Step Back*.

52. Gormley, M. (2023). Personal interview with Jennifer Otter Bickerdike.

53. Copeland, M. *Two Steps Forward, One Step Back*.

54. micki-steele-net. (2010). "An interview with Mark Buchholtz." Available at https://micki-steele-net.tumblr.com/post/640013687963385856/an-interview-with-mark-buchholtz-april-2010. Accessed November 2, 2023.

55. Peterson, D. (2023). Personal interview with Jennifer Otter Bickerdike.

56. Rosenthal, G. (2000). *Behind the Music: The Bangles*. IMDb, S3, E40.

57. miscellaneous publication #15. (2021). *The Bangles on Mouth to Mouth*. March 18. Available at https://youtu.be/T_i_ZglDU1Y. Accessed May 10, 2023.

58. Rosenthal, G. *Behind the Music*.

59. DeYoung, B. *I Need to Know*.

60. Rosenthal, G. *Behind the Music*.

61. Gormley, M. (2023). Personal interview with Jennifer Otter Bickerdike.

62. Philbin, P. (2023). Personal interview with Jennifer Otter Bickerdike.

63. Rosenthal, G. *Behind the Music*.

64. Rosenthal, G. *Behind the Music*.

Chapter 14.

1. Love, C. (2023). Personal interview with Jennifer Otter Bickerdike.

2. banggothebangles. (2017). "The Bangles Story June 23–25, 1989." Available at https://www.youtube.com/watch?v=e-jvyXJ6Hnw&list=PLGp3HEH8K0yHDGMR1smOzqouoQoA9lewe&index=22. Accessed April 8, 2023.

3. DeYoung, B. (2019). *I Need to Know: The Lost Music Interviews*. St. Petersburg, FL: St. Petersburg Press.

4. Peterson, V. (2023). Personal interview with Jennifer Otter Bickerdike.

5. Philbin, P. (2023). Personal interview with Jennifer Otter Bickerdike.

6. Philbin, P. (2023). Personal interview with Jennifer Otter Bickerdike.

7. Stella, J. (2023). Personal interview with Jennifer Otter Bickerdike.

8. Chiccarelli, J. (2023). Personal interview with Jennifer Otter Bickerdike.

9. Chiccarelli, J. (2023). Personal interview with Jennifer Otter Bickerdike.

10. Chiccarelli, J. (2023). Personal interview with Jennifer Otter Bickerdike.

11. Chiccarelli, J. (2023). Personal interview with Jennifer Otter Bickerdike.

12. Philbin, P. (2023). Personal interview with Jennifer Otter Bickerdike.

13. Dean, J. (2023). Personal interview with Jennifer Otter Bickerdike.

14. Peterson, V. (2023). *All Over the Place* liner notes.

15. Caro, M. (2023). "Debbi Peterson (The Bangles)." *Caropop* podcast. S01 E73. Available at https://rss.com/podcasts/thecaropopcast/848495/. Accessed October 5, 2023.

16. Caro, M. "Debbi Peterson (The Bangles)"; DeYoung, B. (2019). *I Need to Know*.

17. Caro, M. "Debbi Peterson (The Bangles)."

18. Peterson, V. *All Over the Place* liner notes.

19. Chiccarelli, J. (2023). Personal interview with Jennifer Otter Bickerdike.

20. Gormley, M. (2023). Personal interview with Jennifer Otter Bickerdike.
21. Gormley, M. (2023). Personal interview with Jennifer Otter Bickerdike.
22. DeYoung, B. *I Need to Know*.
23. DeYoung, B. *I Need to Know*.
24. DeYoung, B. *I Need to Know*.
25. DeYoung, B. *I Need to Know*.
26. Gormley, M. (2023). Personal interview with Jennifer Otter Bickerdike.
27. Peterson, V. *All Over the Place* liner notes.
28. Philbin, P. (2023). Personal interview with Jennifer Otter Bickerdike.
29. Chiccarelli, J. (2023). Personal interview with Jennifer Otter Bickerdike.
30. Chiccarelli, J. (2023). Personal interview with Jennifer Otter Bickerdike.
31. Philbin, P. (2023). Personal interview with Jennifer Otter Bickerdike.
32. Chiccarelli, J. (2023). Personal interview with Jennifer Otter Bickerdike.
33. Caro, M. "Debbi Peterson (The Bangles)."
34. Hann, M. (2013). "The Paisley Underground: Los Angeles's 1980s Psychedelic Explosion." Available at https://www.theguardian.com/music/2013/may/16/paisley-underground-history-80s-los-angeles-psychedelia. Accessed November 1, 2023.
35. Peterson, V. *All Over the Place* liner notes.
36. Peterson, V. (2023). Personal interview with Jennifer Otter Bickerdike.
37. Peterson, V. (2023). Personal interview with Jennifer Otter Bickerdike.
38. Lloyd, R. (1984). "The Bangles' Bright, Shiny Beats." In *LA Weekly*. July 5.

Chapter 15.

1. Partridge, K. (2018). "Why the Bangles, Dream Syndicate & Others Want the Paisley Underground to Rise Again." Available at https://www.billboard.com/music/rock/bangles-dream-syndicate-three-oclock-paisley-underground-8484948/. Accessed September 13, 2023.
2. banggothebangles. (2014). "The Bangles | Limited Edition Picture Disc Interview." April 12. Available at https://www.youtube.com/watch?v=8aPmKaMXrsE&ab_channel=banggothebangles. Accessed March 15, 2023.
3. Partridge, K. "Why the Bangles, Dream Syndicate & Others Want the Paisley Underground to Rise Again."
4. Ivie, D. (2024). "The Bangles Were Always a Democracy." Available at https://www.vulture.com/article/susanna-hoffs-the-bangles-manic-monday-songs.html. Accessed January 5, 2024.
5. Pollack, B. (2012). "They're Playing My Song: Eternal Flame." Available at https://www.songfacts.com/blog/playingmysong/susanna-hoffs-eternal-flame. Accessed November 2, 2023.
6. Caro, M. (2023). "Debbi Peterson (The Bangles)." *Caropop* podcast. S01 E73. Available at https://rss.com/podcasts/thecaropopcast/848495/. Accessed October 5, 2023.
7. Rollins, H. (2023). Personal interview with Jennifer Otter Bickerdike.
8. Rollins, H. (2023). Personal interview with Jennifer Otter Bickerdike.
9. Gormley, M. (2023). Personal interview with Jennifer Otter Bickerdike.
10. Caro, M. "Debbi Peterson (The Bangles)."

11. Lamson, C. (2023). Personal interview with Jennifer Otter Bickerdike.
12. Rathod, D. (2023). Personal interview with Jennifer Otter Bickerdike.
13. Rathod, D. (2023). Personal interview with Jennifer Otter Bickerdike.
14. Rathod, D. (2023). Personal interview with Jennifer Otter Bickerdike.
15. Gormley, M. (2023). Personal interview with Jennifer Otter Bickerdike.
16. Caro, M. "Debbi Peterson (The Bangles)."
17. Branst, L. (1984). "Bangles' Beat Is '80s Sound." In *News-Pilot*. December 14.
18. *Rolling Stone*. (1984). "*All Over the Place*, The Bangles." August 16, page 38.
19. Author Unknown. (1900). "Sussana [sic] Hoffs of the Bangles Intimate Details Article, Picture & Songwords."
20. Schneider, M. (1983). "The Big Bangles Theory." In *Creem*. May.
21. Schneider, M. "The Big Bangles Theory."
22. Gormley, M. (2023). Personal interview with Jennifer Otter Bickerdike.
23. Joe Johnson. (1986). "Bangles on *Late Night*." Available at https://www.youtube.com/watch?v=Tst4WFxi1lY. Accessed November 2, 2023.
24. Lamson, C. (2023). Personal interview with Jennifer Otter Bickerdike.
25. Lloyd, R. (1984). "The Bangles' Bright, Shiny Beats." In *LA Weekly*. July 5.
26. Benarde, S. (1984). "Bangles Pay Dues—Now Ready to Rock." In *Fort Lauderdale News*. September 21, page 74.
27. Hall, M. (1984). "All-Girl Bangles Brings '60s Sound into '80s with Style." In *Austin American-Statesman*. October 12, page 101.
28. Zeller, C. (1984). "The Bangles: *All Over the Place* (Columbia)." Available at https://www.rocksbackpages.com/Library/Article/the-bangles-iall-over-the-placei-columbia. Accessed November 2, 2023.
29. Zebora, J. (1984). "Gutsy All-Girl Bangles Pack Punch in Their Rock." In *Record-Journal*. October 5, page 17.
30. Holden, S. (1984). "Pop: Bangles at the Ritz." Available at https://www.nytimes.com/1984/10/01/arts/pop-bangles-at-the-ritz.html?searchResultPosition=1. Accessed February 17, 2023.
31. Zebora, J. "Gutsy All-Girl Bangles."
32. Rolling Stone. (1984). "Bangles." December 4, issue 436.
33. Lamson, C. (2023). Personal interview with Jennifer Otter Bickerdike.
34. Lamson, C. (2023). Personal interview with Jennifer Otter Bickerdike.
35. Branst, L. "Bangles' Beat Is '80s Sound."
36. Marlowe, J. (1984). "Lauper Proves She's So Unusual." In *Miami News*. October 24, page 24.
37. Lamson, C. (2023). Personal interview with Jennifer Otter Bickerdike.
38. Peterson, D. (2023). Personal interview with Jennifer Otter Bickerdike.
39. Cromelin, R. (1986). "The Bangles: Local Girls Make Good." Available at https://www.rocksbackpages.com/Library/Article/the-bangles-local-girls-make-good. Accessed November 2, 2023.
40. Peterson, V. (2023). Personal interview with Jennifer Otter Bickerdike.
41. Philbin, P. (2023). Personal interview with Jennifer Otter Bickerdike.

42. Philbin, P. (2023). Personal interview with Jennifer Otter Bickerdike.

43. Creem Magazine. (1985). "The Winners CREEM's '84 Rock 'n' Roll Readers Poll, March 1985."

Chapter 16.

1. Ivie, D. (2024). "The Bangles Were Always a Democracy." Available at https://www.vulture.com/article/susanna-hoffs-the-bangles-manic-monday-songs.html. Accessed January 4, 2023.

2. Peterson, D. (2023). Personal interview with Jennifer Otter Bickerdike.
3. Peterson, D. (2023). Personal interview with Jennifer Otter Bickerdike.
4. Gormley, M. (2023). Personal interview with Jennifer Otter Bickerdike.
5. Peterson, D. (2023). Personal interview with Jennifer Otter Bickerdike.
6. McDonald, S. (2023). Personal interview with Jennifer Otter Bickerdike.
7. McDonald, S. (2023). Personal interview with Jennifer Otter Bickerdike.
8. McDonald, J. (2023). Personal interview with Jennifer Otter Bickerdike.
9. McDonald, J. (2023). Personal interview with Jennifer Otter Bickerdike.
10. McDonald, S. (2023). Personal interview with Jennifer Otter Bickerdike.
11. Chiccarelli, J. (2023). Personal interview with Jennifer Otter Bickerdike.
12. McDonald, J. (2023). Personal interview with Jennifer Otter Bickerdike.
13. Lamson, C. (2023). Personal interview with Jennifer Otter Bickerdike.
14. McDonald, S. (2023). Personal interview with Jennifer Otter Bickerdike.
15. Lamson, C. (2023). Personal interview with Jennifer Otter Bickerdike.
16. Stella, J. (2023). Personal interview with Jennifer Otter Bickerdike.
17. Lamson, C. (2023). Personal interview with Jennifer Otter Bickerdike.
18. McDonald, S. (2023). Personal interview with Jennifer Otter Bickerdike.
19. Philbin, P. (2023). Personal interview with Jennifer Otter Bickerdike.
20. Dean, J. (2023). Personal interview with Jennifer Otter Bickerdike.
21. Peterson, V. (2023). Personal interview with Jennifer Otter Bickerdike.
22. Peterson, V. (2023). Personal interview with Jennifer Otter Bickerdike.
23. Peterson, V. (2023). Personal interview with Jennifer Otter Bickerdike.
24. Gormley, M. (2023). Personal interview with Jennifer Otter Bickerdike.
25. Gormley, M. (2023). Personal interview with Jennifer Otter Bickerdike.
26. Gormley, M. (2023). Personal interview with Jennifer Otter Bickerdike.
27. Gormley, M. (2023). Personal interview with Jennifer Otter Bickerdike.
28. Lamson, C. (2023). Personal interview with Jennifer Otter Bickerdike.
29. Gormley, M. (2023). Personal interview with Jennifer Otter Bickerdike.
30. Hoffs, S. (2023). Personal interview with Jennifer Otter Bickerdike.
31. Hoffs, S. (2023). Personal interview with Jennifer Otter Bickerdike.
32. Dean, J. (2023). Personal interview with Jennifer Otter Bickerdike.
33. McDonald, J. (2023). Personal interview with Jennifer Otter Bickerdike.
34. Lamson, C. (2023). Personal interview with Jennifer Otter Bickerdike.
35. Hogan, P. (1989). *The Bangles*. London: Omnibus.
36. Peterson, V. (2023). Personal interview with Jennifer Otter Bickerdike.

Chapter 17.

1. Rifkin, B. (2023). Personal interview with Jennifer Otter Bickerdike.
2. Record Collector. (2019). "Paisley Underground." Available at https://recordcollectormag.com/articles/paisley-underground. Accessed September 27, 2023.
3. Rifkin, B. (2023). Personal interview with Jennifer Otter Bickerdike.
4. Philbin, P. (2023). Personal interview with Jennifer Otter Bickerdike.
5. Philbin, P. (2023). Personal interview with Jennifer Otter Bickerdike.
6. Hoffs, S. (2023). Personal interview with Jennifer Otter Bickerdike.
7. Simmons, S. (1987). "Cyndi Lauper: Doing That Primitive Thing." Available at https://www.rocksbackpages.com/Library/Article/cyndi-lauper-doing-that-primitive-thing. Accessed November 2, 2023.
8. Peterson, D. (2023). Personal interview with Jennifer Otter Bickerdike.
9. Peterson, V. (2023). Personal interview with Jennifer Otter Bickerdike.
10. Trakin, R. (1986). "The Bangles: Making Pop Her-Story or It's a Girl's, Girl's, Girl's World." In *Creem*. June.
11. Trakin, R. "The Bangles: Making Pop Her-Story."
12. Kotero, A. (2023). Personal interview with Jennifer Otter Bickerdike.
13. Grow, K. (2019). "Prince's Unearthed 'Originals:' Collaborators Look Back on the Hits He Passed Along." Available at https://www.rollingstone.com/music/music-features/prince-originals-interview-842940/. Accessed September 28, 2023.
14. Kotero, A. (2023). Personal interview with Jennifer Otter Bickerdike.
15. Kotero, A. (2023). Personal interview with Jennifer Otter Bickerdike.
16. Kotero, A. (2023). Personal interview with Jennifer Otter Bickerdike.
17. Kotero, A. (2023). Personal interview with Jennifer Otter Bickerdike.
18. Kotero, A. (2023). Personal interview with Jennifer Otter Bickerdike.
19. Kotero, A. (2023). Personal interview with Jennifer Otter Bickerdike.
20. Grow, K. "Prince's Unearthed 'Originals.'"
21. Kotero, A. (2023). Personal interview with Jennifer Otter Bickerdike.
22. Philbin, P. (2023). Personal interview with Jennifer Otter Bickerdike.
23. Philbin, P. (2023). Personal interview with Jennifer Otter Bickerdike.
24. Philbin, P. (2023). Personal interview with Jennifer Otter Bickerdike.
25. Rifkin, B. (2023). Personal interview with Jennifer Otter Bickerdike.
26. Rifkin, B. (2023). Personal interview with Jennifer Otter Bickerdike.
27. Philbin, P. (2023). Personal interview with Jennifer Otter Bickerdike.
28. Rifkin, B. (2023). Personal interview with Jennifer Otter Bickerdike.
29. Ivie, D. (2024). "The Bangles Were Always a Democracy." Available at https://www.vulture.com/article/susanna-hoffs-the-bangles-manic-monday-songs.html. January 3, 2024.
30. Balaban, S. (2019). "How Prince Worked His Magic on the Bangles' 'Manic Monday.'" Available at https://www.npr.org/programs/weekend-edition-suday/2019/06/23/735191049/weekend-edition-sunday-for-june-23-2019. Accessed November 2, 2023.
31. Hann, M. (2013). "The Paisley Underground: Los Angeles's 1980s Psychedelic Explosion." Available at https://www.theguardian.com/music/2013/may/16

/paisley-underground-history-80s-los-angeles-psychedelia. Accessed November 1, 2023.

32. Lamson, C. (2023). Personal interview with Jennifer Otter Bickerdike.
33. Lamson, C. (2023). Personal interview with Jennifer Otter Bickerdike.
34. Balaban, S. "How Prince Worked His Magic."
35. Hoff, S. (2023). Personal interview with Jennifer Otter Bickerdike.
36. Tudahl, D. (2022). *Prince and the Parade and Sign O' The Times Era Studio Sessions: 1985 and 1986 (Prince Studio Sessions)*. Lanham, MD: Rowman & Littlefield Publishers.
37. Peterson, V. (2023). Personal interview with Jennifer Otter Bickerdike.
38. Caro, M. (2023). "Debbi Peterson (The Bangles)." *Caropop* podcast. S01 E73. Available at https://rss.com/podcasts/thecaropopcast/848495/. Accessed October 5, 2023.
39. Peterson, D. (2023). Personal interview with Jennifer Otter Bickerdike.
40. Hann, M. "The Paisley Underground."
41. Peterson, V. (2023). Personal interview with Jennifer Otter Bickerdike.
42. Draper, J. (2017). *Prince: Life and Times: Revised and Updated Edition*. London: Chartwell Books.
43. Lamson, C. (2023). Personal interview with Jennifer Otter Bickerdike.
44. Gormley, M. (2023). Personal interview with Jennifer Otter Bickerdike.
45. Lamson, C. (2023). Personal interview with Jennifer Otter Bickerdike.
46. Author Unknown. (1986). "'*Different Light*' LP Sparkler from Bangles." In *Arizona Daily Star*. February 9.
47. Author Unknown. "'*Different Light*' LP Sparkler from Bangles."
48. Rolling Stone. (1984). "Notable News." In *Rolling Stone*, November 8, issue 434.
49. Lev, M. (1986). "Girl Group's Prince Has Come." In *News-Pilot*. Available at https://www.newspapers.com/image/607002219. Accessed January 25, 2023.
50. Hibbert, T. (1987). "The Bangles: Girls on Top." Available at https://www.rocksbackpages.com/Library/Article/the-bangles-girls-on-top. Accessed March 1, 2023.
51. Rapido. (1991). Contributor: Hoffs, Susanna (speaker, female) Identifier: ISRC: CKEY1304972. V224/1 RAPIDO.
52. Hoffs, S. (2023). Personal interview with Jennifer Otter Bickerdike.
53. Hoffs, S. (2023). Personal interview with Jennifer Otter Bickerdike.
54. Kotero, A. (2023). Personal interview with Jennifer Otter Bickerdike.
55. Kotero, A. (2023). Personal interview with Jennifer Otter Bickerdike.
56. Rifkin, B. (2023). Personal interview with Jennifer Otter Bickerdike.
57. Peterson, V. (2023). Personal interview with Jennifer Otter Bickerdike.
58. Caro, M. "Debbi Peterson (The Bangles)."
59. Rollins, H. (2023). Personal interview with Jennifer Otter Bickerdike.

Chapter 18.

1. Gormley, M. (2023). Personal interview with Jennifer Otter Bickerdike.
2. Lamson, C. (2023). Personal interview with Jennifer Otter Bickerdike.
3. Gormley, M. (2023). Personal interview with Jennifer Otter Bickerdike.

4. Gormley, M. (2023). Personal interview with Jennifer Otter Bickerdike.

5. Peterson, D. (2023). Personal interview with Jennifer Otter Bickerdike.

6. Rosenthal, G. (2000). *Behind the Music: The Bangles*. IMDb, S3, E40.

7. Peterson, D. (2023). Personal interview with Jennifer Otter Bickerdike.

8. Peterson, V. (2023). Personal interview with Jennifer Otter Bickerdike.

9. Doyle, T. (2021). "Classic Tracks: The Bangles 'Walk Like an Egyptian.'" Available at https://www.soundonsound.com/techniques/classic-tracks-bangles-walk-egyptian. Accessed October 5, 2023.

10. Lamson, C. (2023). Personal interview with Jennifer Otter Bickerdike.

11. Rifkin, B. (2023). Personal interview with Jennifer Otter Bickerdike.

12. Philbin, P. (2023). Personal interview with Jennifer Otter Bickerdike.

13. Peterson, D. (2023). Personal interview with Jennifer Otter Bickerdike.

14. Peterson, D. (2023). Personal interview with Jennifer Otter Bickerdike.

15. Rosenthal, G. *Behind the Music*.

16. Lamson, C. (2023). Personal interview with Jennifer Otter Bickerdike.

17. Peterson, D. (2023). Personal interview with Jennifer Otter Bickerdike.

18. Peterson, D. (2023). Personal interview with Jennifer Otter Bickerdike.

19. Balaban, S. (2019). "How Prince Worked His Magic on the Bangles' 'Manic Monday.'" Available at https://www.npr.org/2019/06/21/734176868/how-prince-worked-his-magic-on-the-bangles-manic-monday. Accessed September 8, 2024.

20. Philbin, P. (2023). Personal interview with Jennifer Otter Bickerdike.

21. Ivie, D. (2024). "The Bangles Were Always a Democracy." Available at https://www.vulture.com/article/susanna-hoffs-the-bangles-manic-monday-songs.html. Accessed January 5, 2024.

22. Rifkin, B. (2023). Personal interview with Jennifer Otter Bickerdike.

23. banggothebangles. (2014). "The Bangles | Limited Edition Picture Disc Interview." April 12. Available at https://www.youtube.com/watch?v=8aPmKaMXrsE&ab_channel=banggothebangles. Accessed March 15, 2023.

24. Tudahl, D. (2022). *Prince and the Parade and Sign O' The Times Era Studio Sessions: 1985 and 1986 (Prince Studio Sessions)*. Lanham, MD: Rowman & Littlefield Publishers.

25. Hoskins, Z. (2022). "Dance / Music / Sex / Romance." Available at https://princesongs.org/author/dmsradmin/. Accessed October 3, 2023.

26. Philbin, P. (2023). Personal interview with Jennifer Otter Bickerdike.

27. Gormley, M. (2023). Personal interview with Jennifer Otter Bickerdike.

28. banggothebangles. "The Bangles | Limited Edition Picture Disc Interview."

29. Philbin, P. (2023). Personal interview with Jennifer Otter Bickerdike.

30. Mojo. (2022). "MOJO Time Machine: The Bangles Walk Like an Egyptian to Number One." Available at https://www.mojo4music.com/time-machine/1980s/mojo-time-machine-the-bangles-walk-like-an-egyptian-to-number-one/. Accessed October 5, 2023.

31. Doyle, T. "Classic Tracks."

32. Doyle, T. "Classic Tracks."

33. Hoffs, S. (2023). Personal interview with Jennifer Otter Bickerdike.

34. Peterson, V. (2023). Personal interview with Jennifer Otter Bickerdike.
35. Peterson, V. (2023). Personal interview with Jennifer Otter Bickerdike.
36. Harris, W. (2011). "Susanna Hoffs of the Bangles." Available at https://www.avclub.com/susanna-hoffs-of-the-bangles-1798228045. Accessed October 5, 2023.
37. Lamson, C. (2023). Personal interview with Jennifer Otter Bickerdike.
38. Caro, M. (2023). "Debbi Peterson (The Bangles)." *Caropop* podcast. S01 E73. Available at https://rss.com/podcasts/thecaropopcast/848495/. Accessed October 5, 2023.
39. Igleheart, W. (2023). Personal interview with Jennifer Otter Bickerdike.
40. Gormley, M. (2023). Personal interview with Jennifer Otter Bickerdike.
41. Gormley, M. (2023). Personal interview with Jennifer Otter Bickerdike.
42. Philbin, P. (2023). Personal interview with Jennifer Otter Bickerdike.
43. Philbin, P. (2023). Personal interview with Jennifer Otter Bickerdike.
44. Gormley, M. (2023). Personal interview with Jennifer Otter Bickerdike.
45. Gormley, M. (2023). Personal interview with Jennifer Otter Bickerdike.
46. Peterson, V. (2023). Personal interview with Jennifer Otter Bickerdike.
47. Caro, M. "Debbi Peterson (The Bangles)."
48. Philbin, P. (2023). Personal interview with Jennifer Otter Bickerdike.
49. DeYoung, B. (2019). *I Need to Know: The Lost Music Interviews*. St. Petersburg, FL: St. Petersburg Press.
50. Peterson, D. (2023). Personal interview with Jennifer Otter Bickerdike.
51. Podany, A. 2023). Personal interview with Jennifer Otter Bickerdike.
52. DeYoung, B. *I Need to Know*.
53. Peterson, V. (2023). Personal interview with Jennifer Otter Bickerdike.
54. Peterson, V. (2023). Personal interview with Jennifer Otter Bickerdike.
55. Rosenthal, G. *Behind the Music*.
56. Doyle, T. "Classic Tracks."
57. Rosenthal, G. *Behind the Music*.
58. Doyle, T. "Classic Tracks."
59. Rosenthal, G. *Behind the Music*.
60. Doyle, T. "Classic Tracks."
61. Peterson, D. (2023). Personal interview with Jennifer Otter Bickerdike.
62. Copeland, M. (2021). *Two Steps Forward, One Step Back*. London: Jawbone Press. Kindle Edition.
63. Doyle, T. "Classic Tracks."
64. Caro, M. "Debbi Peterson (The Bangles)."
65. Kasza, T. (2023). Personal interview with Jennifer Otter Bickerdike.
66. Peterson, D. (2023). Personal interview with Jennifer Otter Bickerdike.
67. Banda, M. (2023). Personal interview with Jennifer Otter Bickerdike.
68. Banda, M. (2023). Personal interview with Jennifer Otter Bickerdike.
69. Peterson, D. (2023). Personal interview with Jennifer Otter Bickerdike.
70. Peterson, D. (2023). Personal interview with Jennifer Otter Bickerdike.
71. Caro, M. "Debbi Peterson (The Bangles)."
72. DeYoung, B. *I Need to Know*.

73. Peterson, D. (2023). Personal interview with Jennifer Otter Bickerdike.
74. Peterson, D. (2023). Personal interview with Jennifer Otter Bickerdike.
75. Peterson, D. (2023). Personal interview with Jennifer Otter Bickerdike.
76. Peterson, V. (2023). Personal interview with Jennifer Otter Bickerdike.
77. Igleheart, W. (2023). Personal interview with Jennifer Otter Bickerdike.
78. DeYoung, B. *I Need to Know*.
79. Peterson, Dave. (2023). Personal interview with Jennifer Otter Bickerdike.
80. Peterson, Dave. (2023). Personal interview with Jennifer Otter Bickerdike.
81. Gormley, M. (2023). Personal interview with Jennifer Otter Bickerdike.
82. Peterson, D. (2023). Personal interview with Jennifer Otter Bickerdike.
83. McDonald, S. (2023). Personal interview with Jennifer Otter Bickerdike.
84. McDonald, J. (2023). Personal interview with Jennifer Otter Bickerdike.
85. Hoffs, S. (2023). Personal interview with Jennifer Otter Bickerdike.
86. Hoffs, S. (2023). Personal interview with Jennifer Otter Bickerdike.
87. Peterson, V. (2023). Personal interview with Jennifer Otter Bickerdike.
88. Trakin, R. (1986). "The Bangles: Making Pop Her-Story or It's a Girl's, Girl's, Girl's World." In *Creem*. June.
89. Hoffs, S. (2023). Personal interview with Jennifer Otter Bickerdike.
90. Lamson, C. (2023). Personal interview with Jennifer Otter Bickerdike.

Chapter 19.

1. Hilburn, R. (1986). "Robert Hilburn: Summer Pop Has Arrived on Airwaves." In *Los Angeles Times*. Available at https://www.latimes.com/archives/la-xpm-1986-04-19-ca-622-story.html. Accessed October 5, 2023.
2. Peterson, V. (2023). Personal interview with Jennifer Otter Bickerdike.
3. DVDGuy2012. (2011). *The Bangles Canadian TV Interview 1986 Part #1*. January 4. Available at https://youtu.be/GFntqkReyTc. Accessed April 4, 2023.
4. DVDGuy2012. *The Bangles Canadian TV Interview*.
5. banggothebangles. (2021). "The Bangles | The Wide Awake Club | June 1986." August 7. Available at https://www.youtube.com/watch?v=XVFE9jiKl6Q&ab_channel=banggothebangles. Accessed March 27, 2023.
6. Lamson, C. (2023). Personal interview with Jennifer Otter Bickerdike.
7. Taylor, J. (1986). "Bangles Have Arrived—via Bus: Now Pit Stops Are High on the Charts." In *Times-Advocate*. March 6, page 84.
8. Taylor, L. (1985). "Bangles Jangle Their Way up the Pop Charts." In the *Messenger-Inquirer*. Available at https://www.newspapers.com/image/378790201. Accessed January 25, 2023.
9. Peterson, D. (2023). Personal interview with Jennifer Otter Bickerdike.
10. Harrington, R. (1986). "The Bangles: Baubles & a Beat." Available at https://www.washingtonpost.com/archive/lifestyle/1986/04/08/the-bangles-baubles-38/f32f9c2e-d7b5-4028-9e6a-baf001289159/. Accessed October 6, 2023.
11. Igleheart, W. (2023). Personal interview with Jennifer Otter Bickerdike.
12. Banda, M. (2023). Personal interview with Jennifer Otter Bickerdike.
13. Sweeting, A. (1985). "Americans in Paris." In *Melody Maker*. March 2.

14. Igleheart, W. (2023). Personal interview with Jennifer Otter Bickerdike.
15. Igleheart, W. (2023). Personal interview with Jennifer Otter Bickerdike.
16. *Metal Priestesses Podcast*. (2021). "Episode 10: Linda Ronstadt and Susanna Hoffs!" Available at https://www.youtube.com/watch?v=SxQXyddJqCY. Accessed May 19, 2023.
17. Igleheart, W. (2023). Personal interview with Jennifer Otter Bickerdike.
18. Wilson, R. (2023). Personal interview with Jennifer Otter Bickerdike.
19. Wilson, R. (2023). Personal interview with Jennifer Otter Bickerdike.
20. Popson, T. (1986). "Bangles Hit It Big; Bassist Floats into Zen Consciousness." In *Chicago Tribune*. May 2, 1986.
21. Wilson, R. (2023). Personal interview with Jennifer Otter Bickerdike.
22. Wilson, R. (2023). Personal interview with Jennifer Otter Bickerdike.
23. Wilson, R. (2023). Personal interview with Jennifer Otter Bickerdike.
24. Wilson, R. (2023). Personal interview with Jennifer Otter Bickerdike.
25. Corvalan, M. (2023). Personal interview with Jennifer Otter Bickerdike.
26. Harrington, R. "The Bangles: Baubles & a Beat."
27. Sweeting, A. (1985). "The Bangles." Available at https://www.rocksbackpages.com/Library/Article/the-bangles. Accessed January 20, 2023.
28. Lababedi, I. (2015). "Interviews, News, Slideshows." Available at https://rocknyc.live/oldies-but-goldies-bangles-for-sale-interview-from-1985.html. Accessed September 11, 2024.
29. Popson, T. "Bangles Hit It Big."
30. Cromelin, R. (1986). "The Bangles: Local Girls Make Good." Available at https://www.rocksbackpages.com/Library/Article/the-bangles-local-girls-make-good. Accessed October 6, 2023.
31. Harrington, R. "The Bangles: Baubles & a Beat."
32. Cromelin, R. "The Bangles: Local Girls Make Good."
33. Rifkin, B. (2023). Personal interview with Jennifer Otter Bickerdike.
34. No Author. (1986). "The Bangles Make Noise at the Beacon." In *Newsday*.
35. Gormley, M. (2023). Personal interview with Jennifer Otter Bickerdike.
36. Trakin, R. (1986). "Honking Off Dudes." In *Creem*. May.
37. Holdship, B. (1987). "I Like the Monkees." In *Creem*. December. Available at https://monkees.coolcherrycream.com/articles/1987/04/creem-presents. Accessed October 6, 2023.
38. DVDGuy2012. *The Bangles Canadian TV Interview 1986 Part #2*.

Chapter 20.

1. Lamson, C. (2023). Personal interview with Jennifer Otter Bickerdike.
2. Lamson, C. (2023). Personal interview with Jennifer Otter Bickerdike.
3. Lamson, C. (2023). Personal interview with Jennifer Otter Bickerdike.
4. Lamson, C. (2023). Personal interview with Jennifer Otter Bickerdike.
5. Hoffs, S. (2023) Personal interview with Jennifer Otter Bickerdike.
6. Balaban, S. (2019). "How Prince Worked His Magic on the Bangles' 'Manic Monday.'" Available at https://www.npr.org/2019/06/21/734176868/how-prince-worked-his-magic-on-the-bangles-manic-monday. Accessed October 10, 2023.

Notes

7. *Metal Priestesses Podcast.* (2021). "Episode 10: Linda Ronstadt and Susanna Hoffs!" Available at https://www.youtube.com/watch?v=SxQXyddJqCY. Accessed May 19, 2023.

8. Lamson, C. (2023). Personal interview with Jennifer Otter Bickerdike.

9. Peterson, V. (2023). Personal interview with Jennifer Otter Bickerdike.

10. Teicholz, T. (2006). "Susanna Hoffs Walks Like a—Rockstar No, a Mom—Rockstar/Mom." Available at https://web.archive.org/web/20061018205847/http://www.jewishjournal.com/home/preview.php?id=16541. Accessed October 10, 2023.

11. Hoffs, S. (2023). Personal interview with Jennifer Otter Bickerdike.

12. Hoffs, S. (2023). Personal interview with Jennifer Otter Bickerdike.

13. Teicholz, T. "Susanna Hoffs Walks Like."

14. Copeland, M. (2021). *Two Steps Forward, One Step Back*. London: Jawbone Press.

15. Gormley, M. (2023). Personal interview with Jennifer Otter Bickerdike.

16. Gormley, M. (2023). Personal interview with Jennifer Otter Bickerdike.

17. Copeland, M. *Two Steps Forward, One Step Back*.

18. https://www.instagram.com/p/Cxb9VIes58r/.

19. Tudahl, D. (2022). *Prince and the Parade and Sign O' The Times Era Studio Sessions: 1985 and 1986* (*Prince Studio Sessions*). Lanham, MD: Rowman & Littlefield Publishers.

20. Peterson, V. (2023). Personal interview with Jennifer Otter Bickerdike.

21. Peterson, D. (2023). Personal interview with Jennifer Otter Bickerdike.

22. Peterson, V. (2023). Personal interview with Jennifer Otter Bickerdike.

23. Balaban, S. "How Prince Worked His Magic."

24. Hoffs, S. (2023). Personal interview with Jennifer Otter Bickerdike.

25. Rifkin, B. (2023). Personal interview with Jennifer Otter Bickerdike.

26. Rifkin, B. (2023). Personal interview with Jennifer Otter Bickerdike.

27. Peterson, V. (2023). Personal interview with Jennifer Otter Bickerdike.

28. Peterson, V. (2023). Personal interview with Jennifer Otter Bickerdike.

29. Peterson, D. (2023). Personal interview with Jennifer Otter Bickerdike.

30. Peterson, D. (2023). Personal interview with Jennifer Otter Bickerdike.

31. Peterson, D. (2023). Personal interview with Jennifer Otter Bickerdike.

32. Jensen, D. (1986). "Capitol Radio Interviews: Susanna Hoffs, Debbi Peterson." Available at http://cadensa.bl.uk/uhtbin/cgisirsi/?ps=JuCwT4x0Vm/WORKS-FILE/104820018/9. Accessed February 4, 2023.

33. Hibbert, T. (1987). "The Bangles: Girls on Top." Available at https://www.rocksbackpages.com/Library/Article/the-bangles-girls-on-top. Accessed October 10, 2023.

34. Peterson, V. (2023). Personal interview with Jennifer Otter Bickerdike.

35. Peterson, D. (2023). Personal interview with Jennifer Otter Bickerdike.

36. Peterson, V. (2023). Personal interview with Jennifer Otter Bickerdike.

Chapter 21.

1. Harris, W. (2011). "Susanna Hoffs of the Bangles." Available at https://www.avclub.com/susanna-hoffs-of-the-bangles-1798228045. Accessed October 11, 2023.

2. Cost, J. (2009). "A Conversation with Susanna Hoffs and Matthew Sweet." Available at https://magnetmagazine.com/2009/07/20/qa-with-susanna-hoffs-and-matthew-sweet/. Accessed October 11, 2023.

3. *Metal Priestesses Podcast*. (2021). "Episode 10: Linda Ronstadt and Susanna Hoffs!" Available at https://www.youtube.com/watch?v=SxQXyddJqCY. Accessed May 19, 2023.

4. Ireland, K. (2023). Personal interview with Jennifer Otter Bickerdike.

5. Peterson, V. (2023). Personal interview with Jennifer Otter Bickerdike.

6. Peterson, V. (2023). Personal interview with Jennifer Otter Bickerdike.

7. Hoffs, S. (2023). Personal interview with Jennifer Otter Bickerdike.

8. Gormley, M. (2023). Personal interview with Jennifer Otter Bickerdike.

9. Smith, B. S. (2023). Personal interview with Jennifer Otter Bickerdike.

10. Griffin, S. (2023). Personal interview with Jennifer Otter Bickerdike.

11. Hann, M. (2013). "The Paisley Underground: Los Angeles's 1980s Psychedelic Explosion." Available at https://www.theguardian.com/music/2013/may/16/paisley-underground-history-80s-los-angeles-psychedelia. Accessed October 11, 2023.

12. Peterson, Dave. (2023). Personal interview with Jennifer Otter Bickerdike.

13. Stella, J. (2023). Personal interview with Jennifer Otter Bickerdike.

14. Lamson, C. (2023). Personal interview with Jennifer Otter Bickerdike.

15. Stella, J. (2023). Personal interview with Jennifer Otter Bickerdike.

16. Gormley, M. (2023). Personal interview with Jennifer Otter Bickerdike.

17. Peterson, V. (2023). Personal interview with Jennifer Otter Bickerdike.

18. Peterson, D. (2023). Personal interview with Jennifer Otter Bickerdike.

19. Peterson, D. (2023). Personal interview with Jennifer Otter Bickerdike.

20. Wilson, R. (2023). Personal interview with Jennifer Otter Bickerdike.

21. Peterson, D. (2023). Personal interview with Jennifer Otter Bickerdike.

22. Griffin, S. (2023). Personal interview with Jennifer Otter Bickerdike.

23. Peterson, V. (2023). Personal interview with Jennifer Otter Bickerdike.

24. DeYoung, B. (2019). *I Need to Know: The Lost Music Interviews*. St. Petersburg, FL: St. Petersburg Press.

25. Bell, M. (Year Unknown). "The Bangles." Publication Unknown.

26. Peterson, V. (2023). Personal interview with Jennifer Otter Bickerdike.

Chapter 22.

1. Copeland, M. (2021). *Two Steps Forward, One Step Back*. London: Jawbone Press.

2. Rosenthal, G. (2000). *Behind the Music: The Bangles*. IMDb, S3, E40.

3. Kasza, T. (2023). Personal interview with Jennifer Otter Bickerdike.

4. Trakin, R. (1986). "The Bangles: Making Pop Her-Story or It's a Girl's, Girl's, Girl's World." In *Creem*. June. Available at http://www.rocksbackpages.com/Library/Article/the-bangles-making-pop-her-story-or-its-a-girls-girls-girls-world. Accessed October 13, 2023.

5. Igleheart, W. (2023). Personal interview with Jennifer Otter Bickerdike.

6. Igleheart, W. (2023). Personal interview with Jennifer Otter Bickerdike.

7. *Metal Priestesses Podcast.* (2021). "Episode 10: Linda Ronstadt and Susanna Hoffs!" Available at https://www.youtube.com/watch?v=SxQXyddJqCY. Accessed May 19, 2023.
8. Stella, J. (2023). Personal interview with Jennifer Otter Bickerdike.
9. Trakin, R. "The Bangles: Making Pop Her-Story."
10. Griffin, S. (2023). Personal interview with Jennifer Otter Bickerdike.
11. Philbin, P. (2023). Personal interview with Jennifer Otter Bickerdike.
12. Hoffs, S. (2023). Personal interview with Jennifer Otter Bickerdike.
13. Rifkin, B. (2023). Personal interview with Jennifer Otter Bickerdike.
14. Diamond, B. (2023). Personal interview with Jennifer Otter Bickerdike.
15. Podany, A. (2023). Personal interview with Jennifer Otter Bickerdike.
16. Hoffs, S. (2023). Personal interview with Jennifer Otter Bickerdike.
17. Maitreya, S. (2023). Personal interview with Jennifer Otter Bickerdike.
18. Maitreya, S. (2023). Personal interview with Jennifer Otter Bickerdike.
19. Peterson, V. (2023). Personal interview with Jennifer Otter Bickerdike.
20. Igleheart, W. (2023). Personal interview with Jennifer Otter Bickerdike.
21. Igleheart, W. (2023). Personal interview with Jennifer Otter Bickerdike.
22. Banda, M. (2023). Personal interview with Jennifer Otter Bickerdike.
23. Igleheart, W. (2023). Personal interview with Jennifer Otter Bickerdike.
24. Kasza, T. (2023). Personal interview with Jennifer Otter Bickerdike.
25. Peterson, D. (2023). Personal interview with Jennifer Otter Bickerdike.
26. Rosenthal, G. *Behind the Music.*
27. Peterson, V. (2023). Personal interview with Jennifer Otter Bickerdike.
28. Igleheart, W. (2023). Personal interview with Jennifer Otter Bickerdike.
29. Kasza, T. (2023). Personal interview with Jennifer Otter Bickerdike.
30. Igleheart, W. (2023). Personal interview with Jennifer Otter Bickerdike.
31. Clerk, C. (1987). "The Bangles: Globe Trotters." In *Melody Maker.* Available at https://www.rocksbackpages.com/Library/Article/the-bangles-globe-trotters. Accessed October 13, 2023.
32. Kasza, T. (2023). Personal interview with Jennifer Otter Bickerdike.
33. Lamson, C. (2023). Personal interview with Jennifer Otter Bickerdike.
34. Rosenthal, G. *Behind the Music.*
35. Rosenthal, G. *Behind the Music.*
36. Rosenthal, G. *Behind the Music.*
37. Peterson, D. (2024). Personal email.
38. Gormley, M. (2023). Personal interview with Jennifer Otter Bickerdike.
39. Hoffs, S. (2023). Personal interview with Jennifer Otter Bickerdike.
40. Igleheart, W. (2023). Personal interview with Jennifer Otter Bickerdike.
41. Creem. (1987). Readers Poll. In *Creem* magazine. April.

Chapter 23.

1. banggothebangles. (2014). "The Bangles | Limited Edition Picture Disc Interview." April 12. Available at https://www.youtube.com/watch?v=8aPmKaMXrsE&ab_channel=banggothebangles. Accessed March 15, 2023.

2. banggothebangles. "The Bangles | Limited Edition."

3. Ireland, K. (2023). Personal interview with Jennifer Otter Bickerdike.

4. Ireland, K. (2023). Personal interview with Jennifer Otter Bickerdike.

5. Clerk, C. (1987). "The Bangles: Globe Trotters." In *Melody Maker*. March 28.

6. Clerk, C. "The Bangles: Globe Trotters."

7. *Metal Priestesses Podcast*. (2021). "Season 2 Episode 3: Debbi and Vicki Peterson of the Bangles." Available at https://www.youtube.com/watch?v=GgKIB0aSZfM. Accessed May 19, 2023.

8. Hoffs, S. (2023). Personal interview with Jennifer Otter Bickerdike.

9. Hoffs, S. (2023). Personal interview with Jennifer Otter Bickerdike.

10. Hoffs, S. (2023). Personal interview with Jennifer Otter Bickerdike.

11. Live Nation Clubs and Theaters. (2016). *The Bangles | Green Room Tales | House of Blues*. June 14. Available at https://youtu.be/8XgoI1Y7_hU. Accessed May 17, 2023.

12. Hoffs, S. (2023). Personal interview with Jennifer Otter Bickerdike.

13. Hoffs, S. (2023). Personal interview with Jennifer Otter Bickerdike.

14. Gormley, M. (2023). Personal interview with Jennifer Otter Bickerdike.

15. Gormley, M. (2023). Personal interview with Jennifer Otter Bickerdike.

16. Caro, M. (2023). "Debbi Peterson (The Bangles)." *Caropop* podcast. S01 E73. Available at https://rss.com/podcasts/thecaropopcast/848495/. Accessed October 5, 2023.

17. Diamond, B. (2023). Personal interview with Jennifer Otter Bickerdike.

18. *Metal Priestesses Podcast*. "Season 2 Episode 3: Debbi and Vicki Peterson."

19. Hoffs, S. (2023). Personal interview with Jennifer Otter Bickerdike.

20. Hoffs, S. (2023). Personal interview with Jennifer Otter Bickerdike.

21. Peterson, D. (2023). Personal interview with Jennifer Otter Bickerdike.

22. Peterson, D. (2023). Personal interview with Jennifer Otter Bickerdike.

23. Parwati, A. (Date unknown). "MTV reportage 1987—February 23, 1987 Officially Declared as Bangles Day." Available at https://www.youtube.com/watch?v=1qOhiLvFHf8. Accessed October 18, 2023.

24. Peterson, D. (2023). Personal interview with Jennifer Otter Bickerdike.

25. DeYoung, B. (2019). *I Need to Know: The Lost Music Interviews*. St. Petersburg, FL: St. Petersburg Press.

26. IMDb. *The Allnighter*. https://www.imdb.com/title/tt0092537/.

27. DeYoung, B. *I Need to Know*.

28. Gormley, M. (2023). Personal interview with Jennifer Otter Bickerdike.

29. Peterson, V. (2023). Personal interview with Jennifer Otter Bickerdike.

30. Peterson, V. (2023). Personal interview with Jennifer Otter Bickerdike.

31. Hoffs, S. (2023). Personal interview with Jennifer Otter Bickerdike.

32. DeYoung, B. *I Need to Know*.

33. Dean, J. (2023). Personal interview with Jennifer Otter Bickerdike.

34. sab67d. (2001). "Review of *The Allnighter*." Available at https://www.imdb.com/review/rw0240830/. Accessed October 25, 2023.

35. DeYoung, B. *I Need to Know*.

36. Rolling Stone. (1987). "Worst Mother and Child Reunion." In *Random Notes*. Issue 515–516. In *Rolling Stone*. New York: Rolling Stone Licensing LLC.

37. Gold, T. (1987). "A Bangle Bares All in a Teen Flick Directed by Her Mom." Available at https://people.com/archive/a-bangle-bares-all-in-a-teen-flick-directed-by-her-mom-vol-27-no-23/. Accessed October 25, 2023.

38. No Author. (1989). "The Allnighter." In *Los Angeles Weekly*. April 20.

39. Gold, T. "A Bangle Bares All."

40. Gold, T. "A Bangle Bares All."

41. Lamson, C. (2023). Personal interview with Jennifer Otter Bickerdike.

42. DeYoung, B. *I Need to Know*.

43. Clerk, C. "The Bangles: Globe Trotters."

44. Scoppa, B. (1987). "Tom Petty: Less Is More, More or Less." In *Creem*. Available at https://www.rocksbackpages.com/Library/Article/tom-petty-less-is-more-more-or-less. Accessed October 25, 2023.

45. Orlean, S. (1987). "The Bangles: California Girls." In *Rolling Stone* magazine, March 26.

46. DeYoung, B. *I Need to Know*.

47. DeYoung, B. *I Need to Know*.

48. Lamson, C. (2023). Personal interview with Jennifer Otter Bickerdike.

49. Valentine, K. (2020). *All I Ever Wanted: A Rock 'n' Roll Memoir*. Austin: University of Texas Press, 275. Kindle Edition.

50. Hoffs, S. (2023). Personal interview with Jennifer Otter Bickerdike.

51. Hoffs, S. (2023). Personal interview with Jennifer Otter Bickerdike.

52. Hoffs, S. (2023). Personal interview with Jennifer Otter Bickerdike.

53. Hoffs, S. (2023). Personal interview with Jennifer Otter Bickerdike.

54. Peterson, V. (2023). Personal interview with Jennifer Otter Bickerdike.

55. Peterson, V. (2023). Personal interview with Jennifer Otter Bickerdike.

56. Orlean, S. "The Bangles: California Girls."

57. Hoffs, S. (2023). Personal interview with Jennifer Otter Bickerdike.

58. Orlean, S. "The Bangles: California Girls."

59. Hoffs, S. (2023). Personal interview with Jennifer Otter Bickerdike.

60. miscellaneous publication #15. (2021). *The Bangles on Mouth to Mouth*. March 18. Available at https://youtu.be/T_i_ZglDU1Y. Accessed May 10, 2023.

61. Orlean, S. "The Bangles: California Girls."

62. Bell, M. (1988). "It's Those Hazy Crazy Bangles!!" Available at https://www.rocksbackpages.com/Library/Article/its-those-hazy-crazy-bangles. Accessed October 25, 2023.

63. Rolling Stone. (1987). "Letters to the Editor." In *Rolling Stone*. Issue 499. New York: Rolling Stone Licensing LLC.

64. Peterson, V. (2023). Personal interview with Jennifer Otter Bickerdike.

65. *Metal Priestesses Podcast*. "Season 2 Episode 3: Debbi and Vicki Peterson."

66. *Metal Priestesses Podcast*. "Season 2 Episode 3: Debbi and Vicki Peterson."

67. Bell, M. (1988) "It's Those Hazy Crazy Bangles!!"

68. *Metal Priestesses Podcast*. "Season 2 Episode 3: Debbi and Vicki Peterson."

69. Peterson, V. (2023). Personal interview with Jennifer Otter Bickerdike.

70. Brown, J. (2009). *Rick Rubin: In the Studio*. Toronto, ON: ECW Press. Kindle Edition.

71. Scoppa, B. (1988). "Bangles Do the Loosen Up." In *Cashbox*. November 19.

72. Morton, R. (1988). "Bring on the Dancing Dogs?" In *Record Mirror*. February 13.

73. DeRiso, N. (2017). "30 Years Ago: The Bangles Rock Out for 'Less Than Zero,' but Trouble Looms." Available at https://diffuser.fm/the-bangles-hazy-shade-of-winter/. Accessed January 5, 2024.

74. banggothebangles. (2017). "The Bangles Story 23–25 June 1989." Available at https://www.youtube.com/watch?v=e-jvyXJ6Hnw&list=PLGp3HEH8K0yHDGMR1smOzqouoQ0A9lewe&index=22. Accessed April 8, 2023.

75. ScottishTeeVee. (2018). *The Bangles—Walking Down Your Street—1988 & Interview*. Available at https://www.youtube.com/watch?v=c76LiN74FC4&ab_channel=ScottishTeeVee. Accessed March 28, 2023.

76. banggothebangles. "The Bangles Story 23–25 June 1989."

77. Lamson, C. (2023). Personal interview with Jennifer Otter Bickerdike.

78. Rosenthal, G. *Behind the Music*.

79. Rice, S. (2023). Personal interview with Jennifer Otter Bickerdike.

80. col1234. (2021). "6. The Bangles." *64 Quartets*. Available at https://64quartets.wordpress.com/2021/03/19/6-the-bangles/. Accessed November 3, 2023.

81. Rosenthal, G. *Behind the Music*.

82. Peterson, D. (2023). Personal interview with Jennifer Otter Bickerdike.

83. DeYoung, B. *I Need to Know*.

84. DeYoung, B. *I Need to Know*.

Chapter 24.

1. DeYoung, B. (2019). *I Need to Know: The Lost Music Interviews*. St. Petersburg, FL: St. Petersburg Press.

2. Peterson, D. (2023). Personal Interview with Jennifer Otter Bickerdike.

3. Peterson, D. (2023). Personal Interview with Jennifer Otter Bickerdike.

4. ScottishTeeVee. (2018). *The Bangles—Walking Down Your Street—1988 & Interview*. Available at https://www.youtube.com/watch?v=c76LiN74FC4&ab_channel=ScottishTeeVee. Accessed March 28, 2023.

5. Scoppa, B. (1988). "Bangles Do the Loosen Up." In *Cashbox*. November 19.

6. Willman, C. (1989). "Facts and / or Fables about the Bangles." *The Los Angeles Times*. April 9, page 348.

7. banggothebangles. (2022). "The Bangles | USA Today | October 1988." February 19. Available at https://youtu.be/oALusQM06ac. Accessed May 4, 2023.

8. Scoppa, B. "Bangles Do the Loosen Up."

9. Scoppa, B. "Bangles Do the Loosen Up."

10. Peterson, D. (2023). Personal interview with Jennifer Otter Bickerdike.

11. Scoppa, B. "Bangles Do the Loosen Up."

12. Peterson, D. (2023). Personal interview with Jennifer Otter Bickerdike.

13. DeYoung, B. *I Need to Know*.

14. Scoppa, B. "Bangles Do the Loosen Up."
15. Caro, M. (2023). "Debbi Peterson (The Bangles)." *Caropop* podcast. S01 E73. Available at https://rss.com/podcasts/thecaropopcast/848495/. Accessed October 5, 2023.
16. Igleheart, W. (2023). Personal interview with Jennifer Otter Bickerdike.
17. Scoppa, B. "Bangles Do the Loosen Up."
18. Igleheart, W. (2023). Personal interview with Jennifer Otter Bickerdike.
19. Igleheart, W. (2023). Personal interview with Jennifer Otter Bickerdike.
20. Parwati, A. (2021) "The Bangles MTV Interview Recording." November 2, 1988. Available at https://youtu.be/BC4nkvh8XnI. Accessed April 13, 2023.
21. Ivie, D. (2024). "The Bangles Were Always a Democracy." Available at https://www.vulture.com/article/susanna-hoffs-the-bangles-manic-monday-songs.html. Accessed January 5, 2024.
22. Author Unknown. (1988). "Bangles Offer 'Everything.'" In *Rolling Stone* October 19, 1988, issue 357.
23. Caro, M. "Debbi Peterson (The Bangles)."
24. Igleheart, W. (2023). Personal interview with Jennifer Otter Bickerdike.
25. DeYoung, B. *I Need to Know.*
26. Guterman, J. (1988). "'A Different Light' The Bangles." In *Rolling Stone*, issue 540, page 86.
27. Le Femme Makita. (2008). "The Bangles Arsenio Hal 1989 Part 1." December 14. Available at https://www.youtube.com/watch?v=qEpvTelKOAM. Accessed March 29, 2023.
28. Willman, C. "Facts and / or Fables."
29. Willman, C. "Facts and / or Fables."
30. Willman, C. "Facts and / or Fables."
31. Morton, R. (1988). "Bring on the Dancing Dogs?" In *Record Mirror* February 13.
32. banggothebangles. (2022). "The Bangles | USA Today | October 1988." Available at https://youtu.be/0ALusQMo6ac. Accessed May 4, 2023.
33. Parwati, A. (2022). "The Bangles ET Inside Music October 1988." May 30. Available at https://youtu.be/mCOa_mplXr8. Accessed April 12, 2023.
34. Parwati, A. "The Bangles ET Inside Music October 1988."
35. Peterson, D. (2023). Personal interview with Jennifer Otter Bickerdike.
36. DeYoung, B. *I Need to Know.*
37. McDonald, S. (2023). Personal interview with Jennifer Otter Bickerdike.
38. DeYoung, B. *I Need to Know.*
39. Peterson, D. (2023). Personal interview with Jennifer Otter Bickerdike.
40. Igleheart, W. (2023). Personal interview with Jennifer Otter Bickerdike.
41. Triplett, G. (2009). "Susanna Hoffs Strolling Down Memory Lane." Available at https://eu.oklahoman.com/story/entertainment/music/2009/08/07/susanna-hoffs-strolling-down-memory-lane/61375860007/. Accessed October 25, 2023.
42. DeYoung, B. *I Need to Know.*
43. DeYoung, B. *I Need to Know.*
44. Rosenthal, G. *Behind the Music.*

45. Rockportraits. (2014). "The Bangles." In *Rockportraits*. Available at https://rockportraits.wordpress.com/2014/09/24/the-bangles/. Accessed October 25, 2023.

46. Peterson, D. (2023). Personal interview with Jennifer Otter Bickerdike.

47. Live Nation Clubs and Theaters. (2016). "The Bangles | Green Room Tales | House of Blues." June 14. Available at https://youtu.be/8XgoI1Y7_hU. Accessed May 17, 2023.

48. Live Nation Clubs and Theaters. "The Bangles | Green Room Tales | House of Blues."

49. Scoppa, B. "Bangles Do the Loosen Up."

50. Gormley, M. (2023). Personal interview with Jennifer Otter Bickerdike.

51. Igleheart, W. (2023). Personal interview with Jennifer Otter Bickerdike.

52. Peterson, D. (2023). Personal interview with Jennifer Otter Bickerdike.

53. Rosenthal, G. *Behind the Music*.

54. Banda, M. (2023). Personal interview with Jennifer Otter Bickerdike.

55. Rockportraits. "The Bangles."

Chapter 25.

1. Michael Steele FanChannel. (2014). "Interview with the Bangles—Amsterdam 1989." July 28. Available at https://youtu.be/9baxuCzDsno.

2. Michael Steele FanChannel. "Interview with the Bangles—Amsterdam 1989."

3. Ivie, D. (2024). "The Bangles Were Always a Democracy." Available at https://www.vulture.com/article/susanna-hoffs-the-bangles-manic-monday-songs.html. Accessed January 5, 2024.

4. Rosenthal, G. (2000). *Behind the Music: The Bangles*. IMDb, S3, E40.

5. Ivie, D. "The Bangles Were Always a Democracy."

6. Aoitoritori. (2012). "The Bangles Interview (1989 Japan)." March 19. Available at https://www.youtube.com/watch?v=yj0_x7PRgRM&list=PL7BC7EC808AB39B05&index=29. Accessed April 4, 2023.

7. Cavanagh, D. (1990). "The Bangles: *Greatest Hits*." Available at https://www.rocksbackpages.com/Library/Article/the-bangles-igreatest-hitsi-. Accessed June 2, 2023.

8. Gleason, H. (1989). "The Bangles: Santa Monica Civic Auditorium, Los Angeles CA: Heroines Take a Fall." Available at https://www.rocksbackpages.com/Library/Article/the-bangles-santa-monica-civic-auditorium-los-angeles-ca. Accessed November 5, 2023.

9. Gleason, H. "The Bangles: Santa Monica Civic Auditorium."

10. Blair, I. (1989). "A Different Bangles." Available at https://www.chicagotribune.com/news/ct-xpm-1989-04-02-8903310983-story.html. Accessed November 2, 2023.

11. Blair, I. "A Different Bangles."

12. Drumsoloterror. (2010). "The Bangles Interviewed on UK TV circa 1989: Ruby Wax." January 24. Available at https://www.youtube.com/watch?v=zmyvJWoEh2k. Accessed March 29, 2023.

13. Strauss, D. (1989). "Lightweight Bangles Don't Dazzle—or Disappoint." In *Los Angeles Times*. September 2.

14. Hilfman, G. (2023). Personal interview with Jennifer Otter Bickerdike.

15. Hilfman, G. (2023). Personal interview with Jennifer Otter Bickerdike.
16. Hilfman, G. (2023). Personal interview with Jennifer Otter Bickerdike.
17. Lynskey, D. (2003). "We're the Mrs Robinsons of Rock." Available at https://www.theguardian.com/music/2003/mar/14/artsfeatures.shopping. Accessed November 3, 2023.
18. Lloyd-Bisley, I. (2023). Personal interview with Jennifer Otter Bickerdike.
19. Lloyd-Bisley, I. (2023). Personal interview with Jennifer Otter Bickerdike.
20. Ellen, B. (1989). "No Sex Please, We're Bangles." Available at https://www.rocksbackpages.com/Library/Article/no-sex-please-were-bangles. Accessed January 20, 2023.
21. Kotero, A. (2023). Personal interview with Jennifer Otter Bickerdike.
22. Caro, M. (2023). "Debbi Peterson (The Bangles)." *Caropop* podcast. S01 E73. Available at https://rss.com/podcasts/thecaropopcast/848495/. Accessed October 5, 2023.
23. DeYoung, B. (2019). *I Need to Know: The Lost Music Interviews*. St. Petersburg, FL: St. Petersburg Press.
24. Peterson, V. (2023). Personal interview with Jennifer Otter Bickerdike.

Chapter 26.

1. Rosenthal, G. (2000). *Behind the Music: The Bangles*. IMDb, S3, E40.
2. Hilfman, G. (2023). Personal interview with Jennifer Otter Bickerdike.
3. Michael Steele FanChannel. (2014). "Interview with the Bangles—Amsterdam 1989." July 28. Available at https://www.youtube.com/watch?v=jmNsa0OhC_M.
4. Ellen, B. (1989). "No Sex Please, We're Bangles." Available at https://www.rocksbackpages.com/Library/Article/no-sex-please-were-bangles. Accessed January 20, 2023.
5. Ellen, B. "No Sex Please, We're Bangles."
6. Rosenthal, G. *Behind the Music*.
7. Caro, M. (2023). "Debbi Peterson (The Bangles)." *Caropop* podcast. S01 E73. Available at https://rss.com/podcasts/thecaropopcast/848495/. Accessed October 5, 2023.
8. Rosenthal, G. *Behind the Music*.
9. Rosenthal, G. *Behind the Music*.
10. Rosenthal, G. *Behind the Music*.
11. Banda, M. (2023). Personal interview with Jennifer Otter Bickerdike.
12. Sendejas, J., Jr. (2016). "I Was There: The Day the Bangles Played on Beltway 8." Available at https://www.houstonpress.com/music/i-was-there-the-day-the-bangles-played-on-beltway-8-9012727. Accessed November 5, 2023.
13. col1234. (2021). "6. The Bangles." *64 Quartets*. Available at https://64quartets.wordpress.com/2021/03/19/6-the-bangles/. Accessed November 3, 2023.
14. Gormley, M. (2023). Personal interview with Jennifer Otter Bickerdike.
15. Rosenthal, G. *Behind the Music*.
16. Gormley, M. (2023). Personal interview with Jennifer Otter Bickerdike.
17. DeYoung, B. (2019). *I Need to Know: The Lost Music Interviews*. St. Petersburg, FL: St. Petersburg Press.
18. Hoffs, S. (2023). Personal interview with Jennifer Otter Bickerdike.

19. DeYoung, B. *I Need to Know*.
20. Caro, M. "Debbi Peterson (The Bangles)."
21. Caro, M. "Debbi Peterson (The Bangles)."
22. Peterson, V. (2023). Personal interview with Jennifer Otter Bickerdike.
23. Peterson, V. (2023). Personal interview with Jennifer Otter Bickerdike.
24. DeYoung, B. *I Need to Know*.

Epilogue

1. Author Unknown. (2004). "*Doll Revolution* Review: The Bangles." Available at https://entertainment.ie/uncategorized/the-bangles-doll-revolution-177715/. Accessed March 6, 2024.
2. Feliciano, K. (2003). "The Bangles." Available at https://web.archive.org/web/20090425171816/http://www.ew.com/ew/article/0,,488189,00.html. Accessed March 6, 2024.
3. Tucker, K. (2011). "The Bangles Are Back, and Still Clever as Ever." Available at https://www.npr.org/2011/09/26/140437708/the-bangles-are-back-and-still-clever-as-ever. Accessed March 6, 2024.
4. Keefe, J. (2011). "Review: The Bangles, *Sweetheart of the Sun*: If There's a Knock on *Sweetheart of the Sun*, It's in the Individual Lead Vocals." Available at https://www.slantmagazine.com/music/the-bangles-sweetheart-of-the-sun/. Accessed March 6, 2024.

Legacy

1. Copeland, M. (2021). *Two Steps Forward, One Step Back: My Life in the Music Business*. London: Jawbone Press.
2. Powers, A. (2000). "Pop Review: Resuming an Interrupted Conversation." Available at https://www.nytimes.com/2000/10/04/arts/pop-review-resuming-an-interrupted-conversation.html. Accessed March 6, 2024.
3. Caro, M. (2023). "Debbi Peterson (The Bangles)." *Caropop* podcast. S01 E73. Available at https://rss.com/podcasts/thecaropopcast/848495/. Accessed October 5, 2023.
4. Hann, M. (2013). "The Paisley Underground: Los Angeles's 1980s Psychedelic Explosion." Available at https://www.theguardian.com/music/2013/may/16/paisley-underground-history-80s-los-angeles-psychedelia. Accessed November 6, 2023.
5. Hoffs, S. (2023). Personal interview with Jennifer Otter Bickerdike.
6. Smith, B. S. (2023). Personal interview with Jennifer Otter Bickerdike.
7. Smith, B. S. (2023). Personal interview with Jennifer Otter Bickerdike.
8. Smith, B. S. (2023). Personal interview with Jennifer Otter Bickerdike.
9. Cameron, J. (2023). Personal interview with Jennifer Otter Bickerdike.
10. Kotero, A. (2023). Personal interview with Jennifer Otter Bickerdike.
11. Griffin, S. (2023). Personal interview with Jennifer Otter Bickerdike.
12. de la Garza, L. (2023). Personal interview with Jennifer Otter Bickerdike.
13. Salazar, B. (2023). Personal interview with Jennifer Otter Bickerdike.
14. Wong, E. (2023). Personal interview with Jennifer Otter Bickerdike.

15. de la Garza, L. (2023). Personal interview with Jennifer Otter Bickerdike.
16. Peterson, D. (2023). Personal interview with Jennifer Otter Bickerdike.
17. Kasza, T. (2023). Personal interview with Jennifer Otter Bickerdike.
18. Stella, J. (2023). Personal interview with Jennifer Otter Bickerdike.
19. Maitreya, S. (2023). Personal interview with Jennifer Otter Bickerdike.

INDEX

2 Tone Records, 81, 101
"7 and 7 Is," 114
415 Records, 126
5150 (Van Halen), 245

A&M Records, 87, 90
ABC, 117
Actors Studio, 256
A-ha, 252
Aisha, 17–29
Akron Beacon-Journal (newspaper), 304
Albers, Josef, 45
albums by Bangles
   All Over the Place, 130–142, 146, 151–152, 157, 162, 168, 172–174, 180–184, 189, 227, 250, 270, 274
   Bangles, 110, 277
   Different Light, 173, 182, 185–186, 190, 193–202, 205–207, 211–213, 216–218, 223, 227, 238–240, 245–247, 250, 253–255, 264, 270–274, 290
   Doll Revolution, 309–310
   Everything, 269–270, 274–281, 286–291, 299, 304
   Ladies and Gentlemen...The Bangles!, 84
   Sweetheart of the Sun, 309–310
All Over the Place (Bangles), 130–142, 146, 151–152, 157, 162, 168, 172–174, 180–182, 189, 227, 250, 270, 274

"All Through the Night," 187
All You Need Is Cash (film), 223
The Allnighter (film), 256–258, 287
American Bandstand (TV show), 117–118, 187
American Film Institute, 80
America's Got Talent (TV show), 67
Anderson, Rusty, 192
Apollonia 6, 169–170, 174
Apollonia 6 (Apollonia 6), 170
Arizona Daily Star (newspaper), 176
Arsenio Hall Show (TV show), 277
Aukerman, Milo, 36–37, 73, 83, 114
Austin Powers: The Spy Who Shagged Me (film), 309
awards/nominations
   Best Female Singer, 246
   Best Group Video, 223
   Best International Group, 252
   Best New Group, 152
   British Phonographic Industry Award, 252–253
   "MTV Video Music Awards," 142, 223, 259
   Rock 'n' Roll Readers Poll, 152, 244–246

Bacall, Lauren, 75
Bachman-Turner Overdrive, 87
Back Door Man (magazine), 25
Backstage Pass, 33, 86

Banda, Marji Mize
  early years of, 14–16, 20, 80, 102, 105–109
  as fan club president, 107–108, 196, 207, 276, 284, 302–303
  reflections of, 14–16, 20, 80, 102, 105–109, 196, 207, 239, 284–285, 302–303
  on tension in band, 196, 239, 284–285, 302–303

Bangles
  albums of, 84, 110, 130–142, 146, 151–152, 157, 162, 168, 172–174, 180–190, 193–202, 205–207, 211–218, 223, 227, 232–245, 247–258, 264–281, 286–291, 299, 304, 309–310
  All Over the Place, 130–142, 146, 151–152, 157, 162, 168, 172–174, 180–182, 189, 227, 250, 270, 274
  awards/nominations, 223, 252–253, 259
  Bangles, 110, 277
  benefit concerts, 82–83, 310
  branding, 72, 229–231
  breakdowns and, 292–293, 297, 302–303, 306–307
  breaking up, 284–285, 297–308, 312
  celebrity status and, 143–151, 174–176, 203–295, 309–314
  commercials, 83–84, 254
  comparisons to, 90, 97–99, 110–111, 121, 145–147, 167, 178, 184, 232, 262–263, 311
  costumes and, 141–143, 158, 166–171, 175–178, 205–206, 223–231, 243–255, 262, 304
  day named for, 255
  Different Light, 173, 182, 185–186, 190, 193–202, 205–207, 211–213, 216–218, 223, 227, 238–240, 245–247, 250, 253–255, 264, 270–274, 290
  Doll Revolution, 309–310
  early years of, 72–102, 119–120
  equality and, 125–126, 154–160, 175–176, 196–200, 224–241, 257–261, 276–283, 294–295, 305–308, 311
  Everything, 269–270, 274–281, 286–291, 299, 304
  fame and, 143–151, 174–176, 203–295, 309–314
  fan club, 107–108, 196, 207, 276, 284, 302–303
  first album, 130–142, 146, 151–152, 157, 162, 168, 172–174, 180–182, 189, 227, 250, 270, 274
  first EP, 91–92, 97–102, 107–108, 110, 126–127, 134, 205, 270, 277
  first LP, 130–142, 146, 151–152, 157, 162, 168, 172–174, 180–182, 189, 227, 250, 270, 274
  first recordings, 74–77, 83–84, 91–92
  first shows, 82–83, 88–94
  first single, 73–77, 81, 83–84
  first tour, 102–110
  free concerts, 303–304
  headlining shows, 165–166, 206–222, 280–283
  Ladies and Gentlemen…The Bangles!, 84
  last show together, 310
  legacy of, 311–314
  managers, 87–91, 101–102, 124–128, 132, 135–136, 141–144, 151–160, 175, 180–192, 200, 212–213, 218–219, 226–228, 244, 248, 252–256, 265, 282–284, 306–308, 311
  mentors, 21–22, 149–150, 167, 222, 239–240
  music videos, 108, 141–143, 148, 157–158, 164, 167, 171–178, 198, 205–206, 220–231, 247–257, 266–268, 286, 290–294, 307

as new band name, 100–102
producers, 24–28, 68, 87–91, 97,
    101–102, 110, 116, 124–127, 130–139,
    143–146, 154, 157, 166, 180–202, 211,
    218–219, 229–233, 240, 247, 258–261,
    264–273, 277, 282–288, 299–300,
    309–310
promoting, 72–81, 93, 150–168, 186–190,
    208–253, 278–280, 306–308
reuniting, 309–310
Rock 'n' Roll Readers Poll, 152, 244–246
as role models, 108, 289, 312
session musicians and, 127, 138,
    190–194
success of, 102–202, 205–295, 299–314
Sweetheart of the Sun, 309–310
tensions within, 153–163, 175–179,
    189–202, 217–221, 227–245, 257–263,
    269–287, 291–295, 299–308, 312
tour managers, 88–89, 102–107, 113,
    142, 145, 148–150, 156, 159–162,
    173–175, 180–183, 189–190, 202, 206,
    214–216, 227, 242
tours, 102–122, 143–166, 206–234,
    242–259, 263–269, 280–292,
    299–305, 309–310
transitioning from Bangs, 101–102
see also Aisha; Bangs; Colours; Fans;
    Muze; Those Girls
Bangles (Bangles), 110, 277
Bangles Day, 255
Bangles 'N Mash, 107–108
Bangs
    branding, 72
    concerts, 82–83
    early years of, 72–102, 119–120
    first EP, 91–92, 97–102
    first recordings, 74–77, 83–84, 91–92
    first shows, 82–83, 88–94
    first single, 73–77, 81, 83–84
    name changes and, 72, 100–102

promoting, 75–78, 80, 93
success of, 72–102, 119–120
transitioning to Bangles, 101–102
see also Bangles
Bartek, Steve, 265
Barton, Steve, 37
Basil, Toni, 187–188
"Be With You," 294
Beach Boys, 57, 94, 191
Beastie Boys, 255
"Beat on the Brat," 23
Beatlemania, 6, 223, 251–253
Beatles
    albums of, 170, 269
    fans of, 5–9, 12–15, 17, 19, 21, 24, 49, 60,
        63–67, 93, 115, 144, 147, 153, 156, 158,
        161, 170, 223, 251–253, 275–276, 309
    films of, 7, 15, 101
    influence of, 12–15, 17, 19, 21, 24, 63–67,
        71–72, 93, 100, 107, 111, 115, 121, 147,
        161, 173, 196, 262
    Lennon assassination, 43, 60, 64
    members of, 7, 9, 17, 19, 41, 43, 57, 60,
        63–64, 156, 191, 199, 205, 231, 253,
        265, 276
    session musicians and, 191
    tribute to, 309
Beauty and the Beat (Go-Go's), 97,
    146, 263
Belafonte, Harry, 13
benefit concerts, 82–83, 303–304, 310
Bennett, Brenda, 169–170
Best Female Singer, 246
Best Group Video, 223
Best International Group, 252
Best New Group, 152
Best, Pete, 19
Beyond the Valley of the Dolls (film),
    248
Big Maybelle, 215
Big Star, 201

Billboard (magazine), 77, 97, 102, 152, 164, 167, 187, 205, 219, 222–223, 250, 267, 280, 294, 310
Billboard 200, 164
Billboard Hot 100, 187, 219, 222–223, 250, 267, 280, 294
Billboard Top 100, 152
Bingenheimer, Rodney, 22–23, 69–70, 73–74, 76, 81, 84
Birmingham High School, 67
"Bitchen Summer/Speedway," 84
Black Flag, 23, 39, 58, 73–74
Black 'N Blue, 152
"Black Slacks," 68
Blackie's, 37
Blade, Richard, 111–112
Blasters, 70
Blondie, 56, 91
Blood on the Saddle, 122
Blue, Vicki, 24
Blue Cheer, 74
Bo Diddley, 24
Bolan, Marc, 34
Bon Jovi, 152, 223, 252, 278
Bon Jovi, Jon, 278
Bonnie and Clyde (film), 47
Bono, 235–236
Boomtown (David & David), 271
Boomtown Rats, 102
Born to Run (Springsteen), 119–120
Botting, Steve
  engagement to Debbi Peterson, 299
  marriage to Debbi Peterson, 302
  as production manager, 299, 302, 304–305
  reflections of, 302, 304–305, 307
  as sound man, 299, 302, 304–305
  as tour manager, 242, 302, 304–305
Bowie, Angela, 23
Bowie, David, 23
Bradley, Tom, 255

branding efforts, 72, 229–231
breakdowns, 292–293, 297, 302–303, 306–307
Breakfast at Tiffany's (film), 255
breakup of Bangles, 284–285, 297–308, 312
British Phonographic Industry Award (BRIT), 252–253
"Broken Wings," 218
Bruce Springsteen & the E Street Band Live (Springsteen), 245
Buchholtz, Mark, 128
Buffalo Springfield, 6, 41, 146
Bush, Kate, 246, 252
Byrds, 6, 41, 68, 93, 128, 146

Caligula (film), 55
"Call on Me," 74
Calle, Jacob, 303–304
Cameo, 252
Cameron, Julie
  background of, 9–12, 16–18
  at Bangles concert, 216
  early bands of, 9–12, 16–18
  early years of, 8–12, 16–20
  education of, 8–11, 19–20
  reflections of, 312
Cannes Film Festival, 80
"Can't Buy Me Tequila," 9
Capitol Records, 49, 165
Carlisle, Brenda, 146, 253, 258, 264
Carter, June, 122
Cash, Johnny, 122
Cashbox (magazine), 270
Cassavetes, John, 80
Cathay de Grande, 89, 94, 119
CBS, 119, 125, 130, 138, 141, 199
CBS International, 119
CBS/Sony, 141
celebrity status, 143–151, 174–176, 203–295, 309–314

Centipede (video game), 280
"Change of Heart," 222
Channel 3, 82
Charley, "Ranking" Roger, 104
Chateau Recorders, 91
Cheers (TV show), 80
Cher, 231
Chicago Tribune (newspaper), 176, 209, 211, 289
Chiccarelli, Joe, 132–133, 135, 137–138, 155
Child, Desmond, 278
Chilton, Alex, 201
Chinatown (film), 25
Chong, Rae Dawn, 54–55
"Christopher," 184, 205, 247. *See also* Prince
Ciniero, Joel, 11–12, 16, 18
Circle Jerks, 23
Clapton, Eric, 191, 252
Clark, Dick, 117–118
Clark, Petula, 49
Club 88, 93
Colasanto, Nick, 80
Collins, Judy, 50
Colours, 70–73
Columbia
　A&R executive at, 119–121, 123–129, 151–152
　music video with, 205–206
　promotion efforts and, 218–219, 236–237
　recording with, 130, 133–134, 138–139, 151–152, 161, 168, 180–181, 188, 199–201, 218–219, 224, 233, 236–237, 247, 306
　session musicians and, 127, 138
　signing with, 119–121, 123–129, 161, 180–181, 199–200, 233
　see also Sony
commercials, making, 83–84, 254

Copeland, Miles
　on equality in band, 125–126, 232–233, 258–261, 311
　I.R.S. Records and, 88–90, 101, 110
　as manager/producer, 87–91, 97, 101–102, 110, 124–127, 138, 143, 146, 154, 166, 180, 193–195, 218–219, 232–233, 258–261, 282–284
　reflections of, 88–91, 124–127, 193–195, 218, 232–233, 258–261, 282–284, 303–305, 311
　replacement of, 282–284, 303
　on tension in band, 193–195, 232–233, 258–261, 282–284, 303–305
Copeland, Stewart, 195, 232, 261, 282, 309
Corona del Mar High School, 115
Corvalan, Maria, 115–116, 210
Cosmopolitan (magazine), 292
Coverdale, David, 242
Cowley, Erin, 77
Cowsill, Barbara, 21
Cowsill, Susan, 21
Cowsills, 21–22
Cox, Andy, 104
Crawford, Joan, 45
Creem (magazine), 97, 111, 146, 152, 167–168, 187, 201, 211, 213, 233, 244–245
Cruise, Tom, 231
Crystals, 99
Cult, 134
Cure, 245
Cusack, Joan, 256
Cutting Crew, 263

Daily Sundial (newspaper), 100, 144
Dale, Dick, 84
Damned, 86
Dancing Waters, 94
D'Arby, Terence Trent, 237
David & David, 271

Davis, Andrew, 54
Davis, Greg, 122–123
De Palma, Brian, 55
Dean, Joanna "Spock," 86, 88, 114, 133–134, 158, 162, 257
Deathwatch (film), 45
Def Jam, 264
depression, coping with, 27–28, 39–40, 116, 182, 241–242, 259, 282–283
Descendents, 36, 73, 82–83, 114
"Desire," 247
Desperately Seeking Susan (film), 264
Diamond, Brian, 235–236, 253
Diana, Princess, 223
Diddley, Bo, 24
Different Light (Bangles), 173, 182, 185–186, 190, 193–202, 205–207, 211–213, 216–218, 223, 227, 238–240, 245–247, 250, 253–255, 264, 270–274, 290
Directing Workshop, 80
Doll Revolution (Bangles), 309–310
Donovan, 49
Don't Miss Wax (TV show), 290
"Don't Stop," 20
Downey, Robert Jr., 143
DownKiddie, 74–75, 83
Downton Abbey (TV show), 46
"Downtown," 49
Drakoulias, George, 264–265
Dream Syndicate, 94–95, 140
"Dreamboat Annie," 20
Driftwood, 29, 32
Dulcimer Works, 50
Duran Duran, 251–252, 263
Duritz, Adam, 309
Dylan, Bob, 49, 128

E., Sheila, 169, 176
Eat 'Em and Smile (Roth), 245
The Ed Sullivan Show (TV show), 5–6, 21, 71–72, 158
Eliot, T. S., 11
Elkind, Lynn, 34–35, 39, 41–44, 63–64, 66, 84
Ellen, Barbara, 300–301
Elliot, Cass, 233
Ellis, Bret Easton, 68, 264
Elton Duck, 114
EMI Records, 187
English Beat, 101–104, 110, 121, 146, 148, 228
Eno, Brian, 97
Entertainment Weekly (magazine), 309
equality issues, 125–126, 154–160, 175–176, 196–200, 224–241, 257–261, 276–283, 294–295, 305–308, 311
Eraserhead (film), 55
Esiason, Boomer, 231
Esquire (magazine), 71
"Eternal Flame," 275–276, 279–280, 286–290, 294, 300
The Eternal Return (Shear), 187
"Every Breath You Take," 195
Everything (Bangles), 269–270, 274–281, 286–291, 299, 304

Faith (Michael), 280–281
Falcon Crest (TV show), 170
Fame (film), 161
fame, attaining, 143–151, 174–176, 203–295, 309–314
fan club, 107–108, 196, 207, 276, 284, 302–303
Fancher, Lisa, 28
Fans, 33–41, 73, 131
fashion/costumes, 141–143, 158, 166–171, 175–178, 205–206, 223–231, 243–255, 262, 304
Faulty Products, 90–91, 97–98, 100, 102, 110, 112, 127, 166

Feliciano, Kristina, 309
Fellini, Federico, 69
Fig, Anton, 254
Film X, 52
Fine Young Cannibals, 104
Fleetwood Mac, 20, 67
"The Fog Song," 9
"Following," 202, 253
Fowley, Kim, 24–28, 68, 116
Fox, Jackie, 24
Fox, Michael J., 177
Frankie Goes to Hollywood, 152
free concerts, 303–304
"Freebird," 35
Freud, Sigmund, 47
Friday Night Videos (TV show), 223
Fun Tour, 148–151

Gabriel, Peter, 245, 252
Galli-Boivin, Deborah, 263
Garcia, Jerry, 281
Gary, Bruce, 17
Garza, Lucia de la, 312–313
Gazzara, Ben, 80
Gehry, Frank, 51
"Getting Out of Hand," 74–77, 81, 83, 123–124
Getty Museum, 39, 41
Gibson, Debbie, 289
Gira, Michael, 82
"Glamorous Life," 169
Gleason, Holly, 289
Glens Falls Post Star (newspaper), 304
Godard, Jean-Luc, 69
Go-Go's
  breakup of, 167–168
  comparisons to, 90, 97–99, 110–111, 121, 145–147, 167, 178, 184, 232, 262–263, 311
  early years of, 22–23, 33, 58, 81–82, 88–90
  members of, 22–23, 117, 146–147, 253–254, 258–259, 264
  record deal for, 81–82, 88–90, 97
  style of music, 81–82, 88–90, 97–99, 110–111, 145–147
  success of, 97–100, 253–254, 258–259, 262–263
"Going Down to Liverpool," 133–135, 143, 146, 294
Goldberg, Michael, 98, 147
The Goonies (film), 167, 186
"The Goonies 'R' Good Enough," 167
Gormley, Mike
  on equality in band, 125–126, 154–160, 175, 200, 282–283
  as manager, 87–91, 101–102, 124–128, 132, 135–136, 141–144, 151–160, 175, 180–192, 200, 212–213, 218–219, 226–228, 244, 248, 252–256, 265, 282–284
  reflections of, 87–91, 101–102, 124–128, 135–136, 141–144, 154–160, 175, 181–192, 200, 212–213, 218–219, 252–256, 282–284, 304–305
  replacement of, 282, 284, 303
  on tension in band, 154–160, 175, 200, 218–219, 282–284, 304–305
Graceland, 286
Gracie, 109, 199
Grass Roots, 65
Grateful Dead, 281
Gray, Chas, 88
Greek Theatre, 216
Green on Red, 94–95
Greg Kihn Band, 121
Grier, Pam, 256

Griffin, Sid
  Jem Records and, 75
  Long Ryders and, 38, 85, 94–95
  reflections of, 38–39, 60, 75, 85, 90–91, 94–95, 108, 116, 128, 226–227, 230, 234, 312
  Unclaimed and, 38–39, 85
The Guardian (newspaper), 173
Guess Who, 65
Guns N' Roses, 60
Gutierrez, Louis, 88, 95–96, 195, 247

The Haircut (film), 80
Hall, Arsenio, 277
Hall of Fame, 252, 309, 314
A Hard Day's Night (Beatles film), 7, 15
Hard Rock Cafe, 263
Harrison, George, 7, 156, 191, 253, 276
Harrison, Mrs., 9–10
Harry, Debbie, 64
Harvard University, 45
Haskell, Jimmie, 137
"Hazy Shade of Winter," 77, 111, 264–267, 275
Heart, 20, 29
"Heatwave," 16
Help! (Beatles album), 170
Help! (Beatles film), 15, 101
Hemophilia Foundation, 49
Hendrix, Jimi, 174
Hepburn, Audrey, 76, 225
Herald Examiner (newspaper), 93
"Hero Takes a Fall," 140–143, 157–158, 164, 170–172, 175–178, 180, 205, 215, 219, 230
Hewitt, Don, 51–52
Hilburn, Robert, 110–111, 205
Hilfman, Greg "Harpo," 290–292, 299
Hill, Christopher, 263
Hills, Amanda. *See* Podany, Amanda Hills
Hoffs, Jesse, 49

Hoffs, John, 46, 49, 52–53, 56–58
Hoffs, Joshua, 45–51
Hoffs, Susanna
  background of, 45–60
  as Best Female Singer, 246
  career of, 72–201, 205–295, 299–314
  early bands, 57–58, 65–109, 119–120
  early years of, 44–60, 63–64
  education of, 50–57
  family of, 45–58, 77–80, 143, 256–257
  first recordings, 74–77, 83–84, 91–92
  leaving Bangles, 305–308
  as solo artist, 284, 295, 305–306, 308
  success of, 72–201, 205–295, 299–314
  see also Bangles
Hoffs, Tamar, 45–51, 54, 80, 143, 256–257
Hogan's House of Music, 17
Hole, 60
Hollywood Bowl, 49, 309
Hollywood Reporter (newspaper), 257
Honeydrippers, 152
Hong Kong Cafe, 41, 66, 70
Hoodoo Gurus, 263
Hookers, 174
Hornsby, Bruce, 134
Houston, Whitney, 246, 287
"How Is the Air Up There?," 91
Huey Lewis and the News, 142, 252
Hynde, Chrissie, 145, 246

"I Am Your Singer," 9
"I Got Nothing," 167, 186
"I Want a New Drug," 142
Idyllwild Arts Academy, 56
"If She Knew What She Wants," 186–188, 213, 215, 218, 223
Iggy Pop, 23
Igleheart, Walker
  as keyboardist, 190, 199, 290–291
  reflections of, 190, 199, 207–209, 233, 239–241, 244, 273–276, 280, 284

on tension in band, 233, 239–241, 244, 284
on tours, 190, 199, 207–209, 233
"Iko Iko," 281
"I'm in Line," 91, 111
"I'm on Fire," 22
"In a Different Light," 205
"In Your Room," 275, 279–280
International Ballet School West, 51
INXS, 119, 245
Ireland, Kathryn, 224, 248–250
I.R.S. Records, 88–90, 101, 110

Jackson, Michael, 164
Jackson 5, 190
Jagger, Mick, 240
James, Ethan, 74
Jane Eyre (Brontë), 48
"Jealous Girl," 174, 184
Jefferson Airplane, 65
Jem Records, 75
Jett, Joan, 24–28
Joel, Billy, 125, 222
Johnson, Betsey, 230
Johnson, Joe, 179
Jones, Jill, 169–170
Jones, Marti, 188–189
Jones, Oran "Juice," 264
Josie and the Pussycats, 100, 289

Kaaboo Festival, 310
Kahne, David
    as producer, 126–127, 130–139, 146, 157, 180–202, 211, 229, 240, 247, 270–273, 299–300
    reflections of, 182, 195
    replacement of, 271–273, 282
Kalberg, Bruce, 82–83
Kamali, Norma, 230
Kasza, Toni, 7–8, 22, 117, 195–196, 233, 240, 242, 313
Katrina and the Waves, 134

Kaye, Carol, 115
Kaye, Lenny, 39
K-Earth 101, 77
Kelly, Tom, 274–275, 277, 286–287
Kerckhoff Coffee House, 29
Kereakes, Theresa, 23, 93
Keystone, 126
King, Carole, 67
"Kiss," 206
KISS, 275
KNAC, 81
Knack, 17, 35, 40
Knightsbridge Hotel, 292
"Knockin' on Heaven's Door," 281
Kotero, Apollonia, 169–171, 177, 293–294, 312
Kraftwerk, 97
KROQ, 23, 69, 76, 81, 111, 141
"Kyrie," 218

La De Das, 91
La Dolce Vita (film), 251
LA Girls, 33
LA Weekly (newspaper), 10, 81, 94, 99, 139, 145, 257
Ladies and Gentlemen...The Bangles! (Bangles), 84
Laird Studios, 256
Lamson, Chris
    on equality in band, 156, 159–160, 257
    reflections of, 88–89, 103–107, 142, 145, 148–150, 156, 159–162, 173–175, 189–190, 202, 214–216, 227, 242, 257–259, 267, 305
    replacement of, 242
    on tension in band, 156, 159–162, 202, 227, 242, 257–259
    as tour manager, 88–89, 102–107, 113, 142, 145, 148–150, 156, 159–162, 173–175, 180–183, 189–190, 202, 206, 214–216, 227, 242, 257

Larkin, Joan, 25
Last, 29, 58, 74, 93
Late Night with David Letterman (TV show), 217, 254
Lauper, Cyndi, 148–151, 167, 187, 222, 246, 274
Le Bon, Simon, 251–252
Led Zeppelin, 242–243, 265–266
Lee, Arthur, 65
legacy of Bangles, 311–314
"Legend in Your Own Time," 12
Lennon, John, 41, 43, 57, 60, 63–64, 156, 265, 276
Lennon, Julian, 253
Lennox, Annie, 246
Leon, Craig, 91
Leonard, David, 173
Leonard, Peggy, 173
Less Than Zero (film), 264, 267
"Let It Go," 190
Letterman, David, 217, 254–255
Leviton, Mark, 100
Lhasa Club, 100
Life, 16–17
Lifes Rich Pageant (R.E.M), 245
"Like a Rolling Stone," 49
"Like a Virgin," 274
Linda Lindas, 312–313
Lindsay, Mark, 280
Listen Like Thieves (INXS), 245
LL Cool J, 264
Lloyd, Robert, 81–82
Lloyd-Bisley, Ian, 116, 292–293
Long Beach State University, 20
Long Ryders, 38, 85, 94–95
Lords of the New Church, 86
Los Angeles Harbor College, 19
Los Angeles Personal Direction (LAPD), 87–91
Los Angeles Times (newspaper), 93, 97, 99, 110, 151, 205, 290

Love, 65, 68, 114
Love, Courtney, 130
"Love Me Do," 6, 67
Lowe, Rob, 263

Madness, 81
Madonna, 104, 142, 213, 225, 229, 246, 262, 274, 295
Magic Mountain, 118–121
Maitreya, Sananda, 237–238, 313–314
Maltin, Leonard, 257
Mamas and Papas, 6, 13, 76, 81, 191, 233
Mamis, Toby, 23–24, 28
"Manic Depression," 174
"Manic Monday," 164–165, 169–174, 179, 182–190, 205–209, 212–215, 218–220, 235, 247, 258, 266, 313
Martin, George, 252–253, 309
Mary Poppins (musical), 13
The Mary Tyler Moore Show (TV show), 121
Masque, 29–30
May, Brian, 252
McCartney, Paul, 9, 156, 199, 231, 276
McCreary, Peggy, 185, 222
McDonald, Jeff, 94, 121, 155–156, 162–163, 200–201, 279
McDonald, Steve, 97, 121, 123, 155–157, 200, 279
McDonnell, Evelyn, 28
McKee, Maria, 59
McQueen, Steve, 45
Meditation Garden, 286
Meet the Beatles! (Beatles), 49
Melody Maker (magazine), 144, 162, 208, 211, 241, 250, 258
Melvoin, Wendy Ann, 175, 220, 274
mentors, 21–22, 149–150, 167, 222, 239–240
Mercury, Freddie, 217
Mercury Records, 87, 127

Metal Priestesses Podcast (podcast), 208
Metallica, 60
Meyer, Russ, 248
Michael, George, 206, 280–281
Michigan Daily (newspaper), 146–147
"Mickey," 187
Midnight Cowboy (film), 47
Minutemen, 74
"Mirror in the Bathroom," 102
Mitchell, Joni, 13, 51
Mize, Marji. *See* Banda, Marji Mize
Mojo (magazine), 26, 28
Monkees, 68, 213, 245
Monroe, Marilyn, 45
Moon Sound Studios, 164
"More Than Meets the Eye," 136
Morrissey, 70
Moss, Kate, 238
Mötley Crüe, 60, 152
Mouth to Mouth (TV show), 262
Mr. Mister, 218
MTV, 102, 108, 111, 142, 148, 164, 172, 205, 209, 220–223, 235, 243, 253–254, 259, 262. *See also* music videos
"MTV Video Music Awards," 142, 223, 259
Music Connection (magazine), 100
Music Machine, 94
music videos
   "Be With You," 294
   "Eternal Flame," 279–280, 286–290, 294, 300
   filming, 141–143, 157–159, 167, 205–206, 223–226, 247–249, 254, 307
   "Going Down to Liverpool," 143, 294
   "The Goonies 'R' Good Enough," 167
   "Hazy Shade of Winter," 266–267
   "Hero Takes a Fall," 141–143, 157–158, 164–165, 171–172, 175–178, 205, 230
   "If She Knew What She Wants," 223
   "In Your Room," 279–280

"Manic Monday," 205–206
   popularity of, 108, 141–143, 148, 157–158, 164–165, 167, 171–178, 220–231, 247–257, 266–268, 290–294
   "The Real World," 205
   "Walk Like an Egyptian," 223–225, 248–249, 251–254
   "Walking Down Your Street," 247–249
Musicians Contact Service, 63
Muze, 29–33, 131
MV3 (TV show), 111
"My Sharona," 35

Nadia Kapiche, 114, 128
Nebraska (Springsteen), 287
Nelson, Prince Rogers, 185. *See also* Prince
Nelson, Willie, 171
Ness, Mike, 37
Neville Brothers, 281
New Musical Express (magazine), 293, 300
New York Daily News (newspaper), 304
New York Dolls, 23
Newman, Thomas, 264
Newsday (TV show), 212
News-Pilot (newspaper), 144, 149
Newton-John, Olivia, 271, 287
Nicks, Stevie, 117, 252
Nimoy, Leonard, 45, 51, 78, 143
Nimoy, Sandi, 51, 78
NME (magazine), 293, 300
NO MAG (fanzine), 82–84, 98
"No Mag Commercial," 83–84
Nolte, Joe, 29, 58, 99
Nolte, Mike, 58
"Norwegian Wood," 12
"Not Like You," 193
NPR, 310
Nuart Theatre, 52
Nuggets (Kaye), 39
The Nutcracker (ballet), 4

Oberman, Ron, 126–127
Odyssey, 76
Oedipus Rex (Sophocles), 140
Oingo Boingo, 87, 132, 265
Old Friends concert, 266
One Life to Live (TV show), 212
Ono, Yoko, 57, 229
Ontkean, Michael, 256
Our Lady of Lourdes Catholic school, 7–8, 13–14

Pacino, Al, 208
Paisley Underground, 94–95, 108, 140, 310
Palace, 165, 171, 219–220, 274
Palisades Park, 255
Palmer, Arnold, 207
Palomino Club, 67
"Park It Under a No Parking Sign," 9
The Partridge Family (TV show), 21
Patterson, "Phast" Phreddie, 25–26, 117
Paul, Scott, 36
Paul Revere and the Raiders, 83, 99, 280
Paul Revere Junior High School, 46
People (magazine), 212
Pesavento, Sandy, 25
Pet Sounds (Beach Boys), 94
Peterson, Dave, 3–6, 14–16, 66, 84, 138, 197, 199–200, 227
Peterson, Debbi
  background of, 3–9, 13–30
  career of, 33–41, 63–202, 205–295, 299–314
  early bands, 9–44, 63–109, 119–120
  early years of, 3–9, 13–44
  education of, 7–9, 13–14, 19, 31–32, 41
  engagement of, 299
  family of, 3–7, 13–15, 18, 66, 78–79, 84, 105–106, 108, 138, 197, 199–200, 227, 255
  first recordings, 74–77, 83–84, 91–92
  journal of, 31–33, 41, 66, 68, 70, 89, 105

  marriage of, 302, 307
  success of, 72–202, 205–295, 299–314
  wedding of, 302
  see also Bangles
Peterson, Jeanne, 3–7, 13, 18, 105–106, 108, 255
Peterson, Milt, 3–7, 13, 18, 105–106, 108, 255
Peterson, Pam, 3–6, 13–15, 108
Peterson, Vicki
  background of, 3–30
  career of, 33–44, 63–202, 205–295, 299–314
  early bands, 9–44, 63–109, 119–120
  early years of, 3–44
  education of, 7–11, 19, 39–40, 44
  family of, 3–7, 13–15, 18, 66, 78–79, 84, 105–106, 108, 138, 197, 199–200, 227, 255
  first recordings, 74–77, 83–84, 91–92
  success of, 72–202, 205–295, 299–314
  see also Bangles
Petrie, Mary, 46–48, 51–55
Petty, Tom, 234, 258
Philbin, Peter
  as A&R executive, 119–121, 123–134, 137, 151–152, 157, 165, 172, 181–187
  reflections of, 119–121, 123–134, 137, 151–152, 156–157, 165, 172, 181–187, 190–192, 235
  signing deals with, 123–129
Phillips, John, 233
Phillips, Michelle, 81
Phillips, Randy, 284, 294
Picasso museum, 216
Pier 84, 231
Pippin's, 39
Piucci, Matt, 71
Plant, Robert, 242–243, 253
Plugz, 73

Podany, Amanda Hills
  background of, 8–30
  at Bangles concert, 216
  career of, 43–44, 63–64, 70–109
  early bands, 9–44, 63–64, 70–109
  early years of, 8–44
  education of, 8–11, 19, 40–44
  leaving band, 43–44, 63, 66
  reflections of, 81, 193, 236
Podany, Jerry, 43–44
Police, 87, 89–90, 166, 195, 232–233, 261
Pollock, Jackson, 45
Pop, Iggy, 23
Post Star (newspaper), 304
Powers, Ann, 311
Presley, Elvis, 24, 286
Preston, Billy, 191
Pretenders, 276
Prince
  albums of, 164, 169
  Bangles and, 164–166, 169–179, 183–187, 205–206, 212–222, 243, 247, 257, 287
  Revolution and, 164–166, 172–173, 175, 220, 274
  writing songs, 164–165, 172–173, 183–184, 205–206, 212–213, 247
  promotion efforts, 39, 54, 72–81, 93, 150–168, 186–190, 208–253, 278–280, 306–308
"P.S. I Love You," 6
Psychedelic Furs, 150–151
Public Enemy, 264
"Purple Rain" (song), 171
Purple Rain (film), 164, 169
"Pushin' Too Hard," 83
Pussycat Theater, 29

Q (magazine), 176
Quaid, Randy, 248–249
Queen, 136, 217

The Queen Is Dead (Smiths), 245
Queen of Hearts, 34
Quercio, Michael, 94–96

Radio City Music Hall, 150
Radio Tokyo, 74, 83–84
The Radio Tokyo Tapes (compilation), 84
Rain Parade, 71, 94
Rainbow Room, 264
Raitt, Bonnie, 51
Ramones, 23, 57, 91
Rathod, David, 142–143
Ratt, 152
Reagan, Nancy, 83
Reagan, Ronald, 95
"The Real World," 91, 111, 117, 127, 150, 205
Record-Journal (newspaper), 146
Recycler (newspaper), 59–60, 63–64, 66, 68
Redd Kross, 39, 58, 94, 97, 121, 155, 279
Reed, Lisa, 67
Reed, Lou, 97
Reed, Paul, 115–117
R.E.M., 119, 140, 245, 288, 295
Replacements, 86, 134, 245
reunion of Bangles, 309–310
Revolution, 164–166, 172–173, 175, 220, 274
Rew, Kimberley, 133–134
Rhino Records, 93
Rice, Stephen, 267
Richard, Little, 24, 248–250
Richards, Keith, 34, 126, 270
Rifkin, Bobby "Z"
  Prince and, 164, 172–173, 177–178, 185, 212, 220
  reflections of, 164, 172–173, 177–178, 182, 185, 212, 220, 235
  Revolution and, 164, 172–173, 220
Ringo, 17, 205, 276
Rivers, Joan, 145, 179
Roback, David, 52, 56–57, 60, 64–65, 71, 74–75, 84–85

Roberts, Jill, 67
"Rock & Roll Nightmare," 188
Rock Against Drugs (RAD), 36
Rock and Roll Hall of Fame, 252, 314
Rock 'n' Roll Readers Poll (1984), 152
Rock 'n' Roll Readers Poll (1986), 244–246
Rocky III (film), 121
Rodeo, 114
Rodgers, Nile, 167
Rodney on the ROQ (radio show), 23, 69, 76, 81
Rodney's English Disco, 23
role models, 108, 239–240, 289, 312
Rolling Hills High School, 8–10, 12
Rolling Stone (magazine), 22, 98, 147, 175–176, 257–259, 261–263, 277, 289
Rolling Stones, 24, 99, 270
Rollins, Henry, 32, 37–38, 73–74, 141, 179
Romeo Void, 130
Ronettes, 99
Ronstadt, Linda, 16, 49–51, 77, 190, 223
Ross, Diana, 295
Roth, David Lee, 245
Roxy, 110
Rubin, Rick, 264–265
Rumours (Fleetwood Mac), 67
Runaways, 24–28, 68, 114–117, 128
Rush, 87

Sacramento Bee (newspaper), 98, 111
Saigon, 82
Salazar, Bela, 313
Salvation Army, 93–95
Saturday Night Live (TV show), 223
"Save It for Later," 102
Scarface (film), 208
Schock, Gina, 254
Schorr, Genevieve, 208, 215
Scorsese, Martin, 55

Seeds, 83, 99
Sensible Shoes, 66, 70
"September Gurls," 201
session musicians, 127, 138, 190–194
Shaffer, Paul, 254
Shangri-Las, 24, 99
Shantih, 11–12
Shear, Jules, 167, 186–187, 213
She's So Unusual (Lauper), 149, 187
Sigerson, Davitt, 271–273, 277, 287–288
Silva, John, 85
Simon, Carly, 12
Simon, Carmi, 50–51, 77
Simon, Paul, 77, 265–266
Simon and Garfunkel, 9, 77, 111, 265–266
Sing, Lauri, 34
Sioux, Siouxsie, 246
Sire Records, 76–77
Slane Castle, 217
Slant (magazine), 310
"Slice" commercial, 254
Slow Children, 114
Smith, Patti, 69, 229
Smiths, 245
Snakefinger, 114
So (Gabriel), 245
Social Distortion, 23, 36–37, 121
Solid Gold (TV show), 118
Sony, 139, 141, 151, 183, 233, 236–237, 253, 260, 267, 269. *See also* Columbia
Sound Factory, 189–190
The Sound of Music (musical), 13, 50
Sparkletones, 68
Spector, Phil, 191
Spielberg, Steven, 167
Spin (magazine), 259–261
Spinal Tap, 243

Spock Hotel, 86, 114, 117, 128, 133, 140
Springfield, Dusty, 49
Springsteen, Bruce, 119–121, 218, 245, 286–287
Spurrier, Jeff, 97
"Standing at the Station," 9
"Standing in the Hallway," 193
Standing on the Beach (Cure), 245
Star Trek (TV show), 143
Star Wars (film), 52
Starlight Club, 89
Starr, Ringo, 17, 205, 276
Start, Brix Smith, 226, 312
Starwood, 70
Statue of Liberty, 223
"Steady," 187
Steele, David, 104
Steele, Michael "Micki"
  career of, 114–117, 128–130, 139–202, 207–295, 300–302, 305–309
  depression and, 27–28, 116, 241–242, 282
  early bands, 24–28, 114–117, 128
  early years of, 24–28, 114–117, 128–130
  joining Bangles, 128–130
  leaving Bangles, 305–309
  Runaways and, 24–28, 114–117, 128
  success of, 139–202, 207–295, 300–302, 305–309
  see also Bangles
Steinberg, Billy, 274–277, 286–287
Stella, Joe, 106, 132, 156, 227, 234, 313
"Steppin' Out," 83
Sternberg, Liam, 187–188
Stevens, Cat, 13
Stevenson, Bill, 73
Stewart, Rod, 87
Stiefel, Arnold, 284, 294, 306
Sting, 166, 232, 261, 283
Stony Island (film), 54–55

Streisand, Barbra, 218
success, attaining, 102–202, 205–295, 299–314
Sullivan, Ed, 5–6, 21, 71–72, 158
Summers, Andy, 232, 261, 309
Sundance Film Festival, 80
Sunset Sound Studios, 167, 173, 220
Supremes, 247, 295
Sweet, Matthew, 309
Sweet, Rachel, 275
Sweetheart of the Sun (Bangles), 309–310
Sweetwater Cafe, 20–23, 29

Talk Show (Go-Go's), 146, 263
Talking Heads, 57, 245
Tapestry (King), 67
Taylor, James, 192
Taylor, John, 251–252
Teardrop Explodes, 72
Teen Angel (film), 22
Telluride Film Festival, 80
tensions, coping with, 153–163, 175–179, 189–202, 217–221, 227–245, 257–263, 269–287, 291–295, 299–309, 312
Then & Now…The Best of the Monkees (Monkees), 245
This Is Spinal Tap (film), 243
Thomas, Sue, 25
Those Girls, 41–44, 63–64, 70
Three O'Clock, 94, 96, 247
"To Sir, with Love," 161
Toni and the Movers, 114
Top 40, 247
Toronto Film Festival, 80
tours, 102–122, 143–166, 206–234, 242–259, 263–269, 280–292, 299–305, 309–310
Tower Records, 216
Tramps, 255

Translator, 37
Troubadour, 33, 35, 41–42, 49–50
"True Colors," 274
True Colors (Lauper), 222
Tucker, Ken, 310
Turner, Tina, 240, 246
Turtles, 99
Twiggy, 223
Twilley, Dwight, 22
"Twist and Shout," 263
Twisted Sister, 152

U2, 235–236, 245
UB40, 292
UCLA, 19, 22, 29, 34, 40, 45, 85, 88
Unclaimed, 38–39, 85
Under the Cherry Moon (film), 184
Universal Studios, 80
University of California, Berkeley, 53–59, 64–66, 77, 84
University of California, San Diego, 114
US Top 40, 247
USA Today (newspaper), 270–271

Vacation (Go-Go's), 263
Valentine, Kathy, 147, 259
Van Halen, 245
Vanian, Dave, 86
Vega, Carlos, 192
Velvet Underground, 64
View (newspaper), 36
Vincent, Vinnie, 275
Vocal Group Hall of Fame, 309

"Walk Like an Egyptian," 187–189, 194, 218–219, 223–228, 231, 235, 247–254, 266
"Walking Down Your Street," 193, 195, 247, 249–250
Wall of Voodoo, 87–88, 112, 132
"Want You," 117

Warfield Theatre, 214–216
Warwick, Dionne, 49
Washington Post (newspaper), 211
W.A.S.P., 152
Watts, Charlie, 17
Wax, Ruby, 290
Wayne, John, 115
Weir, Bob, 281
Weis, Gary, 223–225, 248–249
Welcome to the Real World (Mr. Mister), 218
West, Sandy, 25–28
Weston, Doug, 33
Wham!, 152, 281
"When Doves Cry," 164, 178
Whisky a Go Go, 22, 29, 36, 59, 93–94
White, David, 274
White Album (Beatles), 269
"White Rabbit," 65, 213
Who, 24
Who Put the Bomp (fanzine), 24, 28
"Whole Lotta Shakin'," 215
Wiedlin, Jane, 22–23, 117, 264
Williams, Lucinda, 134
Williams, Tony, 222
Wilson, Ann, 246
Wilson, Brian, 190
Wilson, Rebecca, 209–210, 229
The Wizard of Oz (film), 120
Wonder, Stevie, 17, 238
Wong, Eloise, 313
Wood, Natalie, 225
"Words of Love," 67
World's Most Dangerous Band, 254
Wrecking Crew, 191
Wynn, Steve, 94–95, 114, 124, 140

Yale University, 45, 53, 56
Yardbirds, 99
YouTube, 36, 179

Z, Bobby, 164, 172–173, 177–178. *See also* Rifkin, Bobby
Zed Records, 73
Zeller, Craig, 146
Zilinskas, Annette
  background of, 3, 66–67
  career of, 82–96, 99, 103–105, 112–114, 117–129, 205, 310
  early bands, 69–73
  early duos, 67–68
  early years of, 3, 66–76
  family of, 66–67, 71, 74, 82
  leaving Bangles, 123–124, 127
  rejoining Bangles, 310
  success of, 82–96, 99, 103–105, 112–114, 117–129, 205, 310
  see also Bangles
Zombies, 252